195/99/00

STALIN'S INDUSTRIAL REVOLUTION

SOVIET AND EAST EUROPEAN STUDIES

Editorial Board

The National Association for Soviet and East European Studies exists for the purpose of promoting study and research on the social sciences as they relate to the Soviet Union and the countries of Eastern Europe. The Monograph Series is intended to promote the publication of works presenting substantial and original research in the economics, politics, sociology and modern history of the USSR and Eastern Europe.

For other titles in this series, turn to page 365.

STALIN'S INDUSTRIAL REVOLUTION

POLITICS AND WORKERS, 1928–1932

HIROAKI KUROMIYA
KING'S COLLEGE, CAMBRIDGE

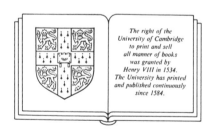

The right of the
University of Cambridge
to print and sell
all manner of books
was granted by
Henry VIII in 1534.
The University has printed
and published continuously
since 1584.

CAMBRIDGE UNIVERSITY PRESS

CAMBRIDGE

NEW YORK   NEW ROCHELLE   MELBOURNE   SYDNEY

Published by the Press Syndicate of the University of Cambridge
The Pitt Building, Trumpington Street, Cambridge CB2 1RP
32 East 57th Street, New York, NY 10022, USA
10 Stamford Road, Oakleigh, Melbourne 3166, Australia

338.947

First published 1988

K96ω

Printed in the United States of America

Library of Congress Cataloging-in-Publication Data
Kuromiya, Hiroaki.
Stalin's industrial revolution.
Bibliography: p.
1. Central planning – Soviet Union.   2. Soviet Union –
Economic policy – 1928–1932.   3. Soviet Union – Industries
– History.   4. Labor and laboring classes – Soviet Union –
History.   5. Soviet Union – Politics and Government – 1917–
1936.   6. Stalin, Joseph, 1879 – 1953.   I. Title.
HC335.4.K87   1988   338.947   87-25010

m.R.   ISBN 0 521 35157 X

British Library Cataloging in Publication applied for.

Contents

Acknowledgments

The present book has grown out of a Ph.D. dissertation written at Princeton University. My thanks for financial support are due to the Department of History, the Shelby Cullom Davis Center for Historical Studies, and the Committee for European Studies of Princeton University, all of which supported my graduate tenure from 1980–81 to 1984–85; the Russian Research Center of Harvard University, which awarded me an Andrew W. Mellon postdoctoral fellowship in 1985–86; and King's College, Cambridge, which has enabled me to complete this work by electing me to a Research Fellowship.

The bulk of the research has been done in the United States at Princeton's Firestone Library, the Library of Congress, the New York Public Library, and Harvard's various libraries. The Lenin Library, the Institute for Scientific Information for Social Sciences Library, the State Historical Library, all in Moscow; the Library of the International Labour Office in Geneva, the Hoover Archive in Stanford, and the Library of the University of Illinois at Urbana-Champaign have also been helpful. I wish to acknowledge my gratitude here to these institutions and their staffs, particularly to Dr. Orest Pelech, the former bibliographer of Slavic materials at Princeton.

Much of whatever that is good in this book is due to my teachers, colleagues, and friends, to all of whom I wish to express my deep gratitude. My greatest debt is to Cyril E. Black, who had guided me throughout my graduate tenure at Princeton. His support, encouragement, advice, and inspiration were invaluable. I owe a special debt to Sheila Fitzpatrick, whose influence on me has been unparalleled. William J. Chase, Sally Ewing, Loren R. Graham, Carol S. Leonard, Roberta Thompson Manning, Norman M. Naimark, Gilbert Rozman, Lynne Viola, Mark Von Hagen, and Richard S. Wortman have read all, or large parts, of the manuscript and provided me with much valuable advice. I have tried to follow them in revising the manuscript, but any remaining shortcomings are of course my responsibility. I have also benefited from discussion with many specialists in the United States, Britain, and Japan, particularly John Barber, Stephen F. Cohen, Linda Cook, Paddy Dale, R. W. Davies, Orlando Figes, J. Arch Getty, George Liber, Catherine Merridale, Anne Dickason Rassweiler, and Lewis H. Siegelbaum.

Parts of Chapters 3 and 4 appeared earlier in slightly different version in the journals *Soviet Studies* and *Slavic Review*. I wish to thank the editors for permission to incorporate those articles here. I also wish to thank the Houghton Library of Harvard University for permission to use materials from the Trotsky Archives, and Mary Byers, Russell Hahn, Frank S. Smith, and Douglas Weiner for having facilitated the publication of this book by Cambridge University Press.

Last but not least, my dear thanks go to Yitzhak Brudny, Sally Ewing, and Carol S. Leonard, who have supported and encouraged me through many difficult times.

April 1987   HIROAKI KUROMIYA

Author's note

Soviet administration

This brief note is intended to give the general reader a basic idea of the Soviet political and administrative structure in the period discussed in this book.

The government of the Soviet Union was composed of the Council of People's Commissars, or a cabinet of ministers, appointed by the All-Union Central Executive Committee of Soviets. The committee acted in the name of the supposedly supreme authority in the state, the All-Union Congress of Soviets, when the Congress was not in session. This structure was basically replicated down the administrative hierarchy: Union Republic (SSR) – region (*oblast'* or *krai*, composed of several former *guberniia*) – department (*okrug*, abolished in the summer and autumn of 1930) – and district (*raion*). For example, the Russian Republic had its own Council of People's Commissars, All-Russian Central Executive Committee, and All-Russian Congress of Soviets.

The Soviet government was actually dominated by the All-Union Communist Party, the only legal political party that ruled the country in the name of the proletariat. The party leadership consisted of the Politbureau, the most important decision-making organ, appointed by the Central Committee of the Communist Party, which acted in the name of the supposedly supreme authority in the party, the All-Union congress of the party, when the congress was not in session. The congress also elected the Central Control Commission, the supreme disciplinary organ of the party, which often held joint plenums with the Central Committee. The party hierarchical structure was largely parallel to the governmental structure: Union Republic Communist Party (e.g., Ukrainian Communist Party) – regional committee (*obkom* or *kraikom*) – departmental committee (*okrkom*) – district committee (*raikom*). The party also had a cell (or a committee) in factories and governmental and social organizations. The Komsomol, the Communist Youth League, had an organizational structure similar to the party's.

The Soviet economic year

Before 1931 the Soviet economic year ran from 1 October to 30 September of the succeeding year, and in this book is indicated by an oblique (as 1928/29 or 1929/30). By contrast, calendar years are referred to as 1928–29 or 1929–30. After the so-called special quarter, October–December 1930, economic and calendar years coincided. The First Five-Year Plan was originally projected for the five economic years from 1928/29 to 1932/33, namely, from October 1928 to September 1933; at the close of 1932, however, the plan was declared to have been fulfilled in four years and three months.

Transliteration

In transliterating Slavic words and proper names I have used the Library of Congress system. In the text and footnotes, however, I have followed common English usage for those names familiar to general readers, for example, Trotsky and Kharkov rather than Trotskii and Khar'kov (or Kharkiv).

Introduction

This is a book about the rapid and vast industrial transformation that took place in the Soviet Union in the period of the First Five-Year Plan, 1928–32. It was a momentous event that, along with the simultaneously promoted collectivization of agriculture, comprised what is usually known as Stalin's revolution from above. Stalin's industrial revolution embodied a special vision of the October Revolution – the creation of industrial socialism, a system deemed superior to capitalism. The slogan of the revolution was, Overtake and Surpass the Advanced Capitalist Countries. The Bolsheviks had long been fascinated with the most advanced technology and scientific management (Fordism and Taylorism) in these countries, the adoption of which in the Soviet Union, they believed, was a prerequisite to socialism.[1] The possibility of building socialism in one country was taken for granted; rather, the very survival of the country was believed to depend on rapid industrialization. In his impassioned speech in February 1931, Stalin spoke of Russian history as one of "continual beatings due to backwardness," beatings by the Mongol khans, the Swedish feudal lords, the Polish-Lithuanian pans, the Anglo-French capitalists, and the Japanese barons, and he declared: "We are fifty to one hundred years behind the advanced countries. We must cover this distance in ten years. Either we do this, or they will crush us."[2] The sense of international isolation and an inevitable international class war contributed to the breakneck speed of Stalin's industrialization. It was conceived as a

[1] For Soviet scientific management after the October Revolution, see Tatur, "*Wissenschaftliche Arbeitsorganisation.*" (*Note:* The complete citations of all articles referred to in the notes are found in the Bibliography.)
[2] Stalin, *Sochineniia,* 13:38–39. The more detailed global contexts of the Stalin years are explored in Von Laue's controversial works: *Why Lenin? Why Stalin?,* "Stalin in Focus," and "Stalin Reviewed."

great leap from a relatively backward country to an ultramodern industrial power.

This leap reflected the contradiction of the October Revolution itself: a proletarian revolution in a predominantly peasant country, or "revolution against *Das Kapital*" in Antonio Gramsci's famous expression. Because Karl Marx assumed that socialism would be built on the basis of the productive capacity of advanced industrial capitalism, the Bolsheviks believed that a historically unprecedented leap would be necessary to build socialism in the Soviet Union. The decision to take the leap in the late 1920s was preceded by a heated theoretical debate on industrialization,[3] with theoretical disagreements often developing into political divisions within the party. Almost all participants in the debate assumed, however, that investment capital for industrial development had to be somehow "pumped out" of the agrarian sector (whose population still accounted for over 80 percent of the total population of the country in 1926), because there were no other sources: the Soviet Union neither expected to obtain necessary aid from the Western capitalist countries nor possessed external colonies to exploit. (In any case, the exploitation of colonies, believed to be a capitalist method, was ruled out.) The debate revolved mainly around how to pump out the resources without breaking civil peace with the peasantry.

It remains a controversial issue whether the resources for industrial development were actually provided by the countryside, which, against the widely accepted assumption of the industrialization debate, was brutally attacked and extensively transformed.[4] Historians concur, however, that national consumption was severely squeezed: per capita consumption did not rise but declined from 1928 to 1932.[5] The burden of industrialization weighed heavily on the entire population, affecting different social groups to different degrees. Yet even the most favored industrial working class, in whose name the Bolshevik party ruled, found its standard of living

---

[3] Erlich, *The Soviet Industrialization Debate.*
[4] Note particularly the famous article by Alec Nove, "Was Stalin Really Necessary?" Nove and James R. Millar exchanged views in several articles on this topic in the early 1970s. Their discussion is summarized in "A Debate on Collectivization: Was Stalin Really Necessary?" See also Ellman, "Did the Agricultural Surplus Provide the Resources for the Increase in Investment in the USSR during the First Five-Year Plan?" The debate was triggered by a stimulating Soviet work by Barsov, *Balans stoimostnykh obmenov mezhdu gorodom i derevnei.*
[5] Barsov, *Balans stoimostnykh obmenov mezhdu gorodom i derevnei*, p. 90.

substantially lower in 1932 than in 1928.[6] To paraphrase Nikolai Bukharin's criticism of Stalin's industrialization plan, it appeared as if the "present-day life" of the population were supported by "future bread."[7]

Stalin's industrialization gained impressive achievements at the expense of the population: it laid the foundations for the post–World War II rise of the Soviet Union to a world power. In discussing Stalin's industrial revolution, Soviet historians tend to emphasize its dazzling accomplishments and minimize its staggering costs, and Western historians tend to do just the opposite.[8] Even when historians appreciate both the achievements and costs, they seem to be preoccupied with the question of whether the former were worth the price paid, or whether the revolution was really necessary.[9] As a result, the central question of *how* the Soviet political leadership made the mobilization of the resources politically possible remains largely unexamined. It is this question that the present book addresses.[10]

[6] The real wages of Moscow industrial workers in 1932, for example, were "53% of their 1928 level and in 1937 63.5%." Barber, "The Standard of Living of Soviet Industrial Workers," p. 116, citing an unpublished Soviet dissertation. For somewhat lower figures of the urban living standard, see Vyas, *Consumption in a Socialist Economy*, pp. 119–20.

[7] Bukharin criticized the plan as an attempt to "build 'present-day' factories with 'future bricks.' " Cohen, *Bukharin and the Bolshevik Revolution*, p. 296.

[8] For Soviet and Western historiographies, see Lel'chuk, *Sotsialisticheskaia industrializatsiia SSSR i ee osveshchenie v sovetskoi istoriografii*; Olegina, *Industrializatsiia SSSR v angliiskoi i amerikanskoi istoriografii*; and Hough, "The Cultural Revolution and Western Understanding of the Soviet System," in Fitzpatrick (ed.), *Cultural Revolution in Russia, 1928–1931*. For discussion of Soviet industrialization in general: Zaleski, *Planning for Economic Growth in the Soviet Union, 1918–1932*; Jasny, *Soviet Industrialization*; Hunter, "The Overambitious First Five-Year Plan," with comments by Robert Campbell, Stephen F. Cohen, and Moshe Lewin; and Wheatcroft, Davies, and Cooper, "Soviet Industrialization Reconsidered."

[9] See note 4 and Von Laue's work cited in note 2. E. H. Carr, the author of the multivolume *History of Soviet Russia* (which covers the years 1917–29) and a historian widely known as having adamantly refused to make a moral judgment on historical events, has actually stated that "where hungry and illiterate masses had not yet reached the stage of revolutionary consciousness, revolution from above was better than no revolution at all." Carr, *The Russian Revolution from Lenin to Stalin*, p. 190.

[10] The forthcoming volumes of R. W. Davies's multivolume series *The Industrialisation of Soviet Russia* (which is expected to concentrate on the economic aspects of the industrialization drive) and my mainly political and social study will be mutually supplementary. The first two volumes of the series dealing with the collectivization of agriculture were published in 1980: *The Socialist Offensive* and *The Soviet Collective Farm*. Note also the recent case study of a giant construction project, Rassweiler, "Dneprostroi, 1927–1932."

The central organizing theme of the book is that Stalin sought to enable the mobilization by presenting the industrialization drive, like the cultural revolution of the same period, as class war.[11] The drive imposed enormous tasks upon all the institutions, organizations, and individuals involved whose strengths and capabilities, however high their ambitions, often failed to live up to the tasks. The institutions and organizations were purged of those deemed politically unreliable who were often branded as "class enemies" and "wreckers." The factories were reorganized along the lines of one-man management to ensure maximum industrial efficiency and political mobilization. The trade unions were deprived of a relatively autonomous status in the Soviet political structure, and the working class as a whole was forced to bear up and live in destitution. Some segments of the working class, including the one traditionally identified as its hard core, fell out of political favor with Stalin and his group within the party leadership. However, the Stalinist group made efforts to preserve the political identity of the working class against the alleged "class enemies." The class-war atmosphere facilitated the articulation of committed workers, Communists, and Komsomols, whose prejudices and aspirations in turn helped the political leadership to shake up the various institutions and organizations and place them under police control. The concept of class war, economically costly though it was, was politically powerful enough to make the mobilization of vast resources possible. As class war, Stalin's industrialization was of a historically unprecedented type.

This book shifts the focus somewhat from high politics and illuminates the intricate interaction among the political and economic demands of the leadership in industrialization, the objectives and capabilities of various institutions and organizations involved in its implementation, and the vision, passion, commitment, and resentments of the affected social groups, particularly the industrial workers. It also shows the complexity of the social processes, the actual impact of various organizational policies, and the motivation for their shifts. In short, this book examines the class-war political process of industrialization in the social, economic, and institutional contexts of the period itself, rather than from the perspective of the 1930s and after.

[11] For the cultural revolution, see Fitzpatrick, "Cultural Revolution as Class War," in Fitzpatrick (ed.), *Cultural Revolution in Russia*.

The concept of class war was part and parcel of Marxism and Leninism, to which Stalin claimed to be heir. Indeed he spoke the language of class war throughout the period under discussion. In May 1928, for example, he declared: "No, comrades, our class enemies still exist. They not only exist, they are growing and trying to take action against the Soviet government." He therefore appealed for "strengthening the readiness of the working class for action against its class enemies."[12] The language was more than rhetoric. Stalin and many other Bolsheviks suspected that the kulaks, or well-to-do peasants, the NEPmen, or private businessmen and traders, the "bourgeois," or non-Communist specialists, and many other survivors from the old regime were exploiters and speculators, inheritors of old bourgeois ideology and values, and therefore actual and potential enemies.

Stalin's industrialization was not just any kind of rapid industrialization but one that also sought to remove the kulaks and NEPmen rapidly, replace the "bourgeois" specialists with a "proletarian intelligentsia," and supersede a market economy with a centrally planned economy. It signified for the Bolsheviks a proletarian class war, a struggle of socialist planning against capitalist market forces.

This war was not necessarily a new experience to the Bolsheviks. In the heady years of the civil war that followed the October Revolution, a series of economic measures evolved into what was subsequently to be called "war communism."[13] They included the virtually wholesale nationalization of industry, the maximum centralization of industrial production and distribution, the forced requisition of grain from the peasants, the elimination of money and regular markets, the rationing of food and other basic consumer goods, and egalitarian payments. It is controversial whether these measures stemmed from the exigencies of the civil war or from Bolshevik ideology itself. Whatever the case, it appeared to many Bolsheviks as if the anarchy and spontaneity of capitalist market relations had been conquered by the "conscious" policy of proletarian dictatorship. However, no serious economic planning was realized, and peasant rebellions were ubiquitous. The economy collapsed in ruins. The chaotic economy of the period was

[12] Stalin, *Sochineniia*, 11:69–70.
[13] For the latest Western work on war communism, see Malle, *The Economic Organization of War Communism*.

later dubbed with some self-mockery as the "most accomplished form of the proletarian natural-anarchistic economy."[14]

In 1921 the Bolsheviks were forced to retreat: war communism was replaced with the New Economic Policy (NEP) to restore both the economy and civil peace with the peasantry. NEP reinstated market relations between town and country and forsook most of the characteristics of war communism, thereby allowing the private sector to revive.

The economy's "commanding heights" (large-scale industry, banking, and foreign trade) were kept in the hands of the state, however. Many institutions of war communism had survived, most notably Vesenkha, the Supreme Council of National Economy, which retained control of industry.[15] To promote overall economic planning, Gosplan, the State Planning Commission, was founded in 1921.[16] The activities of these institutions were monitored by Rabkrin, the People's Commissariat for Workers' and Peasants' Inspection, which was created in 1920 and soon became a powerful apparatus through the merger in 1923 with the Central Control Commission of the Communist Party.[17] Rabkrin was aided in its work by the GPU (or OGPU), the State Political Administration, which grew out of the state security police, the Cheka, borne by the October Revolution and bred by the civil war. All these institutions were to play a prominent role in Stalin's industrialization drive.

NEP postponed war on the market forces for an unspecified period, and instead declared competition with them. Skillful price maneuvering in the markets was assumed to ensure the accumulation of the capital necessary for industrialization at the expense of peasant income but not of civil peace. Throughout NEP, however, the fear that the markets would take the upper hand haunted the Bolshevik government, which did not hide an emotional aversion to its rivals. Price maneuvering in the markets, politically necessary as it was, was seen by many Bolsheviks as an unheroic business, as

[14] Kritsman, *Geroicheskii period Velikoi Russkoi Revoliutsii*, p. 122.

[15] For the history of Vesenkha, see Drobizhev, *Glavnyi shtab sotsialisticheskoi promyshlennosti.*

[16] For the foundation of Gosplan and its role in economic planning in the 1920s, see Zvezdin, *Ot plana GOELRO k planu pervoi piatiletki.*

[17] For the history of Rabkrin, see Ikonnikov, *Sozdanie i deiatel'nost ob"edinennykh organov TsKK-RKI v 1923–1934 gg.*

attested to by the fact that during NEP the years of war communism came to be nostalgically remembered as "the heroic period of the great Russian Revolution."[18]

The civil peace of NEP meant class conciliation in Bolshevik parlance: conciliation with the market forces, and with the peasants, particularly the kulaks regarded as a rural bourgeoisie. On the whole, a similar conciliation with the "bourgeois" specialists had been maintained.[19] The class-conciliatory policy was politically expedient. The Bolsheviks did not indiscriminately distrust the "bourgeois" specialists, nor did the Bolsheviks blindly trust them. Rather, before 1928 the Bolsheviks expediently assumed that NEP had allowed the majority of the "bourgeois" specialists not to be actively hostile to the Soviet government.[20] Hard won as civil peace had been, before 1928 no prominent political leader dared to speak openly against it.

The crisis of NEP in 1927–28, with which the present book begins, led quickly to the abrogation of class conciliation and the onset of class war in both industry and agriculture. At the sixteenth party conference in April 1929, a Rabkrin reporter declared that the time had come for war and that "*we have already become engaged.*"[21] It became an all-out war involving all parties. This book seeks to analyze how it was fought.

This study of industrialization does not dismiss the notion of "revolution from above," but challenges some assumptions implicit in it, thereby supplementing the findings, and supporting the most important implication, of recent Western works on other aspects of Stalin's revolution. The revolution appears in these works not merely as a revolution from above but also as one that was to some extent politically pressed and supported "from below."[22] So uncritically have Western historians assumed that Stalin intimidated and terrorized the whole society that the question of popular support has largely escaped them. The concept of class war itself was in fact intended to gain the support of the working

---

[18] Kritsman, *Geroicheskii period Velikoi Russkoi Revoliutsii.*

[19] Bailes, *Technology and Society under Lenin and Stalin,* chap. 2.

[20] Note the very important article by Bogushevskii, "Kanun piatiletki," p. 489.

[21] *XVI konferentsiia VKP(b),* p. 446 (Ia. A. Iakovlev). Emphasis in the original.

[22] Chase, *Workers, Society, and the Soviet State;* Fitzpatrick, "Cultural Revolution in Russia in 1928–1932," "The 'Soft' Line on Culture and Its Enemies," and "The Russian Revolution and Social Mobility"; Viola, *The Best Sons of the Fatherland.*

class. In this book I discuss the extent and mode of both workers' resistance and support, and suggest that workers' support provided the basis for the survival of the Stalinist regime that emerged from the revolution.[23]

[23] Fitzpatrick, *Education and Social Mobility in the Soviet Union*, "Stalin and the Making of a New Elite," and "The Russian Revolution and Social Mobility." Filtzer, *Soviet Workers and Stalinist Industrialization*, focuses almost exclusively on workers' resistance as if they were an undifferentiated political whole.

Part I

1927 – 1928

1

From NEP to the socialist offensive

The politics of the New Economic Policy (NEP) has been a highly controversial topic in Western scholarship. In the last two decades or so some scholars, who acknowledge themselves to be revisionists, questioned the so-called totalitarian school, arguing that bolshevism was no single, monolithic ideology, and that there had been alternatives in the 1920s to the Stalinist course. According to one of the most ardent revisionist scholars:

Compared to the Stalinist order that followed, the distinctive feature of NEP – of the Soviet twenties – was the existence of significant social pluralism within the authoritarian framework of the one-party dictatorship. For, while the party's monopoly of political power was zealously defended, pluralism and diversity in other areas [were] officially tolerated and even encouraged.

In economic life, the private sector played the most important role in the production and trade of consumer goods, and the "immense peasant majority which still constituted over eighty per cent of the population, lived and worked remote from party or state control." In its social, cultural, and intellectual spheres, NEP was a "comparatively pluralistic and liberal order."[1]

As these revisionists also acknowledge, NEP initially was a "strategic retreat" forced by the economic collapse of 1920–21. According to another account, NEP remained a retreat throughout:

Russian society remained highly volatile and unstable during the NEP period. The Bolsheviks feared counter-revolution, remained preoccupied with the threat from "class enemies" at home and the capitalist nations abroad, and constantly expressed dissatisfaction with NEP and unwillingness to accept it as an outcome or permanent settlement of their Revolution. . . .

[1] Cohen, *Bukharin and the Bolshevik Revolution,* pp. 270–73.

3

NEP remained a retreat, and the Bolsheviks' mood remained belligerent and revolutionary.[2]

Although the party leadership may have tolerated if not encouraged a degree of pluralism and diversity, there were those in the party whose temperament tended to be "hard" on pluralism and diversity. The "hard-liners" pressed for proletarian or Communist hegemony in all spheres of life and attacked the "bourgeois" or non-Communist elements in society – technical experts, kulaks, NEPmen, teachers, bureaucrats, artists, etc.[3] Even the moderates in the party never disclaimed this ultimate goal of proletarian dictatorship. The difference revolved mainly around timing: the moderates regarded the goal in terms of decades, whereas the hard-liners could not possibly tolerate such procrastination. Before 1928 the party leadership as a whole conformed to the class-conciliatory (evolutionary) rather than the class-war (revolutionary) approach, because it needed the cooperation of experts and peasants to restore an economy ruined by the war, the revolution, and the civil war. As Sheila Fitzpatrick has correctly argued concerning the politics of culture in 1921–27, NEP was "neither liberal nor non-Communist, as its opponents believed," but "a policy of *expedient accommodation with the intelligentsia, on non-negotiable terms laid down by the party leadership and without institutional guarantees.*"[4]

The politics of NEP in other spheres, however, was not necessarily predicated upon nonnegotiable terms or without institutional guarantees. Agricultural policy, for instance, was based at least to some extent on negotiable terms with the peasants and had an institutional guarantee, i.e., the market. It is in this sphere that the most serious crisis of NEP, the grain crisis, occurred in late 1927.

The grain crisis

The grain procurement difficulties were not new. Throughout the 1920s the "goods famine," a chronic phenomenon, had caused sporadic procurement difficulties. The peasants had often gained the upper hand in the market over the state industrial sector, which had failed to provide peasants with necessary commodities. The

[2] Fitzpatrick, *The Russian Revolution*, p. 2.
[3] Fitzpatrick, "Cultural Revolution in Russia, 1928–1932."
[4] Fitzpatrick, "The 'Soft' Line on Culture and Its Enemies," p. 267. Emphasis in the original.

party leadership had portrayed the politics of agriculture during NEP in typically Bolshevik parlance as a constant fighting against the kulak and the building of a *smychka* (alliance) with the middle peasant while relying upon the poor peasant.

The leadership feared, however, that the *smychka* might be terminated by the middle peasant at any moment, depending on the market situations: there remained a mutual distrust between the party and the peasants, including the middle peasants. In an unpublished speech at the July 1928 plenum of the Central Committee, L. M. Kaganovich, a rising star in the party leadership, frankly admitted this mutual distrust:

Some comrades are ready to depict the problem in the following way: formerly the middle peasant was so ideal and so fine that he applauded all the measures of the Soviet government, but now he has suddenly stood up against us. This is not true. The middle peasant ... has always been discontent to a certain degree, because the union [*soiuz,* or *smychka*] means that there are certain contradictions between the peasantry and the proletariat. We shall overcome these contradictions in the process of [socialist] construction.[5]

This prediction was to prove too optimistic.

Before the crisis became evident in late 1927, according to N. A. Uglanov, then head of the Moscow Committee of the party, nothing appeared to be particularly ominous, and in any case the Stalin-Bukharin majority of the party remained united against the L. D. Trotsky-G. E. Zinoviev-L. B. Kamenev opposition ("United" or "Left" Opposition), which, the majority contended, sounded an unduly strong alarm about the kulak threat.[6] But the chronic "goods famine" had intensified already in the summer of 1927, when the deterioration of international relations, especially the breaking of diplomatic relations with Britain, produced a war scare causing a run on the shops and markets. In the autumn and winter of 1927–28 price policies, inflation pressures, and failures of procurement organizations combined to cause a serious crisis in grain procurements.[7] In October 1927 the state collections of grain were only two-thirds of those of October 1926, and in November and December they fell below half the levels of the previous year.[8]

---

[5] Trotsky Archives, T 1835.
[6] Trotsky Archives, T 2815.
[7] Carr and Davies, *Foundations of a Planned Economy,* chap. 2, and Lewin, *Russian Peasants and Soviet Power,* chap. 9.
[8] Carr and Davies, *Foundations of a Planned Economy,* Table 7.

The party leadership responded in panic by resorting to "extraordinary" or "emergency" measures: the notorious Article 107 of the Criminal Code, which stipulated "deprivation of liberty" against speculators, was extensively applied to peasants holding or suspected of holding grain. According to A. I. Rykov's account of July 1928, the party employed such measures as the "least evil," a regrettable, short-term necessity.[9] Yet these measures led here and there to arbitrary administrative "excesses" and the "infringement of revolutionary legality" such as house-to-house searches for grain, which, Stalin admitted, "worsened the political situation in the country and created a threat to the *smychka*."[10]

This threat to the cardinal tenet of NEP divided the party leadership into those who adhered to NEP (Bukharin, Rykov, M. P. Tomskii, N. A. Uglanov, and others) and those who increasingly challenged NEP while ostensibly defending it (Stalin, V. M. Molotov, L. M. Kaganovich, V. V. Kuibyshev, G. K. Ordzhonikidze, A. I. Mikoyan, A. A. Andreev, K. E. Voroshilov, and others).[11] Bukharin and his associates considered the grain crisis a "result of secondary factors: the state's unpreparedness, poor planning, inflexible price policies, and negligent local officials."[12] By contrast, the Stalin group came to contend that the crisis was a "grain strike" and an "expression of the first serious action, under the conditions of NEP, undertaken by the capitalist elements of the countryside against the Soviet government."[13]

This class-war interpretation of the Stalin group was hardly new in essence. Market relations, in its view, reflected class relations, and the spontaneity of the market was the enemy, or antithesis, of

[9] Trotsky Archives, T 1835 (July 1928 plenum of the Central Committee).

[10] Stalin, *Sochineniia*, 11:205–6. Somewhat frightened, A. A. Andreev, then secretary of the Northern Caucasus party committee, wrote to his wife on 27 January 1928: "Now, in earnest, I have to give directions to restrain the zealots." Andreev, *Vospominaniia, pis'ma*, p. 209.

[11] According to Tucker, even before 1928 there were latent differences between Stalin and Bukharin concerning how to build socialism. Tucker, *Stalin as Revolutionary*, pp. 395–420. See also Cohen, *Bukharin and the Bolshevik Revolution*, p. 266, where he argues that there were taking shape contrary views on collectivization, investment policy, and the tempo of industrial growth on the eve of the fifteenth party congress in December 1927 and before news of the grain crisis. For the party struggle in the 1920s, see Daniels, *The Conscience of the Revolution*.

[12] Cohen, *Bukharin and the Bolshevik Revolution*, p. 283.

[13] Kaganovich's speech at the July 1928 plenum of the Central Committee in the Trotsky Archives, T 1835, and Stalin, *Sochineniia*, 11:45 (speech at the April 1928 plenum of the Central Committee).

planning or proletarian "consciousness." For instance, Mikoyan, the people's commissar of trade, declared in February 1927, well before any sign of a serious grain crisis appeared: "The market is an arena in which all branches of the economy, all class interests of the country find their reflection and clash."[14] Eight months later he stated more boldly:

By building a socialized sector in the apparatus of distribution and by consolidating its victory over private-capitalist elements, we will bridle market spontaneity, introduce more and more elements of planning principle into the market, and, bypassing private capital, pave the way for economic relations of the socialist city to the petty bourgeois countryside.[15]

At about the same time, shortly before the grain crisis came to light, a journal of the People's Commissariat of Trade claimed that in the sphere of trade, there had been no restoration period, but only a "reconstruction period," that is, an offensive against the private sector. This was certainly an overstatement, but in the 1920s the administrative elimination of private traders indeed proceeded at what was called "dizzyingly quick" tempos: in the early 1920s, retail trade was almost entirely in the hands of private traders, whose share, however, rapidly declined to 37.0 percent by the economic year 1926/27.[16] The journal also suggested that in light of goods famines and other "negative features" of the economy, a *"regulated distribution, rationing, extended to the entire population"* might have to be put into force.[17] This prediction proved true.

All this suggests that even before 1928 the state was turning increasingly away from negotiations in the market with the peasants. It was much easier to attack market forces than to maneuver them skillfully. This temptation was particularly strong in the People's Commissariat of Trade. In their examination of the Soviet economic policy of 1926–27, R. W. Davies and S. G. Wheatcroft have concluded that the extraordinary measures were to a large extent a "natural continuation of the activities and state-

---

[14] *3 sessiia TsIK Soiuza SSR 3 sozyva*, p. 834.

[15] *Voprosy torgovli*, 1927, no. 1 (October), p. 6.

[16] *Voprosy torgovli*, 1927, no. 1 (October), pp. 45–46. For the administrative pressure against private traders in 1926–27, see also *3 sessiia TsIK Soiuza SSR 3 sozyva*, p. 857 (A. I. Mikoyan) and *3 sessiia TsIK Soiuza SSR 4 sozyva*, pp. 243 (M. I. Frumkin) and 347 (A. I. Rykov).

[17] *Voprosy torgovli*, 1927, no. 1 (October), p. 63. Emphasis in the original.

ments of Narkomtorg [People's Commissariat of Trade] and Vesenkha during 1927 in favor of administrative control and rapid
industrialization."[18] Even Bukharin conceded at the July 1928
plenum of the Central Committee: "Once we had from the very
beginning taken over too many articles of supply on the part of
government institutions, naturally we were forced to resort to
extraordinary measures."[19]

The response of the Stalin group to the grain crisis was much more
resolute than had been publicly stated at that time. As early as 18
January 1928, V. V. Kuibyshev, then head of Vesenkha, frankly
stated to its party members that "if there was a choice between the
industrialization program and equilibrium in the market, the market
must give way" and that the market situation could be "one current,
but a Communist and Bolshevik has always been and is able to swim
against the current."[20] The most important factor under the conditions of proletarian dictatorship, emphasized Kuibyshev, was the
subjective factor, or "will and energy of the party": "The will of the
party can create miracles . . . and is creating and will create miracles
despite all these market phenomena."[21] A few weeks later Kuibyshev
declared to the presidium of Vesenkha that "the will of the state has
smashed the market [*gosudarstvennaia volia slomila kon"iunk-
turu*]."[22] These statements evidently challenged the entire premise of
NEP, namely, market relations between agriculture and industry,
and were in no way acceptable to Bukharin and his allies.

This premise, however, had its own contradiction: although they
deemed market relations indispensable to the restoration of the
economy, the Bolsheviks had always counterposed a planned, socialist economy to the market economy of NEP. The problem revolved

[18] Davies and Wheatcroft, "Further Thoughts on the First Soviet Five-Year Plan,"
p. 798.
[19] Trotsky Archives, T 1901.
[20] "V. V. Kuibyshev i sotsialisticheskaia industrializatsiia SSSR," p. 56, and Davies,
"Some Soviet Economic Controllers – III," pp. 27–28. At this point, however,
Stalin's position may have been wavering. According to M. Reiman, only three
weeks before Kuibyshev delivered the speech, Stalin had reversed his previous
position and supported the proposal by G. V. Chicherin, the people's commissar of
foreign affairs, for a slackening of state monopoly in foreign trade as a way out of
the economic difficulties (Reiman, *Die Geburt des Stalinismus*, pp. 27, 74–75,
132–33, 246–56). By April 1928 Stalin was to return to his previous position and
denounce the proposal as a concession to capitalism. Stalin, *Sochineniia*, 11:55.
[21] "V. V. Kuibyshev i sotsialisticheskaia industrializatsiia SSSR," p. 56.
[22] Quoted in Bogushevskii, "Kanun piatiletki," p. 478.

largely around the question of timing: the Stalin group appeared convinced that the time was drawing near to overcome the market once and for all, but the Bukharin group contended that the time lay still far ahead. The grain crisis was the decisive event, as Mikoyan suggested in June 1929:

Had it not been for the grain difficulties, the question of strong collective farms and of machine-tractor stations would not have been posed *precisely at this moment* with such vigor, scope, and breadth. Of course we would have inevitably come to grips with this task sometime, but it is a question of timing.[23]

Because it was generally acknowledged that by 1927–28 the restoration of the economy had been largely completed, the attack on the market and the kulaks appeared to the Stalin group to be justified. In the meantime, Stalin used a maximalist approach to refute the Bukharin group. In April 1929 Stalin declared:

NEP by no means implies *complete* freedom for private trade, the *free* play of prices in the market. NEP is freedom for private trade within *certain* limits, within *certain* boundaries, *with the proviso that the role of the state as the regulator of the market is guaranteed*. . . . [Bukharin] wants to put a brake on the role of the state as the regulator of the market. . . . What can there be objectionable in the fact that the state, state industry, is the supplier, without middlemen, of goods for the peasantry, and that the peasantry is the supplier of grain for industry for the state, also without middlemen?[24]

Stalin almost declared an end to negotiations in the market with the peasants.

In 1928–29 anti-NEP feelings grew intense among Bolsheviks, who came close to identifying the "influences of NEP" (*nepovskie vliianiia*) with "petty bourgeois spontaneity."[25] At a session of the Politbureau of the Central Committee held on the eve of the sixteenth party conference in April 1929, Mikoyan accused A. I. Rykov, a leader of the Bukharinist "Right," of screaming about "maintaining NEP." This means, contended Mikoyan, "pulling the

---

[23] Mikoian, *Problema snabzheniia strany i rekonstruktsiia narodnogo khoziaistva*, p. 60 (emphasis in the original). See also Davies, *The Socialist Offensive*, p. 120. As early as the spring of 1928 a delegate from the Urals to the All-Russian Central Executive Committee declared: "We have been somewhat distracted from this task [collectivization] thanks to the New Economic Policy." *II sessiia VTsIK XIII sozyva*, p. 69.

[24] Stalin, *Sochineniia*, 12:43, 45, 48. Emphasis in the original.

[25] See, for example, *II plenum TsKK sozyva XV s'ezda VKP(b)*, p. 216. See also D. B. Riazanov's remark in *3 sessiia TsIK Soiuza SSR 4 sozyva*, p. 162.

party back to 1921 when we had to convince the party members of the necessity of NEP."[26] In the same vein, A. A. Andreev, an important regional party leader and a staunch supporter of Stalin, declared to the April 1929 plenum of the Central Committee: "The NEP as a system, gradually transformed, will die out and be replaced by another policy of the proletarian government. That's the point."[27]

Stalin's maximalist approach, however, was not so much theoretical as political. If, as he contended, the class struggle intensified, the fighting ability of the party naturally became a central concern of the Stalin group. An official from Rabkrin, the state control agency, indeed contended that the grain crisis revealed that the local party and Soviet organizations had lost their fighting ability by "preferring friendship and peace with the kulak to the direct and accurate execution of our [party] orders."[28] In early 1928, to promote grain collections, Stalin and his associates went around the countryside purging the local party and Soviet institutions of allegedly "degenerate elements" and bringing "to the fore new, revolutionary cadres."[29] The young A. S. Chuianov, who in the wake of the "Great Purge" in the late 1930s was to become first secretary of the Stalingrad *obkom* of the party, was one such "new, revolutionary" cadre.[30] In an appeal to "all party organizations" dated 13 February 1928 (which was not published at that time) Stalin urged the secretaries of party organizations to work "not for the sake of their jobs but for the sake of the revolution."[31]

At the end of March 1928, when the immediate difficulties of grain procurements had been overcome by coercive measures, Andreev, then head of the North Caucasus party committee, declared that the party had come out of the grain crisis "considerably stronger and considerably mightier" than when the crisis had begun.[32] At the April 1928 plenum of the Central Committee Stalin

[26] Quoted in Kuz'min, *V bor'be za sotsialisticheskuiu rekonstruktsiiu*, pp. 53–54.
[27] Quoted in Abramov, *O pravoi oppozitsii v partii*, p. 43.
[28] See A. Ia. Iakovlev in *XVI konferentsiia VKP (b)*, p. 446.
[29] Stalin, *Sochineniia*, 11:2, 4, 13, 16, 19, 35, 47, 71, 131–32, and 12:36.
[30] As party plenipotentiary, Chuianov participated in the grain procurement campaign in the Kuban in the North Caucasus. A typical First Five-Year Plan *vydvizhenets* (promotee), he was selected in 1929 as a "party thousander" and sent to Lomonosov Mechanical Institute in Moscow. Chuianov, *Na stremnine veka*, pp. 35–36, 38.
[31] Stalin, *Sochineniia*, 11:11.
[32] *Molot*, 31 March 1928.

declared that the party and the government had "scored a signal victory" on the grain front, because

we have put our procurement and party organizations in the localities on a sound, or more or less sound, footing, having tested their combat readiness [*boevaia gotovnost'*] in practice and purged them of blatantly corrupt elements who refused to recognize the existence of classes in the countryside and were reluctant to "quarrel" with the kulaks.[33]

In May 1928 Stalin appealed to the Komsomol to "strengthen the readiness for action of the working class."[34] At the July 1928 plenum of the Central Committee, Kaganovich defended the "political-administrative measures and Article 107" as "having served the economic policy of the proletariat," and emphasized that the measures had demonstrated a "valuable thing," namely, that the party had "demonstrated its *fighting ability* [*boesposobnost'*]."[35]

The Right considered that the "excesses" caused by the extraordinary measures threatened civil peace and market relations with the peasantry, whereas in the view of the Stalin group the "excesses," deplorable though they might have been, demonstrated the "fighting ability" of the "new, revolutionary cadres." The Stalin group may have used this argument simply to justify its radical policy. Yet despite the Right's warning that the measures had jeopardized civil peace, Stalin repeatedly declared that the party would resort to extraordinary measures if necessary.[36] In his speech to a joint plenum of the Central Committee and the Central Control Commission in April 1929, Stalin suggested that in a revolutionary situation what was dangerous was not so much excess as moderation:

Point out even one political measure taken by the party that has not been accompanied by excesses of one kind or another. The conclusion to be drawn from this is that we must combat excesses. But can one *on these grounds* decry the line itself, which is the only correct line?[37]

In the following years Stalin and his supporters did in fact resort to the much more radical policy of wholesale collectivization, and more "excesses" would ensue. By May–June 1928 the successful outcome of the first showdown with the peasants undoubtedly emboldened Stalin to do more decisive battle.

[33] Stalin, *Sochineniia*, 11:47.
[34] Ibid., 11:67–70.
[35] Trotsky Archives, T 1835.
[36] Stalin, *Sochineniia*, 11:46 (April 1928) and 174 (July 1928).
[37] Ibid., 12:92. Emphasis in the original.

The Shakhty affair

The grain crisis was a "catalyst" that accelerated the political, economic, social, and cultural events leading to Stalin's revolution from above.[38] The crisis in fact led to the cancellation of class conciliation in the industrial sphere as well. According to Stalin, the slogan of NEP in industry was as follows:

> Since Communists do not yet properly understand the technique [*tekhnika*] of production; since they have yet to learn the art of management, let the old technicians and engineers – the experts – carry on production, and you, Communists, do not interfere with the technique of the business; but while not interfering, study technique, study the art of management tirelessly, in order later on, together with the experts who are loyal to us, to become true managers of production, true masters of the business.[39]

This administrative practice predicated upon class conciliation too came to be questioned immediately after the grain crisis.

As suggested earlier, the immediate cause of the crisis was disequilibrium caused by large-scale industrial investment and concomitant inflation pressures, which turned the terms of trade against the countryside. Capital investment in "census industry" (large-scale industry) in fact increased steadily from 1,003,000,000 rubles in 1925/26 to 1,333,000,000 in 1926/27, and to 1,679,000,000 in 1927/28.[40] In 1925–27 Soviet planners, particularly party members and radical nonparty specialists in Gosplan, the State Planning Commission, pressed for high plan targets "to a level which was incompatible with equilibrium on the market." Simultaneously, Vesenkha pushed forward with ever higher levels of investment. As R. W. Davies and S. G. Wheatcroft have argued, "Important developments of thought and policy" of an industrialization program

[38] Bogushevskii, "Kanun piatiletki," p. 461.
[39] Stalin, *Sochineniia*, 13:36.
[40] Carr and Davies, *Foundations of a Planned Economy*, Table 17. For the definition of census industry, see ibid., note D. (" ' Census' industry included industrial units [*zavedeniya*] which had the qualification [*tsenz*] of employing sixteen workers or more, in the case of units which used mechanical motive power, and thirty workers or more, in the case of those which did not.") The majority of industrial workers were employed in census industry: 89.2% in 1929, 92.7% in 1930, and 93.3% in 1931. *Narodnoe khoziaistvo SSSR* (1932), p. 414.

that was incompatible with NEP took place *before* 1928, and "in circles far wider than the Stalin group."[41] In 1926–27, however, the initial drive for industrialization had created a host of grave problems. In the much publicized case of the Kerch Metallurgical Factory in the Crimea, for example, construction costs had reached sixty-six million rubles by June 1928, three and half times the planned costs.[42] Such overexpenditures threatened to jeopardize other projects. The widespread practice of "spontaneous construction," or construction without permission of the industrial and financial authorities, also disturbed the Bolshevik government. When, for example, the director of the Moscow Rubber Trust obtained permission from the Russian Republic's Vesenkha to build a factory and when it came to the budgeting and planning of construction, it turned out that the factory had already been built.[43] Such management surely involved double accounting and other financial irregularities, leading the authorities to suspect that industry hid enormous resources.

Industrial managers for their part complained bitterly about the capricious work of the planning institutions (Gosplan and Vesenkha), which changed plans constantly, with operation (or construction) resumed and halted accordingly; and managers had to work without definitive plans for several months. The construction of a metallurgical factory in the Far East, for example, collapsed in bureaucratic chaos. According to its director's account, a "very fine program" had been adopted. But in January 1928 a telegram came: "Stop [the construction]." In February another telegram came: "Start." In March yet another telegram: "Suspend." In April: "Credits have been curtailed." And in May a "funny telegram": "Stop the construction of the factory, but find construction funds on the spot."[44] It was the red tape of the plan-

[41] Davies and Wheatcroft, "Further Thoughts on the First Soviet Five-Year Plan," p. 798. See also Davies, "Some Soviet Economic Controllers – II," p. 390. According to Valentinov, who worked on the editorial staff of the Vesenkha newspaper in the 1920s, beginning in late 1926, and especially from 1927 onward, the government began to depart noticeably from NEP. See Valentinov (Vol'skii), *NEP i krizis partii posle smerti Lenina*, p. 248.

[42] Khavin, *Kratkii ocherk istorii industrializatsii SSSR*, p. 70.

[43] Bogushevskii, "Kanun piatiletki," p. 527.

[44] *IX Dal'nevostochnaia kraevaia partiinaia konferentsiia*, p. 48. For a similar case in the Urals, see Busygin, *Pervyi direktor*, pp. 33–36, 59–68.

ning agencies, contended the managers, that caused "spontaneous construction," "noncredit work," and overexpenditure.

Quite understandably, factories were also inclined to obtain the "latest achievement of technology,"[45] but in the process a large amount of foreign currency was often wasted on equipment that turned out to be unnecessary or unfit for the factories. Such mismanagement prompted Rabkrin and the Central Control Commission to remove engineers and technical directors whose activity was allegedly "suggestive of deliberate counterrevolutionary activity."[46] Apparently the Donbas industrial leaders had been under considerable pressure. At the fifteenth party congress in December 1927 G. Lomov, then director of the Donbas Coal Trust, openly challenged the threat of punishment he perceived: "Try to put somebody [of us] on trial in these conditions of ours."[47]

Within a few weeks after the congress, however, Lomov reversed his attitude dramatically (probably under the pressure of the party leadership or the GPU)[48] and warned the Donbas coal-mining administration in a strong tone that hinted of future trouble:

We will mercilessly "excoriate" all the managers and chief engineers of the large, medium, and small coal-field administrations, including their removal from work, if non-credit work, overexpenditure, or budget indiscipline is discovered.[49]

[45] *Khoziaistvo i upravlenie*, 1927, nos. 7–8, p. 113.

[46] See the case of the technical director of the Southern Steel Trust, Adam Svitsyn, discussed in *XVI konferentsiia VKP(b)*, pp. 506–7, 557, and *Vseukrainskaia proizvodstvennaia konferentsiia rabochikh metallistov zavodov Iugostali*, 1:163. Svitsyn was removed by a resolution of 22 February 1928 by the Politbureau and the presidium of the Central Control Commission. He was subsequently arrested by the GPU. In January 1928 Rabkrin conducted an investigation into the work of Southern Steel. As of 1 October 1928, foreign equipment worth 15.6 million rubles remained unused in storehouses, and equipment worth only 5 million rubles had been put into operation (Ikonnikov, *Sozdanie i deiatel'nost' ob"edinennykh organov TsKK-RKI v 1923–1934 gg.*, p. 312). Some managers, specifically those of the southern metallurgical industry, were so independent of the control of the industrial authorities in Moscow that they were to be called "feudal princes" (*kniaz'ia-feodaly*), a phrase that suggests those purged in the mid- and late 1930s. Bogushevskii, "Kanun piatiletki," p. 509.

[47] *XV s"ezd VKP (b)*, 2:1059.

[48] If Avtorkhanov is correct in saying that the Shakhty affair can be traced back to the end of 1927, Lomov may well have been under pressure. (See Avtorkhanov, *Tekhnologiia vlasti*, p. 24.) On 5 or 6 February 1928 Lomov informed a meeting of chief engineers and other higher technical staff of Donbas Coal that a "counterrevolutionary conspiracy" had been discovered in the Donbas. *Materialy k otchetu TsKK VKP (b) XVI s"ezdu VKP (b)*, p. 40.

[49] *Vestnik Donuglia*, no. 28 (15 January 1928), p. 4 (G. Lomov) (emphasis in the original). See also no. 27 (1 January 1928), pp. 1–2 (E. Abakumov).

On 1 February 1928 the government issued a special order against "spontaneous construction," which, it warned, would "destroy the reconstruction plan of the national economy."[50]

It was in this political context that in March 1928 the Soviet press announced that the security police had uncovered a "counterrevolutionary plot" in the Shakhty coal mines of the Donbas, in which "bourgeois" engineers and other persons associated with the coal-mining industry were alleged to have engaged in sabotage and treason.[51] The accusation included every possible detail ranging from the singing of the tsar's anthem and rude treatment of workers (these acts were attributed to the closed esprit de corps of engineers) to intentional delays in the compilation of plans for capital construction, constant revisions of already completed plans for no other reason than sabotaging economic planning, criminal waste of foreign currency, intentional flooding of mines, sabotage of equipment. All these were ascribed to wrecking staged in cooperation with the foreign powers and former mine owners living abroad to undermine the industrialization drive that would "have strengthened the proletarian dictatorship," thereby making a return to capitalism difficult.[52]

This Shakhty affair became a significant incident in the history of the Soviet Union that, along with the grain crisis, marked the turning point from the class-conciliatory NEP to the class-war policy of 1928–31. The affair unleashed an attack on the previously privileged, educated groups in all spheres of life. It is unclear whether Stalin masterminded the Shakhty trial.[53] What is clear is that he skillfully used it to discredit the class-conciliatory NEP, which he had come to suspect to be a political obstacle to rapid industrialization. The April 1928 plenum of the Central Committee, almost certainly reflecting his view, declared that the Shakhty affair signified "new forms and new methods of bourgeois counterrevolution against proletarian dictatorship and against socialist industrialization."[54]

Intelligentsia under fire

[50] *Sobranie zakonov*, 1928, I, 12–102.

[51] Fifty-three men were implicated in the trial in May–June 1928, and five were executed. For a detailed account of this affair, see Bailes, *Technology and Society under Lenin and Stalin*, chap. 3.

[52] See *Ekonomicheskaia kontrrevoliutsiia v Donbasse*.

[53] For a view stressing Stalin's initiative in staging the trial, see Avtorkhabnov, *Tekhnologiia vlasti*, pp. 24–27. For an account by a Western observer, see Lyons, *Assignment in Utopia*, pp. 114–33.

[54] *KPSS v rezoliutsiiakh*, 4:84–85.

Figure 1.1. Defendants at the Shakhty trial; in the front are defense law-yers. From *Ekonomicheskaia kontrrevoliutsiia v Donbasse. Itogi Shakhtin-skogo dela. Stat'i i dokumenty* (Moscow, 1928).

As the accusations of the Shakhty trial indicated, the GPU, the State Procuracy (a division of the People's Commissariat of Justice that was responsible for the general supervision of Soviet legality and exercised extensive powers including criminal prosecution), and other vigilantes had feared that "bourgeois" specialists, or at least part of those employed by the Soviet government, might sabo-tage Bolshevik industrialization for political and emotional reasons. The problem of resource constraints appeared to those vigilantes not so much an economic as a political one. All the troubles that plagued the industrialization drive in 1925–27 were almost a priori attributed to the actions of "bourgeois" specialists. The experience of 1925–27 led Stalin and his advisers to suspect that industry was far from willing or able to mobilize all the resources available and use them most effectively. The Communist managers, the party organizations, and the trade unions all appeared to the Stalin group to have become politically complacent because of class-conciliatory management.[55]

The Stalin group used the Shakhty affair to reshape the political structure of industry. The institutions and organizations involved in industrialization were to be purged of those "bourgeois" and other nonparty specialists deemed politically suspect, and the factories were to be reorganized along the lines of one-man management of the Communist manager.[56]

purging of politically suspect

The industrialization drive

Industrialization was a cardinal feature of modernization in the Soviet Union as in other societies. Moreover, the Bolsheviks believed that their political base was the industrial working class and that industrialization would therefore ultimately widen their political base by increasing the ranks of workers, which in 1928 accounted for a mere 3 percent of the population. The supremacy of industrial interests over agricultural interests was taken for granted by the Bolsheviks. One of the assumptions of the industrialization debate during NEP was that investment capital for industrialization had to be provided by the agrarian sector through marketing; without coercion, it was expected to supply raw materials for industry, to provide exports needed to pay for imports of industrial equipment, to satisfy the demands of expanding industry for labor, and to furnish food for the growing industrial work force. The grain crisis appeared to Stalin and his supporters to dash this expectation. In early 1928, in the midst of the grain crisis, Stalin declared: "We cannot allow our industry to be dependent on the caprice of the kulaks."[57]

The grain crisis caused great concern among the party leadership

---

[55] See Stalin, *Sochineniia*, 11:59, *KPSS v rezoliutsiiakh*, 4:86–87, and *Sputnik agitatora dlia goroda*, 1928, no. 8, p. 18, no. 10, p. 19. According to Reiman, a government circular of 22 March 1928 signed by M. I. Kalinin and A. I. Rykov blamed the local party and government organizations for not being in shape for fighting against "sabotage," and declared that, given the grave situation, their "lack of energy" was a "crime against the cause of the proletariat." See Reiman, *Die Geburt des Stalinismus*, pp. 296–99.

[56] See chaps. 2 and 3, this volume.

[57] Stalin, *Sochineniia*, 11:5.

about the tempo of industrialization. As early as January 1928, N. A. Uglanov, whose Moscow Committee was to provide the Right's organizational support, declared to the Politbureau that the crisis was due to the fast tempo of industrialization.[58] At the end of January he told the Moscow Committee that large construction projects already initiated (such as the Dnepro Hydroelectric Dam) should be curtailed so as to channel investment into the consumer goods industries vital to market relations with the peasantry.[59]

At about the same time V. V. Kuibyshev expressed a diametrically opposite view, which was essentially the view of the "Left Opposition" that industrial goods were in short supply because industry lagged behind agriculture:

The general line of the party in favor of heavy industry, means of production, is principally correct not only because the development of the country to socialism proceeds along this line ... but also because it is the only possible way in our economic situation.[60]

Whether or not this general line of the party was the only possible way was a big bone of contention throughout 1928. Certainly, as Uglanov argued, there were alternatives such as a reduction in capital investment and shift of resources to the consumer goods industries. In fact, in the first few months of 1928 both investment and current resources were temporarily transferred to the consumer goods industries.[61]

The industrialization drive, however, did not slacken, and the total investment plan for industry was in fact further boosted.[62] Meanwhile, the political screws tightened for those Communists and nonparty specialists within the government who stood on the moderate side concerning industrialization. Particularly hard hit were the People's Commissariats of Agriculture and Finance, "the custodians of the market economy and of financial orthodoxy" and the commissariats that put up the "most stubborn resistance to forced industrialization."[63] Since the mid-1920s, these commissariats (which, under the influence of nonparty experts, actively sought

[58] Tetiushev, "Bor'ba partii za general'nuiu liniiu protiv pravogo uklona VKP(b) v period mezhdu XV i XVI s″ezdami," p. 6, citing archival material.

[59] *Vtoroi plenum MK VKP (b)*, pp. 11–12.

[60] "V. V. Kuibyshev i sotsialisticheskaia industrializatsiia SSSR," pp. 57–58.

[61] Carr and Davies, *Foundations of a Planned Economy*, pp. 310–11.

[62] Ibid.

[63] Carr, *The Russian Revolution from Lenin and Stalin*, pp. 108 and 132.

to maintain balance in the market between demand and supply and between capital expenditure and capital accumulation) had been in a sustained conflict with Gosplan and Vesenkha (which advocated the subordination of finance to planning and of the interests of agriculture to those of industry).[64] In the spring of 1928, N. D. Kondrat'ev (former deputy minister of food under the 1917 provisional government, and the most influential economist in the two commissariats of the Soviet government in the 1920s), his deputy A. L. Vainshtein, and other nonparty experts were removed from positions of influence in the commissariats; even Bukharin was compelled to denounce them.[65]

In May 1928 Stalin openly and unequivocally supported Kuibyshev's rapid industrialization. On 28 May Stalin delivered a speech entitled "On the Grain Front" at the Institute of Red Professors, Bukharin's "ideological bailiwick." The talk not only was "his most extreme public statement to date on peasant agriculture"[66] but also a declaration of support for an ambitious industrialization drive:

> We must maintain the present rate of development of industry; we must at the first opportunity speed it up in order to pour goods into the rural areas and obtain more grain from them, to supply agriculture, and primarily the collective farms and state farms, with machines, so as to industrialize agriculture and to increase the proportion of its output for the market.
>
> Should we, perhaps, for the sake of greater "caution," retard the development of heavy industry so as to make light industry, which produces chiefly for the peasant market, the basis of our industry? Not under any circumstances! That would be . . . suicidal; it would mean . . . transforming our country into an appendage of the world capitalist system of economy.[67]

A partial record of his talk was published in *Pravda* on 2 June 1928. According to one account, this bold declaration, clearing away the hesitation and confusion caused by the grain crisis, "literally revived spirits and inspired confidence" among industrial managers.[68] Whatever the case, by the summer and autumn of 1928 the claims of industry indeed increased to such a degree that the party and

[64] Carr and Davies, *Foundations of a Planned Economy,* chaps. 29 and 37.
[65] Ibid., pp. 311 and 736. For Kondrat'ev and his group, see Jasny, *Soviet Economists of the Twenties,* pp. 158–78.
[66] Cohen, *Bukharin and the Bolshevik Revolution,* p. 285. See also Avtorkhanov's first-hand account in *Tekhnologiia vlasti,* pp. 11–15.
[67] Stalin, *Sochineniia,* 11:93.
[68] Bogushevskii, "Kanun piatiletki," p. 537.

industrial leadership had to moderate them, urging the "self-limitation" of industry.[69] Stalin and his associates, while carefully moderating the claims of industry, used the growing enthusiasm for industrialization to fight the Bukharin group within the party leadership. On the one hand, Vesenkha, headed by Kuibyshev, was said to have employed an "amazing tactic." "The logic of bureaucratic interest [*vedomstvennost'*] and interest in a peaceful life [*zhitie*]" should have pushed the Vesenkha leadership to seek an "easy plan" in both quantitative and qualitative terms. Instead, it pushed forward with ever higher targets, assuming "a burden almost beyond its strength."[70] Vesenkha went so far as to overstate grossly the effectiveness of capital investment in its fight against the moderates (although Vesenkha was constantly attacked by Rabkrin for this reason).[71]

On the other hand, the Stalin group not only inspired confidence in industrialization but also awakened what was called "industrial self-consciousness" (*industrial'noe samosoznanie*) throughout the country.[72] Ambitious investment plans aroused regional self-interests, and the regional leaders struggled for resources. Such "self-consciousness" was politically useful for the Stalin group, as D. B. Riazanov quite aptly remarked at the sixteenth party conference in April 1929: "Every speaker from this platform ends with the conclusion: 'Give us a factory in the Urals, and to hell with the Rightists!' [Laughter] 'Give us a power station, and to hell with the Rightists!'[Laughter]"[73] The Rightists found themselves on the defensive in such an intense struggle for resources. At the fifth All-Union Congress of Soviets in May 1929, which formally adopted the First Five-Year Plan, a delegate declared:

[69] See editorial in *Pravda*, 14 September 1928. See also Carr and Davies, *Foundations of a Planned Economy*, p. 316.

[70] Bogushevskii, "Kanun piatiletki," pp. 532 and 535. On 7 October 1928 Kuibyshev wrote to his wife that because he could not cut down capital investments he had to shoulder a task (cost reduction) that was "almost beyond the strength" of industry. See Kuibyshev et al., *Valerian Vladimirovich Kuibyshev*, p. 287, and *O Valeriane Kuibysheve*, p. 240.

[71] Bogushevskii, "Kanun piatiletki," p. 533.

[72] Bogushevskii and Khavin, "God velikogo pereloma," pp. 349, 355, and 359. This kind of manifestation of regional interests constitutes a main theme of Kirstein, *Sowjetische Industrialisierung – geplanter oder spontaner Prozeß?*

[73] *XVI konferentsiia VKP (b)*, p. 214. See also Carr and Davies, *Foundations of a Planned Economy*, p. 893.

I've got the impression that every speaker has come here for money. It seems as if Comrade Rykov [a leader of the Right and then chairman of the Council of People's Commissars] sat on an enormous chest full of money and as if we came out and said:
—Give us a factory.
—What factory?
—An automible factory, which costs a billion [rubles]!
—Please take it.
Then another came out:
—We need a factory.
—What factory?
—Give us an automobile factory.
—Here you are.[74]

It appeared as if people were caught by the illusion of building "present-day" factories with "future bricks."[75]

Three factors contributed to the ascendancy of Stalin's radical policy. First, the forced grain collections were not an unnatural continuation of the growing control of market relations by administrative measures already evident by the time of the grain crisis. Second, when in early 1928 the party, determined to fight against the kulaks (and the middle peasants), "brought to the fore new, revolutionary cadres," their militancy threatened to erupt beyond the control of the center. Whereas such eruptions frightened the moderates within the party leadership into forming a faction, these eruptions appeared to the Stalin group to demonstrate the party's fighting ability. According to V. M. Molotov's account, the party promoted the *"unleashing of the revolutionary forces* of the working class and poor and middle peasants."[76] Third, already in 1925–27 there had taken place important developments of thought and policy toward an industrialization program that was incompatible with NEP. The grain crisis only prompted industrialists like Kuibyshev to press further for rapid industrialization, and the struggle for resources pushed up the industrialization plans. Clearly optimism

---

[74] *5 s͞ezd Sovetov [SSSR]*, 5:3.
[75] In September 1928 Bukharin, in his famous article "Note of an Economist," criticized Stalin's rapid industrialization plan as an attempt to "build 'present-day' factories with 'future bricks.'" Cohen, *Bukharin and the Bolshevik Revolution*, p. 296.
[76] *Biulleten' 3-ei leningradskoi oblastnoi konferentsii VKP (b)*, 1:33 (emphasis in the original). For a similar argument, see Fitzpatrick, "Cultural Revolution in Russia," p. 35. Chapter 5 of this book discusses these "revolutionary forces" in more detail.

and foolhardiness overrode the concern that civil peace would collapse and that it was impossible to "build 'present-day' factories with 'future bricks.' "

This optimism made the rapid industrialization drive embodied in the Five-Year Plan (1927/28–1932/33) of revolutionary magnitude. The optimal variant of the plan formally adopted in May 1929 and retrogressively effected in October 1928, rejecting a retardation of growth rates, projected a 236 percent increase in gross industrial output (in 1926/27 prices) and a 110 percent increase in labor productivity; the plan heroically assumed that a 35 percent decline in industrial costs, along with a substantial decline in the retail prices of consumer goods, would raise the real wages of industrial workers by more than 70 percent.[77]

The plan was apparently influenced in one way or another by the Left Opposition's "superindustrialization" plan. When he addressed the November 1928 plenum of the Central Committee, Ia. B. Gamarnik, then secretary of the Belorussian Communist Party, implicitly revealed the influence of the ousted Leftists on the Five-Year Plan:

We are strongly against the Left's plan, Trotsky's anti–middle peasant, antipeasant, essentially counterrevolutionary plan, but we are for a taut, intensified tempo of industrialization of our country so as not only to gain a decisive position of industry in our national economy but also to overtake and surpass the capitalist countries in the shortest possible time.[78]

Yet already in 1928–29 Stalin's industrialization drive began to overbid the Left's superindustrialization and rapidly removed market relations from the economy.[79] Stalin and his associates considered the grain crisis of 1927–28 in terms of clashing class interests, so that the crisis strengthened the class-war mentality, which further undermined market relations.

The fight against the market gained unexpected momentum in the autumn of 1929, when the Western capitalist countries were

---

[77] The details of the plan, which was drafted in both optimum and basic variants, are in *Piatilentnii plan narodno-khoziaistvennogo stroitel'stva SSSR*, 3 vols. Because the productivity of labor was assumed to rise sharply, urban unemployment was expected to persist even in 1932/33. The plan projected a mere 32% increase in the number of workers and employees.

[78] Quoted in Vaganov, *Pravyi uklon v VKP (b) i ego razgrom*, p. 179.

[79] For the view that the Left did not envisage the rapid removal of market relations, see Erlich, *The Soviet Industrialization Debate*, and Day, *Leon Trotsky and the Politics of Economic Isolation*.

assaulted by what was to be known as the Great Depression. Economic planning appeared to free the Soviet economy of all the vagaries of the market that gripped the Western economies. Bolshevik "consciousness" seemed to triumph over market spontaneity.

In sum, the economic crisis of 1927–28 quickly turned into a political crisis, because the class-conciliatory political framework of NEP appeared to Stalin and his group to be ill suited to class-war politics. To cope with the grain crisis, they reorganized the party and government institutions in the countryside. As Stalin, Andreev, and Kaganovich remarked, the reorganization helped to revive the fighting ability of these institutions (which, however, would prove insufficient in the heady days of 1929–30). Considering the problem of resource constraints not so much in economic as in political terms, the Stalin group then used the Shakhty affair to reshape the political structure in industry for the class-war socialist offensive. In April 1929 Stalin declared that the new period demanded "new methods of struggle, the regrouping of our forces, the improvement and strengthening of our organizations."[80]

[80] Stalin, *Sochineniia*, 12:27.

Part II

1928 – 1929

2

The purges of the apparatus

"Long live the GPU!" After the Shakhty affair was made public, it was reported that the miners in the Donbas praised the GPU by inscribing this phrase on trolleys.[1] According to another partisan account, "Very many workers [declared that] there are only two organizations we trust: Rabkrin and the GPU."[2] The GPU and Rabkrin were to prove the most reliable organs in the implementation of industrialization. Almost all other organizations, and even some segments of the party itself, were thought by the Stalin group to be ill equipped for the new radical policy. Stalin used the Shakhty affair to discredit the old, class-conciliatory style of work and to introduce a new style in accordance with the class-war policy.

The style of work was closely connected with the staff of the institutions who made and implemented important decisions. The composition of the staffs of the institutions appeared to Stalin and his advisers to pose heavy constraints on the new policy. Addressing the sixteenth party congress in the summer of 1930, Stalin clearly and accurately discussed how the party leadership had sought to overcome these perceived constraints since 1928:

> The essence of the socialist offensive lies . . . in organizing the reconstruction of the entire practical work of the trade-union, cooperative, Soviet, and all other mass organizations to fit the requirements of the reconstruction period; in creating in them a core of the most active and revolutionary cadres, pushing aside and isolating the opportunist, trade-unionist, bureaucratic elements; in expelling from them the alien and degenerate elements and promoting new cadres from below.[3]

[1] Gornorabochii, 1928, no. 15 (23 April), p. 6.
[2] III plenum TsKK sozyva XV s'ezda VKP(b), p. 57.
[3] Stalin, Sochineniia, 12:311–12.

27

The purge–recruitment campaign was a deliberate attempt by the party leadership to reorient the political, economic, and social institutions of the country. This campaign encompassed the cultural and scientific establishments as well: in 1928, the Stalin group unleashed factional struggles and often intervened in favor of the hard (class-war) line.[4] This state of affairs undoubtedly created a pervasive war atmosphere in society.

The purge of the government institutions

After the civil war ended, the introduction of class-conciliatory policies in the first half of the 1920s induced and allowed many former tsarist state officials and other nonparty experts who had earlier refused to cooperate with the Bolsheviks to work for the new Soviet regime. Although the Bolsheviks suspected their political loyalty, the party leadership came to see their service as indispensable in restoring an economy ruined by the war, the revolution, and the civil war. According to 1929 data on some two and a half million employees in the government and trade institutions, officials who had worked for the tsarist regime accounted, for example, for 16.2 percent of the People's Commissariat of Finance employees, and 8.3 percent, 5.4 percent, 4.8 percent, 4.2 percent, and 3.9 percent of the judicial organizations, the People's Commissariat of Trade, Soviet executive committees, Central Statistical Administration, and the People's Commissariat of Labor, respectively. If one counts those petty officials who had worked in the tsarist government, the "holdover" rate jumped, for example, to 37.3 percent, 27.7 percent, 22.2 percent, and 17.0 percent for the People's Commissariat of Finance, the People's Commissariat of Trade, judicial organizations, and Soviet executive committees, respectively.[5] In addition to the "holdovers," a significant number of so-called class aliens and former Mensheviks and SRs, or Socialist

---

[4] Fitzpatrick (ed.), *Cultural Revolution in Russia, 1928–1931;* Brown, *The Proletarian Episode in Russian Literature, 1928–1932;* Joravsky, *Soviet Marxism and Natural Science, 1917–1932;* Graham, *The Soviet Academy of Sciences and the Communist Party, 1927–1932;* Jasny, *Soviet Economists of the Twenties;* Solomon, *The Soviet Agrarian Debate;* Barber, *Soviet Historians in Crisis 1928–1932.*
[5] Lebed', *Ukreplenie apparata proletarskoi diktatury,* pp. 10–11. Pashukanis and Ignat, *Ocherednye zadachi bor'by s biurokratizmom,* p. 50, cite much lower rates.

Revolutionaries, whose political loyalty the Bolsheviks also suspected, worked in the various institutions.[6] In the Central Union of Consumer Societies, for example, as of 1 July 1929, 191 of 2,509 officials were alleged to be "class aliens" (former nobles, hereditary honored citizens, clergymen, merchants); the social backgrounds of another 325 were "unknown"; and "many aliens" were said to have disguised their background as "peasants" or "petty bourgeois" (*meshchane*).[7]

Statistics are often deceptive, and in this case, the issue was not so much numerical as qualitative. As of 1 October 1929, the "holdovers" who had occupied the highest positions in the tsarist government (*sanovniki*, ministers, and others) accounted for only 2 percent of the officials of the All-Union People's Commissariats. Yet 81.1 percent of these holdovers still held the "commanding posts in the highest echelons of the Soviet state government."[8] Indeed, the heads or deputy heads of many departments of such important economic institutions as the People's Commissariat of Finance, Vesenkha, and Gosplan were "bourgeois" experts, former Mensheviks, or SRs.[9] It appeared to the Bolsheviks that the commanding heights of the economy were not firmly in their hands, and that even those Communists holding top positions were often nominal bosses who allowed subordinate nonparty experts to act as virtual commanders. This insecurity became a persistent nightmare to Stalin and his advisers. On the other hand, it was a source of encouragement to those nonparty officials and experts who hoped to "soften" Bolshevik policy from within "by means of cooperating in its formulation and execution."[10] The Bolsheviks remained politically suspicious of them at heart.

---

[6] The Mensheviks were moderate Marxists, who had long been in political conflict with the Bolsheviks, whereas the SRs inherited the populist movement of the nineteenth century.

[7] *Soiuz potrebitelei*, 1929, no. 11, p. 34.

[8] Bineman and Kheinman, *Kadry gosudarstvennogo i kooperativnogo apparata SSSR*, p. 33.

[9] According to N. Valentinov, a former Menshevik who in the 1920s was the de facto editor of the Vesenkha newspaper, *Torgovo-promyshlennaia gazeta*, in Vesenkha and Gosplan there was a semilegal Menshevik group, the "League of Observers," composed of prominent figures such as V. G. Groman and L. B. Kafengauz, who occupied the highest positions in these institutions. See Valentinov, *NEP i krizis partii posle smerti Lenina*.

[10] This is discussed by Azrael, *Managerial Power and Soviet Politics*, pp. 38–39, 48–49, 213.

As early as 1926–27, when pressure began to be applied against market forces, the Bolsheviks came to believe that some "bourgeois" and ex-Menshevik specialists were no longer willing to co-operate with the government. Because their cooperation had been based on the mutual acceptance of a moderate policy, namely NEP, any subtle move against it was resisted by these nonparty specialists. The records of the trials staged against them in 1930–31 indicate that irreconcilable mutual distrust emerged before 1928. At the Menshevik trial in March 1931, N. D. Kondrat'ev, a prominent "neonarodnik" who in the 1920s was the most influential economist in the People's Commissariats of Finance and Agriculture, for example, was heard to testify that until 1926 he was able to cooperate actively with the Soviet government, but that thereafter it became impossible to do so.[11] A. M. Ginzburg (an ex-Menshevik who headed the important Industrial Planning Department of Vesenkha in 1926–29) similarly testified that the new line of economic policy appeared to him "to liquidate NEP, which had created certain grounds for the Mensheviks to work with the Soviet government."[12] V. G. Groman (another prominent ex-Menshevik who was a member of the Gosplan presidium) therefore was alleged to have "worked energetically" to reverse the policy and to "deepen and broaden NEP" back to the level of 1923–25.[13]

In 1928 the grain crisis and the Shakhty affair signified the breakdown of the working relationship based on NEP between these officials and experts and the Soviet government. At the so-called Industrial Party trial in November 1930, defendant after defendant – all "bourgeois" specialists – testified that the new offensive of 1927–28 pushed them away from cooperation.[14] The same motive was consistently cited by the defendants at the Menshevik trial in March 1931 for their alleged resumption of organized fighting against the Bolsheviks. A. L. Sokolovskii, an ex-Menshevik and a Vesenkha consultant in the late 1920s, for example, maintained that he had found himself "absolutely confused and disoriented" by the new offensive and that he had come to adopt "Babel's phrase that for the common goals it is

[11] Protsess kontrrevoliutsionnoi organizatsii men'shevikov, p. 207.
[12] Ibid., pp. 74 and 400.
[13] Ibid., p. 69.
[14] Protsess "Prompartii", passim, especially pp. 90, 159, and 177.

possible to form a bloc with the devil and the grandma."[15] The defendants in these trials were accused of "wrecking" the industrialization drive. In light of the circumstances of the trials, one neither can nor should take these testimonies at face value: it is impossible to assume that their statements accurately reflected the defendants' state of mind. Yet they do seem to mirror the way in which the Stalin group viewed the defendants. In other words, the testimonies indicated this group's own mind: it no longer trusted nonparty officials and experts in staging a new offensive but rather regarded them as potential allies of the "devil," or the "class enemies" – the kulaks, foreign capitalists, former Russian factory owners residing abroad – allegedly intent on overthrowing the Bolshevik government. This distrust is hardly surprising because even within the party Stalin's hard line met considerable resistance.

The purge campaign was an inevitable consequence of the breakdown of the working relationship based on NEP. The Shakhty affair was followed by purges of state and economic institutions without clear instructions from Moscow. In Leningrad, for example, in 1928, 1,100 officials were removed from their posts for job-related "errors and misconduct"; one-quarter of them were tried.[16] Financial officials in particular were brought en masse before the court for their alleged "collusion" with private traders, a euphemism for undertaxation.[17] The November 1928 plenum of the Central Committee resolved that the "present government institutions are still saturated with elements of old officialdom and remnants of the former ruling classes in whom hatred of the Soviet regime still resides," and called for a "radical purge" of the government and cooperative institutions.[18]

These piecemeal purges were followed in April 1929 by a call at the sixteenth party conference for a general purge from these institutions of "corrupt elements, those who pervert Soviet laws, collude with kulaks and NEPmen, hinder the struggle against red tape and condone it, and take a high-handed and bureaucratic approach to

---

[15] *Protsess kontrrevoliutsionnoi organizatsii men'shevikov*, pp. 103 and 440. For an "alliance with the devil," see also N. N. Sukhanov's testimony, ibid., p. 390. For these Menshevik economists, see Jasny, *Soviet Economists of the Twenties*.

[16] Konstantinov, Ivanov, and Zubarev, *Leninskie traditsii partiino-gosudarstvennogo kontrolia*, p. 60. For other cases, see *XVI konferentsiia VKP(b)*, p. 461.

[17] Fabrichnyi, *Chastnyi kapital na poroge piatiletki*, p. 43.

[18] *KPSS v rezoliutsiiakh*, 4:143.

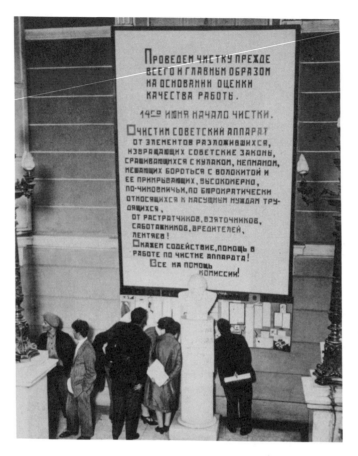

Figure 2.1. Announcement of a purge campaign at the State Bank (June 1929). Courtesy of the David King Collection, London. The announcement reads:

Let us conduct the purge, first and foremost, on the basis of the quality of work.

The purge begins on 14 June.

Let us purge the Soviet government apparatus of corrupt elements, those who pervert Soviet laws, collude with kulaks and NEPmen, hinder the struggle against red tape and condone it, and take a high-handed and bureaucratic approach to the vital needs of workers!

Let us purge embezzlers, bribe takers, saboteurs, wreckers, and loafers!

Let us promote and assist the purge of the apparatus!

All to aid the [purge] commission!

the vital needs of workers." These elements, the resolution declared, "neither wish to nor can execute our [the party's] laws and directives and, in this respect, are unreliable." The purge was also intended to stimulate the "mass promotion of workers and peasants into the apparatus."[19] A few weeks after the conference, on 23 May 1929, when the fifth All-Union congress of Soviets was discussing the Five-Year Plan for approval, the Soviet press announced that the GPU had discovered "wreckers" in the railway and gold-mining industries. The chief alleged "wreckers" were N. K. Von Meck (former hereditary noble, major shareholder of the Moscow-Kazan railway, and later, director of the economic section of the Central Planning Administration of the People's Commissariat of Transport) and P. A. Pal'chinskii (former leader of the Central War Industries Committee during World War I, deputy minister of trade and industry in Kerensky's provisional government, and later professor at the Leningrad Mining Institute). They were sentenced to be shot, and, the report concluded, the sentences had been carried out.[20] The GPU announcement added to the class-war atmosphere and facilitated the purge campaign.

[margin note: Shot as report was announced]

The campaign was a costly operation from the point of view of industry because it distracted and mobilized many workers away from production. As in other campaigns, a "patronage" (*shevstvo*) system was employed: workers from the factory bench were supposed to offer "assistance" to state institutions. For example, workers from the Moscow Electric Factory helped Rabkrin to purge the People's Commissariat of Finance, and workers from Trekhgorka helped to "cleanse" the Central Council of Consumer Societies. The campaign embodied the pro-worker, antibureaucratic spirit characteristic of Stalin's revolution from above, and the Stalin leadership appeared willing to pay the price for gaining workers' popularity. Turov, a worker from the Moscow Electric Factory, proved helpful: he declared to Rabkrin in August 1929 that *our purge is still mild.* In the State Taxation Administration of the People's Commissariat of Finance, for instance, thirty-nine out of seventy-five employees are former ministerial officials. Only one is purged as 'category one' [i.e., class enemy]. . . . it is necessary to shake more resolutely the tsarist officials, the has-beens, and the worthless out of government

[margin note: patronage – where workers helped the purges]

[19] Ibid., 4:227, and *XVI konferentsiia VKP(b)*, pp. 462 and 465.
[20] *Pravda*, 24 May 1929.

institutions."[21] When workers' brigades inspected the People's Commissariat of Finance, they found that private traders were in huge arrears with their taxes. The workers interrogated tax inspectors, who maintained that it was impossible to collect the taxes. The workers, outraged, declared: "If you can't collect [the taxes], give us the right. We'll collect [them]."[22] The workers threatened to take over the apparatus. At the club of Aviakhim Factory No. 1, workers urged a purge of the Russian Republic's People's Commissariat of Labor and demanded a mass promotion of workers:

There was not a speaker who did not stick a finger into the most tender spot.
— You have as many assistants and also officials as you like. But where are worker-*vydvizhentsy* [promotees]?
— There are four, timidly said Bakhutov [of the commissariat]. Laughter in the hall. But Comrade Severinov did not allow [the audience] to be satisfied even with this answer:
— Not four, but only two. Those who were sent by the central committee of the union are not workers from the factory bench. In this fundamental issue, the commissariat's position has turned out indefensible. . . .
— We'll have ten workers, declared Bakhutov.
— Not ten. We have to proletarianize the commissariat by forty percent or so, demanded the workers.[23]

According to data submitted at the sixteenth party congress in June–July 1930, 1,153 officials of the People's Commissariat of Finance were investigated and 169 were purged, 21 as "enemies of Soviet power."[24] From Vesenkha, 229 of 2,556 were purged, 20 as enemies of Soviet power; and from the People's Commissariat of Transport and Gosplan, 737 of 3,640 and 213 of 2,554, respectively, were purged, 105 and 37 for being enemies of Soviet power.[25] The Russian Republic's People's Commissariat of Agriculture lost 60.3 percent of its staff as a result of the purge.[26] Overall, by 1931, 1,256,253 state employees had been investigated, and 138,293, or 11 percent, were purged. Of those purged, 23,000 were classified as category one (enemies of Soviet power). In their stead,

[handwritten margin notes: 1153 investigated - 169 purged; 11% of those investigated were purged]

[21] *Izvestiia TsIK SSSR*, 3 September 1929. Emphasis in the original.
[22] *XI z'izd Komunistychnoi partii (bil'shovykiv) Ukrainy* (hereafter *XI z'izd KP(b)U*), p. 190.
[23] *Izvestiia TsIK SSSR*, 6 September 1929.
[24] *Chistka sovetskogo apparata*, p. 22.
[25] Ibid.
[26] *XVI s'ezd VKP(b)*, p. 316.

12,000 workers were promoted into government institutions.[27] Those charged with being enemies of Soviet power were barred from taking any positions in the state or cooperative institutions. When I. A. Akulov of Rabkrin told a Leningrad party conference in June 1930 that 11,445 had so far been purged as category one from the government and deprived of all civil rights, he was asked: "Where are they going to go?" He responded:

We did not ask the question: where are they going to go? We were faced with the task of freeing the government from hostile elements. Category one – this is for all intents and purposes an element hostile to us. Yet outright wreckers we do not purge but put in the hoosegow with the aid of the GPU.[28]

The Stalin group was ideologically and emotionally inclined to assume that the old officials and experts were poitically unreliable or even suspect. This assumption led the group to employ violent purges to remove perceived institutional constraints on the class-war policy in general and rapid industrialization in particular: those officials deemed politically suspect or unreliable were removed, and those workers believed to be politically reliable were promoted to support the new policy. The custodian of financial orthodoxy, the People's Commissariat of Finance, for example, was effectively transformed by the purges into a sort of "revenue-raising department which no longer controlled expenditure."[29] Similarly, the Central Statistical Administration, purged of many experts, was closed down in late 1929 and most of its activities were transferred to Gosplan's statistical economic sector. Economic statistics were thus forcefully subordinated to central economic planning.[30]

The purge of the party and trade unions

If the old officials and experts were perceived by the Stalin group as hostile to the class-war policy, some segments of the party and other

[27] Ezhegodnik sovetskogo stroitel'stva i prava na 1931 g. (za 1929/30 god), p. 303; Rabota NK RKI SSSR ot V k VI Vsesoiuznomu s'ezdu Sovetov, p. 43, and Za tempy, kachestvo, proverku, 1931, no. 1 (April), p. 51.
[28] Biulleten' 3-ei leningradskoi oblastnoi konferentsii VKP(b), 4:17.
[29] Carr, The Russian Revolution from Lenin to Stalin, p. 150.
[30] Ekonomicheskaia zhizn', 27 December 1929, and Seliunin and Khanin, "Lukavaia tsifra," pp. 188–89.

bureaucracies appeared far from ready for the policy. The group feared that its command might be ignored by the various bureaucracies. According to Stalin, one of the lessons he drew from the Shakhty affair was the necessity for "checking fulfillment." He contended in April 1928 that "as far as checking fulfillment is concerned, things could not be worse than they are in all spheres of administration—in party, in industry, in the trade unions."[31] This issue was part of the broader one of bureaucratism, which Stalin feared might hinder the implementation of his revolutionary policy. In May 1928 he declared to the eighth Komsomol congress:

> Bureaucracy is one of the worst enemies of our progress. It exists in all our organizations—party, Komsomol, trade unions, and industrial management.... The trouble is that it is not a matter of the old bureaucrats. Comrades, it is a matter of the new bureaucrats, bureaucrats who sympathize with the Soviet government, and finally, Communist bureaucrats. The Communist bureaucrat is the most dangerous type of bureaucrat. Why? Because he masks his bureaucracy with the title of party member. And, unfortunately, we have quite a number of such Communist bureaucrats.[32]

One is tempted to see here the same logic that Stalin was to employ in the late 1930s.

In 1928–31, the Stalin group took the campaign against bureaucratism seriously. At the April 1928 plenum of the Central Control Commission, V. P. Zatonskii, a leader of the commission, candidly declared that it was necessary to "somewhat release the pulled-up reins" and "slightly let the workers have the possibility of criticizing us [Communists]" in order to eliminate "whatever discredits party members in the eyes of the workers"; furthermore, "it would be much better to do so now" than when the workers started taking action on their own.[33] The sixteenth party conference in the spring of 1929 adopted, along with the Five-Year Plan, a resolution entitled "On the Achievements and Next Tasks of the Struggle against Bureaucratism." As E. H. Carr has correctly pointed out, this was the "first specific resolution ever devoted by a major party assembly to the problem of bureaucracy."[34] In order to fight bureaucratism, the party leadership mobilized the working class for "self-criticism"

[31] Stalin, *Sochineniia*, 11:61–62.
[32] Ibid., 11:70–71.
[33] *II plenum TsKK sozyva XV s"ezda VKP(b)*, pp. 108–10.
[34] Carr, *Foundations of a Planned Economy*, p. 308.

against and control over "bureaucrats." The politics of 1928–31 thus assumed a peculiar tone of mass politics.

The Stalin group considered the fight against bureaucratism within the party largely in terms of "human material." According to G. K. Ordzhonikidze, the question of the apparatus was "first of all a question of cadres."[35] If the Communist bureaucrats were indeed "the most dangerous type of bureaucrats," as Stalin contended, the struggle against them naturally became a central task. In fact, the grain crisis in 1928 had already caused the party leadership to purge the rural party organizations of alleged "bureaucrats" and "corrupt elements." No overall data on the results of these screenings are available, but according to the data concerning seven *oblast'* and *guberniia* organizations, an average of 12–13 percent of their members were expelled.[36] By the end of the year the Stalin group was determined to resort to a general cleansing of the party. The November 1928 plenum of the Central Committee declared a "verification of the present party composition and . . . the most resolute *purge* of its socially alien, bureaucratized, and degenerate elements, and other hangers-on."[37]

Purges played a critically important role in the Soviet Union, where the lack of political pluralism often created factions within the ruling party. According to a Rabkrin official,

In the prerevolutionary period such wavering comrades left the Bolshevik party and found asylum in other opportunist parties. Now in the period of the dictatorship of the poletariat . . . the presence in the country of other political parties is impossible. Hence all who seek an active political life try to join the ranks of our party.[38]

In April 1929 Stalin spoke more specifically of the reason why the party was to be subjected to a general cleansing:

There can be no doubt that bureaucratic elements exist not only in the economic and cooperative, trade union, and Soviet organizations, but also in the organizations of the party itself. Since the party is the guiding force of all these organizations, it is obvious that purging the party is the essential condition for thoroughly revitalizing and improving all the other organizations of the working class.[39]

[35] Ibid., p. 157.
[36] *XVI konferentsiia VKP(b)*, p. 592. See also Rigby, *Communist Party Membership in the USSR*, pp. 176–77.
[37] *KPSS v rezoliutsiiakh*, 4:148. Emphasis in the original.
[38] Korotkov, "K proverke i chistke proizvodstvennykh iacheek," p. 84.
[39] Stalin, *Sochineniia*, 12:13.

The 1929–30 cleansing was the first general purge since 1921. If the 1921 purge was conducted in order to force the Communists to adjust to the task of "restoration," or NEP, the 1929–30 purge was dictated, according to the Central Control Commission, by the need to make the party "more capable of fighting, more homogeneous, and more mobilized for the fight against bureaucratism and other distortions of the class line" in order to "reconstruct" the economy.[40]

To be sure, the Stalin group directed the general purge against the Bukharin sympathizers within the party. Yet this does not fully explain the motive behind the group's actions, if only because the whole series of intraparty struggles prior to the Stalin–Bukharin confrontation had not led to any general purge. According to the sixteenth party conference resolution,

> The purge now being undertaken must clear the ranks of the All-Union Communist Party of those ["alien, unreliable, and corrupted"] elements and thereby strengthen its mobilization readiness for the socialist offensive, to strengthen further the party's authority and faith in the party, and attract new urban proletarian and rural labor strata to the side of the party.[41]

With or without the Bukharin faction, the Stalinist leadership would have resorted to a general purge of the party to strengthen its "mobilization readiness for the socialist offensive." The data of the 1929–30 purge bear out this view.

The purge ran from May 1929 to May 1930, and some 170,000 (or approximately 11 percent of the current membership) were expelled. (Subsequent rehabilitations of the 36,000 initially purged reduced the rate to 8 percent.)[42] The alleged reasons for expulsion ranged from "defects in personal life and conduct" (anti-Semitism, participation in religious rites, etc.), 21.9 percent; political "passivity," 17 percent; and "alien elements or connection with alien elements," 16.9 percent; to criminal offenses, 12.3 percent. Those expelled for "factional activity and other violations of party discipline" accounted for only 10 percent.[43] The purge affected far wider circles than those deemed "Rightists."

The Stalinist leadership simultaneously recruited workers en

[40] *XVI konferentsiia VKP(b)*, p. 593 (E. Iaroslavskii). See also *KPSS v rezoliutsiiakh*, 4:239.
[41] *KPSS v rezoliutsiiakh*, 4:240.
[42] Ribgy, *Communist Party Membership in the USSR*, pp. 178–79.
[43] *XVI s'ezd VKP(b)*, p. 340.

masse to reactivate the party. The loss of membership cause by the 1929–30 purge was more than offset by the new recruits, a phenomenon that distinguished the 1929–30 purge from the 1921 and 1933–34 purges. In fact, the number of members (including candidates) rose from 1,305,854 in 1928 to 1,535,362 in 1929, 1,677,910 in 1930, and 2,212,225 in 1931.[44] New worker Communists were recruited mainly from among rank-and-file activists engaged in "social activities," that is, holding elected positions in trade unions, Soviet, Komsomol, cooperative, and other organizations. Of those factory workers who had entered the party in the second half of 1929, for example, as many as 94.7 percent were reported to be activists.[45]

At the sixteenth party congress, Stalin declared that the party had "re-formed its own ranks in battle order."[46] L. M. Kaganovich followed by emphasizing that the purge had strengthened "the ideological and organizational fighting ability" of the party.[47] Certainly one should not take this subjective judgment at face value. The purge of 1929–30 was much more limited in scope than that of 1921, which had expelled some 30.3 percent of the current membership.[48] Yet the 1929–30 purge highlighted the victory of the Stalin group and pressed a clear line of policy upon the party members. One Communist declared to the October 1928 joint plenum of the Moscow Committee and the Moscow Control Commission of the party: "Nobody wants to kindle intraparty quarrels; nobody wants to dispute; and all want our leaders to take a clear and unequivocal line."[49] Evidently the purge satisfied such demands. In the leadership, too, a "clear unequivocal line" was imposed. At the April 1929 joint plenum of the Central Committee and the Central Control Commission, S. V. Kosior, the Ukrainian party leader, declared: "One cannot allow free critics in our Politbureau who answer for nothing, who do not help us in work and do not fight against difficulties."[50] The purge–recruitment campaign imposed an unequivocal line on the party and brought in new activists in place of those branded as "bureaucratized

---

[44] Rigby, *Communist Party Membership in the USSR*, p. 52.
[45] *Sostav VKP(b) k XVI s˝ezdu*, p. 45.
[46] Stalin, *Sochineniia*, 12:316.
[47] *XVI s˝ezd VKP(b)*, pp. 58, 90–91. Indeed, this view was repeatedly emphasized in the press during the purge campaign. See, for example, *Leningradskaia pravda*, 30 January 1930.
[48] *XVI s˝ezd VKP(b)*, p. 323.
[49] Trotsky Archives, T 2783 (Strel'tsov).
[50] Quoted in Vaganov, *Pravyi uklon v VKP(b) i ego razgrom*, p. 228.

and corrupted." From the point of view of the Stalinist leadership, this shake-up appeared to strengthen the party's "mobilization readiness" and "fighting ability."

In 1928–29 the Stalin group took the shake-up of the trade unions equally seriously, if only because these mass organizations turned out to be dominated by the "Rightists," particularly the most influential leader, M. P. Tomskii. The unions were strong during NEP. In late 1926 Tomskii boasted of them:

> How can they [the Council of People's Commissars and the All-Union Central Executive Committee] be independent of us, when the unions unite 90 percent of the working class; when we, the unions, have six representatives in the presidium of the All-Union Central Executive Committee, forty-four representatives in the committee itself, four in the presidium of the All-Russian Central Executive Committee, and forty-seven in the committee itself; when we have a consultative vote in the Council of People's Commissars on every question, when the council cannot decide a single question concerning the life of the workers without our final decision in the matter; when we have the right to remove or postpone from the agenda of any high state organ any given question by a mere phone call: No, just a moment; you want to discuss such and such a matter, but you have not asked us our opinion; we want to make a final decision on this matter; be so kind as to postpone that item. We know of no case when this has been refused us. The unions have the right to call upon any people's commissar to appear before them to make a report, and no one of them has the right to refuse on the grounds that he is not formally responsible to the unions.[51]

Moreover, Tomskii was a full member of the Politbureau, the most important decision-making body in the country, from 1922 through July 1930. If they were indeed so powerful, the unions' political stance was an important political issue.

It is often asserted that the unions had sided with the Right within the party leadership because of their opposition to the rapid industrialization drive of the Stalin faction.[52] This view is not wrong, but it is a somewhat misleading simplification, since the unions were not explicitly opposed to rapid industrialization per se. Given widespread unemployment, the unions hoped that rapid industrialization would alleviate unemployment. As early as July 1927, they supported a bold industrialization plan.[53] In August and September

---

[51] Tomskii, *Profsoiuzy SSSR i ikh otnosheniia k kompartii i sovetskomu gosudarstvu*, pp. 39–40.

[52] See, for example, Sorenson, *The Life and Death of Soviet Trade Unionism*, pp. 283–84, and Deutscher, *Soviet Trade Unions*, chap. 4.

[53] Carr and Davies, *Foundations of a Planned Economy*, p. 909.

1928 the central committee of the metal workers' union repeatedly pressed for more rapid industrialization and greater capital investments than those proposed by the economic authorities.[54] L. I. Ginzburg of the All-Union Central Council of Trade Unions, a Rightist, constantly criticized Vesenkha for its "low" production targets and capital investments.[55] While compiling the control figures for 1928/29, the unions pressed for an even higher target of production growth (22 percent) than that proposed by Vesenkha (18.6 percent).[56] At the eighth trade union congress in December 1928, representatives of individual unions and regional union councils, like regional party leaders at the sixteenth party conference, came forward with demands for more resources and for more new factories in their own particular interests.[57] The congress not only failed to challenge Vesenkha's ambitious five-year plan but also accused Vesenkha of underestimating the production capacity of industry; Kuibyshev, in turn, blamed the unions for having demanded the impossible, namely, as much as a 300 percent economic growth in five years.[58] At the fifth Gosplan congress in March 1929, a representative of the Ukrainian metal workers' union declared that even the optimal plan (ten million tons of iron and 85,000 tons of copper) was a *"necessary minimum."*[59]

The unions actually struggled for resources. They chose the tactic of pressing for rapid industrialization in order to obtain more resources for wages, labor protection, and housing, and to alleviate unemployment and the chronic goods famine that had adversely affected workers.[60] At the eighth trade union congress, Ginzburg demanded that Vesenkha project a much higher employment plan, and declared: "If you want a 95 percent growth in the productivity of labor, create conditions for growth, and create normal and healthy working conditions."[61] In principle, union leaders were in favor of rapid industrialization insofar as it would not call for sacrifices on the part of the working class. In reality, they did not

[54] *Torgovo-promyshlennaia gazeta* (hereafter *TPG*), 17 August 1928.
[55] See, for example, *TPG*, 14 September 1928.
[56] See L. I. Ginzburg's account in *Problemy rekonstruktsii narodnogo khoziaistva SSSR na piatiletie*, p. 436.
[57] *VIII s˝ezd professional'nykh soiuzov SSSR*, pp. 372–449.
[58] Ibid., pp. 391 and 411.
[59] *Problemy rekonstruktsii narodnogo khoziaistva SSSR na piatiletie*, p. 523 (Fesenko). Emphasis in the original.
[60] *TPG*, 14 September 1928, and *VIII s˝ezd professional'nykh soiuzov SSSR*, p. 411.
[61] *VIII s˝ezd professional'nykh soiuzov SSSR*, pp. 411 and 413.

regard such an industrialization drive as feasible or possible. Addressing the seventeenth party congress in 1934, Tomskii recalled the position the union leadership, if not the rank and file, took in 1928: "Formally, we stood for industrialization, but in fact . . . where could the party get the resources for its great program of industrialization? We didn't see such resources."[62] Thus, at the fifth Gosplan congress, which endorsed Vesenkha's ambitious plan, Ginzburg resisted by declaring that even the minimal plan (which projected an 85 percent growth in the productivity of labor in five years) was "very difficult."[63]

As E. H. Carr and R. W. Davies have pointed out, the trade unions were "in a cleft stick": "They could not resist the principle of planning, which in any case meant the expansion of industry, and of the industrial proletariat. Yet planning meant the submission of the unions to the planning authorities."[64] Nowhere was the dilemma of the unions more pronounced than in the wage issue. If the economy as a whole was to be planned, wages too had to be subjected to planning, which, in operational terms, meant central regulation. From the mid-1920s on, the state in fact increasingly intervened in wage fixing, and a uniform state regulation came to supersede collective agreements as a determinant of the wages of the employees of all government institutions. This intervention evoked strong reactions from the Union of Soviet and Trade Employees. At the seventh trade union congress in December 1926, M. Gegechkori of that union, for instance, bitterly complained that because of state regulation of wages, the union could no longer fight against management and therefore was deprived of authority in the eyes of the workers.[65] The unions as a whole accepted the principle of state regulation, but they did not allow the principle to extend fully to their main constituency, the industrial proletariat.[66]

The ambivalence of the trade unions with regard to industrialization and planning appeared to Stalin and his associates to deprive the unions of the fighting ability for industrialization. Unable to find a way out, the unions sought their raison d'être in fighting against their traditional foe – managers. As a matter of fact, in the

[62] *XVII s˜ezd VKP(b)*, p. 250.
[63] *Problemy rekonstruktsii narodnogo khoziaistva SSSR na piatiletie*, p. 439.
[64] Carr and Davies, *Foundations of a Planned Economy*, p. 549.
[65] *VII s˜ezd professional'nykh soiuzov SSSR*, pp. 152–54. See also p. 184.
[66] Carr and Davies, *Foundations of a Planned Economy*, pp. 542–44.

summer of 1928 the union leadership entered a state of war with the managerial authorities over the issues of labor discipline and labor productivity. The unions responded angrily to ever intensifying managerial pressure for stricter labor discipline and greater productivity. In June 1928, S. P. Birman, the tough director of the Southern Steel Trust, infuriated the trade unions by openly assailing the workers for lack of discipline in work.[67] At the November 1928 plenum of Vesenkha, I. I. Shvarts of the miners' union contended that the managers were "blockheads" (*shliapy*) and that this was the main reason for economic "counterrevolutionary" activity (the Shakhty affair) and low labor productivity.[68] Birman was reported to have "declared war" on the unions at the plenum.[69] At the November 1928 plenum of the Ukrainian Communist Party, Kosior sharply criticized the unions for describing the managers as "enemies of the working class."[70] Shortly thereafter, at the eighth trade union congress, Tomskii contended that the managers threw all the responsibility for their own defects and mismanagement onto the workers, and he urged the managers to "use your brains a little better."[71]

When economic planning was replacing market relations, it appeared to the Stalin group to be axiomatic that the unions' functions had to change accordingly. The unions, however, seemed to the group to be obsessed with the old struggle of labor and management, a legacy of a market economy.[72] When in the view of the Stalin group it was imperative to fight for labor discipline and labor productivity, the unions proved unable to fight, because to do so, they believed, would only aid their foe and, consequently, curtail their bargaining power. The April 1929 joint plenum of the Central Committee and the Central Control Commission thus savagely denounced the unions:

The trade unions, which are called upon to play a decisive role in building socialist industry, in increasing labor productivity and discipline, in organiz-

---

[67] *Vseukrainskaia proizvodstvennaia konferentsiia,* 1:166. Similar conflicts occurred at a plenum of the Ukrainian metal workers' union in March 1929 and other meetings. *TPG,* 16 April 1929.
[68] *TPG,* 1 December 1928.
[69] Bogushevskii, "Kanun piatiletki," p. 517.
[70] Kosior, *Vybrani statti i promovy,* p. 195.
[71] *VIII s"ezd professional'nykh soiuzov SSSR,* p. 201.
[72] See Kaganovich's talk to the union leaders quoted in Fitzpatrick, "Stalin and the Making of a New Elite," p. 387.

ing the production initiative of the working class and of socialist competition, and also in instilling class values in the new strata of the proletariat, must resolutely rid themselves of all remnants of shoppist exclusiveness [*tsekhovaia zamknutost'*] and trade unionism, as well as bureaucratic inattention to the workers and disregard for the task of defending the day-to-day needs and interests of the working class.[73]

This last contention may sound strange, because the Stalin group attacked the unions for counterposing the defense of workers' economic interests to the promotion of labor productivity and discipline. In 1928–29 the group actually redefined the "needs and interests" of the working class to "fit the requirements of the reconstruction period." The new, politically expedient concept radically departed from what the Stalin group saw as the old obsession of the unions.

The Stalin group found it politically convenient to contend that the "defense" and the "production" functions of the unions constituted a "dialectical unity."[74] Certainly it did not mean that there were no contradictions between the two. Yet it did mean that they could be "synthesized" in a particular way under the conditions of a planned economy: the unions were able to perform the two functions by aiding the managers to maximize both production and wages, more specifically not only by watching management but also by pointing out and helping management eliminate defects and bureaucratism that frustrated the production activity and initiative of workers. In this way, the unions were expected to help management maximize production and productivity, and, by implication, workers' wages as well. At the sixteenth party congress Kaganovich declared that such activity was the real concern for the needs of workers.[75]

Certainly this argument was not incomprehensible to the unions because, under certain circumstances, growth in production and productivity could result in an increase in wages. The argument, however, sounded to the trade union leaders like a familiarly capitalist pretext for imposing sacrifices on workers (indeed, workers' real wages were declining at this time), curtailing their bargaining

---

[73] *KPSS v rezoliutsiiakh*, 4:184.
[74] See, for example, L. Nedachin, "Zashchitnaia rabota profsoiuzov i sotsialisticheskoe sorevnovanie," *Pravda*, 24 October 1929, and Kaganovich's remark that the two functions were two sides of the same coin in *XVI s'ezd VKP(b)*, p. 64.
[75] *XVI s'ezd VKP(b)*, p. 64.

power, and relegating the unions to a subordinate position in the factories.[76] Such a self-image was hard for the union leadership to accept. At the eighth trade union congress, Tomskii ardently defended the factory trade union committees (which were under attack for their alleged disinclination for the drive for productivity) by referring to their revolutionary past.[77]

The unions demonstrated to the Stalin group their resolution to fight for their autonomy in the Soviet political system. The trade unions were neither state nor party organizations, but voluntary associations of workers. In this sense they were independent of both the state and the party. As Tomskii's boast clearly indicated, however, during NEP the unions had enjoyed enormous authority in the making of national policy. They also did not disavow complete independence from the party but rather always acknowledged its guidance; and in the last analysis, Tomskii and other leaders were almost all party members. Nevertheless, the unions, like many other organizations, had retained a relatively autonomous position during NEP.

It was this autonomy that doomed the trade unions. In 1928–29 the Stalin group attacked it as "trade unionism" because the autonomy did not assure compliance with the party line and in fact provided a strong organizational basis for the Right: Tomskii formed an alliance with Bukharin. On the eve of the eighth trade union congress, the Central Committee resolved to send Stalin's staunch supporter, Kaganovich, to the presidium of the All-Union Central Council of Trade Unions as a standing member. Tomskii obstinately resisted the resolution on the grounds that Kaganovich would create a "dual center."[78] Tomskii and his associates were defeated and accused of trying to make a "principality" (*knia-*

---

[76] In March 1929 Gulyi, of the People's Commissariat of Labor of the Ukrainian Republic (which had closely cooperated with the unions in working out various issues related to labor), declared to a conference devoted to the problem of labor discipline: "Industrial managers have arranged to demand that the unions and labor organs and even the party cells 'serve them.' " Naturally angered, managers repeatedly interrupted Gulyi. *Ekonomicheskaia zhizn'*, 3 March 1929.

[77] *VIII s˝ezd professional'nykh soiuzov SSSR*, p. 201. The factory commmittee was a primary trade union organization in the factory. After the 1917 Revolution, the independent factory committees were incorporated into the trade union hierarchy.

[78] *XVI s˝ezd VKP(b)*, p. 276; *KPSS v rezoliutsiiakh*, 4:195–96; *Pravda*, 26 October 1929 (N. Evreinov). See also Cohen, *Bukharin and the Bolshevik Revolution*, p. 301; Daniels, *The Conscience of the Revolution*, p. 348; and Koch, *Die bol'ševistischen Gewerkschaften*, p. 120.

zhestvo) out of their union domain. The April 1929 joint plenum of the Central Committee and the Central Control Commission declared:

> Comrades Bukharin, Rykov, and Tomskii have taken the highly dangerous course of setting the unions against the party. In fact, they are pursuing a policy of weakening party leadership of the union movement, concealing the shortcomings in union work, covering up trade-unionist tendencies and instances of bureaucratic petrification in a part of the union apparatus, and representing the party struggle against the shortcomings as a Trotskyist "shake-up of the trade unions."[79]

Tomskii left his position after the eighth union congress and was officially removed from the post in June 1929.[80]

Following Tomskii's removal, the Stalin group subjected trade unions, like the party and government institutions, to purges. At the sixteenth party conference, the former Komsomol leader, L. A. Shatskin, urged the conference to "purge the unions of trade union-ists."[81] Kaganovich, who evidently supervised the purge operation carried out by Rabkrin, emphasized that the trade union organizations had to be "refreshed" and that the essence of the whole issue was "*selection of new people and replacement of the old.*"[82] According-ing to Tomskii, the Stalin group decided to remove the "entire leadership" (*vsia golovka*) of the unions.[83]

The upshot was a radical replacement of the old union cadres. In 1929 many union leaders, among others Tomskii, I. I. Lepse of the metal workers' union, and G. N. Mel'nichanskii of the textile work-ers' union, were removed from their posts and transferred to their erstwhile archenemy, Vesenkha.[84] As of 1 April 1930, 59.5 percent of the All-Union Central Council of Trade Unions members were removed; and 51.7 percent of its presidium members, 67.5 percent of the unions' central committee members, 71.5 percent of the

[79] *KPSS v rezoliutsiiakh*, 4:185.
[80] *Trud*, 2 June 1929.
[81] *XVI konferentsiia VKP(b)*, pp. 115–16.
[82] *Trud*, 30 January 1930. Emphasis in the original.
[83] *XVI s″ezd VKP(b)*, p. 144.
[84] *Sobranie zakonov*, 1930, II, 31–85, 51–301. See also Koch, *Die bol'ševistischen Gewerkschaften*, pp. 90–91, and *Vsia Moskva*, 1930, p. 44. Lepse died immediately after he was assigned a position in Vesenkha (*Trud*, 5 October 1929). In 1930 the board of the Union Coal Trust, for example, was composed mainly of former leaders of the central committee of the miners' union and therefore was nicknamed the "trade union [board]." Paramonov, *Uchit'sia upravliat'*, pp. 148–49.

board of the unions' departments, and 68.1 percent of the factory committees were replaced.[85] In turn, 250 shock workers were promoted to the Central Council and the unions' central committees.[86]

The Stalin group attacked the unions for their autonomy, which did not ensure compliance with the party line. Certainly, in any case, the unions, like the party itself, were bound to be shaken up as a result of the new policy. Yet it was because of the autonomy that the Stalin group purged the unions so extensively and often violently. The purge of the railway workers' union, for instance, was said to have been conducted in the following way:

If the purge of the party or government institutions continued for a month or two in the provinces, the apparatus of the central committee of the union had been purged for nine months. As they say, it was purged with sand, washed, thrashed, whacked, and scratched in seven waters.[87]

A violation of "proletarian democracy" though the purge may have been, declared Kaganovich to the sixteenth party congress,

Comrades, it has long been known that for us Bolsheviks democracy is no fetish; for us proletarian democracy is a means for arming the working class and for a better execution of its socialist tasks, and therefore we arm the unions by all our organizational practice.

He relentlessly shook up the unions for the sake of "arming the unions in conformity to the tasks of socialist construction."[88]

One important institutional consequence of the purges of the government and trade unions was that Rabkrin, the state control agency in charge of the purges, came to play an increasingly prominent role in the industrialization drive. (Undoubtedly the GPU too played a critically important part, but as a secret police, it had its own functions that supported Rabkrin from the secret side of police activity.) Even before the purge, Rabkrin became increasingly im-

---

[85] Kornilov, "Povyshenie roli partiinykh organizatsii v khoziaistvennom stroitel'stve (1926–1932 gg.)," p. 91, citing *K XVI s~ezdu VKP(b). Materialy k organizatsionnomu otchetu TsK VKP(b)*, vol. II (Moscow, 1930), p. 197. The purge also "uncovered" many former Mensheviks, SRs, and "class aliens" (former Whites) in the union organizations. (See, for example, the case of the miners' union in *Rabochaia gazeta*, 11 September 1929.) As of 1 October 1928, 27.8% of the Central Council's senior officials had formerly belonged to other political parties, but the rate dropped sharply to 5.3% by October 1931. *Udarnik*, 1932, no. 2, p. 57.

[86] *XVI s~ezd VKP(b)*, P. 664. For the shock workers, see chap. 5, this volume.

[87] *Partiia i X s~ezd zheleznodorozhnikov o zh.-d. transporte*, p. 91.

[88] *XVI s~ezd VKP(b)*, p. 63.

portant as "policy makers in agriculture, industry and planning."[89] A number of factors accounted for its ascendancy. Rabkrin was a creation of the Soviet government and therefore was not tarnished by any direct link with the old regime; it was headed by Stalin's close associate, G. K. Ordzhonikidze, and was organizationally merged (and so worked jointly) with the Central Control Commission, which supervised the purges of the party; and it had the highest rate of party "saturation" of all the people's commissariats: in 1929, 48.3 percent of the Rabkrin staff were party members or candidate members, whereas the average rate for all the commissariats was only 24.8 percent.[90]

As early as April 1929, a speaker complained about Rabkrin's deep involvement with industrial affairs at the Communist Academy's Institute for Soviet Construction: Rabkrin had "recently gone along the lines of studying problems that are posed by Gosplan and various scientific research institutes," but there was in fact "quite a lot of wrecking in the apparatus of Soviet administration." He was asked: "Who, then, will inspect the economy?"[91] At the sixteenth party conference in April 1929, a Rabkrin representative showed considerable zeal for intervening with what he called the "unwieldy, monstrous bureaucratic apparatus of Vesenkha."[92] In the course of 1929, Rabkrin engaged in industrial planning to such an extent that in late 1929 one commentator, perhaps sarcastically, went so far as to call for the merger of Gosplan and Rabkrin.[93] Through the purges Rabkrin, along with the GPU, emerged as the most reliable apparatus of Stalin's revolution.

The purges were carried out at terrible human cost. Hundreds of thousands of people lost their positions; they and their families were stigmatized, and many were imprisoned. The purges entailed huge production costs as well: many workers were mobilized away from the shop floor, and normal production flows were interrupted here and there. The purges, moreover, incurred enormous administrative costs: experienced and skilled officials were removed, and far less experienced and far less skilled workers, peasants, and Com-

[89] Davies, *The Socialist Offensive*, p. 399.
[90] Bineman and Kheinman, *Kadry gosudarstvennogo i kooperativnogo apparata SSSR*, pp. 32, 86, 93.
[91] Pashukanis and Ignat, *Ocherednye zadachi bor'by s biurokratizmom*, p. 68.
[92] *XVI konferentsiia VKP(b)*, p. 510 (A. I. Gurevich).
[93] *TPG*, 11 October 1929 (M. Artamonov).

munists were brought in. The apparatus ceased to function in normal, routine fashion. It is not difficult to imagine the extent of
administrative confusion caused by the purges. In the statistics sector of the central committee of the teachers' union, for instance, a
"near catastrophe" resulted from the purge of three officials.[94]

Yet it appeared to the Stalinist leadership (which considered the
problem of resource constraints not so much in economic as in
political terms) that the political gain of the purges overrode all
other concerns. Those elements deemed unreliable were forced out
of the apparatus, and those seen as politically reliable and militant
were put in their stead. At great human, economic, and administrative costs, the purges thus forced the apparatus to become more
responsive to the class-war industrialization drive. On the one
hand, as industrialization and collectivization were accelerated in
1929–30, the apparatus would appear to the leadership to be still
disappointingly inept and invite further purges. On the other hand,
as a result of continuous purges and constant exhortation on the
part of the leadership, some sections of the apparatus would prove
militant beyond the control of the leadership. This would only add
chaos to the administrative confusion.[95]

[94] *Pravda,* 3 September 1930.
[95] See chap. 6, this volume.

3

The shake-up of industrial enterprises

In November 1928 a speaker declared at a session of the All-Russian Central Executive Committee: "Wrecking is an exception, an isolated phenomenon, and not a constant phenomenon onto which we can dump our inability to work. A large portion of the defects in our construction depends on our inability to work, not on some wicked will. This has to be understood."[1] A few weeks later the chairman of the Ukrainian Central Executive Committee emphasized that the Shakhty affair was typical of all industrial enterprises.[2] Despite the seeming contradiction of these statements, their implications were clear: that there were serious defects in the work of industry and that all industrial enterprises were to be reorganized in accordance with the imperatives of industrialization.

In the wake of the Shakhty affair the industrial enterprises too were subjected to purges. A number of engineers deemed politically suspect were arrested and put on trial. In the Donbas, by 1931 half of all engineers and technical workers were arrested.[3] In the transportation sector, 4,500 "wreckers" were "removed" by mid-1931.[4] At the so-called Industrial Party trial in November 1930, L. K. Ramzin, the chief defendant, maintained that the Industrial Party had held a membership of approximately 2,000, or 6–7 percent of the engineering cadres in the country.[5] Presumably, these members were arrested or purged. No doubt, the purges, however economi-

---

[1] *III sessiia VTsIK XIII sozyva*, 16:12 (V. P. Miliutin).
[2] *4 sessiia TsIK Soiuza SSR 4 sozyva*, 26:6 (G. Petrovskii).
[3] Bailes, *Technology and Society under Lenin and Stalin*, p. 150.
[4] Kuibyshev, *Stat'i i rechi*, p. 78.
[5] *Protsess "Prompartii,"* pp. 52, 148–49. According to Trifonov, "not more than 2,000 to 3,000" proved to be "wreckers" (*Ocherki istorii klassovoi bor'by v SSSR v gody NEPa*, pp. 160–61).

cally irrational, were intended to make the factories politically alert and responsive to the class-war policy.

Yet the shake-up of the factories entailed more than purges. It was in the factories that industrial policies were actually executed and that mass politics that characterized the revolutionary years actually took place. The rapid industrialization drive and the creation of a planned economy required maximum managerial efficiency and accountability. To this end, the political leadership sought to reorganize the factories not only by purges but also by the institutionalization of *edinonachalie*, or one-man management.

One-man management had long been controversial in the party since the civil war years. Concerns for managerial efficiency and iron labor discipline conflicted with collegiate management, a principle deemed more democratic. One-man management also appeared to many Bolsheviks and workers to repudiate the revolutionary watchword of workers' control.[6] The introduction of NEP further complicated the issue: the factory nominally operated according to one-man management, but managerial power was actually divided between the Red director and the chief (typically "bourgeois") engineer, or the technical director; moreover, it was often shared by the party and trade union representatives who were jealous of power. Workers' control was assumed irrelevant to the market economy of NEP. In 1928, this managerial style appeared to the Stalin group to be woefully ill equipped for a class-war industrialization drive and a new, nonmarket economy.

The problem of one-man management reemerged immediately after the Shakhty affair. In early 1929 the party embarked on a public campaign for one-man management, which culminated in September 1929 with the Central Committee's special resolution on the principle.[7] In 1928–29, the institutionalization of one-man management had three objectives. First, it was to eliminate the managerial dualism of the Red and the technical directors and to establish the sole managerial command of the former. Second, one-man management was to be complemented by controls both from above and from below. Third, it was to eliminate the triple managerial parallelism of the director, the party secretary, and the factory trade union committee chairman. The reorganization of the factories along the

---

[6] For this controversy see Carr, *The Bolshevik Revolution*, pp. 187–91.
[7] "Postanovlenie TsK VKP (b) o merakh po uporiadocheniiu upravleniia proizvodstvom i ustanovleniiu edinonachaliia," *KPSS v rezoliutsiiakh*, 4:310–17.

lines of one-man management created a new regime in which single managerial command and multiple controls over management would in theory work together to ensure maximum managerial accountability and efficiency.

One-man management and managerial accountability

After the Shakhty affair, warnings were voiced that Soviet power was under the "technological yoke of the Tartars" (the "Tartars" being "bourgeois" specialists) and that the Communists' lack of technical expertise was therefore "politically dangerous."[8] In the 1920s the Communist (Red) managers were incomparably inferior to their nominal subordinates ("bourgeois" specialists) in terms of education in general and technical expertise in particular. Reflecting the party's social basis, nearly nine out of every ten Communist managers did not have even an elementary education, whereas the majority of engineers had secondary and higher educations. According to one survey, as of 1 October 1929, 84.9 percent of 1,542 directors of industrial enterprises and institutions were Communists. But 88.4 percent of these did not have even an elementary education, and only 34 (or 2.6 percent) of them had completed higher education. On the other hand, 62.1 percent of 2,459 deputy and assistant directors were non-Communists; 76.6 percent of these non-Communists had some form of higher, secondary, or primary education, 47.0 percent having completed higher education.[9]

Stalin used the Shakhty affair to press on the party the political imperative of creating a "proletarian intelligentsia" that would solve the dichotomy between "Red" and expert, thereby eliminat-

---

[8] *Rabochaia gazeta*, 8 September 1928 (Ia. Rudzutak, a Politbureau member), and *Pravda*, 4 March 1928 (A. Iakovlev of Rabkrin).

[9] *Inzhenerno-tekhnicheskie kadry promyshlennosti*, pp. 47, 52. As of the same date, 48 of 51 directors in the Donbas coal mines, the stage of the Shakhty affair, were Communists. But 43 of these were *praktiks*, i.e., those with no formal education. On the other hand, 28 of 30 chief engineers were non-Communists, only one being a *praktik*. Renke, *Kadry inzhenerno-tekhnicheskogo personala kamennougol'noi promyshlennosti Donetskogo basseina*, p. 10. Similarly, in 1929 only 3 of the 125 leading industrial managers in Moscow had a higher education. L. Faber, "Nabor 'tysiachnikov' i zadachi podgotovki krasnykh spetsialistov," *Partiinoe stroitel'stvo*, 1930, no. 15, pp. 21–22.

ing the rationale for class-conciliatory management.[10] According to Sheila Fitzpatrick, from 1928 on, hundreds of thousands of workers, peasants, and Communists were in fact sent to engineering schools.[11]

There was the more immediate task of making management more loyal to party policy and more capable of fighting for industrialization. The purge of specialists, for one, was intended to serve this end. Crash courses were set up for Red directors to improve their technical skills.[12] Simultaneously, the political leadership sought to eliminate the institutional framework of class-conciliatory management. Stalin maintained in April 1928 that the 1926 "Model Regulations" of factory management conferred "practically all the rights on the technical director [chief engineer], leaving to the general [Red] director the right to settle conflicts, to 'represent,' in short, to twiddle his thumbs."[13] The Model Regulations in fact conferred on the technical (typically "bourgeois") director the "whole management of technical-production matters" in the factory. Welcoming the 1926 regulations, the specialist journal *Inzhenernyi trud* had jovially declared that the "maintenance of one-man management in the factory" was a "fetish."[14] In the Donbas coal mines managers had been barred by collective agreements from interfering with the "matters and work of engineering-technical personnel." The managers were not allowed to take any action against them in connection with mismanagement or technical errors without the decision of the engineering-technical section of the miners' union.[15] At the Shakhty trial, the defending engineers were accused of having prevented the managers from intervening in "operative work" in the mines.[16] Stalin contended that the Red directors were also responsible for this state of affairs because they, having lost the sense of class struggle, had become the "rubber stamps" or "followers" of "saboteurs and specialist-wreckers."[17] Worse still, according to Stalin,

[10] Stalin, *Sochineniia*, 11:36–38, 58–61; *KPSS v rezoliutskiialkh*, 4:84–93, 111–18; and Fitzpatrick, "Stalin and the Making of a New Elite."

[11] Fitzpatrick, *Education and Social Mobility in the Soviet Union*, chap. 9.

[12] *Sovetskaia intelligentsia*, chap. 2, sect. 3.

[13] Stalin, *Sochineniia*, 11:58. Stalin referred to Circular No. 33 of USSR Vesenkha in *TPG*, 31 March 1926.

[14] *Inzhenernyi trud*, 1926, no. 6, p. 238.

[15] *Vestnik Donuglia*, no. 38 (15 June 1928), p. 7.

[16] *Ekonomicheskaia kontrrevoliutsiia v Donbasse*, p. 26.

[17] See Stalin, *Sochineniia*, and Ia. A. Iakovlev, deputy people's commissar for Rabkrin, in *XVI konferentsiia VKP(b)*, pp. 454–59, 553.

the directors were unwilling to confront their errors.[18] He urged
that the 1926 regulations be replaced by new ones that would "alter
the conditions of work of the managerial cadres and help them to
become real and absolute masters [*polnovlastnye khoziaeva*] of
their job."[19] Rabkrin took the lead in the replacement.[20]

In early 1929 the old regulations were replaced by the new "Basic
Rules on the Rights and Duties of Administrative, Technical, and
Managerial Personnel."[21] By concentrating managerial command in
the director's hands, the new rules were said to "eliminate the possibility of the presence in the enterprise of two directors – 'technical'
and 'Red' " and to institutionalize one-man management (*edinolichie*) in the factory.[22] An editorial in *Torgovo-promyshlennaia
gazeta*, an organ of Vesenkha, declared to the managers: "Rights are
given. . . . You have to consolidate them in practice."[23] The principle
of one and only one director was further elaborated by the September
1929 resolution on one-man management and the new "Model Regulations of Production Enterprises" issued in January 1930.[24] The
director thus acquired sole managerial command in the factory. One-
man management eliminated the dual power of Red and technical
directors and granted the former a vast range of rights and responsi-
bilities, not only for general administration, but for organizational-
technical problems as well. It was expected to ensure a tougher class
line in the factory and to allow the director to mobilize all the
factory's resources for industrialization by improving managerial
efficiency.

Power is seldom free of responsibility. One-man management
implied not only sole managerial command but strictly individual
managerial responsibility for the wielding of power and the results

[18] See Stalin's account in *Sochineniia*, 1(14):59.
[19] Ibid., 11:58.
[20] *Za ratsionalizatsiiu*, 1928, no. 8, p. 16. Vesenkha failed to take the initiative.
Inzhenernyi trud, 1928, no. 8, p. 246. It should be noted that it was Rabkrin that
was most concerned about the lack of individual responsibility of Soviet officials.
See, for example, Ordzhonikidze, *Stat'i i rechi*, 2:157.
[21] *TPG*, 2 February 1929, and *Za ratsionalizatsiiu*, 1928, no. 8, p. 16.
[22] *Trud*, 2 February 1929, and *TPG*, 20 January, 2 and 3 February 1929. Apparently, *edinolichie* carries fewer hierarchical implications than does *edinonachalie*,
which was employed in the September 1929 resolution and became the standard
term thereafter. Süß, *Der Betrieb in der UdSSR*, p. 571, seems to get this point
wrong.
[23] *TPG*, 2 February 1929.
[24] *Gosudarstvennoe predpriiatie*, pp. 104–9.

of its use, in particular the fulfillment of plan targets. Just like any other administrator, however, the Soviet manager wanted power rather than responsibility. In 1929 some managers went so far as to claim "dictatorship in production."[25] I. A. Kraval' of Vesenkha had to take them to task: "Some [managers] have gone too far in their pretensions."[26] They were accused of considering one-man management "unlimited power" and of assuming that they now could do whatever they pleased.[27] However, they openly disclaimed the sole responsibility for the fulfillment of production targets: they sought to share responsibility with the party and union organizations.[28]

The investment of managerial power in a person who was rather weak in technological matters but willing to avoid taking responsibility for the use of power was necessitated by the class-war policy, but it did not promise well in terms of managerial accountability. Moreover, the new economic system lacked an effective mechanism of rendering management accountable. In a capitalist society, competition in the market tests managerial competence, with incompetence and mistakes often resulting in bankruptcy. While it eliminated this anarchy in the market, the centrally planned economy rid itself of the control of the market. When the party leadership granted managers one-man management with all its powers, it also sought to make managerial accountability an integral part of the planned economy.

Even at the high point of NEP the factory was not at all accountable, partly because of overcentralized industrial management. In the 1920s the factory was not a full-fledged juridical body but was directly subordinated to a trust, which in turn was subordinated to a chief administration (*glavk*) of Vesenkha. The trust directly managed its factories, which therefore did not get involved in the market on their own account and were thus "depersonalized," a peculiar

---

[25] Quoted in *Trud*, 6 March 1929. Even I. Tolstopiatov, deputy people's commissar of labor and chairman of the State Commission for the Improvement of Labor Discipline set up in Februuary 1929, emphasized: "The director has to be the dictator in the factory." *Ekonomicheskaia zhizn'* 6 March 1929, and *Voprosy truda*, 1929, no. 8, p. 14.

[26] Quoted in *Trud*, 6 March 1929.

[27] *Pravda*, 12 September 1929; *Inzhenernyi rabotnik*, 1930, nos. 5–6, p. 4; *Rabochaia gazeta*, 27 February, 26 March 1930; *Izvestiia Stalingradskogo okrkoma VKP(b)*, 1930, nos. 7–8, p. 19; *XI z'izd KP(b)U*, pp. 432, 667; *Gornorabochii*, 1929, no. 45 (8 December), p. 12.

[28] See the meeting of some thirty top-level managers in *TPG*, 5 April 1929. Only one of them opposed collective responsibility.

Soviet expression meaning lack of personal power, initiative, and responsibility.[29] The factory was said to occupy "a purely parasitical position," comfortably free from the control of the market. The relationship between the trust and its factories, according to one account, consisted in the principle that the factory "took according to its needs and gave according to its ability"; it was "accountable for nothing, and at the same time had no rights"; and the psychology of the factory director was "extremely consumerist."[30] According to V. P. Zatonskii, an outspoken representative of Rabkrin, the "awful centralization" could be explained "not only by the bureaucratic influence of old specialists, not only by the fact that we had inherited an old apparatus that is still a burden on us, but also by our poverty during war communism, by our low cultural level, and by the fact that very often we could not rely on anybody."[31]

Whatever the reason, already before the Shakhty affair, while economic planning was being centralized, factory operation was being decentralized in order to transfer more discretionary powers from the trust to the factory director and to strengthen the latter's managerial accountability.[32] This measure, taken by the new 1927 law on industrial trusts, was expected to "emancipate" the factories from their trust.[33] But the trust, jealous of power and distrustful of its subordinates, continued to keep its factories under "tutelage." Therefore, it was emphasized, the factories could not "grow normally" and their leaders (directors) were brought up as "irresponsible commisars."[34] After the Shakhty affair, the Central Control Commission and Vesenkha had to exert pressure on the trusts "to a sufficiently brutal degree."[35]

From a more practical point of view, managerial accountability meant the managerial ability to account for all credits and debits, to cut operating costs, and to generate capital for investment. The new

[29] Lakin, *Reforma upravleniia promyshlennost'iu v 1929/30 g.*, p. 24.
[30] S. Birman, "Promfinplan i khozraschet," *Puti industrializatsii*, 1931, no. 8, pp. 3–4.
[31] *XV s'ezd VKP(b)*, 1:469.
[32] "Polozhenie o gosudarstvennykh promyshlennykh trestakh," in *Sobranie zakonov*, 1927, I, 39–392; "Tipovoe polozhenie o proizvodsvennom predpriiatii, vkhodiashchem v sostav tresta," in *TPG*, 14 October 1927. As a matter of fact, these clearly stipulated one-man management (*edinolichie*), a principle that remained only on paper.
[33] *Ekonomicheskaia zhizn'*, 28 October 1928 (M. B. Grossman of Rabkrin).
[34] *Sputnik agitatora dlia goroda*, 1928, no. 14, p. 17.
[35] See Ia. A. Iakovlev in *Leningradskaia pravda*, 12 March 1929.

law regarding industrial trusts was an attempt to eliminate the factory's parasitical position and to make it an accountable production unit by granting it more discretionary powers and by imposing on it the principle of *khozraschet* (cost accounting). In a market economy like NEP this principle meant commercial accounting, or a profit and loss principle. Yet in the late 1920s, market relations ironically were being squeezed out of the socialized sector of the economy: already in 1925–26, the "sale of the product of state industry lost the character of 'free' trade, and its realization assumed an organized, planned character."[36] Therefore, despite the decentralization of industrial management, the factory proved no more subject to the control of the market than before.[37] As more and more resources were invested in industry, this lack of control over the factory increasingly disquieted the party leadership.

Enthusiasm for industrialization was inseparable from struggle for resources, and managers made every effort to obtain as large an investment as possible for their own trusts or plants. In 1928–29 the discussion of the First Five-Year Plan gave birth to a tense atmosphere among managers. At the second Ukrainian party conference in April 1929 a Rabkrin representative declared:

We are all impatient; all workers are impatient; local organizations are impatient – impatient to reconstruct their factories as soon as possible and industrialize them according to the latest word in technology. But . . . if we throw about our resources and powers for all factories and enter into vast construction work without calculating the effectiveness of the factories, and without comparing the effectiveness of one factory with another. . . . , then the mistakes of the Five-Year Plan will be at least ten times as many as those we have made already.[38]

In spite of repeated warnings, managers sought to outmaneuver the party and the government.

---

[36] Iakovleva, *Razvitie dogovornykh sviazei gosudarstvennoi promyshlennosti SSSR*, p. 263. See also Drobizhev, "Nekotorye osobennosti metodov upravleniia promyshlennost'iu v SSSR v 1926–1932 godakh," p. 38.

[37] Accordingly, the concept of *khozraschet* ceased to imply "profit or loss." Instead it was linked with "production economy" to be achieved by overfulfilling production targets. (See, for example, L. Gintsburg, "Sovetskoe predpriiatie v period sotsialisticheskoi rekonstruktsii," *Sovetskoe gosudarstvo i revoliutsiia prava*, 1930, no. 2, p. 105.) The difference between planned and actual costs became the criterion of the success of factory operation. But the pressure to fulfill production plans overrode the pressure to reduce costs.

[38] *Drukha konferentsiia Komunistychnoi partii (bil'shovykiv) Ukrainy*, p. 318 (A. I. Gurevich).

The Stalino Metallurgical Factory in the Donbas, which caused a heated controversy at the sixteenth party conference in April 1929, illustrates this problem. In January 1929 the factory completed a 690-page plan for an extensive reconstruction, demanding seventy-two million rubles for the following five years.[39] According to S. P. Birman, then director of the Southern Steel Trust to which the Stalino Factory belonged, the construction of a blast furnace and Bessemer steel workshop, a cardinal feature of the plan, had started in December 1928 according to the "affirmed plan."[40] Shortly thereafter, on 28 December, the Council of Labor and Defense (a commission attached to the Council of People's Commissars that had the right to issue its own decrees and instructions) ordered the factory to stop the construction.[41] The director of the factory declared, however, that he had already laid the foundations and spent a million rubles. Having inspected the factory, Rabkrin's special task force denounced him for having "hurriedly invested a ruble in order later on to elicit hundreds."[42] On 27 February 1929 the Central Control Commission and Rabkrin disapproved the plan submitted by the factory and proposed instead to utilize existing plants more efficiently and to cut new investments down to twenty million rubles.[43] At the sixteenth party conference, a speaker from Rabkrin who had directed the investigation of the factory insisted that the factory had started the construction before the plan was submitted to the trust and the government for review. Another Rabkrin leader interjected: "It's time to give up this practice."[44]

It is not clear what actually happened, but in light of the complaint lodged by G. Lomov of Donbas Coal at the fifteenth party congress,[45] the claim of the factory and Southern Steel may well have been valid. On the other hand, this case illustrates the fact that investments amounting to "several hundred million rubles" gravely concerned Rabkrin, which considered it imperative to achieve maxi-

---

[39] Volodin, *Po sledam istorii*, p. 203. According to another source, it was 54 million rubles. *Drukha konferentsiia Komunistychnoi partii (bil'shovykiv) Ukrainy*, p. 182.

[40] *Drukha konferentsiia Komunistychnoi partii (bil'shovykiv) Ukrainy*, p. 230.

[41] Volodin, *Po sledam istorii*, p. 205.

[42] Belen'kii, *Rezul'taty obsledovaniia NK RKI kapital'nogo stroitel'stva VSNKh SSSR*, pp. 16–17. S. I. Syrtsov termed this widespread practice "insurance." *Pravda*, 5 August 1929.

[43] Volodin, *Po sledam istorii*, pp. 203–4.

[44] *XVI konferentsiia VKP(b)*, p. 508 (A. I. Gurevich and Ia. A. Iakovlev).

[45] See chap. 1, note 47, this volume.

mum results with a minimum expenditure.[46] It was declared at the second conference of the Ukrainian Communist Party in April 1929 that "we are accustomed to regarding a million rubles as inconsiderable. . . . It often turns out that we get money and then use it negligently: the more money the less economy."[47]

The concern about waste quickly turned into anger and suspicion when Rabkrin found a "conscious understatement of the existing capacity of the factory."[48] Rabkrin suspected that the managers overstated the amount of investment needed and understated the actual capacity of production at a time when maximum cost-effectiveness was essential. Perhaps the Southern Steel affair was a classic case of what János Kornai has called the "softening" of budget constraints in socialist nonmarket economies: because the factory has its losses "almost automatically compensated by the state" and thus does not fear bankruptcy, its demands become "almost insatiable."[49] This problem is familiar today, but it was alarmingly novel in the late 1920s.

Emphasizing the need to monitor managerial activities closely, Rabkrin consciously promoted control "from below" as a substitute for the control of the market:

How is the activity of unsuccessful leaders of both joint-stock companies and some enterprise or other in capitalist society corrected? It is corrected by competition and bankruptcy. If a joint-stock company built glass factories the way we build the Sergiev Factory [whose constructions costs turned out to be five times more than the normal costs], it would collapse disgracefully, and the technical leader or the engineer who built such a factory would not get any post in any enterprise of a capitalist society for the rest of his life. This control of the market, the control by bankruptcy, the control by the ruin of a career, we have to replace by organized controls by the working class.[50]

Control from below (or "social control") by workers and their organizations was economically expensive because it took workers

[46] *XVI konferentsiia VKP(b)*, pp. 460, 509, 558.
[47] *Drukha konferentsiia Komunistychnoi partii (bil'shovykiv) Ukrainy*, p. 282.
[48] *XVI konferentsiia VKP(b)*, pp. 456. Rabkrin contended that a renewed open hearth furnace would produce more than 300,000 tons of steel, whereas the factory's plan projected only 210,000 tons. See *O rekonstruktsii zavodov Iugostali*, pp. 21, 30, 60, and Volodin, *Po sledam istorii*, p.203. For a more detailed account of the Southern Steel affair, see Fitzpatrick, "Ordzhonikidze's Takeover of Vesenkha," pp. 158–60.
[49] See Kornai, *Contradictions and Dilemmas*, pp. 6–51.
[50] *Pravda*, 4 March 1928 (A. Iakovlev of Rabkrin). For a similar discussion, see Mikoyan in *3 sessiia TsIK Soiuza SSR 3 sozyva*, pp. 858–62.

away from productive activity. Expensive though it was, contended Rabkrin, control had to become an integral mechanism of Soviet management, an indispensable tool with which to hold managers accountable:

> It is clear that social control costs a lot of money, but is it true that the expenditure is unproductive? Of course not. It is said that capitalists do not have such control. But capitalists bear more costs than we do, only the expenditure goes in a different direction. In capitalism, a certain number of firms crash every year. This means that a given firm has made so many mistakes that it is not in a position to compete with other firms. . . . Yet we expend money on social control, knowing that this will insure us against a number of mistakes that may arise.[51]

Clearly Rabkrin was quite conscious that in Soviet society, market control did not exist or function as it did and still does in capitalist society. Control from below was a deliberate mechanism that, together with "control from above," was expected to replace "spontaneous" market control and without which there would be no predictable management. For all productivist similarities, Stalinist industrial management differed sharply from "scientific management" in the West precisely in this crucial aspect.

In the political context of 1928–30, control from below also meant "proletarian control" over "bourgeois" specialists and their alleged "followers" (Communist managers), thereby invoking the revolutionary memory of workers' control and class-war mentality among workers. According to Stalin, it was precisely lack of control from below that stupefied the Communist managers and helped the alleged "wreckers."[52]

"Control" (*kontrol'*) often confuses students of Soviet administration because of its ambiguity. It is usually said that control was distinct from management (*upravlenie*): as Lenin conceived it, workers' control meant overseeing and ensuring the propriety of managerial action by checking, inspecting, and verifying it – in other words, supervision external to management per se.[53] This definition of control, however, was expedient as well as politically powerful. The concept of control was analogous to that of "revolutionary legality":

---

[51] Belen'kii, *Rezul'taty obsledovaniia NK RKI kapital'nogo stroitel'stva VSNKh SSSR*, p. 18.

[52] Stalin, *Sochineniia,* 11:61–62, 73 and 13:36.

[53] For a thoughtful clarification of the meaning of "control," see Avrich, "The Bolshevik Revolution and Workers' Control in Russian Industry."

Revolutionary legality demanded that administrative decisions should be at once legal, and thus in line with central regulations, and expedient, which meant that a decision went beyond a strictly formal approach. . . . Revolutionary legality was such a powerful ideological principle precisely because it incorporated both views [views stressing the importance of either expediency or formality] and thus allowed Soviet administrators and legal theorists to grope toward a new type of legal form which could somehow embrace legality and expediency.[54]

The concept of control too demanded that managerial decisions be at once legal and expedient. (In a similar vein, one-man management aimed at expediency, and in having sole managerial responsibility it sought to guarantee legality.) In other words, control, like revolutionary legality, was an open-ended concept.

This open-endedness created constant tensions with one-man management, as we shall see presently. Yet workers' control at this time was politically expedient and well suited to the pro-worker and antibureaucratic political atmosphere the party leadership sought to create. Moreover, control was an important means of initiating workers into the realm of administration: it was intended to familiarize workers with management and to help the managers make correct decisions and execute them properly and creatively. Thus, control assumed peculiar "democratic" functions. It was claimed in 1929 and 1930 that one-man management not only granted enormous powers to management but also required "severalfold multiplied control" from below to "prevent unlimited [managerial] despotism [*svoevlastie*]."[55]

The Shakhty affair prompted Stalin to call for the strengthening of twofold control from above and in particular from below. Stalin declared in 1928 that control from above was still far from sufficient, but that, moreover, it was "by no means the chief thing now," which was rather "control from below."[56] In order to reveal (and prevent) managerial mistakes, improprieties, and red tape, the party leadership promoted various forms of control from below — the promotion of workers into administrative-technical positions, self-criticism, temporary worker control commissions, the "light cavalry" of the Komsomol, production conferences, the

[54] Ewing, "Social Insurance in Russia and the Soviet Union, 1912–1933," chap. 4.
[55] *Izvestiia Severo-Kavkazskogo kraevogo komiteta VKP(b)*, 1930, no. 2, p. 8, and *Partrabotnik*, 1929, no. 21 (45), p. 50.
[56] Stalin, *Sochineniia*, 11:73.

shock movement.[57] In practice, however, the open-ended nature of control often turned control into a heavy constraint on management. Managers angrily contended that control was nothing but intervention in managerial prerogatives.

This problem was vividly highlighted by the debate at the sixteenth party conference between S. P. Birman, and Ia. A. Iakovlev, deputy people's commissar for Rabkrin. In essence, Birman denounced various forms of control and "tutelage" on the part of the workers, the party, and the unions, and, in particular, Rabkrin's "sadistic" harassment of managers with countless investigations. The managers, Birman contended, were closely bound by the "control-punitive deviations" of various organizations, and were discouraged from taking the initiative; they needed flexibility and maneuverability if they were to operate plants effectively. He claimed that only trust in the managers could create in them self-confidence and a sense of responsibility.[58]

There was a good deal of truth to his argument, which was apparently supported by many managers. Yet Iakovlev considered Birman's claim against control to be tantamount to a call for a "peculiar bloc of the controller and the controlled," or "collusion [*sgovor*] for the purpose of concealing mistakes."[59] Iakovlev declared emphatically:

If a temporary worker control commission or an organ of Rabkrin or a group of light cavalry or an organ of the unions uncovers defects and openly tells workers about them, then this will be the best aid [for management].[60]

He denounced the managers for seeking another kind of aid, "coordination" (with the party and union organizations), that is, collective responsibility, which would nullify control and compound managerial mistakes and bureaucratism. The point resided, underscored Iakovlev, not in the excess of control but in the establishment of one-man responsibility and command.[61]

The manager's absolute autonomy could easily have become des-

---

[57] For these, see Carr and Davies, *Foundations of a Planned Economy*, chap. 18, and Carr, *Foundations of a Planned Economy*, vol. 2, chap. 51. See also chap. 5, this volume.

[58] *XVI konferentsiia VKP(b)*, pp. 492–501. As a matter of fact, he used the phrase "control-punitive deviations," not at the conference, but in his article that appeared at the very time of the conference. *TPG*, 27 April 1929.

[59] *XVI konferentsiia VKP(b)*, p. 574.

[60] Ibid., pp. 574–55. Emphasis in the original.

[61] Ibid., pp. 448–54.

potic, and this was what the Soviet political leaders quite rightly understood. Though Birman carefully worded his speech at the conference, he was more explicit at a Vasenkha plenum held a few weeks before the conference: "In Southern Steel there does not exist one-man management in managerial leadership," but only "one-man responsibility of management to everybody."[62] He meant that only one-man responsibility was imposed on the managers whereas all sorts of control undermined their one-man command: Rabkrin imposed the impossible on managers. But Iakovlev apprehended that they sought one-man command free of control while rejecting one-man responsibility and insisted that control was essential to the establishment of managerial authority and accountability.

The Stalin group used the Shakhty affair to enhance the "fighting ability" of industrial management. The affair created an atmosphere of class vigilance and forcefully alerted managers to what appeared to the group to be the political danger of their technical ignorance. On the one hand, the party leadership started a campaign for sending hundreds of thousands of workers, peasants, and Communists to engineering schools in order to create a "proletarian intelligentsia" technologically competent and politically loyal to the regime. On the other hand, the leadership launched a campaign for reconstituting the political and managerial structure in industry in readiness for the rapid industrialization drive.

The institutionalization of one-man management was a hallmark of this reorganization. It granted Communist managers sole managerial command to mobilize all the factory's resources. This was to be complemented by workers' control, which was ideally to help managers make full use of their powers in an accountable and "democratic" fashion. The political framework that the campaign for one-man management sought to establish, according to Stalinist rhetoric, would allow (or compel) the managers to "develop into real leaders" capable of "fighting" for the rapid industrialization drive.

The troika and one-man management

While purging them, the Stalin group reoriented the party and union organizations in the factories along the lines of one-man

---

[62] *Pravda*, 6 April 1929.

management. This realignment provided a new framework of relations for the troika consisting of management (director), the party cell (secretary), and the factory trade union committee (chairman). The institutionalization of one-man management sought to establish sole managerial command by eliminating not only the dualism of the Red and the technical directors but also the managerial parallelism (or bloc) of these three organizations. On the one hand, one-man management was intended to make management strong, efficient, and accountable. On the other hand, it was intended to reorient the party and union organizations toward the new offensive by gearing their activity both to the control of management and to the political and social mobilization of workers.

When NEP was introduced in 1921, the unions disavowed any involvement in management (which now operated the factory on market principles) because they assumed that it was "impossible at the same time to manage a factory on the basis of commercial accounting and to be the spokesman and guardian of the economic interests of hired workers."[63] It was for this reason that union leaders like Tomskii consistently defended the principle of one-man management during NEP.[64] The same principle of nonintervention also applied to the party cell. Although the factory director was most likely to be a member of the party, the primary functions of the cell (i.e., the overall political guidance of the factory) was considered strictly distinct from managerial functions. At least theoretically, the troika was not a managerial organ.[65]

The troika, however, was not at all stable during NEP. One-man management was very often superseded by two forms of troika: either a "triple bloc" or "triple parallelism." In the former case, the troika, allegedly existing cozily in a "family circle" but manipulated freely by "bourgeois specialists,"[66] formed a bureaucratic alliance. The workers therefore reportedly lost trust in the party and union organizations, with the result that labor discipline plummeted. In the latter case, the party and union organizations, assuming managerial functions, undermined one-man managerial command.

[63] Tomskii, *Stat'i i rechi*, pp. 8, 44, 68, 85–86, 117, 119, 146.

[64] *XIV s"ezd VKP(b)*, p. 734; *XV konferentsiia VKP(b)*, pp. 357–60 (D. B. Riazanov); *Trud*, 14 July 1927 (V. Dmitriev); Murashev, *Profsoiuzy i sotsialisticheskoe stroitel'stvo*, p. 13.

[65] *Khoziaistvo i upravlenie*, 1926, no. 12, pp. 12–17, and *Proletarii*, 28 October 1931.

[66] See the case of the Donbas coal mines in *Komsomol'skaia pravda*, 12 May 1928.

There were at least two obvious and universal reasons for the instability of the troika: the tendency for bureaucratic organizations to protect each other against controls both from above and from below, and the tendency for them to struggle for power.

More important, the instability was actually rooted in the contradictory position of the troika (particularly the factory trade union committee) implicit in NEP. With the progress of the industrialization drive, the contradiction was all the more evident and appeared to the Stalin group to have created a political crisis in the factories.

As Lenin emphasized at the introduction of NEP in 1921–22, the unions assumed two important tasks: the promotion of the national economy as a whole and the protection of the immediate economic interests of workers, or the "production" and the "defense" roles. The former required aid for management to promote production and the latter, protection against managerial abuse and bureaucratism. Because NEP operated on market principles with the work force quoted on the market, Lenin emphasized that contradictions could arise between the unions' two functions.[67]

As the pressure for industrialization mounted in the second half of the 1920s, the contradictions became more evident than before from the point of view of the troika. When the troika emphasized production, it tended to result in a "triple bloc," pushing the "defense" function to the back and dismissing demands for wage hikes as "money grubbing."[68] Having neglected the interests of workers, the troika tended then to turn to the other extreme, triple parallelism, with the party and union organizations frequently interfering with management on the workers' behalf. The unions and the party thus tended to become either "adjuncts to management" or control organizations usurping managerial functions.[69]

The contradictions had been evident well before the Shakhty affair came to light in March 1928. The triple bloc had caused a wave of strikes back in 1925, at the peak time of NEP, when the "threefold bloc" of the troika pressed for intensified labor "at the expense of the workers."[70] An organ of the All-Union Central Council of Trade Unions sarcastically declared that such a bloc, or "collu-

[67] Lenin, *Polnoe sobranie sochinenii*, 44:341–353, 494–500.
[68] See, for example, the case of Smolensk in the Smolensk Archive, WKP 33, p. 236; WKP 296, p. 3.
[69] *Trud*, 7 March 1929 (editorial), and *Golos tekstilei*, 18 October 1929.
[70] *XIV s"ezd VKP(b)*, pp. 723, 735, 741. See also Carr, *Socialism in One Country*, 1:393–34, 399–401.

sion," was a "good method" of undermining the authority of the party and union organizations in the eyes of workers.[71]

In 1926 the troika, attacked both from above and from below, was said to have eliminated its bloc. According to Tomskii's account at the fifteenth party conference in November 1926, however, the unions now tended to go from *"from active support* [for managers] *always and everywhere"* to "another nasty deviation," namely, *"passivity"*: the unions stayed to the side even when managers did "obviously wrong things" and when "workers' demands were absolutely right."[72]

This kind of bloc came under fierce attack in 1928, when the Shakhty affair and other "wrecking" and scandals came to light. The Stalin group did not confine the attack to these troubled regions, but mounted it nationwide.[73] Encouraged, the discontented workers came out to declare that the "director is the head, the factory committee is the tail," and that the "factory committee and administration are one family."[74] The authority of the unions declined sharply, and strikes took place "without the unions' knowledge."[75] The unions feared that they would become "generals without an army."[76] The unions in the troubled Artemovsk industrial center were attacked with particular rigor both from above and from below.[77] In May 1928 an article in the unions' newspaper, *Trud*, vividly described the activity of a mine union committee at Shcherbinovsk in Artemovsk:

Women wheelers went [to the mine manager]:
—Give us warm coats, to which we have the right according to the collective agreement.

[71] *Vestnik truda*, 1926, no. 10, pp. 13–14.
[72] *XV konferentsiia VKP(b)*, p. 274. Emphasis in the original.
[73] See, for example, *Sputnik agitatora dlia goroda*, 1928, no. 8, pp. 17–23, no. 10, pp. 21–22; *Trud*, 11, 12, 25 May, 6 July 1928; *Molot*, 12 July 1928; *Izvestiia Donskogo okrkoma VKP(b)*, 1928, no. 17 (August), p. 6 ("O sostoianii raboty treugol'nika [iacheika, FZMK i administratsiia]"); *Izvestiia TsK VKP(b)*, 1928, no. 27 (10 September), p. 16; 1929, nos. 11–12 (24 April), p. 23.
[74] *Rabochaia gazeta*, 26 August 1928, and *Trud*, 6 July 1928 (the Makeevka industrial complex in the Donbas).
[75] *VIII s"ezd professional'nykh soiuzov SSSR*, p. 26. For strikes in the Donbas, see also *Trud*, 5 July 1928; *Komsomol'skaia pravda*, 12 May 1928; *Sputnik agitatora dlia goroda*, 1928, no. 6, p. 4.
[76] See the case of the Far East, where labor-management conflict had occurred over the head of the unions, in *IX Dal'nevostochnaia kraevaia partiinaia konferentsiia*, p. 104.
[77] For the Artemovsk scandal, see Carr, *Foundations of a Planned Economy*, 2:141.

—No, you don't.

—According to the old agreement, we don't, but we do according to the new one.

—I'm not giving you any.

—If you don't, we'll walk out.

Then the manager made a telephone call:

—Mine committee? Chairman, please. Listen. Wheelers are hounding me. They're demanding coats. They've taken it into their heads to threaten me. I'm going to kick them out.

—All right, go ahead.

In came a militiaman and took them out.

Always ready to render service, the RKK [Assessment-Conflict Commission, the first instance of settling labor disputes] resolved that because the wheelers violated item 3 of the mine regulations, firing was considered legitimate.

Twelve days later it turned out that the wheelers were right. They were reinstated and the manager removed; but it was difficult for the union committee to recover its authority.[78]

Closely linked with the "triple bloc" were violations of party and union "democracy." Like the bloc, this problem was nothing new at all, but it became politically important in 1928, when the Stalin group sought to shake up the entire political structure in the factories. As early as February 1928, V. Polonskii, a leader of the Moscow Committee of the party and a Stalin loyalist, declared:

First, the shop cell [of the party] convenes and decides the candidates [for factory committee elections]. Then the factory cell convenes and decides the candidates, and so on. It seems as if there were no suppression, but in reality a situation is created in which workers say: "You decide everything, and nothing is left for us."[79]

At the Frunze Factory in Moscow, a reelection of the factory committee took place in the spring of 1928. A man called Makarov received only 150 votes, but the election committee announced that 360 votes were cast for him. In the following year no candidate for the committee received more than 150 votes out of 800 workers present at the election meeting.[80] At the June 1928 plenum of the Moscow Committee of the party, a worker by the name of Lazareva from the Vysokovsk Factory declared that the workers "cursed" the party and the union without hesitation: "Neither the factory com-

[78] *Trud*, 25 May 1928.

[79] *Rabochaia Moskva*, 5 February 1928.

[80] *Golos tekstilei*, 26 April 1928, and *Izvestiia TsK VKP(b)*, 1929, nos. 23–24 (25 August), pp. 3–5.

mittee nor the party nor the Soviet government will do at all."[81] At
the Red Perekop Factory in Yaroslavl, which employed 14,000
workers, an all-factory conference elected a delegate to the eighth
trade union congress (to be held in December 1928) whom the
party had not endorsed because of his alleged antiparty activity.[82] A
Secret Police report in the Smolensk Archive dated the summer of
1928 characterized the political mood of workers in the Tomskii
Factory:

[Workers claim that] party work will not do at all. Our chiefs beginning
from Stalin and Rykov on down live at the expense of workers, while our
self-seekers [*shkurniki,* referring to the party cell members] do not allow us
to say anything about this. If you say so, you'll be [taken] to the proper
quarters right away.[83]

As V. P. Zatonskii emphasized, the party leadership considered it
necessary to release the reins slightly and let the workers criticize
the Bolsheviks.

The triple bloc and violations of party and union "democracy"
discredited the troika in the eyes of workers. The case of the Yartsevo
Textile Factory in Smolensk is particularly illustrative. In this factory, which in 1928–29 employed some 7,000 workers, the troika
had long been vying for power.[84] In June 1928 there occurred serious
unrest among the workers in conjunction with a corruption scandal
in Smolensk and the campaign for the intensification of labor in the
factory. Workers adopted a resolution against intensified labor, and
only after the intervention of the central committee of the textile
workers' union did they withdraw their opposition.[85]

Then, in the first half (October–April) of the 1928/29 economic
year, the failure to fulfill the plan targets pressed management hard
to intensify labor; moreover, management decided to lay off 300
(500, according to some accounts) of the 1,000 "superfluous" workers who had been unnecessarily hired because of "sloppy recruitment." According to one account, the party cell emphasized that the
layoff would affect only those who retained land holdings in the
countryside. According to another account, the party collaborated

[81] Quoted by Molotov in *Pravda,* 4 July 1928.
[82] Gurevich, *Za uluchshenie partiinoi raboty,* pp. 10–11.
[83] WKP 144, "Politicheskoe sostoianie uezda," p. 1.
[84] See for example, WKP 294, pp. 164–65 (July 1927).
[85] Fainsod, *Smolensk under Soviet Rule,* pp. 51 and 311, and *Golos tekstilei,* 26
June, 18 July, 11 August 1928.

with the factory committee in making up a list of workers to be laid off. The selection, however, was "random," and the list included as many as 1,000 workers. "Protectionism, favoritism, and nepotism" were reported to be widespread. "No worker was sure of tomorrow." One worker declared: "If my wife or I am fired, I'll shoot six bullets into whoever is responsible." Labor discipline and production dropped off, and the factory appeared on the "black list." Workers demonstratively boycotted factory meetings. They were said to believe that "in government as in the trusts, bourgeois and [former] factory owners have established themselves, who want to revenge themselves on us workers for having taken their factories."

In the spring (March or April) of 1929 the central committees of the party and the textile workers' union sent out special teams of organizers to the factory. The committee for the layoff set up by the factory union committee was dissolved, and the factory union committee itself was disbanded. The entire troika was removed, including Okhalin, the director, and Davydov, the chairman of the factory committee. The new chairman of the committee was sent from Moscow—Rishchev, head of the cultural department of the central committee of the textile workers' union.[86] Stoliarov, new director, promoted one-man management and pressed for labor discipline, but some party members opposed one-man management, contending that workers were suffocated and could not even breathe.[87]

The other tendency of the troika, triple managerial parallelism, appeared to the Stalin group to be equally dangerous politically. It was a mere reverse of the triple bloc. The party and union organizations regarded themselves as the masters of the factory, in which the troika fought for power.[88] In the LSPO Factory in Leningrad, for instance, the relation between the manager and the factory committee's chairman, both Communists, was far from harmonious: "They sit side by side in a room and don't want to say hello to each other when some conflict arises."[89] During NEP, "syndicalist" or antimanagerial feelings were frequently manifested, and

---

[86] "Doklad orgpartgruppy TsK VKP(b) o sostoianii raboty na Iartsevskoi manufakture," dated 20 September 1929 in WKP 150. See also WKP 377, p. 32, WKP 150, p. 46; *Izvestiia TsIK SSSR*, 23 July 1929; *Golos tekstilei*, 6 June 1929. For a very similar case at the Red Echo Factory in Vladimir, see *Golos tekstilei*, 26 April 1929.

[87] *Pravda*, 5 July 1929.

[88] *Partrabotnik*, 1928, no. 18, pp. 32–34; *TPG*, 17 June 1929.

[89] *XXIV Leningradskaia gubernskaia konferentsiia VKP(b)*, p. 103.

workers' demands for restricting administrative powers of management persisted.[90] Reflecting their mood against management, the trade unions went to considerable lengths to depict managers as "petty tyrants."[91]

During NEP, like their leadership in Moscow, the factory trade union committees had retained considerable autonomy in the factories. In a factory in Zaporozhye, for example, when a Rabkrin commission came to investigate the factory committee, the committee had disputed for three weeks whether the commission (state organ) was entitled to investigate an elected organ of the union (nonstate organization).[92] A report came from the Donbas in late 1928 that "workers are terrorizing the engineer-technical personnel . . . and are resorting to *volynki* [dawdling or a euphemism for strikes] and getting their wages raised," and that the miners' union committees "support them . . . and recommend *volynki.*"[93] In a factory in Yegorevsk, it was said in early 1929 that if workers were asked who was master on the shop floor they would answer without hesitation: "The union."[94]

The party cell, for its part, often sought supremacy in the factory. The case of Moscow is of particular interest. At the January–February 1928 plenum of the Moscow Committee of the party, N. A. Uglanov, then head of the committee and one of the prominent leaders of the emerging Right, repeatedly blamed the party cell for its pretensions. Emphasizing the necessity for giving the manager a freer rein in the factory, Uglanov declared: "The director has to become the director. . . . It is the director who is responsible [for production]. This is the essence. This has to be understood."[95] Nevertheless,

---

[90] See, for example, D. B. Riazanov's criticism in *XV konferentsiia VKP(b)*, p. 361. M. Rubinshtein, "Protiv perezhitkov stariny na nashei fabrike," *Sputnik kommunista*, 1928, no. 17, p. 66; *Moskovskii proletarii*, 1927, no. 40 (28 October), p. 6; *Vtoroi plenum MK VKP(b)*, p. 69.

[91] *XV konferentsiia VKP(b)*, pp. 321, 367. See also Etchin, *Partiia i spetsialisty*, p. 61. Some managers did in fact behave as such. See, for example, the director of the 5 October Factory in Vladimir, reported in *Golos tekstilei*, 27 August 1929.

[92] *II plenum TsKK sozyva XV s˝ezda VKP(b)*, p. 107.

[93] *Ekonomicheskaia zhizn'*, 25 December 1928 (G. Lomov).

[94] *TPG*, 9 April 1929.

[95] *Vtoroi plenum MK VKP(b)*, pp. 27–28. See also his speech in November 1927 in *XVI Moskovskaia gubernskaia konferentsiia VKP(b)*, p. 181. On the other hand, Uglanov emphasized the necessity for improving the relations of the troika (*XV konferentsiia VKP*[b], p. 296, and *Ekonomicheskaia zhizn'*, 2 March 1929). Evidently he referred to the troika not as a managerial organ but as a form of communication and cooperation of the troika's three bodies.

doubt was expressed: "Who manages the factory, the director or the [party] cell?" Uglanov replied that the cell and its secretary had to guide (*napravliat'*) the factory, whereas the director had to manage (*upravliat'*) it. He went on to say that party secretaries self-righteously considered themselves managerially competent and emphasized that the directors needed more autonomy.[96] "Young party members," however, contended that Uglanov's emphasis on managerial authority would "narrow the role of the party cells and workers," and accused the Moscow Committee of having "taken the course that favored the specialists." The grass-roots feeling against the managerial-technical personnel provoked by the Shakhty affair prompted another Rightist, E. F. Kulikov, to claim that after the February 1928 plenum of the Moscow Committee the managers had been "puffed up" (*podniali nosy*).[97]

The troika thus appeared to the Stalin group to have created "triple power" and a lack of command (*beznachalie*) in the factories, as the 21 February 1929 circular of the Central Committee on labor discipline pointed out.[98] Each body of the troika claimed its own say in the selection of personnel, disciplinary measures against violators of labor discipline, and a variety of purely operational measures such as the transfer of workers from one job to another. The party and union organizations, in defense of their right to intervene, contended that otherwise they would lose their authority among workers.[99] The troika thus created a situation in which management could not allocate the work force according to production needs.[100]

The union's unsuccessful intervention needlessly discredited its authority among workers. Even when the union quite rightly refused to intervene, it also jeopardized its authority:

Because of the union's intervention with the management of production, its role is totally distorted in the eyes of workers. . . . A worker goes to his

---

[96] *Vtoroi plenum MK VKP(b)*, pp. 41–43.

[97] *Rabochaia Moskva*, 26, 27 April 1928, and N. Morozov-Vorontsov, "O treugol'-nike," *Sputnik kommunista*, 1928, no. 8, p. 23. Apparently there were disagreements on the issue among the Rightists. People like Uglanov who were interested in orderly business, preferred efficient management, whereas people like Kulikov who were concerned with power politics in the factories, contested managerial autonomy.

[98] "Pis'mo TsK VKP(b) vsem partiinym organizatsiiam o podniatii trudovoi distsipliny," in *KPSS v rezoliutsiiakh*, 4:169–75.

[99] *Sputnik kommunista*, 1928, no. 8, pp. 24–25. *TPG*, 5, 21 March 1929; *Leningradskaia pravda*, 15 March 1929.

[100] Etchin (ed.), *O trudovoi distsipline*, p. 46.

foreman to request a transfer from one machine to another, and the foreman says, "I'll be glad to [help you], but what will the union [say]?" The worker goes to the union bureau [of the shop], which refuses his request. He is discontented: "The union does not defend us." Yet another example: A worker refuses to carry out the foreman's order. Instead of taking action immediately in accordance with factory regulations the foreman goes to the union representative to get his approval to impose a penalty for insubordination. Such facts as these attest to a sheer distortion of the role of the union worker, because the union worker and the manager "coalesce," as it were, in the person of the former. Meanwhile, such "coalescence" is absolutely intolerable from the viewpoint of methods of guiding the workers: *the union worker* influences the workers first of all by methods of *education and persuasion* (and coercion in the form of social influence); *the manager* approaches the workers first of all with administrative orders, i.e., by totally contrary methods. This is why the "coalescence" in the union worker of union and managerial functions cannot but *break the unions away from the masses of workers.*[101]

These examples suggest at least two important things. First, sole managerial command did not exist on the shop floor. Second, from the point of view of workers, "triple power" could easily turn into a "triple bloc," if, as the first example shows, the unions did not satisfy workers' demands.

In the late 1920s a political crisis thus emerged in the factories: the troika, caught between a triple bloc and triple parallelism, appeared to the party leadership to be unable to mobilize the working class for rapid industrialization. Moreover, neither the bloc nor the parallelism was conducive to managerial efficiency and accountability. This state of affairs invited political intervention from above. The party leadership responded by institutionalizing one-man management.

One-man management excluded the party and union organizations from the managerial domain. Particularly noteworthy was the government's 6 March 1929 decree that gave management the right to one-man decisions without prior clearance from the factory RKK (Assessment-Conflict Commission) to impose penalties (including firing) on violators of labor discipline.[102] Managers had long complained that the workers' side of the RKK, which was equally represented by labor and management, undermined managerial power

[101] V. Riabokon', "Edinonachalie, 'treugol'nik' i massy," *Partiinoe stroitel'stvo*, 1929, no. 1, pp. 13–14. Emphasis in the original.
[102] *Izvestiia TsIK SSSR*, 7 March 1929.

and left the factory "without a master."[103] This managerial right had been legalized in late 1927, but the unions' resistance kept it from being put into practice.[104] Similarly, management was now able to assign the workers to the wagescale table without the approval of the RKK, thereby excluding the trade unions even more from the wage domain.[105]

More generally, one-man management dictated not managerial but political and social roles to the party and union organizations. (Accordingly, they assumed not managerial but political and social responsibility.) They were supposed neither to "collude" nor to compete for power with management, but to aid it by educating and organizing workers in the spirit of "proletarian discipline." The party cell was expected to "guide the social, political, and economic life of the factory so as to ensure the execution of the party's principal orders by the union and managerial organs." The factory trade union committee was expected to become an "energetic organizer of the production activity and initiative of workers," listen to management's reports, investigate problems with production, make suggestions for improvement, and see to it that they were actually implemented by management. By struggling against managerial bureaucratism that frustrated workers' production activity and initiative, according to the oft-quoted rhetoric, the unions were expected to synthesize their "production" and "defense" functions — "two sides of the same coin."[106]

There remained much ambiguity, however, about the precise role of each of the troika's three bodies. The party and union organizations were strictly forbidden to intervene in managerial questions, but were encouraged both to aid management and to control or monitor management. In the real world, these two functions often contradicted each other. This ambiguity and contradic-

[103] *Vestnik truda*, 1926, nos. 7–8, pp. 105, 108; *Ocherednye problemy truda*, pp. 52, 315–18, 353–54; *TPG*, 24 February 1929; *Ekonomicheskaia zhizn'*, 3 March 1929 (I. Kraval' of Vesenkha).

[104] Kuz'min, *V bor'be za sotsialisticheskuiu rekonstruktsiiu*, p. 65, and *Professional'nye soiuzy SSSR, 1926–1928*, p. 459. For the uneasy compromise of workers' and management's interests in the RKK in the 1920s, see McAuley, *Labour Disputes in Soviet Russia*, chap. 2.

[105] This right was made public in the model collective agreements for 1931 (*Trud*, 13 November 1930). But an Ivanovo collective agreement for 1930 clearly stipulates this managerial right. *Kollektivnyi dogovor*, pp. 22 and 66.

[106] *KPSS v rezoliutsiiakh*, 4:313–14 (September 1929 resolution on one-man management); and *XVI s˝ezd VKP(b)*, p. 64 (L. M. Kaganovich).

tion continued to undermine one-man management. Nevertheless, the distinction between control and intervention was important both in principle and in practice. It corresponded roughly to the distinction between what political scientists call "policy questions" (questions with policy implications) and "routine (operational) questions."[107] The case of the AMO Factory in Moscow illustrates this issue.

In 1929 there developed a serious controversy between the director of the Automobile Trust, M. L. Sorokin, and the director of the factory, I. A. Likhachev, as to how to restructure the factory. The controversy was not settled within the trust or in the party's Moscow Committee, and Likhachev took the issue to Ordzhonikidze, then chairman of Rabkrin and of the Central Control Commisssion, who then put the issue on the agenda of the Politbureau of the Central Committee. The troika – Likhachev, the party secretary, S. S. Igantov, and the chairman of the factory committee, F. Labutin – was invited, together with all members of the Moscow Committee and K. V. Ryndin, chairman of the party's Moscow Control Commission, to the Politbureau session on 23 January 1930. Likhachev and Ignatov, both full party members, did not take Labutin along because he was a candidate member at that time. Stalin insisted, however, that the chairman of the factory committee be present regardless of his party status and that the issue not be discussed until Labutin came to the session. Labutin, found in a public bathhouse (fortunately that day was a factory holiday), was immediately taken in his underwear to the Kremlin by car.[108] Why did Stalin insist on Labutin's participation? Because this issue was not a "routine question" but a "policy question," and Stalin and other Politbureau members wanted multiple inputs into decision making. Indeed, if this had been a "routine question," it would not have been discussed by the Politbureau at all. In other words, one-man management excluded the party and union organizations from the domain of "routine questions," but not from that of "policy questions," in which they had the duty to intervene.

This case may raise as many questions as it answers, particularly because the distinction between routine and policy questions is not always a clear one. Yet such ambiguities are not confined to the

107 For these, see Hough, *The Soviet Prefects*, pp. 81–86.
108 See Ignatov's memoir in *Direktor I. A. Likhachev*, pp. 49–50.

Soviet administrative system, but in one form or another are inherent in other administrative systems.[109] With all its uncertainties and contradictions, one-man management was a step toward efficient management. The director of the Putilov Factory, V. F. Grachev, had earlier complained: "We are more often in meetings and sessions than we are in production. This disgrace has to be eliminated. . . . We have too many coordinations, reports, and whatnot, of all kinds."[110] The institutionalization of one-man management was a response to such complaints. While the party organization retained its overall political leadership in the factory, the factory trade union committee lost much of its bargaining power.

The new regime

The new regime that the political leadership sought to create in the factories was characterized by the peculiar combination of sole managerial command and multiple controls over management. Dictatorial though one-man management may have appeared, the new regime in the factory was fundamentally distinct from the military regime in two respects. In the Soviet military, sole command was introduced gradually from 1924 and, as in industry, decisively from 1929 onward by eliminating the dualism of the commander and the political commissar.[111] But the military, in which order and discipline were imperative, entirely lacked a motive for capital accumulation and was free from control from below, whereas this motive and control from below were deemed essential in industry.

The abrogation of market forces eliminated both the control and the stimulus they provided to the economy. As early as March 1927, Komsomol leader L. A. Shatskin emphasized the need to replace the control and incentive by Bolshevik "consciousness":

You know, comrades, that in our industry the stimulus is lacking that drove forth capitalist industry, that is, the stimulus of individual profit – the main-spring and the nerve of capitalist production. For the purpose of developing

---

[109] See Hough, *The Soviet Prefects*, pp. 83–84.
[110] Quoted in *Krasnaia gazeta*, 29 September 1929. In the late 1920s the director of the Tagil Works in the Urals, for instance, spent 20% of his work time coordinating managerial questions with various organizations. Bogushevskii and Khavin, "God velikogo pereloma," p. 364.
[111] Iovlev, "K istorii bor'by partii za perekhod k edinonachaliiu v Krasnoi Armii."

industry we can put in its place only the conscious participation of the masses of workers in the construction of socialist production. Without such mass participation we will not be able to build up socialist production.[112]

In September 1927, Stalin, in response to the question posed by the First American Labor Delegation as to what in the Soviet Union served in place of profit, maintained: "The consciousness that the workers work not for capitalists but for their own state, for their own class, is a tremendous motivating force in the development and perfection of our industry." Stalin cited as examples of such stimuli the trade unions' control over management and workers' participation in management through production conferences, and argued that these were "permanently operating forces" in Soviet industry.[113]

By contrast, the Soviet military dismissed appeals to consciousness as a legacy of revolutionary romanticism.[114] At the sixteenth party congress K. E. Voroshilov, the people's commissar for military and naval affairs, proudly spoke of the privilege the military enjoyed, namely, freedom from the self-criticism campaign.[115] The campaign was directed mainly against industrial managers[116] and was an important control from below in industry. In January 1930 Stalin wrote to Maksim Gorky, who was skeptical about the campaign:

We cannot do without self-criticism. We simply cannot, Aleksei Maksimovich. Without it, stagnation, corruption of the apparatus, growth of bureaucracy, sapping of the creative initiative of the working class, are inevitable. Of course, self-criticism provides material for our enemies. You are quite right about that. But it also provides material (and a stimulus) for our advancement, for unleashing the constructive energies of the working people, for the development of competition, for shock brigades, and so on. The negative aspect is counterbalanced and *out*weighed by the positive aspect.[117]

The new regime in the factories was perhaps neither "despotic," as Western scholars would have us believe, nor "democratic," as Soviet scholars claim. Conceptual ambiguities implicit in "control" constantly created practical tensions between "dictatorship" and

---

[112] *V Vsesoiuznaia konferentsiia VLKSM*, pp. 83–84.
[113] Stalin, *Sochineniia*, 10:119–22. For production conferences, see chap. 5, this volume.
[114] I owe this point to Von Hagen, "School of the Revolution."
[115] *XVI s˝ezd VKP(b)*, pp. 285–86.
[116] Managers complained that 80% of self-criticism was directed against themselves. *III plenum TsKK XV s˝ezda VKP(b)*, pp. 22, 30.
[117] Stalin, *Sochineniia*, 12:173. Emphasis in the original.

"democracy" and between the needs for discipline and for mobilization. Whatever the rhetoric, the class-war policy and the emerging planned economy gave rise to a new regime that was expected to ensure maximum managerial efficiency and accountability and to facilitate the mobilization of workers for the industrialization drive.

4

The crisis of proletarian identity

The Stalinist leadership had to overcome not only institutional constraints but also social constraints to promote the rapid industrialization drive. It perceived that the class-war policy alienated from the party almost all social groups except the industrial working class and possibly the poor peasants and rural workers. This alienation was a serious problem, but even more serious was what might be called a dual "crisis of proletarian identity": in 1928–29 the Stalin group came to question its own traditional concept of the poletariat; and the proletariat itself, or to be exact, the workers of the older generation, perceived a crisis of their own identity in production.

Three factors played a critically important role in the crisis: the declining standard of living, which agitated both the political leadership and the workers; the influx of new workers into the factories, which diluted the old working class; and the destabilizing impact of industrial modernization on the old order in the factories. To be sure, even before 1928 the relationship between the party and the working class was not as amicable as the party leadership wished: in the early 1920s the economic devastation led to a wide breach between them; in the summer of 1923 and autumn of 1925 there were waves of industrial workers' strikes, a fact that attested to certain strain in their relationship;[1] moreover, industrial modernization and the influx of new workers were nothing new. Nevertheless, before 1928, particularly in the mid-1920s, the party leadership managed to improve its political relationship with the working class through the vigorous proletarianization of the party and the steady recovery of

---

[1] Carr, *The Interregnum*, pp. 92–96, and chap. 3, note 70 this volume. For party–worker relations in the 1920s, see Chase, *Workers, Society and the Soviet State*, chap. 7, and Rosenberg, "Smolensk in the 1920s."

the economy and the standard of living; and the magnitude both of the influx of new workers and of industrial modernization was rather limited. In 1928–29, however, the declining standard of living, the growing numbers of new workers, and the acceleration of industrial modernization combined to upset older, skilled workers and to cause the party leadership to redefine its political relationship with the working class.

Politically, the crisis manifested itself in the fact that in 1928–29 the Stalin group perceived growing manifestations of so-called opportunism and petty bourgeois spontaneity among the workers. The emerging "Rightists" in the party leadership were particularly intent on emphasizing workers' discontent with the party. N. A. Uglanov, a noted Rightist and secretary of the Moscow Committee of the party, maintained in the spring of 1928 that now, "in contrast to the time of the fifteenth party congress" in December 1927, the workers were in a "more critical mood toward the party leadership": "We work hard and will work even better, but you leaders, please commit fewer errors, and we won't have such affairs as the Shakhty affair."[2] On another occasion, Uglanov went so far as to suggest that workers were not on the side of the leadership: "In another factory [in Moscow], when the secretary of a [party] cell came out against an oppositionist and said that he must be arrested, three-quarters of the workers present started making a fuss and declared that they would desert such a meeting. . . . GPU measures alone are not enough."[3]

Yet even Stalin's supporters were not reticent. At the April 1928 plenum of the Central Control Commission, V. P. Zatonskii warned: "Comrades, especially those who work directly in the factories, know that workers demand free elections," which "formerly coincided with the Menshevik claim."[4] Perhaps the workers' claims were not as articulated as Zatonskii claimed. For instance, at the

---

[2] Quoted from the archives in Vaganov, *Pravyi uklon v VKP(b) i ego razgrom*, 2nd ed., pp. 97 and 176. In June 1928 the deputy people's commissar of finance, M. Frumkin, wrote to the Politbureau: those who appeared in workers' and soldiers' meetings knew well that "the peasants' mood against us" strongly affected the workers and soldiers. Trotsky Archives, T 1693.

[3] Trotsky Archives, T 2668 (speech of 25 September 1928).

[4] *II plenum TsKK sozyva XV s'ezda VKP(b)*, pp. 109–10. See also his article in *Rabochiaia gazeta*, 13 April 1928. For the "Menshevik" demands for free elections, see also *Materialy k XVIII chrezvychainoi Smolenskoi gubernskoi konferentsii VKP(b)*, p. 21.

Menshevik trial in March 1931, M. P. Iakubovich (a former deputy director of the supply section of the People's Commissariat of Trade) maintained that in 1928–29 it seemed to them that "in the proletariat there is a lot of unformulated, latent discontent." He went on to say:

We did not think that we had to arouse discontent that did not exist in worker circles. If we had thought that discontent did not exist, then perhaps we would not have come to the tactic we employed [i.e., alleged opposition to the Bolshevik government] and would not have come to participate in the Menshevik party.

Iakubovich further maintained: "We assumed [in 1928–29] that discontent existed [among workers] and that it was necessary only to formulate and sharpen it. . . . I have to tell you that it was no secret to anyone that there was a lot of discontent in the country."[5]

Whatever the case, by mid-1929 the working class no longer seemed to the Bolsheviks to have "the strictly preserved proletarian outlook that it had five or six years ago."[6] Clearly, party leaders perceived that proletarian "consciousness," which in Bolshevik parlance implied working-class identification with the party, was rapidly losing ground before the growing influence of "deviant" political moods.

The Rightists may not have perceived this state of affairs as a crisis of proletarian identity, because, according to them, it was the policy of the party that was to blame. In fact, in September 1928, Uglanov declared that "it is not necessary now to sharpen the struggle against petty bourgeois moods in the proletariat."[7] Yet the Stalin group came to question its own assumption about the relationship between the party and the working class. As much as it may have stemmed from political expediency, this perception did reflect a social and political crisis taking place in the factories.

The declining standard of living

In mid-1927 Soviet industrial workers appear to have enjoyed a standard of living they had never enjoyed before: their real wages

[5] *Protsess kontrrevoliutsionnoi organizatsii men'shevikov*, pp. 166, 272–73. See also pp. 410 and 413–14.
[6] *Visnyk profrukhu Ukrainy*, 1929, no. 12 (June), p. 6.
[7] Quoted from the archives in Titov, Smirnov, and Shalagin, *Bor'ba Kommunis- ticheskoi partii s antileninskimi gruppami i techeniiami*, p. 274

were said to have risen by about 11 percent over the 1913 level, and the average workday had decreased to seven and half hours from ten hours in 1913.[8] In 1923–27 a working-class family's expenditures on food accounted for 42–46 percent of its wages, a substantial decrease from 80 percent during the civil war and 57 percent on the eve of World War I.[9]

Yet in late 1927, when the grain crisis emerged, the real wages of workers started to decline mainly because of the rising retail prices of agricultural produce. According to a government report, the first quarter of the 1927/28 economic year (October–December 1927), when the first signs of the grain crisis appeared, recorded a 1.5 percent decline in real wages from the last quarter of the preceding economic year (July–September 1927).[10] According to studies by the People's Commissariat of Labor the real wages of Moscow workers decreased by 1.3 percent from the first half of 1927/28 to the same period of 1928/29.[11] At the eighth trade union congress in December 1928 a representative of the Northern Caucasus openly complained that because of the rising cost of living real wages were "not maintained."[12] In the spring of 1929 an official of the Russian Republic's People's Commissariat of Labor frankly stated that "we have some decline in real wages."[13] In July 1929 the information bulletin of the Leningrad Committee of the party reported the committee's 3 July resolution to the effect that rising prices "were leading to some decline in real wages."[14]

The grain crisis prompted the introduction of food rationing in major cities.[15] The chronic goods famine rapidly worsened, and

---

[8] See Valentinov, *NEP i krizis partii posle smerti Lenina*, p. 115; *Ekonomicheskaia obozrenie*, 1927, no. 10, pp. 155–58. See also S. Zagorsky, *Wages and Regulation of Conditions of Labour in the USSR*, pp. 182–83, 194–95.

[9] *Voprosy torgovli*, 1928, no. 3 (December), pp. 17–18, and Kir'ianov, *Zhiznennyi uroven' rabochikh Rossii*, pp. 203–5, 208 (data for the Moscow *guberniia*).

[10] *Svodnye materialy o deiatel'nosti SNK i STO za I kvartal (okt.–dek.) 1927/28 g.*, p. 8.

[11] *Voprosy truda*, 1929, no. 9, pp. 98–99, 104.

[12] *VIII s˝ezd professional'nykh soiuzov, SSSR*, p. 479.

[13] *XIV Vserossiiskii s˝ezd sovetov*, 9:41 (Bakhutov).

[14] *Biulleten' Leningradskogo oblastnogo kimiteta VKP(b)*, 1929, no. 6 (30 July), pp. 30–31, cited in *Industrializatsiia Severo-Zapadnogo raiona v gody pervoi piatiletki*, p. 315. A Moscow trade union leader also declared that "we have some decline in real wages." Strievskii, *Material'noe i kul'turnoe polozhenie moskovskikh rabochikh*, p. 16.

[15] See Shkaratan, "Material'noe blagosostoianie rabochego klassa SSSR v perekhodnyi period ot kapitalizma k sotsializmu." See also Carr and Davies, *Foundations of a Planned Economy*, chap. 27, and Barber, "The Standard of Living of Soviet Industrial Workers, 1928–1941."

long queues appeared everywhere. From September 1928 on, the country ran short of such basic items as salt and kerosene, and "everything got messed up."[16] At the November 1928 session of the All-Russian Central Executive Committee, a delegate from Yaroslavl openly complained about the food situation:

Taking advantage of this opportunity, I want to touch on some issues not related to the budget. The thing is that when we left for this [session], people pointed out all sorts of burning issues to the members of the All-Russian Central Executive Committee. I'll speak about my region. The food situation is very, very bad in our region. Now the situation is such that we appear to have retreated by six or seven years. It looks like 1920–21. There is no bread. The prices have gone up very high. It is impossible to find sixteen kilograms of grain even for six to seven rubles.[17]

A Soviet account of the First Five-Year Plan published in 1936 quite vividly describes the hard life of the country in the early months of 1929:

The appearance of the streets is changing. Only two–three years ago they were crowded with signs of private merchants, *artel*s [cooperatives], and pseudo*artel*s; and show windows attracted shoppers. Now private traders are not seen. The NEPmen have not disappeared, but repainted themselves in protective coloring. Today shop owners, who ran a big business yesterday, are often changing into modest accountants or clerks. They are meek and mild.

The show windows have become empty, and lots of shops are nailed tightly. . . . Here and there the street has the same appearance now as during the stern years of war communism. Cooperative stores are slovenly, shabby, and cluttered. Private eating houses and coffee shops are being closed. Cooperative eating houses are dirty and poor. . . . Life is becoming difficult. . . . Moscow is short of fuel: houses with central heating are poorly heated; worse still are those [only] with tiled stoves. There are huge lines in the wood yards. There is nothing by which to transport wood. People come to unload railroad stations and drag whatever is available directly from the wagons. . . . Ready-to-wear shops and shoe stores are empty. In April and May costumes tailored of homemade wool were sold for 250 rubles in Kuznetskii [a section of Moscow]. Every batch brought over is scratched away in half an hour. Again, as in 1919–20, there have appeared people dressed in leather from top to toe. There disappeared from the streets the expensive fur coats and the provocative, tasteless apparel by which NEPmen were plainly distinguishable to the eye. The streets have turned gray.

---

[16] Bogushevskii, "Kanun piatiletki," p. 468.
[17] *III sessiia VTsIK XIII sozyva*, 15:4–5 (Belov). For similar complaints, see *VIII s'ezd professional'nykh soiuzov SSSR*, pp. 487 and 489, and *II sessiia VTsIK XIV sozyva*, 4:6, 7:9–10, 18–23.

And this was in those weeks when the Five-Year Plan was being examined in Vesenkha, Gosplan, and the government.[18]

Accordingly, the food consumption of workers deteriorated. The urban ("nonagricultural") population of the country ate less grain, meat, and butter, but more potatoes, in 1929 than in 1928. Per capita annual consumption of grain products declined to 169.82 kilograms in 1929 from 174.39 in 1928; of meat, fat, and poultry to 47.50 kilograms from 51.68; and of butter to 2.84 kilograms from 2.97. Instead, per capita consumption of potatoes rose to 108.84 kilograms in 1929 from 87.60 in 1928.[19] (This issue will be discussed further in Chapter 9.) The changes in consumption reflected the worsening lives of workers in 1928–29.

The economic hardships naturally caused great concern within the party leadership. As early as February 1928 Stalin warned in the then-secret letter addressed to all party organizations:

What does the grain procurement crisis imply? What is its significance? What are its probable consequences?

It implies, above all, a crisis in the supply of the working-class areas, high bread prices in these areas, and a fall in real wages of the workers.

It implies, second, a crisis in the supply of the Red Army and discontent among the soldiers.[20]

Stalin repeatedly emphasized the ill effects of the crisis on the working class and the Red Army.[21] Evidently he was most concerned about their political mood. In the summer of 1928, the GPU reported that "in all industrial districts [there is] worker discontent with the bad supply of bread," that the workers at Red Sormovo, Izhevsk, Profintern, Petrovskii, and other factories demanded a review of collective agreements for the purpose of increasing wages to compensate for inflated prices of bread, and that in some factories there were "tendencies toward strikes" and "threats of strikes."[22]

---

[18] Bogushevskii and Khavin, "God velikogo pereloma," p. 330.

[19] Moshkov, *Zernovaia problema v gody sploshnoi kollektivizatsii sel'skogo khoziaistva SSSR*, p. 136, citing archival sources. For details, see E. O. Kabo, "Voprosy potrebleniia," in *Na novom etape sotsialisticheskogo stroitel'stva*, 1:281. *Trud*, 16 May 1929 (Iu. Kalistratov), refers to the declining consumption of a "number of scarce goods."

[20] Stalin, *Sochineniia*, 11:10.

[21] Ibid., 11:5, 39, 43, 167, and 12:46. On 27 January 1928, Andreev wrote in a private letter that "the mood in the countryside has been transferred to the barracks; as a result, discussion about grain [is growing] in the barracks." Andreev, *Vospominaniia, pis'ma*, p. 209.

[22] Cited in a document of the All-Union Central Council of Trade Unions in the Trotsky Archives, T 1829. Strikes took place at the Kuvshinsk Factory in the Urals.

Both the Stalin and the Bukharin factions expressed great concern about the political mood of the working class at the July 1928 plenum of the Central Committee, which provided an arena for bitter dispute between the two factions. The bulk of the record of the plenum has not been published, but the Trotsky Archives contain some excerpts of speeches delivered. From the Right, Uglanov sounded a tocsin:

We cannot address the peasant question separately from the working class. After all, the consumers' point of view speaks inside me, and we are such consumers as represent the proletariat of the city of Moscow, millions strong. We know that a great number of cities have cards or surrogate cards or some restrictive, regulatory measures. Herein lies the whole point. Let us honestly answer the question, Does such a situation in the eleventh year of the revolution not cause doubt and alarm in the working class? I'll frankly tell you, comrades: this squarely puts the masses of workers on the alert. It is necessary to see this in every factory. It goes without saying that if this situation – any kind of interruption in [food] supply, a shortage of foodstuffs, surrogate measures of our [price?] regulations, etc. – persists, it cannot be supported by the working class. This is clear. Such a situation cannot go on for very long. . . . We all know quite well the very nature of the Russian proletariat: a large percentage of it is tied to the countryside, and the degree of vacillation there is transferred to the working class.[23]

V. M. Molotov, a staunch supporter of Stalin, declared in an equally frank manner but with a pretense of optimism:

[Workers] may have to eat not white but black bread. We have to tell workers about this frankly, and they will understand us.
Voroshilov: Quite right.
Workers will understand us if we have to substitute black for white bread in order not to increase the price of bread. In Moscow we will probably have to sell not fresh but frozen meat so as to keep the price index of agricultural products [at a low level].[24]

In August 1928 Molotov noted publicly that the hardship was bound up with "certain sacrifices on the part of the working class."[25] Yet the Stalin group consistently attributed the whole problem to the "class enemy." At the July 1928 plenum, L. M. Kaganovich, for example, contended that the hardships were caused by the "grain strike" of the kulaks.[26]

Workers were not silent about the hardships. Some workers

23 Trotsky Archives, T 1835.
24 Ibid., T 1833.
25 *Pravda*, 5 August 1928.
26 Trotsky Archives, T 1835.

exclaimed "What have we come to!" and "Where are we rushing to with industrialization?"[27] Others complained bitterly about the offensive against the private traders: "Why do you move against the private trader, because he does business better than the co-operative?" "The private trader has had everything, but there is nothing in the cooperative."[28] At the June 1928 session of the All-Union Central Council of Trade Unions, it was reported that the delegates were "not afraid to curse the People's Commissariat of Trade and workers' cooperatives, cursed very sharply their bad organization of [food] supplies," and were angered by the commissariat's "planning" and "regulation" of the market.[29] New workers (so they were described) invariably came forward with the same question: "Why on earth is it that before, two–three years ago, all kinds of foodstuffs were plentiful, but now are in short supply in spite of the claim that we are growing and marching ahead all the time?"[30]

Not only new workers posed such questions. At a meeting with Stalin held on 4 May 1929, a delegate from the Donbas miners named Krysin asked the question that "agitated many [workers]" and that he already had posed at meetings with the leaders of the fuel industry and the central committee of the miners' union: "Why have the stores become short of foodstuffs?" Stalin put down his pencil, stood up, and proposed to distinguish the two – technical and "class" – aspects of the problem. Stalin went on to stress the latter aspect:

Grain, meat, butter – all foodstuffs come to us from the village. Yet who until now is the biggest economic force in the village? The private producer and, above all, the kulak. What percentage of the [rural] population is now organized in collective farms in the Donbas?
　— In our Lugansk, nine percent. . . .
　— What percentage of land belongs to the collective farms?
　— Six percent. . . .
That is to say, ninety-four percent of land remains with private owners, a considerable part of the land, and the best part at that, being in the hands of the kulak. The kulak understands that socialism is death for him. . . . [We] have to accelerate collectivization and the construction of state farms,

[27] Zhukov, *Liudi 30-kh godov*, p. 49.
[28] Aksel'rod, *Kak my uchil's' torgovat'*, p. 44, and *XIV Vserossiiskii s'ezd sovetov*, 2:23.
[29] Bogushevskii, "Kanun piatiletki," p. 485. The discussion was not reported in the press.
[30] Mikoian, *Prodovol'stvennoe snabzhenie i nashi zadachi*, p. 5.

arm the collective and state farms with tractors and agricultural machines, teach collective farmers modern methods of agriculture and ways to raise the yield, and then there will be plenty of grain, plenty of meat, and plenty of butter.[31]

Whether Stalin's analysis of food shortages convinced the working class is arguable. What is definite is that he sought to deflect their grievances to the countryside and elicit their political support for the collectivization drive.[32]

The declining standard of living affected all social groups. The party leadership introduced food rationing in order to secure provisions for the workers and thereby win their political support.[33] In June 1929, a resolution of the People's Commissariat of Trade explicitly declared that rationing was a "measure to limit the consumption of these [scarce] goods by the nonlaboring population and a means of satisfying, first of all, the needs of the industrial workers for these goods."[34]

At that time there took place no such violent reaction as the Kronstadt rebellion of 1921. Yet identifiable groups of workers appeared to the Stalin group to be politically and socially disoriented. K. Ia. Bauman, for example, who was soon to take over the Moscow Committee of the party from the Rightist Uglanov, declared to the April 1928 joint plenum of the committee and the Moscow Control Commission that there was "legitimate dissatisfaction with the policies of the Soviet government" among "individual strata of workers."[35] In the autumn of 1929, Kaganovich frankly stated to a Moscow party conference: "There is no need for us to conceal the fact that in a number of cases, discontent with the difficulties – queues, food shortages – captures individual groups of workers."[36] Bauman and Kaganovich had in mind two particularly

---

[31] Zhukov, *Liudi 30-kh godov*, pp. 98–102.
[32] According to Viola, some workers believed that the problem of food shortages lay with the peasants. See Viola, *The Best Sons of the Fatherland*, pp. 60, 230–31.
[33] Mikoian, *Problema snabzheniia strany i rekonstruksiia narodnogo khoziaistva*, pp. 22–24.
[34] Neiman, *Vnutrenniaia torgovlia SSSR*, p. 178. In fact, the top priority of rationing was given to the workers (ibid., p. 173). In 1929–30, the Leningrad industrial workers' rations of bread and meat, for example, were twice as much as those of white-collar employees. See *Leningradskie rabochie v bor'be za sotsializm, 1926–1937*, p. 172.
[35] Quoted in *Moskovskie bol'sheviki v bor'be s pravymi i "levymi" opportunizmom*, p. 246.
[36] *Pravda*, 1 November 1929.

distinctive, easily perceptible groups of workers that were conveniently referred to as "new" and "old."

New and old workers

When in 1928 it embarked on the socialist offensive, the Stalin group deemed it imperative to minimize the differentiation of the working class and close its ranks, because, in Stalin's judgment, the offensive "intensified the class struggle."[37] As much in its political as in its social dimensions, the differentiation of the working class had been a major issue within the party during the 1920s. When confronting the United Opposition in December 1926, Stalin had declared, for instance, that the two marginal strata – the "newcomers from nonproletarian classes" and the "labor aristocracy," or the "most well-to-do portion of the proletariat" – were a "common nutritive medium for opportunism," whether open opportunism or "opportunism camouflaged with 'Leftist' phrases."[38] Like other controversial categories (e.g., kulak), terms like "newcomers" and "labor aristocrats" were politicized, and one is tempted to see them as scarcely more than political labels disguised with a sociological mask.

Certainly the social and the political are not altogether distinct. Indeed, it was precisely by virtue of their social status that the marginal strata of workers appeared to the Bolshevik leadership to be politically suspect. Because they were "not fenced off" from the besieging "bourgeois" and "petty bourgeois" milieus and because they were "isolated" from the core of the working class,[39] the marginal strata of workers were deemed by the Bolshevik leaders a potential "conduit for bourgeois influences on the proletariat."[40] During the 1920s, therefore, the party leadership had made efforts to maintain a certain degree of social homogeneity in the working class as a "barrier" against the surrounding milieus, in order to prevent the "economic heterogeneity [*neodnorodnost'*] of the proletariat" from "growing into political groupings."[41]

---

[37] Stalin, *Sochineniia*, 11:17–8, 269–70, 278–79.
[38] Ibid., 9:10–11.
[39] *Molodaia gvardiia*, 1929, no. 4, p. 54 (L. M. Kaganovich).
[40] *Bol'shevik*, 1926, nos. 21–22, p. 48 (G. Malenkov), and ibid., 1926, nos. 23–24, pp. 38–39 (M. Pitkovskii).
[41] Ibid., 1927, nos. 19–20, p. 64 (M. Brudnyi).

These efforts were closely linked to the wage-scale reform of 1927–29, which had the object of narrowing wage differentials among workers.[42] In 1927–30, as far as wage differentials were concerned, the reform was successful.[43]

Nevertheless, the industrialization drive made it difficult for the working class to close ranks. Political divisions and tensions among the workers were complex and often cut across generational lines, gender, skill levels, work experience, and other characteristics, as William Chase has admirably demonstrated in his book on Moscow workers in the 1920s.[44] While their complexity defies any simplistic categorizations, the political leadership was particularly concerned with the two distinctive groups of workers – "new" and "old."

One should not assume that these categories corresponded strictly to their actual social qualities; specifically, the phrase "new workers" was often stretched to comprise those unskilled and undisciplined workers who were resistant to party, union, and managerial controls. Yet one also should not assume that these terms were pure abstractions devoid of social substance. As will be shown, they applied to those workers who had certain outlooks thought to be characteristic of their social backgrounds, that is, new, unskilled, and poorly paid workers of peasant origin, and skilled and well-paid workers of the older generation.

In the second half of the 1920s the number of industrial workers increased steadily from 2,335,600 in 1926 to 2,479,000 in 1927, 2,690,800 in 1928, 2,921,000 in 1929, and 3,675,000 in 1930.[45]

---

[42] Ibid. Tomskii described this as "elementary class justice." *VII s'ezd professional'nykh soiuzov SSSR*, p. 51. From the unions' point of view, the reform had another object of reducing the proportion of supplementary payments. These payments depended on the "will of management," so that the unions had little "regulating influence" on the actual wages of workers. Naturally, the reform met resistance from the managers (*Zarabotnaia plata i koldogovornaia kampaniia 1927/28g.*, pp. 16–28). Yet this reform was "clearly favoured by the planners, since it made a higher proportion of the wages fund amenable to planning" by increasing the proportion of fixed wage rates in total earnings. Carr and Davies, *Foundations of a Planned Economy*, p. 536.

[43] In terms of decile ratio of highest-to-lowest tenth wages, differentials narrowed from 3.60 in 1926 to 3.33 in 1930. Rabkina and Rimashevskaia, "Raspredelitel'nye otnosheniia i sotsial'noe razvitie," pp. 20–21, and Ellman, "A Note on the Distribution of Earnings in the USSR under Brezhnev," p. 670. See also Zeltyn', "Razvitie form i metodov oplaty truda rabochikh v promyshlennosti SSSR," pp. 146–47.

[44] Chase, *Workers, Society and the Soviet State*.

[45] *Trud v SSSR* (1932), p. 61 (average annual number of workers including factory apprentices of "census industry" or large-scale industry).

Such growth was conducive to qualitative change or differentiation. In almost every discussion of the working class the Bolsheviks noted the danger that the class might split into older, skilled workers with work experience under capitalism and new, young, and unskilled workers who lacked this knowledge.[46] The influx of new workers into the factories brought frequent and more strident alarms: "Every year the working class is being diluted [*razzhizhaetsia*] by a large number of people from other classes, especially from the village."[47] "The ranks of older workers . . . are thinning out every year."[48] To be sure, the problem was partly due to natural attrition through aging. Yet the expansion of industry, the "infiltration" of new peasant workers, and the promotion of workers into full-time administrative positions and higher education accelerated the "dilution." M. Tomskii, head of the trade unions, complained in late 1926 that the peasant youth were "very eager to go to the city for any work at all."[49] Peasants appeared to urban workers to infiltrate the factories "almost imperceptibly."[50] The "dilution" increasingly concerned the party and the trade unions and prompted them to conduct a census of the working class.[51]

The union census held in the spring of 1929 revealed that in spite of the steady addition of new workers the older generation was still predominant: 50.7 percent of those surveyed had first entered industrial work before 1918, or roughly before the October Revolution.[52] The majority of highly skilled and skilled workers (for exam-

[46] *VII s"ezd professional'nykh soiuzov SSSR*, pp. 38–39, 184, 236, 719, 766; *VIII s"ezd professional'nykh soiuzov SSSR*, pp. 28, 31–32, 83–84, 186, 514, 532, 567; *XVI konferentsiia VKP(b)*, pp. 72, 145; *VIII Vsesoiuznyi s"ezd VLKSM*, pp. 22–29. For the diversity of the labor force in Moscow in the 1920s, see also Chase, *Workers, Society and the Soviet State*, chap. 3.

[47] See G. D. Veinberg, of the All-Union Central Council of Trade Unions and the Central Control Commission, in *Trud*, 27 September 1929, and *Torgovo-promyshlennaia gazeta*, 1 September 1929.

[48] Khain and Khandros, *Kto oni–novye liudi na proizvodstve?* p. 4. See also *Kommunisticheskaia revoliutsiia*, 1929, no. 8, pp. 31–32.

[49] *XV konferentsiia VKP(b)*, p. 288.

[50] *Trud*, 5 April 1929, and Burdov, *Profsoiuzy i industrializatsiia*, p. 28; Semenov, *Litso fabrichnykh rabochikh prozhivaiushchikh v derevniakh i politprosvetrabota sredi nikh*, p. 62.

[51] Molotov in *Pravda*, 4 December 1928, and his report to the November 1928 plenum of the Central Committee quoted in Rashin, *Sostav fabrichno-zavodskogo proletariata SSSR*, pp. iii and 125.

[52] *Trud v SSSR* (1926–1930), pp. xii–xiii, 26, 28–29. The average age of the metal workers of this older generation was 37.9 years (my calculation based on *Perepis' rabochikh i sluzhashchikh 1929 g.*, pp. 9, 51).

ple, 92.1 percent and 78.1 percent, respectively, for the metal workers) belonged to this older generation.[53] With an average of fifteen years of work experience in industry, the skilled workers, most of them in their mid- to late thirties, accounted for 33.0 percent of the cotton workers, 21.1 percent of the metal workers, and 13.3 percent of the Donbas miners.[54] With an average of more than twenty years' experience, the highly skilled workers, most of them in their late thirties and early forties, accounted for 9.3 percent of the cotton workers, 4.6 percent of the metal workers, and 23.5 percent of the Donbas coal miners.[55]

This upper stratum was far from homogeneous. On the one hand, the level of party "saturation" and "social activity" (party, union, Soviet, cultural, and cooperative activity) was highest among the highly skilled.[56] On the other hand, even within this group of workers there were many "semipeasants."[57] The highly skilled workers also tended to have had less schooling than the younger generation.[58] The party leadership, however, saw their relatively privileged position within the working class as providing a potential conduit for "influences alien to the proletariat": "liberal reformism" and "opportunism."[59] Numerically "inconsiderable" though they were, the "whole policy of the party and the unions" in the factories was geared to "eradicating" their influences.[60]

[53] *Perepis' rabochikh i sluzhashchikh 1929 g.*, p. 62.

[54] Rashin, *Sostav fabrichno-zavodskogo proletariata SSSR*, pp. 75–79, 84, and *Perepis' rabochikh i sluzhashchikh 1929 g.*, p. 52.

[55] Rashin, *Sostav fabrichno-zavodskogo proletariata SSSR*, pp. 74–85, and *Perepis' rabochikh i sluzhashchikh 1929 g.*, pp. 57–58. The classification by skill is based on the wage-scale tables in force at that time. The high percentage of highly skilled Donbas miners reflects heavy mining labor, which was scaled high on the table.

[56] Of the highly skilled, skilled, semiskilled, and unskilled workers, 16.2, 15.1, 11.8, and 9.5% respectively, were party members. Meyer, *Sozialstruktur sowjetischer Industriearbeiter*, p. 175. For social activity, see Rashin, *Sostav fabrichno-zavodskogo proletariata SSSR*, pp. 145–46.

[57] See, for example, *Rabochaia Moskva*, 30 January 1929.

[58] Rashin, *Sostav fabrichno-zavodskogo proletariata SSSR*, pp. 110–24.

[59] *Bol'shevik*, 1926, nos. 21–22, p. 48, nos. 23–24, p. 39. Some of them were not union members. The party's Central Committee complained in late 1926 that party "saturation" was "insufficient" among the highly skilled. *Izvestiia TsK VKP(b)*, no. 1(74), 10 January 1927, p. 2.

[60] *Bol'shevik*, 1926, nos. 21–22, p. 48. Contemporary Soviet historians usually do not discuss this issue. See, for example, Vdovin and Drobizhev, *Rost rabochego klassa SSSR*, p. 175, where it is stated that after the October Revolution, the "stratum of 'labor aristocracy' ceased to exist." "Aristocrats" were not entirely confined to the older generations, however. For highly skilled "young aristocrats," see N. Potakov, "Aristokraty ot stanka," *Molodaia gvardiia*, 1929 no. 15

In general, before the critical years 1928–29 it was the older, skilled workers who enjoyed good credentials within the party leadership. Certainly this group of workers was also far from homogeneous, and its overall level of party "saturation" and "social activity" was slightly lower than that of the highly skilled workers.[61] Yet this group was not as "aristocratic" as the highly skilled group. Moreover, in the view of the Bolsheviks, the older skilled workers distinguished themselves from the younger generation by their social and political experience: they had learned in the "hard school of class struggle with the capitalists." During NEP the party leadership thus conformed to the traditional assumption that identified the proletarian outlook with these workers.[62] This assumption was well suited to the primary objective of NEP, namely, the restoration of an economy ruined by the war, the revolution, and the civil war.

In 1929 the trade unions maintained that, based on the census, the "influx into the working class of people from the petty bourgeois peasant milieu" was "not as large" as was generally assumed.[63] To be sure, in the 1920s the tight labor market and widespread unemployment limited the number of peasants who could find industrial work. Yet the union census nevertheless clearly revealed a steady (and, in some industries and regions, rapid) movement of peasants into the industrial work force, a fact that augmented fears that peasants were infiltrating the factories through every possible channel. One-fifth of the workers surveyed had first entered industrial work between 1926 and the spring of 1929, and 45 percent of these new workers were children of peasants, a figure nearly as high as that of children of workers (46.3 percent).[64]

(August), pp. 172–75. Of the highly skilled metal workers, 12.9% were below thirty years of age. *Perepis' rabochikh i sluzhashchikh 1929 g.*, p. 51.

[61] Meyer, *Sozialstruktur sowjetischer Industriearbeiter*, p. 175, and Rashin, *Sostav fabrichno-zavodskogo proletariata SSSR*, pp. 145–46.

[62] Note particularly that in April 1926, N. Uglanov, then head of the Moscow Committee of the party, firmly defended skilled workers from grass-roots accusations of their "aristocratic" and "reformist" tendencies. *Pravda*, 25 April 1926.

[63] See the resolution of the presidium of the All-Union Central Council of Trade Unions quoted in Meyer, *Sozialstruktur sowjetischer Industriearbeiter*, pp. 22–23, and N. Evreinov's introduction to Rashin, *Sostav fabrichno-zavodskogo proletariata SSSR*, p. v as well as Rashin's conclusion (p. 169). For a very positive view of the composition of the working class in 1929, see also Shkaratan, *Problemy sotsial'noi struktury rabochego klass SSSR*, pp. 257–58.

[64] *Trud v SSSR* (1926–30), pp. xiii, 28–29. In the Ukrainian metallurgical industry and the Donbas coal mines, children of peasants were predominant among this new cohort, accounting for 61.2 and 68%, respectively (see Meyer, *Sozialstruktur*

Predominantly males in their late teens or early twenties, new workers tended to be unskilled and poorly paid.[65] On the average the unskilled were paid less than half as much as the highly skilled,[66] and therefore were inclined to drift from factory to factory in search of higher wages.[67] The level of party "saturation" and "social activity" was lowest among the new, unskilled workers.[68] Their lack of work experience under capitalism made their political credentials very poor. They were considered "raw" and politically untempered. "It would be a self-deception," one commentator declared in 1929, "to think that these new workers perceive the lessons of the class struggle just as do the older cadres who have learned in the hard school of this struggle."[69]

As the compilers of the trade union census repeatedly pointed out, there were vast regional and professional differences in the census indexes, so that one must avoid hasty generalizations. Moreover, at the time of the census the social and political outlook of the working class was undergoing rapid and significant change. The growing influx of new workers and industrial modernization played a major role in this change.

The influx of new workers into the factories

In the second half of the 1920s individual factories experienced a large influx of new workers. The giant Red Triangle Rubber Plant in

sowjetischer Industriearbeiter, p. 134). Many peasant workers indeed lived in the countryside and commuted to the factories. For this, see Semenov, *Litso fabrichnykh rabochikh*.

[65] For instance, more than half of those in the metal-fabricating industry who had first entered industrial work between 1926 and 1929 were less than 23 years old (*Perepis' rabochikh i sluzhashchikh 1929 g.*, p. 51). In the late 1920s the sexual composition of new workers was rather stable, males accounting for 71–72% (Vdovin and Drobizhev, *Rost rabochego klass SSSR*, 130). According to one analysis, of the new workers in the metal-working industry who had first entered industrial work in 1928–29, only 1.3% in Moscow and 1.1% in Leningrad were highly skilled or skilled (N. Gumilevskii, "Kharakteristika sostava rabochei sily v metallopromyshlennosti," *Metall*, 1930, no. 2, p. 20). The new recruits could not fully compensate for even the natural "attrition" of skilled workers. *Statistika truda*, 1929, nos. 2–3, p. 18.

[66] See note 55, this chapter.

[67] Rashin, *Sostav fabrichno-zavodskogo proletariata SSSR*, pp. 47–63, 76–85, and *Perepis' rabochikh i sluzhashchikh 1929 g.*, pp. 65–72.

[68] See note 56, this chapter, and Meyer, *Sozialstruktur sowjetischer Industriearbeiter*, pp. 171–73.

[69] Korotkov, "K proverke i chistke proizvodstvennykh iacheek," p. 84.

Leningrad quadrupled its work force in five years, reaching 20,000 in 1928.[70] In Belo-Kalitva *raion*, Shakhty *okrug*, in the North Caucasus, the number of workers more than doubled between 1925 and 1927.[71] In 1928 as many as 45 percent of the workers in the Southern Steel Trust, which embraced Ukrainian metallurgical factories, were peasants who allegedly owned and farmed their land and worked in the factories only to "earn a little extra."[72] In the summer of 1928 those with more than five years' continuous work at the Petrovskii Plant, a giant Southern Steel factory, accounted for only 11.5 percent of its work force of 22,000, whereas 2.1 percent were "rich peasants" or "class aliens."[73] In the autumn of 1928 as many as 85 percent of 1,187 workers in the hull workshop of the Baltic Shipbuilding Plant in Leningrad retained holdings of land.[74] The influx of peasants was nothing new, but as industry rapidly developed in the second half of the 1920s, the press sounded frequent warnings that there were "not a few petty bourgeois peasant workers" even in the factories of the vanguard city of Leningrad.[75] The problem was not simply quantitative. Even a small-scale increase had a strong psychological impact upon older workers, who described new workers as "a fly in the ointment."[76]

The contemporary press gives the impression that older, skilled workers reacted as a more or less solid group against the influx of new workers. Older workers saw new workers as uncultured, unskilled, and politically illiterate elements who knew little about the history and discipline of the factories, although the presence of new workers in the factories was not a recent phenomenon, and many workers had themselves once been unfamiliar with industrial work.

---

[70] *VIII s˝ezd professional'nykh soiuzov SSSR*, p. 122. See also *Sputnik agitatora dlia goroda*, 1929, no. 8, pp. 37–38. Among the new workers were peasants, former officers of the Imperial Army, hereditary nobles, etc. Shkaratan, *Problemy sotsial'noi struktury rabochego klassa SSSR*, pp. 244–45.

[71] *Vestnik truda*, 1927, no. 12, p. 97.

[72] *Izvestiia TsIK SSSR*, 26 April 1929.

[73] Ibid., and *Statisticheskoe obozrenie*, 1929, no. 2, p. 50. See also Dukel'skii, *Za sotsialisticheskuiu trudovuiu distsiplinu*, pp. 18–19, and *VI Vsesoiuznaia konferentsiia VLKSM*, p. 384.

[74] *Ekonomicheskoe obozrenie*, 1929, no. 3, p. 7, and *Visnyk profrukhu Ukrainy*, 1929, no. 12 (June), p. 6. This was made clear by a special investigation of new workers conducted nationwide in the autumn of 1928 by the metal workers' union.

[75] See, for example, the case of the Putilov Factory in *Trud*, 29 April 1929.

[76] *Pravda*, 9 April 1929.

New workers were subject to prejudice, discrimination, and harassment. They were the easy target of administrative abuse, especially arbitrary treatment by foremen.[77] Older workers treated new workers "in a lordly manner," ridiculing them as "country bumpkins" (*derevenshchina*), "sandaled people" (*lapotniki*), or "dark people."[78] The new workers had difficulty operating unfamiliar machinery, frequently damaging it and also increasing the number of labor accidents.[79] In the North Caucasus older workers reportedly refused to work in a team with new ones.[80] New workers were even denied the name "worker" because this respectable label misrepresented their origins.[81] In the late 1920s the press reported worsening tensions between older and new workers everywhere.

The impact of new workers on labor discipline was an especially serious problem. Labor indiscipline naturally had many causes, and statistical data do not conclusively indicate that labor discipline actually deteriorated in 1928–29. Yet labor–management relations apparently worsened from the spring of 1928 on, when the Shakhty affair came to light. The Bolsheviks attributed the lack of labor discipline to the disorganizing influences of new workers. In late 1928 a worker from the aforementioned Petrovskii Plant reported that peasant workers were interested less in production than in gambling and drinking, and that they entertained themselves with "fist fighting" (*stenki*).[82] In this factory, with the influx of new workers, the number of penalties for nonfulfillment of administra-

[77] *Sputnik kommunista*, 1928, no. 17, p. 69.

[78] *Rabochaia gazeta*, 12 December 1929; *Vestnik truda*, 1927, no. 12, p. 100; *Molodaia gvardiia*, 1929, no. 14, pp. 58–68, no. 16, p. 53. See also N. Bukharin's speech in *VIII Vsesoiuznyi s˝ezd VLKSM*, p. 29, and M. Tomskii's in *VIII s˝ezd professional'nykh soiuzov SSSR*, p. 32. This was an old phenomenon seen widely in the prerevolutionary years and during NEP as well. See Bonnel (ed.), *The Russian Worker*, p. 39, and Chase, *Workers, Society and the Soviet State*, chaps. 6 and 7.

[79] For instance, in the Ukrainian metallurgical industry, where the influx of new, peasant workers was very rapid, the number of labor accidents increased by 24.4% in 1927–28, whereas it dropped by 2.2% in the Russian Republic (Dukel'skii, *Za sotsialisticheskuiu trudovuiu distsiplinu*, p. 64, and *Trud*, 17 July, 18 September 1929). In one metallurgical factory, 781 of 929 accidents happened to new workers. *TPG*, 7 October 1928.

[80] *Novye kadry promyshlennykh rabochikh i rabota sredi nikh*, p. 10.

[81] *Pravda*, 9 April 1929.

[82] Ibid., 25 December 1928. This pastime apparently survived the October Revolution. For an interesting account of this in the nineteenth century, see Brower, "Labor Violence in Russia in the Late Nineteenth Century."

tive orders tripled in 1928–29.[83] In 1927–28, 79 percent of the penalties for violation of factory regulations in Southern Steel were imposed on unskilled workers, the majority of whom were new, peasant workers.[84] In 1929 some new workers in the Donbas reportedly resorted to "self-maiming" by burning themselves with acid in order to shirk labor.[85] In this coal-mining region "raw peasant masses" migrated from one mine to another in search of better housing and "lighter work quotas." These "rolling stones" (*letuny*) disrupted the tone of work in the mines. Some *desiatniki* (roughly the equivalent of assistant foremen in factories) joined the workers sleeping on the job, while others had to go around workers' lodgings ferreting out malingerers in order to bring them to the mines. This state of affairs apparently irritated older workers, who contended that they had "never witnessed such laxity even under the old regime."[86] The Bolsheviks and older, skilled workers regarded new workers as a heterogeneous (petty bourgeois) element that disrupted "proletarian discipline" in the factories.

Nor did the new workers fit comfortably into the institutional setting of the factory. They felt obliged either to abase themselves in front of "any big or little boss," silently enduring violations of their legitimate interests by management, or to press their demands in "anarchic fashion," thereby circumventing the unions.[87] In pursuit of higher wages, new workers worked overtime (ten to twelve hours a day) on piece rates, which led management to revise work quotas upward and aroused the hostility of older workers.[88] New workers intensified conflicts on the shop floor by pursuing their interests through their own peculiar methods. As a journal of the Central Committee reported in 1929, after such methods failed the new workers resorted to

---

[83] *Izvestiia TsK VKP(b)*, 1929, nos. 14–15, p. 16. It should be noted, however, that the increase in the number of penalties reflected the collapse of managerial authority as a result of the Shakhty affair: factory directors often responded to this crisis simply by imposing more penalties than before. Bogushevskii, "Kanun piatiletki," pp. 509–10, and *XI z'izd KP(b)U*, p. 672.

[84] *Statisticheskoe obozrenie*, 1929, no. 2, p. 51 (based on material from five factories).

[85] *Kommunisticheskaia revoliutsiia*, 1929, no. 6, p. 5.

[86] *Gornorabochii*, 1929, no. 2, p. 2, no. 3, p. 18, and *Pravda*, 16 February 1929. See also *Rabochaia gazeta*, 1 March 1929, and *Predpriiatie*, 1928, no. 12, pp. 11–12.

[87] Burdov, *Profsoiuzy i industrializatsiia*, pp. 29, 63. See also *Izvestiia TsIK SSSR*, 26 April 1929.

[88] *Novye kadry promyshlennykh rabochikh i rabota sredi nikh*, p. 10.

threats, surreptitious beatings, insults to management, rejection of administrative instructions, and discrediting of managerial personnel in front of workers. Embittered by management, they sought to take revenge by wrecking or damaging machines and equipment. At the Krasnokholmsk Factory [a textile factory in Moscow], one worker, angry at being transferred to [lower-paying] work by management, threw a bolt into a printing machine [*krapmashina*], causing twelve thousand rubles in damage.[89]

Sometimes older workers found themselves on the defensive:

The presence in the enterprises of older cadres of skilled workers on the one hand, and of new workers, the majority of whom are engaged in unskilled labor, on the other hand, leads in a number of cases to unsound relations between these groups. New workers [adopt] hostile attitudes toward the older, skilled proletarians, envy their better working conditions, or fawn on them. The skilled workers in turn adopt scornful, haughty attitudes toward new workers, even beat them, and demand [of management] an exclusive right to occupy the best position in production.[90]

Circumventing the established channels of communication and negotiation between labor and management and "anarchically" pressing their demands, new workers threatened the social stability in the factories. Considering the discrimination, harassment, and poor wages to which they were subject, new workers had ample reason to be discontented with the factory establishment. They found themselves treated as "outsiders" and very often behaved accordingly.

New workers brought heterogeneous elements not only into the social and institutional settings of the factory but also into its political life. In 1929 a party journal of the Urals reported:

The new worker, knowing only by hearsay about the prerevolutionary order, is included to see in demands for discipline and honest and intense work something hostile to his own ideas about revolution and freedom. . . . Can we raise the productivity of labor in earnest, if a considerable portion of workers are inclined to see this as exploitation?[91]

New workers reportedly saw no difference between the former capitalist factory owner and the Red director, whom they regarded as an "exploiter."[92] According to a report from the North Caucasus, "abnormal attitudes of new workers toward engineers and technicians"

[89] *Sputnik agitatora dlia goroda,* 1929, no. 8 (April), p. 39.
[90] Ibid.
[91] *Biulleten' Ural'skogo oblastnogo komiteta VKP(b),* 1929, no. 5, p. 1.
[92] *Mettallist,* 1928, no. 40, p. 29, and *Golos tekstilei,* 12 June 1929. See Korotkov, "K proverke i chistke proizvodstvennykh iacheek," p. 84, and Murashov, *Profsoiuzy i sotsialisticheskoe stroitel'stvo,* p. 32.

troubled almost all factories.[93] The unions and the party had great difficulties teaching new workers basic concepts – the differences between capitalist and socialist factories, the "differences between the union and management" – in Bolshevik parlance, "political literacy."[94] In the Donbas coal mines, trade union representatives often found it difficult to teach new workers "political literacy":

In conversation with new workers, we received appalling answers to our questions. For instance, when we asked, "Who is the master of the enterprise?" we were told in one case, "the union," and in another case, "the head miner" [*shteiger*]. "Can the union fire [workers]?" They answered confidently, "Yes." "Who sets work quotas?" The answer was, "The union representatives," and so on.[95]

These "appalling" responses may well have been a tactic directed against the factory establishment. Whatever the case, party leaders feared that the outlook of the new workers posed a threat to political homogeneity in the factories. An illuminating incident occurred in the summer and autumn of 1928 at the Bol'shevik Textile Factory in Ivanovo-Voznesensk. New workers took the side of an assistant foreman and member of the factory committee named Krepikov who called for a strike for higher wages. Krepikov agitated against the factory committee, which he contended had turned into a "gendarmerie," and against the party, which had "deceived the working class." Although it is not clear whether a strike actually took place, his supporters (assistant foremen, new workers, former merchants) frustrated subsequent attempts by the committee to expel him from the union. In reporting the incident, the newspaper of the textile workers' union, *Golos tekstilei*, severely attacked the new workers, calling them "dark people" and contending that they "interpret in their own way anything that takes place around them, and [that they] understand political events in their own way [as well]."[96]

The party leadership maintained that the lack of respect for socialist factories shown by the new workers was part and parcel of their political illiteracy:

These new workers ... have never seen and known what class struggle means, and why and how discipline is needed in the ranks of the proletar-

[93] *Novye kadry promyshlennykh rabochikh i rabota sredi nikh*, p. 13.
[94] *Bol'shevik*, 1926, nos. 23–24, p. 47.
[95] Ibid.
[96] *Golos tekstilei*, 17 November 1928. Some 4,000 out of 14,000 workers were said to be "new workers."

iat. . . . For them the factory is neither the property of the working class that was taken by the working class from the capitalists, nor the creation [*detishche*] of the proletariat that has been erected by Soviet power, but rather a place in which they can earn a little extra to strengthen their own farms.[97]

Perhaps this last contention should not be taken at face value, if only because many new workers did not own a farm, but the meaning is clear. To the party leaders, these "raw" elements, fresh from a "petty bourgeois medium" and unfamiliar with the history and discipline of the factory, were politically ill equipped to cope with the difficulties of rapid industrialization.[98]

As the problems mounted in 1928–29, the mood of the new workers became a matter of increasing concern within the party leadership. In June 1928 L. M. Kaganovich warned Ukrainian miners against capitulating to the mood of new workers, to their lack of discipline and their resistance to the drive for productivity.[99] In early 1929 the Politbureau heatedly discussed this issue.[100] In February 1929 the Central Committee sent out a secret circular and drew particular attention to the mood of new, peasant workers.[101] This circular signaled the beginning of a vigorous press campaign against labor indiscipline. At the sixth Komsomol conference in June 1929, a new worker named Eliseev came under special attack for a letter to a Siberian newspaper in which he had "described extremely clearly the mood of certain strata of new, young workers":

Now the workers live badly. They lived better before. How do we work now? [We] drudge for all we are worth for eight hours, and we cannot relax. If you relax, you'll earn little. Yet all sorts of campaigns are going on here: "Raise Productivity!" "The Regime of Economy," and whatnot. In my opinion, socialist competition means "squeeze the last drops out of the workers." . . .

If we keep living like this, then it will turn out that we have been squeezed, we are squeezed harder now, and we will be squeezed in the future!

---

[97] Korotkov, "K proverke i chistke proizvodstvennykh iacheek," p. 83.

[98] It is symbolic of the Stalin group's distrust of new workers that in 1928, in order to help "fight against Trotskyism," the Central Committee sent out to the *obkom*s and *raikom*s I. Zhiga's book *Novye rabochie* (Moscow, 1928). Zhiga described new workers in a Leningrad factory as susceptible to the influence of enemies of labor policy in the factory. Zhiga, *Ocherki, stat'i i vospominaniia*, pp. 8, 180–288.

[99] *Pravda*, 24 June 1928.

[100] See K. E. Voroshilov's speech in *Leningradskaia pravda*, 10 March 1929.

[101] "Pis'mo TsK VKP(b) vsem partiinym organizatsiiam o podniatii trudovoi distsipliny," in *KPSS v rezoliutsiiakh*, 4:170.

I ask [you] to prove that I am wrong. But it is wrong to say that I am perhaps a counterrevolutionary, that I am against Soviet power, and so on. [You] should not make a fuss. Maybe I work more honestly than those who will answer me. But I cannot understand what is happening now in our country. I have been in production for only a year. Before that I lived in the countryside and thought that the workers lived better in the city. There is no difference [*odin chert*].[102]

Actually Eliseev seemed to understand what was happening and was intensely unhappy with it. The Bolsheviks, for their part, feared that new workers like Eliseev were politically disoriented in the face of revolutionary upheaval. Their native villages were also undergoing rapid change, a fact that contributed to the Bolshevik fear of their political disorientation and opposition to the party's agricultural policy.[103]

The Bolsheviks attached the label "petty bourgeois spontaneity" to the social and political outlook of the new, unskilled workers, an outlook whose influence appeared to grow with the influx of new workers. Lack of discipline, resistance to the push for productivity, "political illiteracy," and "disorientation" were all seen by the Stalin group as manifestations of the petty bourgeois mentality and as signs of a rapid "dilution" of proletarian consciousness. In 1929 some factories resorted to a mass "cleansing" of those new workers suspected of political disorientation under the guise of purging "class aliens," but this easiest yet most disruptive solution was denounced by the party.[104] By 1929 the task of accommodating new workers assumed a high political priority.

[102] *VI Vsesoiuznaia konferentsiia VLKSM*, pp. 353–54.
[103] See, for example, *Visnyk profrukhu Ukrainy*, 1929, no. 12 (June), pp. 8–10; *Molodaia gvardiia*, 1929, no. 14, pp. 60–61; *Bol'shevik*, 1929, no. 22, p. 38.
[104] See the case of Moscow in Davydova and Ponomarev, *Velikii podvig*, p. 239, and Bauman, *Sotsialisticheskoe nastuplenie i zadachi Moskovskoi organizatsii*, p. 59. Note especially the case of the Podolsk Factory near Moscow, where the peasant workers' influence was said to be particularly strong. In October 1928, some workers presented a "program of demands," which included a rise in selling prices for grain and a decrease in agricultural taxes (Krylov and Zykov, *O pravoi opasnosti*, p. 198). In November 1928 M. I. Kalinin visited the factory, where workers' discontent with food shortages was manifest. Kalinin appealed to the workers to "bear a little more," but they shouted him down. He escaped from the angry workers only with the help of the local GPU. *Sotsialisticheskii vestnik*, no. 24 (190), 19 December 1928, p. 15, and no. 25 (191), 9 January 1929, p. 15. In September 1929, seasonal workers, some of whom were "disfranchised," attacked Komsomol members and GPU agents at a Podolsk railroad station with a crowbar and rocks. This incident led to a "cleansing" of the workers in Podolsk. *Komsomol'skaia pravda*, 24, 26 September 1929; *Trud*, 25, 26 September 1929; *Pravda*, 27, 28 September, and 1 October 1929.

The impact of industrial modernization

In the late 1920s party leaders were concerned about "petty bourgeois spontaneity." Factory policy was deliberately directed against it:

The peasant group harbors and cannot but harbor some enmity to the proletarian workers, because labor policy in the factory and the line of development of production are justly and rightly oriented toward the proletarian section of workers.

The policy is designed to further the struggle for the liberation of the workers from economic and ideological peasant appendages. By virtue of this [the policy] cannot but stand in contradiction both to the interests stemming from agricultural activity of the peasant group of workers and to their psychology, which is determined by the existence of petty property and life in the village.[105]

But the party leaders were not necessarily optimistic about the popularity of their policy even among the "proletarian workers." For instance, a variety of productivity campaigns (which began as early as 1924 and continued to intensify, particularly from 1927 onward)[106] were bound to affect adversely not only new workers but also skilled and highly skilled workers. Candid about the sacrifices entailed by the campaigns, Stalin appealed to the workers to bear up under them. Addressing the fifth Komsomol conference in March 1927, he declared:

It is said that rationalization entails certain temporary sacrifices on the part of certain groups of workers, including youth. That is true, comrades. . . . The history of our revolution tells us that not a single important step has been taken that did not involve certain sacrifices on the part of individual groups of our country's working class. . . . It scarcely needs proof that the present insignificant sacrifices will be more than compensated for in the future. That is why I think we should not hesitate to make certain insignificant sacrifices in the interests of the working class as a whole.[107]

Whether the sacrifices were insignificant was arguable, and it may be an indication of his suspicion of the older generation of workers that Stalin appealed to the young Komsomols to stand "in the front ranks" in the rationalization drive.[108] Stalin feared that the status,

[105] Semenov, *Litso fabrichnykh rabochikh*, p. 58.
[106] Chase, *Workers, Society and the Soviet State,* chap. 6, and Carr and Davies, *Foundations of a Planned Economy,* chap. 18.
[107] Stalin, *Sochineniia*, 9:197–98.
[108] Ibid.

skill, and "work culture" of older workers would not favor these sacrifices.[109] If the new workers were "anarchic" from the point of view of the older workers, the older workers were, in the eyes of the new workers, bound together by "collective solidarity":

[Workers'] attitudes toward production, or if I may use this expression, work culture [*trudovaia kul'tura*], are formed in the workers not only over years but over decades. [The attitudes] have been formed under the influence of capitalist relations in the factories. The workers are accustomed to closing ranks and standing firm against the foreman, against the boss. The workers dislike upstarts [*vyskochki*] and bootlickers [*podlipaly*], those who seek to "curry favor" and beat down the piece rates [of fellow workers], those who whisper to the foreman about fellow workers' idleness, and so on and so forth. In this way, "work culture" has been formed.[110]

The work culture of old skilled workers set the pace on the shop floor. In an instrument workshop of the Nev'iansk Plant in the Urals, for instance, the Communists and Komsomols fought for a faster work pace and lower piece rates, but it was skilled molders (*lekal'shchiki*) who actually set the pace and rates in the workshop, because they were irreplaceable and easily gained the upper hand. Their behavior was seen by the Communists and Komsomols as "sabotage."[111] When pressed hard, skilled workers could threaten to walk out. An incident in the rolling mill workshop of the Enakievo Metallurgical Plant in the Ukraine is particularly illustrative. Sometime in 1927 (or 1928) the old skilled workers in the workshop, many of whom had participated in the revolution and civil war, refused to work in protest against an increase in output quotas. The party secretary of the factory, the young N. A. Voznesenskii, who would become the chairman of Gosplan in 1937, summoned the workers to the factory club to talk them into accepting the higher norms. While he emphasized how important the increase was to build socialism, he relentlessly attacked the skilled workers, who, he contended, often drank and failed to show up for work. His speech evoked a cry from the audience: "That's right. How much can we put up with [from them]? Chuck them out." Voznesenskii replied:

---

[109] For the resistance of skilled workers to the drive, see, for example, *Khoziaistvo i upravlenie*, 1927, nos. 4–5, p. 29.

[110] G. Lebedev, "Vziat' novyi kurs," *Molodaia gvardiia*, 1929, no. 16, p. 52.

[111] Ermilov, *Schast'e trudnykh dorog*, pp. 103 and 113. The molders came to work in clean suits and shirts with ties and "looked down on young workers, who in turn, called them 'fastidious.' " Ibid., p. 104.

Unfortunately, we cannot chuck them out. They know and take advantage of this. . . . Today, when every skilled worker counts with us, we allow him a lot. But this is a temporary and forced liberalism. Tomorrow we won't pardon anybody for drinking and truancy.[112]

Firmly committed as it was to the idea that there was no exploitation in the Soviet factories, the party leadership was in no way committed to the "work culture" of old skilled workers that still prevailed during NEP and may indeed have grown stronger in the late 1920s in reaction to the "anarchic" behavior of new workers. In an attempt to do away with this culture, from early 1929 on the Stalin group utilized the shock movement (*udarnichestvo*) and socialist competition to improve labor discipline and increase productivity.[113] At first, these movements were organized by young but skilled workers, who were much freer of the work culture than were the older workers and had a greater stake in the factories than did the new peasant workers. The "greenhorns" (*molokososy*), as the older workers called these younger ones, came into conflict with the work culture and professional pride of older, skilled cadres and aroused their opposition;[114] the older workers attacked the shock workers as "strikebreakers" and "traitors."[115]

At stake were not only the work culture and professional pride but also the professional skills of the older, skilled workers. During NEP the shop floor had a very hierarchical order. The workers, classified according to wage ranks, regarded the system, by the analogy of the tsarist hierarchy of government officials, as a sort of "table of ranks that determined the status and professional authority of each worker in the factory"; and "every worker, who took himself seriously and did not lose self-respect, aspired to climb up the ladder of worker 'ranks' [*chiny*]."[116] In the late 1920s, however, it was widely believed under the impact of industrial modernization that manual labor (skilled and highly skilled jobs of "universal," handicraft type) was already being replaced by semiskilled labor, and the fear of imminent revolutionary change was increasing

[112] Kolotov, *Nikolai Alekseevich Voznesenskii*, pp. 101–7.
[113] For these movements, see chap. 5, this volume, as well as Carr and Davies, *Foundations of a Planned Economy*, chap. 18.
[114] *Molodaia gvardiia*, 1929, no. 16, pp. 52–53, and *TPG*, 26 May 1929.
[115] *Pravda*, 19 August 1929, and Paramonov, *Proizvodstvennye soveshchaniia i sotsialisticheskoe sorevnovanie na Urale*, p. 91.
[116] Antonov, *Svet ne v okne*, p. 39.

among the older generation.[117] One of the most influential Soviet Taylorists, A. Gastev, was an advocate of the "rejuvenation of the proletariat" (*omolozhenie proletariata*) and a "gradual ousting of aged workers."[118] In 1927 he attacked the skilled workers for their "conservatism":

Under the banner of craft knowledge, people instinctively protest against the invasion of any innovative trends into the factories. These skilled workers, these "mockers" do not suspect that by their protest against unskilled workers in the factories they reveal themselves to be the hardened craftsmen,
owners of the craft secret,
against which the all-disclosing science . . . , the all-solving machine, the all-foreseeing organization are struggling. . . . These protestors are miserable private owners of the secret that was superseded by machines very long ago. . . . This resistance, or better to say,
this organic protest,
is a phenomenon of enormous importance.[119]

Gastev and his Central Institute of Labor (TsIT) vigorously promoted this replacement. Yet young metal workers trained in the methods of TsIT faced the hostility of older workers and were forced to organize "illegal cells and circles" for "collective struggle for a new work culture." In 1928 more than a hundred such cells and circles existed in Leningrad alone.[120] In the coal mines management frequently attempted to dissolve the traditional collective organizations of labor (*artels*) and to create in their stead a modern division of labor. (The attempts, however, met with stiff worker resistance and, consequently, had little success in the 1920s.)[121] In the textile industry, where the intensification of labor and the rationalization of production progressed rapidly, the status of skilled workers in production was becoming increasingly insecure. The theory and practice of the so-called functional organization of labor, a division of skilled labor into specialized tasks, which Gastev,

[117] See, for example, *4 sessiia TsIK Soiuza SSR 4 sozyva*, 4:3–4, 6:6–7; *Ratsionalizatsiia promyshlennosti SSSR*, pp. 333–34; and Bystritskii and Serebriannikov, *Novaia bronia podrostkov*, p. 39.

[118] Gastev, *Trudovye ustanovki*, p. 300. For the Taylorist scientific organization of labor, see Tatur, "*Wissenschaftliche Arbeitsorganisation.*"

[119] Gastev, *Trudovye ustanovki*, p. 214. Gastev thus found himself in the position of management he had so vigorously attacked before the revolution. See Hogan, "Industrial Rationalization and the Roots of Labor Militance in the St. Petersburg Metalworking Industry, 1901–1914," pp. 188–89.

[120] *Ustanovki rabochei sily*, 1928, nos. 1–2, p. 68, nos. 3–4, p. 18.

[121] See, for example, *Predpriiatie*, 1926, no. 3, p. 81, and *Vestnik Dongulia*, no. 64 (15 July 1929), p. 13, no. 65 (10 August 1929), p. 12.

following Frederick W. Taylor, described as making skilled labor "vanish," naturally threatened the majority of skilled workers.[122] They resisted the "invasion of innovative trends," while others (assistant foremen, workers in mechanical workshops) remained discontented with their lower status in production compared with the prerevolutionary period.[123] The influx of new workers only made matters worse. In 1928–29 this "peculiar intertwining" of dissatisfied older workers and new, undisciplined workers created "difficulties in the social order" in some textile factories and led to strikes.[124]

Not only were new workers and the rationalization drive altering the traditional life in the factories, but the growing economic difficulties also weighed heavily upon the workers. Moreover, the wage-scale reform conducted from 1927 on contributed to the relative decline in wages of older skilled workers by narrowing wage differentials. Some workers suffered an absolute decline. The official union report of 1928 concluded that the decline in wages caused by the reform had mainly affected "workers with relatively high wages."[125] The reform upset skilled workers because it signified to them a lowering of their status.[126]

---

[122] See, for example, *Ratsionalizatsiia promyshlennosti SSSR*, p. 148. For the practice of the new organization of labor modeled on Taylorism, see, for example, *Trud*, 29 June 1928.

[123] See the resolution of 25 March 1929 of the Central Committee of the party, "O rabote na tekstil'nykh predpriiatiakh," *Izvestiia TsK VKP(b)*, 1929, no. 10 (12 April), pp. 13–15, and *Bol'shevik*, 1929, no. 11, pp. 46–56. At the Red Presnia Textile Factory, resistance to the rationalization drive came "mainly from the most skilled and best-paid workers." *Sputnik kommunista*, 1928, no. 7, p. 61.

[124] Meerzon, *Za perestroiku partiinoi raboty*, p. 6; *Molodai bol'shevik*, 1930, no. 3, p. 25, and Korotkov, "K proverke i chistke proizvodstvennykh iacheek," p. 87. "Small strikes" occurred in Tver around this time (*II plenum TsKK sozyva XV s″ezda VKP[b]*, p. 141). For an interesting case of worker resistance to the drive for productivity at the Yartsevo Factory in Smolensk, see Fainsod, *Smolensk under Soviet Rule*, pp. 51 and 311, and *Golos tekstilei*, 17 April, 26 June, 18 July, 11 August 1928.

[125] *Professional'nye soiuzy SSSR, 1926–1928*, p. 329. For instance, more than 3% of the textile workers suffered pure losses. See also *Materialy k otchetu TK KP(b)G*, p. 74, and *Bol'shevik*, 1928, no. 5, p. 60.

[126] See, for example, Uglanov's speech in *Rabochaia Moskva*, 26 April 1928, and *VIII s″ezd metallistov*, pp. 58–59, 153, 562, 570. See also *Bol'shevik*, 1928, no. 5, p. 60. The situation appears to have been most serious in the textile industry, where the influx of new, unskilled workers also contributed to the narrowing of wage differentials, mainly at the expense of older, highly skilled workers (Kvasha and Shofman, *Semichasovoi rabochii den' v tekstil'noi promyshlennosti*, pp. 104–14). In 1928–29 *Sotsialisticheskii vestnik*, a Menshevik journal then published in

In 1928–29 the factory order familiar to the older, skilled workers was vanishing. Their traditional prestige on the shop floor was declining because of a rapid addition of heterogeneous elements (new workers) and the encroachment of modernization on their work culture, professional pride, and skills.

Though a far cry from political opposition, this loss in status implied politically dangerous moods. While older, skilled workers were more likely than new workers to benefit from the "proletarianization" of party, government, and educational institutions, they appeared to the Stalin group to be unsure of their future and therefore politically disoriented by revolutionary changes. In 1928–29 some "older, skilled workers with long years of experience," as well as new workers, came under attack for their political "backwardness" and "nonproletarian moods."[127] Their "labor aristocratic" reaction against new workers was condemned and, most important, their "trade unionist" tendencies were categorically denounced.[128] This was a serious political problem. These old, skilled workers had been brought up under capitalism and may also have retained a distinct "political culture," which resisted the shake-up of the unions and the tightening of the political screw just as their work culture stood in the way of industrial modernization. Schooled in class struggle with capitalists, these workers had not only experienced a freer and pluralistic trade union movement during the prerevolutionary era but had also dominated the relatively autonomous unions under Tomskii. It was precisely this autonomy that the Stalin group, in its efforts to reorient the whole political structure in the factory along the new, class-war line, denounced as "trade unionism." To this end the Stalin group skillfully used the Komsomol, which was intent on promoting the interests of young work-

---

Berlin, reported strikes caused by the wage-scale reform and the deterioration of working conditions in Moscow at the Liubertsy, Mytishchi, and Red Torch factories, in Leningrad at the Putilov and an unnamed textile factory, in the Donbas at the Enakievo Factory, and at some factories in Sormovo and Orekhovo-Zuevo. See *Sotsialisticheskii vestnik,* nos. 2–3 (168–69), 6 February 1928, p. 20; no. 4 (170), 21 February 1928, p. 14; no. 10 (176), 18 May 1928, p. 13; nos. 7–8 (197–98), 12 April 1929, p. 22; nos. 10–11 (200–1), 25 May 1929, pp. 20–21; no. 12 (202), 14 June 1929, p. 14.

[127] *Trud,* 1 November 1929 (D. Bentsman), and *Pravda,* 26 October 1929 (N. Evreinov).

[128] Ibid.

ers over those of the older generation.[129] This attack was indeed symbolic of the "crisis of proletarian identity" as the Stalin leadership perceived it.

The crisis was both social and political. First, the overall decline of the standard of living disquieted the working class. Second, the growing movement of "newcomers" into the factories "diluted" the working class socially and politically to an alarming degree. Third, nascent industrial modernization was threatening the status of the older, skilled workers on the shop floor. Fourth, the Stalin group abandoned the traditional assumption that proletarian consciousness belonged to this group of workers.

To the Rightists it was politically absurd that the party should rely rather exclusively on such a tiny segment of the population as the industrial working class (which in 1928 accounted for a mere 3 percent of the overall population). It was all the more absurd because even the working class did not appear to be uniformly supportive of the rapid industrialization drive. In its effort to minimize the political differentiation of workers and to promote their solidarity, the leadership therefore constantly reminded workers that they, not the specialists, were the masters, as Ordzhonikidze declared at the eighth trade union congress in December 1928: "If you [specialists] want to eat bread, listen to your master, and your master is the proletariat."[130] The leadership thus used specialist baiting to articulate and protect such social and political homogeneity as existed among the workers by unleashing working-class hostilities against previously privileged groups in production that did not belong to the proletariat.

It was difficult, however, to overcome this crisis: given the rapid tempo of industrialization, investment inevitably took precedence

---

[129] See, Carr, *Foundations of a Planned Economy*, vol. 2, pp. 175–76. (The Komsomol accepted youths between the ages of fourteen and twenty-three, but in 1928 some 16–17% of its members were over twenty-three years of age. For the Komsomol, see Fisher, *Pattern for Soviet Youth*.) Note also that the sixth Komsomol conference in June 1929 placed on its agenda the "reconstruction of trade unions," an item very unusual for the Komsomol and a clear affront to the unions. *VI Vsesoiuznaia konferentsiia VLKSM*, pp. 343–426.

[130] *VIII s˝ezd professional'nykh soiuzov SSSR*, p. 271. After the Shakhty affair, a leader of the miners' union declared: "If a technician treats workers rudely, [should we] beat him in the mug? Yes, beat [him] in the mug." *VI Vsesoiuznyi s˝ezd gornorabochikh SSSR*, p. 195.

over consumption; the influx of new workers was an unavoidable consequence of industrial expansion; and industrial modernization could not have been halted, because it was central to industrialization. This quandary made the attack on the perceived class enemies all the more attractive politically to the leadership.

5

The emergence of new proletarian forces

An American journalist, having visited the Soviet Union to observe Stalin's industrialization drive in progress, reported: "The Soviet Union is a land at war. This is a first and a last impression." He saw there "an atmosphere of militant struggle, a nation under arms living figuratively but effectively under martial law and subsisting on the short rations of a beleaguered state."[1] Stalin's revolution from above, like war between nations, was to a large extent an act of the state. When they initiated the war, Soviet political leaders, like any other political leaders, carefully analyzed social and political forces working for and against it and, as they fought along, made every effort to marshal support.

In January 1930 Stalin wrote to Maksim Gorky:

It cannot be the case that now, when we are breaking the old relations in life and building new ones, when the customary roads and paths are being torn up and new, uncustomary ones laid, when whole sections of the population who used to live in plenty are being thrown out of their comfortable way of life, making way for millions of people who were formerly oppressed and downtrodden – it cannot be the case that the youth should represent a homogeneous mass of people who sympathize with us, that there should be no differentiation and division among them. . . . Naturally, in such "racking turmoil" ["the tremendous breakup of the old and the feverish buildup of the new"], we are bound to have people who are weary, overwrought, worn out, despairing, backsliding, and who, lastly, desert to the camp of the enemy. These are the unavoidable "costs" of revolution.[2]

Stalin could have used the same argument about the working class, which he well knew was far from a "homogeneous mass of people." In 1929 some Bolsheviks argued explicitly against "idealizing the

[1] Knickerbocker, *The Soviet Five-Year Plan and Its Effect on World Trade*, p. 3.
[2] Stalin, *Sochineniia*, 12:174.

working class" as a homogeneous political entity.[3] Stalin and his allies were determined to pay the "unavoidable costs" in order to carry out revolution:

The vanguard, the leader of the [working] class, has sometimes to go against the predominant moods among the workers in the name of the general interests of the entire proletariat.

The vanguard of the working class must stand above the particularistic, cliquish, and shoppist [*tsekhovye*] interests prevailing, at times, in the workers' mood.[4]

These remarks strongly suggest that Stalin's revolution was indeed a revolution from above.

Yet one can also sense in these remarks the leaders' confidence in drawing on the support of "millions of people who were formerly oppressed and downtrodden." Of course, any political leader might misjudge the situation, but no one would be foolish enough to initiate a war that was likely to have no popular support. Where did support, if any, come from? How did the political leadership seek to promote support?

Signs of hope

The militant political atmosphere that accompanied Stalin's revolution from above is often attributed to the "Bolshevik mores of war communism," the "militant, voluntarist political culture and mystique of war communism." As Robert Tucker has argued, this war mentality, as distinct from the "evolutionary NEP culture," constituted an essential component of Stalin's revolution.[5] A. G. Zverev, for instance, tells us how this mentality had shaped the mind-set of his contemporaries. (Zverev was born into a worker's family in 1900, fought in the civil war, joined the party in 1919, worked in the 1920s as a local official in various capacities, was selected and sent in 1930 to the Moscow Financial-Economic Institute as a

---

[3] See for example *Trud*, 1 November 1929 (D. Bentsman). L. M. Kaganovich consistently emphasized this point: *Pravda*, 21 January 1930, and *Rabochaia Moskva*, 1 March 1931.

[4] Korotkov, "K proverke i chistke proizvodstvennykh iacheek," p. 85. A member of the Central Control Commission, Korotkov sat on the commission set up in early 1929 by the Politbureau and the presidium of the commission to deal with the Bukharin faction. Vaganov, *Pravyi uklon v VKP(b) i ego razgrom*, p. 200.

[5] Tucker, "Stalinism as Revolution from Above," pp. 92–93.

"party thousander," and became commissar of finance in 1938, i.e., in the wake of the Great Purges.) He recollected the 1920s in his memoirs published in 1973: "Constant struggle, struggle, and struggle! This [mentality] willy-nilly fostered in the people the thought that that was the way it was, that otherwise nothing could be gained, and that it was the norm of social life."[6]

Militancy was particularly manifest among the youth who had grown up under Soviet power. V. V. Ermilov, for intance, who was born in 1909, experienced the revolution and the civil war as a child, and subsequently became a labor hero under Stalin, maintains that the militant worldview of his generation originated in its childhood experience: "It was in this setting [of October Revolution and the civil war] that in me and my peers our first convictions began to form and the embryo of our future worldview came into being and became stronger."[7] Having thus acquired a "class view" of the world, Ermilov and his peers sincerely believed that the "engineers and other specialists" were "representatives and hirelings of the bourgeoisie."[8] The Shakhty affair unleashed working-class hostilities against the engineers and specialists. The hard line against them undoubtedly met with considerable popular support.

The class-conciliatory NEP fit very uncomfortably into the militant worldview. K. Vorobei, for example, who in 1929 organized a shock brigade in Leningrad, recalls how Soviet youth remained dissatisfied with NEP:

The Komsomols of my generation – those who met the October Revolution at the age of ten or younger – took offense at our fate. When our consciousness was formed and we joined the Komsomol, when we went to work in factories, we lamented that nothing would be left for us to do, because the revolution was gone, because the severe [but] romantic years of civil war would not come back, and because the older generation had left to our lot [only] a boring, prosaic life that was devoid of struggle and excitement.[9]

At the fifth Komsomol conference in 1927 a young member from Samara was quoted as claiming:

I joined the Komsomal in 1923 when I was 14 years old, and actively worked in the organization. But now I am of the opinion that the

---

[6] Zverev, *Zapiski ministra*, p. 54. From the vantage point of the 1970s, however, Zverev warned Soviet youth against "unnecessarily going too far."
[7] Ermilov, *Schast'e trudnykh dorog*, p. 14.
[8] Ibid., p. 132.
[9] Vorobei, *Odin – za vsekh, vse – za odnogo*, p. 13.

Komsomol organization does not do any good. This opinion began to grow in me last year. I would like the Komsomol to be as it was in 1918 – the bell-bottoms, the revolver, and whatnot. This is the type of Komsomol I have in mind. Sometimes there occurs to me this question: what was NEP introduced for? For nothing, I think. At the present time NEP could be canceled immediately, even with the help of brute force.[10]

In 1927 the political leadership assailed this anti-NEP mood as a manifestation of political illiteracy and as a Trotskyist deviation.

Even before 1928, however, many loyal supporters of Stalin anticipated at heart the advent of a heroic socialist offensive that would supersede the prosaic life of NEP. Petro Grigorenko, for example, was born into a farm laborer's family in 1907, experienced the October Revolution and the civil war as a child, and joined the party in 1927 as a loyal supporter of Stalin and a staunch foe of Trotsky. Grigorenko lived in the spirit of civil war and remained belligerent throughout the 1920s: he, like Stalin, wore a military outfit and his father's red hussar's service cap and, when treated badly at school, sensed in its director a living example of a class enemy. When the socialist offensive began in 1928, he and his peers "believed we were at last achieving our goals. The epoch of industrialization and mass collectivization had begun." He emphasizes even half a century after the event that "thinking about this time in my life, I always recall the enthusiasm and passion we Komsomols felt."[11] Indeed, the offensive let loose those whom Stalin referred to as "new, revolutionary cadres."

Stalin's offensive found support even among his archenemies. Soon after the fifteenth party congress, when the offensive against the kulaks started and the industrialization drive gained momentum, many supporters of Trotsky came to see in Stalin's "left course" the triumph of their ideas. In 1928–29 they therefore came to terms with Stalin and willingly took part in promoting the left course.[12] Lev Kopelev, a young Trotskyist (born in 1912) who had considered NEP "the source of all our evils and misfortunes" and had been arrested for his Trotskyist activity, came to think that Stalin's left course was "basically right," because "such an immense

---

[10] V *Vsesoiuznaia konferentsiia VLKSM*, p. 135. In the 1920s the word NEP came to be associated with speculation and new bourgeois strata. Selishchev, *Iazyk revoliutsionnoi epokhi*, p. 196.

[11] Grigorenko, *Memoirs*, p. 28.

[12] Day, *Leon Trotsky and the Politics of Economic Isolation*, pp. 180–81. For a vivid account of this reconciliation, see Deutscher, *The Prophet Outcast*, pp. 62–82.

construction" had started and NEP would soon be terminated. "The issue of the possibility of building socialism in one country," Kopelev recalls of his reconciliation in 1928–29, "was of course principal, but today is secondary, as are the problems of widening intra-party democracy. Now the main thing is to build factories and electric power stations, and to strengthen the Red Army."[13] Many other Trotskyists thought in the same vein. In July 1929 E. A. Preobrazhenskii, K. B. Radek, I. T. Smilga, and other prominent supporters of Trotsky published a joint statement in the Soviet press in which they declared a reconciliation with Stalin and support for his industrial drive: "The realization of the Five-Year Plan will solve the main tasks of the revolution at the present time, and therefore we consider it our Bolshevik duty to take an active part in the struggle for the implementation of the plan."[14] Seven and a half years later, at the Moscow trial in January 1937 Radek still emphasized that he was sincere in that statement: he believed that "the conviction that the accusation of Thermidorism we had made against the Central Committee of the Party was unfounded and that the program of the Five-Year Plan was a program for a great step forward."[15] In October 1929 the president of the State Bank, Iu. L. Piatakov, known as a "superindustrializer" and a former close associate of Trotsky's who had come to terms with Stalin shortly after the fifteenth party congress, gave an impassioned speech at the Council of People's Commissars:

In our work we must adopt the *rates of the Civil War*. Of course I am not saying we must adopt the methods of the Civil War, but that each of us . . . is obliged to work with the same tension with which we worked in the time of armed struggle with our class enemy. *The heroic period of our socialist construction has arrived.*[16]

Stalin's left course disarrayed the Left Oppositionists. In the autumn of 1929 many irreconcilables, including I. N. Smirnov and M. S. Boguslavskii, followed in the footsteps of Radek and others. By the end of 1929 the majority of the several thousand exiled

---

[13] Kopelev, *The Education of a True Believer*, pp. 223–24.

[14] *Pravda*, 13 July 1929.

[15] *Report of Court Proceedings in the Case of the Anti-Soviet Trotskyite Centre*, p. 82.

[16] Quoted in Davies, *The Socialist Offensive*, p. 148. Piatakov was appointed the president of the State Bank in April 1929. *Sobranie zakonov*, 1929, II, 17–96.

Trotskyists came to rapprochement.[17] This was a resounding political victory for Stalin. Moreover, the return to the party of men of talent and experience whose dedication to industrialization was sincere and passionate undoubtedly added to hope and confidence in the left course.

The left course was as much a cause of popular hope as of popular despair. "Now that the laboring people are freed from the yoke of capital," a worker delegate from Smolensk declared at a session of the All-Russian Central Executive Committee, "naturally they seek a new, bright life."[18] How then could one believe in the leadership when life in the country was becoming ever more difficult in sharp contrast with the bright picture depicted by the Five-Year Plan? Indeed, the failure of the leadership to live up to this expectation politically disquieted both the "new" and "old" workers. Yet one did not live by politics alone, nor by bread alone. N. S. Patolichev (born in 1908), for example, maintains that his generation consciously gave up a great deal for the sake of the cause: "Today something extremely necessary is not available. Well, what of it? Tomorrow or in a week it'll be available."[19] Grigorenko (born in 1907) also emphasizes that his generation "did not seek easy lives and material advantages." Hardships enhanced the war atmosphere and stirred the youth's idealistic romanticism. In the late 1920s, "grain was in acute shortage and long bread lines were appearing. Rationing was not far off; neither was famine." But Grigorenko believed that directly "ahead of us lay the route to the complete victory of socialism."[20] An American who experienced Stalin's revolution firsthand has aptly pointed out what "a present-day observer can easily overlook, that is, the genuine upsurge of messianic hopes and revolutionary self-sacrifice," and "a renewal of the revolutionary spirit and a welcome release from the psychological doldrums of NEP, with its undramatic goals and its petty-bourgeois comfort": "The force of this emotion was great among a part of the first postrevolutionary generation, especially among many sons and daughters of the previously underprivileged peasants and factory work-

---

[17] Deutscher, *The Prophet Outcast*, p. 81.

[18] *II sessiia VTsIK XIII sozyva*, p. 327.

[19] Patolichev, *Ispytanie na zrelost'*, p. 170. In the wake of the Great Purges Patolichev became first secretary of the Yaroslavl *obkom* and later first secretary of the Central Committee of the Belorussian Communist Party.

[20] Grigorenko, *Memoirs*, p. 28. For "blind faith in a bright future," see also *Komsomol. Sbornik statei*, particularly N. Lunev's memoirs.

ers." To these sons and daughters, "the purpose of the revolution" was "not merely to advance their own careers, but to create a new society, never known before, in which injustice and inherited social inequities would dissolve in a brotherhood of the proletariat and eventually of all people."[21]

How large and powerful was the constituency of these militant hard-liners, romantic idealists, and true believers? It is not easy to identify them, because there are no results of reliable polls or elections available. Sheila Fitzpatrick, in her examination of the hardliners on culture in the 1920s, has concluded that the support for the proletarian hard line came from "the lower ranks of the party, the Komsomol, and Communist vigilante groups such as the proletarian writers and the militant atheists (Militant Godless)," and that the strength of the hard line in the party was "not so great as to force Stalin, or any other leaders in 1928, to accept it," but that "it was strong enough not to be overlooked."[22] Similarly, R. W. Davies and S. G. Wheatcroft have argued that "important developments of thought and policy" of an industrialization program that was incompatible with NEP took place "in circles far wider than the Stalin group."[23]

It is even more difficult to identify the idealistic, enthusiastic, and committed workers. Yet it is not impossible: they were found predominantly among those who belonged neither to the older cohort of skilled workers nor to the new and unskilled group, and who, therefore, in the judgment of Stalin and his close associates, were free from and critical of "aristocratic opportunism" and "petty bourgeois spontaneity." The shock workers (*udarniki*) and initiators of socialist competition were typical of those young committed workers. As discussed in the Appendix, they were mainly young urban males who had experienced the revolution and the civil war in their teens or younger, first entered industrial work shortly after the revolution, and therefore had had several years of work experience and some skills by the late 1920s. Predominantly party and Komsomol members, they were thus in a position to be critical of both the work culture of older workers and the peasant culture of new arrivals from the countryside. They were new forces in the factories, who, impatient with the given rate of industrialization,

[21] Mosley, "1930–1932," pp. 56–57.
[22] Fitzpatrick, "The 'Soft' Line on Culture and Its Enemies," pp. 269, 287.
[23] See chap. 1, note 18, this volume.

pressed for ever higher tempos; who, free of the old "work culture," promoted industrial modernization; who, intolerant of managerial bureaucratism, pressed for one-man management; who, eager to find "class aliens" in the apparatus, actively sought to be promoted into positions of responsibility; and who, hopeful of tomorrow's gratification, endured today's difficulties. They became the symbol of a new society (as Valentin Kataev vividly depicted them in his famous novel *Time, Forward!*)[24] and provided the Stalin leadership with hopes for a successful industrialization drive.

The shock movement and socialist competition

From 1929 onward a mass campaign called socialist competition swept through the Soviet Union.[25] Factories, workshops, brigades, and individual workers competed for greater production and productivity, cost reduction, and labor discipline. Simultaneously promoted, the shock movement (*udarnichestvo*) played a central role in socialist competition. Workers organized into model or shock brigades (*udarnye brigady*)[26] acted, as it were, as a "vanguard" on the shop floor in promoting not only competition but also other social and political mobilizations.

These movements were not mere propaganda hoopla imposed from above. They sprang from particularistic movements of young workers, who during NEP had been materially disadvantaged and subjected to various forms of discrimination on the shop floor: banding together around young yet relatively skilled workers, ambitious young workers sought to improve their status on the shop floor through these movements. Their aspirations were encouraged by and coincided with the political leadership's interests in the mobilization of available and hidden resources. According to the Komsomol leadership, the movements marked a "consummation of all the

---

[24] The original Russian edition was published in 1932.
[25] For numerous Soviet works on this subject see Oprishchenko, *Istoriografiia sotsialisticheskogo sorevnovaniia rabochego klassa SSSR*, and *Sotsialisticheskaia industrializatsiia SSSR*. For problems involved in the study of these movements, see Drobizhev, "O nekotorykh nedostatkakh metodiki izucheniia politicheskoi i trudovoi deiatel'nosti rabochego klassa SSSR v gody bor'by za postroenie sotsializma."
[26] In the autumn of 1929, the average shock brigade in Moscow consisted of eleven workers, though some had thirty to forty workers. *Pervyi Vsesoiuznyi s˝ezd udarnykh brigad*, p. 64.

production initiatives" undertaken by the Komsomol in the previous few years.[27]

Before the shock movement and socialist competition got under way in 1929, the production initiatives of concerned workers often hit the snag of managerial bureaucratism. The most common form in which workers expressed their initiatives was the production conference in the factory, a forum where administrative-technical personnel, party, union, and Komsomol officials, and old, skilled workers discussed a variety of problems about production and exchanged ideas on how to improve it.[28]

Although in many factories the production conferences managed to mobilize worker activists,[29] worker participation often came to be discouraged by managerial bureaucratism: it was contended that the main reason workers shied away from production conferences was that management ignored their "voice."[30] (It is difficult to ascertain the extent to which this was the case. According to data concerning production conferences in Leningrad, in 1927–28, 78.4 percent of workers' suggestions were adopted, and 69.4 percent were realized by management. The corresponding figures for 1928–29 rose to 83.4 and 81.3, respectively.)[31] According to A. K. Gastev, managers felt that their self-esteem was compromised by workers' initiatives.[32] One might feel annoyed or even offended when criticized by one's subordinates. The director of the Red Triangle Rubber Factory in Leningrad, for example, was attacked as representative of managerial condescension:

It is no good to demand from production conferences serious participation in the rationalization of production, because rationalization has to be based on a strictly scientific foundation and requires a good technical training. The educational composition of workers is such that they are not up to it. When problems of rationalization are discussed at production conferences, workers take little part in the discussion because the problems

[27] *VI Vsesoiuznaia konferentsiia VLKSM*, p. 349.
[28] Carr and Davies, *Foundations of a Planned Economy*, chap. 20; Chase, *Workers, Society and the Soviet State*, chap. 7; and Ostapenko, *Uchastie rabochego klassa SSSR v upravlenii proizvodstvom.*
[29] Chase, *Workers, Society and the Soviet State*, chap. 7.
[30] *Pervye shagi industrializatsii SSSR*, pp. 495–99, and a secret report of the police concerning workers' conferences held in Smolensk in February 1928 (WKP 144).
[31] *Trud i profdvizhenie v Leningradskoi oblasti 1932 g.*, p. 65. Similar figures for the entire country are in *Professional'nye soiuzy SSSR, 1926–1928*, p. 439.
[32] Gastev, *Trudovye ustanovki*, pp. 216–17.

were hardly intelligible to them. There is, however, enormous room for production conferences to raise labor discipline.[33]

In the aftermath of the Shakhty affair, however, managers found themselves on the defensive. Addressing a session of the All-Union Central Executive Committee, which met several weeks after the Shakhty affair came to light, one nonparty delegate named Fomin sharply criticized the managers:

If he [a worker] doesn't fulfill this or that task, he will be transferred to a lower [paid] job. Yet what do we see in relation to the responsible personnel who direct all work? They very often get away with pretty big faults. . . . Two years ago they looked down on the workers at production conferences; and when some worker ventured a remark, he would first be transferred from one workshop to another and then closer to the gates. Of course as a result of this, the workers came to boycott production conferences, and even when they were invited they did not go. Now the situation has changed [because of the Shakhty affair]. The workers are heeded at production conferences. But instead we now hear about a different thing from management: "There is no money, no resources." In other words, workers' suggestions on how to improve production are not given premiums. Meanwhile, however, we have such a characteristic situation: for 150,000-odd rubles we bought machines from abroad, which now lie idle, and the local factory management doesn't know what to do with them. . . . It is necessary to listen carefully to the voice of workers, and then there will not be such incidents as those in the Donbas. We know well that there are still *many reptiles* at the bottom [i.e., in the factories and mines] who sit underground and raise up their heads. If we listen to the voice of the workers, we will quickly crush the reptiles and clear the path.[34]

Certainly the problem was not simply that "reptiles" (i.e., "wreckers") rejected workers' suggestions, but also that the factories, closely bound by the "tutelage" of the trusts, feared initiative from below.[35] In the wake of the Shakhty affair, therefore, Rabkrin pressed hard for the decentralization of factory management. Yet Rabkrin had all along been suspicious of the managerial inclination to evade all sorts of control. For instance, A. Gol'tsman, a Rabkrin leader, sharply attacked managers for their claim that they could not realize workers' suggestions because of a lack of resources:

[33] *VIII s″ezd professional'nykh soiuzov SSSR*, pp. 411–12. This passage of the director was also quoted in an editorial in *Trud*, 7 March 1929.
[34] *3 sessiia TsIK Soiuza SSR 4 sozyva*, pp. 316–17.
[35] *II plenum TsKK sozyva XV s″ezda VKP(b)*, p. 105.

Managers' demands that such resources [with which to realize workers' suggestions] be allocated are attempts to obtain additional resources for themselves. *Workers' suggestions have to be incorporated into the production program and the industrial-financial plan.* . . . Managers are accustomed to devising their production programs without workers' participation and only on the basis of technicians' and specialists' conclusions.[36]

When it was imperative to minimize waste, mobilize all available resources, even discover hidden resources, and thereby maximize production, managerial disregard of the workers' voice was seen by Rabkrin as inadmissible bureaucratism that would have just the opposite effect.

In promoting the self-criticism campaign in the wake of the Shakhty affair, the party leadership used workers' grievances to direct production conferences toward control over management. As early as June 1928 the Central Committee advocated "punishment of those who are guilty of sabotaging" workers' suggestions and called for the "conversion of production conferences into organs of control of the masses." Rabkrin was urged to extend all sorts of assistance to production conferences, which as organs of "control of the masses" were, in turn, to aid Rabkrin.[37] Thus the party leadership vigorously promoted production conferences as workers' control over management, and mounted a constant attack on managerial disregard of workers' suggestions.[38] At a trustwide production conference of Southern Steel in June–July 1928, the secretary of the Central Committee of the Ukrainian Communist Party, A. V. Medvedev, described workers' frustration over the managerial inability to remove "a number of defects in production": "Among workers is created a mood that 'You fight and fight, but you achieve nothing; unless you strike you'll get nothing.' "[39]

Certainly not all workers were so concerned with production. Yet young workers in particular, responsive as they were to leadership's call, willingly took the initiative out of the production conference to implement measures for the rationalization of production and experiment with new work methods. As early as April 1927 the Organization-Distribution Department of the Central Committee

---

[36] Gol'tsman, *Dorogu initsiative rabochikh,* pp. 13–16. Emphasis in the original.
[37] "O samokritike," in *KPSS v rezoliutsiiakh,* 4:97.
[38] See, for example, numerous reports in *Rabochaia gazeta,* 10 April, 29 July, 4 August, 13 September 1928; *III plenum TsKK sozyva XV s˝ezda VKP(b),* p. 64.
[39] *Vseukrainskaia proizvodstvennaia konferentsiia,* 1:142.

reported that young workers' attitude toward rationalization was positive and that they were "the least conservative and the most receptive to the transition to a conveyer, automation, and so on."[40] Indeed, from 1927 on, the industrial centers witnessed the emergence of young workers' shock brigades. In May 1927 the press reported, for instance, that in large factories in Leningrad "initiative shock cores for the rationalization of production are being created spontaneously."[41] From the autumn of 1927 on, shock brigades formed one after another at the Zlatoust Metal Factory in the Urals, which subsequently was dubbed the "cradle of the shock movement and a new organization of labor." One of these brigades, unable to gain support from management, the party, or the union organization, was initially a sort of "underground" organization. This brigade, composed of eleven young workers, soon gained recognition and in the spring of 1928 worked according to "statutes" that included, among others: "To be an example in all spheres of production life"; "To increase the output of production sharply and surpass older workers in labor productivity"; "To eliminate absenteeism completely"; "To prepare the ground for the transition of the entire workshop to the conveyor system."[42] The Zlatoust shock workers were invited to the eighth Komsomol congress in May 1928 as honored guests; *Komsomol'skaia pravda* extolled them as the "prototype of a new worker."[43] In 1928 the brigade system, which used an elaborate division of work, spread around the country under the encouragement of the Komsomol leadership.[44]

In early 1929 the party and the government began to promote vigorously the shock movement and socialist competition. On 16 January 1929, Vesenkha issued an order to encourage the shock

---

[40] *Pervye shagi industrializatsii*, p. 368. For a good case of the use of young workers' brigades to break through worker resistance, see, for example, Ermilov, *Schast'e trudnykh dorog*, pp. 103–4.

[41] *Leningradskaia pravda*, 31 May 1927, quoted in *Pervye shagi industrializatsii*, p. 378.

[42] Quoted in Cheremnykh, "Zarozhdenie i razvitie massovogo sotsialisticheskogo sorevnovaniia," p. 121.

[43] *Komsomol'skaia pravda*, 11 May 1928.

[44] For early shock brigades and competition see, for example, Bespalov and Segal, *Komsomol pod znamenem sotsialisticheskoi ratsionalizatsii*; *Komsomol na fabrikakh i zavodakh k VIII s'ezdu VLKSM*; *Dva goda raboty Ural'skogo komsomola*; *Industrializatsiia SSSR. 1926–1928 gg.*, part III, chap. 2; Finarov, *Kommunisticheskaia partiia – organizator i vdokhnovitel' velikogo trudovogo pod'ema rabochego klassa SSSR v 1926–1929 gg.*; and Rogachevskaia, *Iz istorii rabochego klassa SSSR v pervye gody industrializatsii, 1926–1927 gg.*, pp. 151–71.

brigades, which, the order read, "truly promote the improvement and acceleration of industrial processes, the reduction of costs, the intensification of labor, and the solution of other important economic issues." Vesenkha's chairman, V. V. Kuibyshev, instructed managerial organizations to render all possible assistance both to the existing brigades and to the organization of new ones.[45] In order to lend the new campaigns Leninist orthodoxy, on 20 January 1929 *Pravda* published Lenin's article "How to Organize Competition?" which was written shortly after the October Revolution but remained unpublished until then. In February 1929 the party urged the Komsomol to promote further the shock movement and competition.[46]

These movements freed young workers' concerns and aspirations from the constraints of the old work culture and managerial bureaucratism. According to E. M. Mikulina's popular pamphlet, *Socialist Competition of the Masses,* for which Stalin wrote a foreword in May 1929, the workers at the Moscow Electric Factory, for example, were "infected with the spirit of competition":

At lunch time the workers went to the director's office, crowded round his table and wanted all sorts of questions answered:
— What do you mean about 15 per cent economy in the wall paper? Tell us in plain Russian how much that will be?
— Why hasn't the production programme been hung up yet?
— What are your calculations on economy?
— If we are to compete, then tell us plainly, so we will understand.
— We want a meeting. We want to hold a meeting.
These words went rolling like a wave through the shops, through the departments and through the whole plant. Then came meeting after meeting. . . . Everybody was excited by the questions involved in the terms of competition and by the awards for fulfilling the obligations undertaken.[47]

---

[45] See Order No. 355 of Vesenkha in *Komsomol'skaia pravda* and *TPG,* 17 January 1929. Kuibyshev was "in constant and systematic contact" with the Komsomol at that time. Kuibysheva et al., *Valerian Vladimirovich Kuibyshev,* p. 262.

[46] "Ob ocherednykh zadachakh komsomol'skoi raboty i zadachakh partiinogo rukovodstva komsomolom," in *KPSS v rezoliutsiiakh,* 4:163.

[47] Mikulina, *Socialist Competition of the Masses,* p. 17. The original Russian edition was published in 1929. Mikulina was taken to task for factual inaccuracies in the pamphlets. But Stalin came to her defense: "It *popularizes* the idea of competition and *infects* with the spirit of competition. This is what matters and not a few individual mistakes." Moreover, Stalin rebuffed those who criticized him for having written a foreword to a work by an author unknown in the literary world: "I shall in the future, too, provide forewords only to simple and unassuming pamphlets by simple and unknown authors belonging to the younger forces." Stalin, *Sochineniia,* 12:112–15.

In the assembly shop of the transformer department, a brigade passed a resolution upon hearing a report about socialist competition:

A successful accomplishment of the task we face of reducing the costs (by 13 percent in our factory) and of increasing labor productivity by 17 percent is impossible without our practical participation and help. Entering socialist competition in the face of all workers of the Electric Factory, we promise no absenteeism, not a minute of delay; with regard to other workers we demand of the administration of the factory a strict adherence to the table of penalties. For the purpose of reducing costs we tighten up the working day and ask the Department of Labor Economics to cut our wage rates by 5 percent. We introduce the strictest economy into the spending of raw and other materials. We appeal to all conscious assemblers of the transformer department to follow our suit.
Signed by 1. Minsker, 2. Lukatskii, 3. Savin, 4. Guberman, 5. Kumin, 6. Glukhov, 7. Drozdov.[48]

The brigade's demands were a rate-busting challenge to a work culture that dominated the shop floor. It embarrassed and confused the party cell of the transformer department, which reportedly "did not know what to do."[49]

Welcome though young workers' devotion to production may have been, the managers soon found it rather bewildering: not only did their demands threaten the precarious union–management relations, but they also brought to light managerial defects and conservatism. Therefore, once the shock movement and competition gained momentum, the managers feared them:

At a number of factories management's attitude toward workers has changed for the worse as soon as the latter became shock workers and emphasized the question of the working out of technical-production indexes, demanding a proper supply of raw and other materials and tools.[50]

At the Red Sormovo Factory in Nizhegorod (Nizhni Novgorod), where by the spring of 1929 there were seventy shock brigades embracing 1,000 workers, some administrators shied away from the new movements and rejected the aforementioned order of Vesenkha concerning the shock brigades: "Stop talking rot! Vesenkha's circular about aid to the Komsomol is not authoritative for us."[51]

[48] Ivushkin, Serebrianyi, Timofeev, *Sorevnovanie na "Elektrozavode,"* pp. 49–50.
[49] Ibid.
[50] Ol'khov, *Za zhivoe rukovodstvo sotsialisticheskim sorevnovaniem*, p. 67.
[51] *Komsomol'skaia pravda*, 4 June 1929.

The managers found their "quiet life" disturbed by shock workers and competitive workers.[52] The Stalin group, for its part, used these workers to reorganize the factory troika. Socialist competition was "the best form of expression of self-criticism," declared Ia. A. Iakovlev at the sixteenth party conference in April 1929, where he heatedly argued with the chairman of Southern Steel, S. P. Birman.[53] In its special appeal to the workers, the sixteenth party conference declared: "Competition has to lead to the reorganization of our social and state organizations, above all the trade unions and managerial organizations."[54] In May 1929, in his foreword to Mikulina's pamphlet, Stalin strongly warned against bureaucratism standing in the way of competition:

Certain "comrades" of the bureaucratic type think that competition is just the latest Bolshevik fashion, and that, as such, it is bound to die out when the "season" passes. . . . Other "comrades" of the bureaucratic type, frightened by the powerful tide of competition, are trying to compress it within artificial bounds, to "centralize" the cause of competition, to narrow its scope and thus deprive it of its most important feature – the *initiative* of the masses. . . . Socialist competition must not be regarded as a bureaucratic undertaking. Socialist competition is a manifestation of a practical revolutionary *self-criticism* by the masses, springing from the creative *initiative* of millions of workers. All who, wittingly or unwittingly, restrict this self-criticism and creative initiative of the masses must be brushed aside as an impediment to our great cause.

The bureaucratic danger manifests itself concretely above all in the fact that it shackles the energy, initiative, and independent activity of workers, keeps concealed the colossal reserves latent in the depths of our system, deep down in the working class and peasantry, and prevents these resources from being utilized in the struggle against our class enemies. It is the task of socialist competition to smash these bureaucratic shackles, to afford broad scope for the unfolding of the energy and creative initiative of workers, to bring to light the colossal reserves latent in the depths of our system, and to throw them into the scale in the struggle against our class enemies both inside and outside our country.[55]

This remark is quite characteristic of the pro-worker, antibureaucratic political mood of that time. In July 1929 V. M. Molotov declared that competition was a good means for a radical improve-

[52] Shul'man, *Nashi dostizheniia na fronte sotsialisticheskogo sorevnovaniia*, p. 46.
[53] *XVI konferentsiia VKP(b)*, p. 483.
[54] *KPSS v rezoliutsiiakh*, 4:251.
[55] Stalin, *Sochineniia*, 12:109–10. For a similar warning, see also *KPSS v rezoliutsiiakh*, 4:265.

ment of the factory organizations.[56] In August S. I. Syrtsov emphasized the same point more explicitly:

In the process of socialist competition there comes to light the low quality of management and unskillful administration. The worker . . . begins to make a number of heightened and legitimate demands upon management. He demands that in socialist competition [management] not simply administer but be able to organize the production process so that constant work flows can be secured at all stages. . . . [It is] a more than reasonable demand.[57]

One need not assume that workers' demands were always "more than reasonable," because a number of shock workers were accused of "money-grubbing" attitudes.[58] Yet if workers' demands were indeed "more than reasonable," management found itself on the defensive.

Weak, inefficient management was the last thing the party leadership wanted. Nor was such management favored by the shock workers, because it could not satisfy their demands. For those shock workers concerned about managerial bureaucratism, one-man management did not mean despotism. They demanded order and one-man management, and welcomed the September 1929 resolution by the Central Committee on one-man management as "entirely opportune" because it would eliminate confusion and disorder and establish a "sound regime of labor."[59]

Interestingly enough, while managerial representatives were reticent about one-man management at a July 1929 conference devoted to discussion of socialist competition, the new trade-union leadership emphasized the necessity of one-man management precisely in connection with this "mass movement."[60] The implication was that weak management frustrated workers' initiatives. It turned out that the shock movement and socialist competition compelled management to correct "unskillful administration" and to provide optimal production conditions, that is, to meet "more than reasonable demands." Management had to be strong and efficient to do so.

[56] *Pravda,* 20 July 1929.
[57] Ibid., 13 August 1929. See also *Izvestiia Nizhegorodskogo kraevogo komiteta VKP(b),* 1929, no. 3, p. 4.
[58] See, for example, *Partrabotnik,* 1929, no. 9 (33) (30 April), p. 29, and *Biulleten' TsKK VKP(b) i NK RKI SSSR i RSFSR,* 1929, nos. 2–3, pp. 30–31.
[59] *Pravda,* 8 October 1929 and 15 February 1930; *Rabochaia gazeta,* 23 November, 3 and 13 December 1929; *Za industrializatsiiu,* 8 March 1930.
[60] I. A. Akulov in *Sotsialisticheskoe sorevnovanie na predpriiatii,* p. 39.

Viewed in this perspective, the claim of the party leadership that one-man management was a regime of "production democracy" may well have convinced shock workers.[61]

The shock movement and socialist competition exerted strong pressure for reorganization on the other two bodies of the troika as well, particularly on the union organizations. The eighth trade union congress in December 1928 ended ambiguously: although he nominally retained the leadership until June 1929, Tomskii had given way to the intervention of the Stalin group; moreover, the congress endorsed Vesenkha's ambitious five-year plan, whereas the unions were skeptical of the plan, which would impose significant sacrifices on the working class. The unclear outcome of the congress, according to a report from Leningrad, had "totally disoriented" the union organizations, which did "not know what to do, how to regard the decisions of the congress, how to carry them out, how to interpret them."[62] This was a call for the reorganization of the trade unions.

The old union leadership actually took issue with socialist competition, which it claimed came into being "not from a good life" (*ne ot khoroshei zhizni*), implying that competition could have been dispensed with had the life of the country been better.[63] On 11 April 1929 the Politbureau rejected the plan submitted by the Tariff-Economic Department (at least nominally headed by the Rightist, L. I. Ginzburg) of the All-Union Central Council of Trade Unions concerning the creation of a commission for the "planning of socialist competition," and directed the Organizational Bureau of the Central Committee to devise a plan incorporating measures to promote competition from below.[64] This was a countermeasure on the part of the party leadership against the unions' bureaucratic response. The Organizational Bureau's plan appears to have resulted in the resolution of 9 May 1929 by the Central Committee entitled

---

[61] It is noteworthy in this respect that the September 1929 resolution on one-man management recommended that the chairman of production conferences be appointed on an experimental basis, as assistant to the director exclusively in charge of realizing the resolutions of production conferences and commissions and workers' suggestions. This measure was intended to promote workers' initiative. *KPSS v rezoliutsiiakh*, 4:315.

[62] *VI Vsesoiuznaia konferentsiia VLKSM*, p. 368.

[63] *XVI s˝ezd VKP(b)*, p. 680, and *IX Vsesoiuznyi s˝ezd professional'nykh soiuzov SSSR*, p. 63.

[64] *Industrializatsiia SSSR, 1926–1928*, p. 582.

"Concerning Socialist Competition of the Factories." Condemning bureaucratic attempts to regulate and induce various forms of competition as "schemes established from above," the resolution stipulated that the union organizations direct the "cause of competition."[65] Through the shock movement and competition the Stalin group sought to reorient the unions along new lines with the slogan "Let us turn our faces to production."

In many factories, it was reported that competition unfolded "spontaneously" while the allegedly disoriented unions did not know what to do. One typical report ran:

The trade unions did not pass the examination of leading the workers in socialist competition and the shock movement. The creative enthusiasm of the working class is going over the head of the unions. The shock movement is developing spontaneously.[66]

According to another report, the movement appeared to the old union officials to be so contradictory to their notion of labor and management that they simply "lost their head."[67] In the Donbas, miners' union committees were therefore disbanded.[68] N. Evreinov, one of the few old union leaders who sided with the Stalin group in its attack on the unions, emphasized the significance of socialist competition for the unions:

Socialist competition demands
        a reorganization of union work,
because if the workers enter socialist competition and if they actively fight for the fulfillment of economic plans, the unions, which unite the workers, cannot but stand at their head, cannot make excuses that the economic plans are not their business but the managers'. When the factory enters competition, the unions can no longer respond that way, because the workers themselves correct the unions: "We answer [for the fulfillment of the plans], but you don't?"[69]

In the Yartsevo Textile Factory in Smolensk, whose trouble was discussed earlier,[70] with the removal of the old troika in the spring of 1929 one-man management and socialist competition were simul-

[65] *KPSS v rezoliutsiiakh,* 4:265.
[66] *Sputnik agitatora dlia goroda,* 1930, no. 8, p. 48. For more general observations, see *Trud,* 2 June, 21 August 1929; *Pravda,* 10 and 12 May 1929; *XVI s˝ezd VKP(b),* pp. 63, 191, 514.
[67] *Izvestiia TsK VKP(b),* 1929, nos. 26–27, p. 19.
[68] *Trud,* 3 July 1929.
[69] Ibid., 28 September 1929.
[70] See "The Troika and One-Man Management" (chap. 3).

taneously promoted. According to the report of the organizers sent to the factory by the Central Committee, socialist competition as a "method of mobilizing workers for the struggle with difficulties" had overcome initial resistance and eventually brought about "brilliant results"; and there was a sharp change in workers' attitudes toward production and in their "political orientation."[71]

All in all, whatever the propagandistic nature of these reports, the movement did play a critically important role in the shake-up of the entire political structure in the factories. In August 1929, S. I. Syrtsov, who subsequently got into trouble with Stalin for his candid criticism of the party and government institutions, stated quite frankly:

The meaning of socialist competition lies not only in gaining immediate production effects but also in recasting the workers, party, union, and managerial cadres. There comes a colossal period of the reconstruction of human material. Socialist competition puts each of us under fire, and [our] fitness [as cadres] is checked by its results. Competition recasts and reeducates [us].[72]

The factory committees were deemed "unfit." In 1930 their membership was to be radically replaced by shock workers.[73]

The impact of the shock movement and socialist competition went far beyond the confines of the factories. The emergence of shock workers who were politically and socially active was of enormous importance to the Stalin group, because, according to one commentator, they were new forces and

true vanguard workers, who are capable of solving small and big tasks of the reconstruction period in revolutionary fashion.

Our government needs precisely these worker revolutionaries capable of securing its *fighting ability* in the struggle for socialist construction. The problem of promoting shock workers therefore assumes the most important political significance. . . . *It is necessary to pour into the government hundreds and thousands of shock workers. They will surely promote its reorganization and ensure class lines in its work.*[74]

The political leadership sought to avail itself of the movements, not only to enhance the "fighting ability" of various institutions and

---

[71] "Doklad orgpartgruppy TsK VKP(b) o sostoianii raboty Iartsevskoi manufakture" dated 20 September 1929 in WKP 150.
[72] See note 57, this chapter. Emphasis in the original.
[73] See "The Troika and the Shock Workers" (chap. 7).
[74] *Sputnik agitatora dlia goroda,* 1930, no. 3 (January), p. 53 (D. Reznikov).

organizations, but also to select those workers who were capable of developing technical expertise:

In the process of socialist competition the union, party, and managerial organizations will be able to find *new cadres* of active builders of the socialist economy whom we need so much. I mean not only these cadres who can be immediately taken to some responsible work but also those whom we should send to universities for study. These cadres, in time, will be able to become excellent Red directors and Red specialists about whom we have been talking so much already for over a year.

Now socialist competition gives us the possibilities of distinguishing exactly those cadres of intelligent workers full of initiative whom we need. They have to study in the first place so that in the near future they will occupy the command posts in all the fields of our national economy.[75]

The years 1928–31 were a period of enormous upward mobility for the working class. The initiators of socialist competition and the shock workers not only replaced those cadres deemed "unfit" but also staffed the rapidly expanding bureaucracies and educational institutions en masse. They were not passive promotees but active seekers of promotion (*samovydvizhentsy*).[76] They had a "definite and clear goal for the present and for the future" and "sought to acquire as much knowledge and practical experience as possible in order to be as useful to the new society as possible."[77]

The shock movement and socialist competition played a crucial role in the industrialization drive: they helped the political leadership accelerate the tempo of the drive, promote industrial modernization, reorganize the factory troika along the lines of one-man management, and select ambitious, competent, and politically reliable young workers for promotion. The emergence of these workers as new forces had a mesmerizing effect on party, industrial, and trade union leaders. M. Gegechkori's about-face was a good case in point. He had been firmly opposed to the replacement of collective agreements by the state regulation of wages.[78] But now when workers "voluntarily cut down their wage rates," he maintained, the collective agreements were but an obsolete "bourgeois" practice. He thus went so far as to insist on superseding the collective agreements with agreements for socialist competition, a sort of moral pledge for the govern-

[75] I. A. Akulov in July 1929 in *Sotsialisticheskoe sorevnovanie na predpriiatii*, p. 130.
[76] *2 sessiia TsIK SSSR 5 sozyva*, 11:12. We shall discuss this massive promotion of shock workers in statistical terms in chap. 7.
[77] See Ermilov's memoirs, *Schast'e trudnykh dorog*, p. 76.
[78] See chap. 2, note 65, this volume.

ment.[79] The collective agreements were not formally superseded, but increasingly became more of a moral pledge than a result of bargaining. Whatever the case, there was something in the shock workers that appeared to the leadership to make a radical break with the norm of "capitalist" labor. The emergence of shock workers gave the leadership hope and optimism.

From resistance to adaptation

"One of the stimuli of our work, of our behavior in life," a former shock worker recalls, was "a holy hatred for the enemies of a new socialist life."[80] These "enemies" abounded. Competition changed everyday life on the shop floor. "Everybody up to now had been pursuing a quiet and easy tenor of life at the factory," but "gone for good are the days of leisure and ease."[81] To those who were irritated by leisure and ease, competition was a welcome stimulus; but it was anathema to those who cherished leisure and ease on the shop floor.

Resistance to the shock movement and socialist competition came both from older, skilled workers and from new, peasant workers. The former's "work culture" died hard. Those workers who promoted the rationalization of production were greeted on the shop floor as "aliens" (*chuzhezemtsy*).[82] The emergence of shock workers posed a great threat to the work culture and collective solidarity of older, skilled workers, who had regulated the pace of work and, more generally, dominated the shop floor. Shock workers were thus seen as "scabs" and "traitors," and competition as a "method of compulsion."[83] In Smolensk, workers viewed competition as a "new yoke."[84] In the troubled factory in Yartsevo, some workers initially labeled as a "sponger" the new director, Stoliarov, who promoted both competition and one-man management.[85]

[79] *Nasha gazeta*, 25 September 1929.

[80] Vorobei, *Odin – za vsekh, vse – za odnogo*, p. 12.

[81] Mikulina, *Socialist Competition of the Masses*, pp. 44 and 48.

[82] See, for example, the case of the Donbas in *Proizvodstvennyi zhurnal*, 1929, no. 14 (22 July), p. 8.

[83] *Pravda*, 17 August 1929, and *Izvestiia TsK VKP(b)*, 1929, nos. 26–27 (20 September), p. 16.

[84] "Meterialy k dokladu o polozhenii rabochego klassa po Zapadnoi oblasti po sostoianiiu na 1-oe oktiabria 1929 g.," in WKP 300, pp. 52–53, 56.

[85] See the police report in WKP 150, and *Pravda*, 5 July 1929.

The shock movement and socialist competition greatly intensified labor and hit particularly the unskilled, peasant workers, who, fearing that intensified labor would raise output quotas and decrease their wages, offered strong resistance.[86] Like the Siberian Eliseev, whose letter was quoted in Chapter 4,[87] new arrivals from the countryside resisted socialist competition, characterizing it as "squeezing the last drop of power out of workers."[88] Some peasants and "kulak elements" in the factories allegedly believed that the factories drank peasants' blood, that "collectives [of workers] were started by Antichrists borne out of factory smoke," and that shock workers were "detachments of Antichrists."[89]

Recalcitrant workers often attacked shock workers verbally and physically. In the summer of 1929 at the Zanarskaia Spinning Factory in Serpukhov, for example, two workers who volunteered for intensified labor (simultaneous operation of four machines) were threatened and assaulted by fellow workers. A conference of workers, which convened to discuss the new labor method, turned into a meeting for condemning the two workers and was dispersed by the authorities. Those who assailed the two workers were subsequently put on trial. An assistant foreman and church elder named Gorbatov was sentenced to six months of deprivation of freedom; two workers named Makarenkova and Kochetkova to six and three months of forced labor, respectively.[90]

A number of factories, especially textile factories (where labor was increasingly intensified), rejected the challenge for competition. A group of workers at the Kalinin Factory in Moscow, for example, refused to take part in socialist competition, and found support among "members of the factory committees."[91] At one factory in Bisk in the Altai, the chairman of the factory committee, Semiletov, reportedly conducted "counterrevolutionary agitation" against socialist competition. In October 1929 the presidium of the central committee of the textile workers' union adopted a special resolu-

---

[86] *Izvestiia TsK VKP(b)*, 1929, nos. 26–27 (20 September), p. 16.
[87] See chap 4, note 102, this volume.
[88] *Moskovskie udarniki za rabotoi*, p. 29. See also a letter from a metal worker named Goshev to *Trud*, 3 July 1929, and Schwarz, *Labor in the Soviet Union*, p. 192.
[89] *Vecherniaia Moskva*, 11 February 1930.
[90] *Rabochaia gazeta*, 26 July, 9 August 1929.
[91] *Pravda*, 26 October 1929, and *Trud*, 30 October 1929.

Figure 5.1. Socialist competition: the introduction of the four-loom system (c. 1929–30). From Ernst Glaeser and F. C. Weiskopf, *Der Staat ohne Arbeitslose. Drei Jahre "Fünfjahresplan"* (Berlin, 1931).

tion against the factory committees' cringing before "petty bourgeois spontaneity."[92]

Workers perceived adverse effects of the shock movement and socialist competition on their wages. In the summer of 1929 an interesting incident took place in the Lenin Tea-Weighing Factory in Moscow. In July the factory was challenged for competition by a tea-weighing factory in Odessa, which proposed raising the output quotas from 6,000 200-gram packs of tea per day per eleven-worker team. The challenge was accepted and then gracefully forgotten. In August the Moscow factory hired unemployed workers to substitute for those on summer vacation. Nine of those temporary workers, somehow familiar with Odessa's challenge and evidently encouraged by the favor accorded to shock workers in other factories, proposed raising the output quota to 6,600 packs against their competitors. This proposal caused "more than hostile" reac-

[92] Ibid.

tion on the part of the "permanent" workers, who contended that the temporary workers were motivated by "selfish interests": they wanted to remain in the factory as permanent workers. The nine workers nevertheless fulfilled the raised quotas, and on 25 August management agreed to keep them in the factory as permanent workers. The following day 314 workers, or 80 percent of the factory work force, gathered in the dining hall to accuse the nine workers of having accepted Odessa's challenge and demanded that they be fired. The press characterized this incident as a "counterrevolutionary attack" and its ring leaders as "aliens" to the workers: Fillipova, a "former Menshevik"; Demidov, a former party member who had been expelled from the party for "embezzlement"; Emel'ianova, the "wife of a bandit banished to the Solovki Islands"; and Cheremisova, a "notorious hooligan."[93]

On 22 October 1929 a strike occurred in the pipe-cutting workshop of the Il'ich Plant in the Donbas. Twenty-seven workers walked out and set up a picket line; the striking workers organized a delegation, which went around the factory calling other shops to join them. The reason for the strike was their dissatisfaction with the piece rates revised in conjunction with competition. Management put the new rates into effect without notifying the interested workers and without any explanation. Reporting the strike, the Ukrainian trade union journal, *Visnyk profrukhu Ukrainy*, started with a rather sympathetic heading, "[Managerial] Red-Tape Has Led to a Strike," but ended by condemning the ringleaders – the owner of a "large farm," a *khutor* (or noncommunal, independent peasant), shirkers, and loafers.[94]

The press often reported that the shock movement and socialist competition led recalcitrant workers to "wreck" shock workers' machines. For example, in 1929 at the Violin Mine in the Donbas, miners saw the conveyor and coal cutters as the "enemy" that had come down to the face to force out human labor, decrease wages, and belittle the skill of "hereditary miners." A bolt was thrown into the conveyor of Drift 10. Workers would not leave their barracks and refused to work.[95] It was also reported that in the Donbas coal mines there were "many instances of intentional damage to coal

[93] *Pravda*, 30 August 1929, and *Trud*, 31 August 1929.
[94] *Visnyk profrukhu Ukrainy*, 1929, no. 23, pp. 30–31. According to *Trud*, 5 November 1929, the strike occurred on 26 October 1929.
[95] Galin, *Perekhod*, pp. 52–66.

cutters."[96] In the Red Metal Worker Machine-Building Factory in Vitebsk, "wreckers" reportedly damaged machines "almost every day" and threw in "pieces of scrap iron to cause a shutdown."[97]

In October 1929 an illuminating incident took place in the Proletarka Textile Factory in Tver. Vasilii Sizov, a worker and a party member, volunteered to operate two machines simultaneously in order to raise productivity. But his fellow workers began to harass and threaten him. A "riot against machines" occurred: one day a bolt was pitched into Sizov's machine. On the day when the entire shop was to start simultaneous operation of two machines following Sizov's initiative, all the machines were found covered with inscriptions: "I've broken a machine. I challenge others to do the same thing"; "Let's compete for the breakage of machines"; "Reptiles! What are you doing? For whom?"; "Hang yourself, or you'll be strangled." The ringleaders were put on trial in January 1930. Among others, I. I. Ivanov, an assistant foreman who had allegedly been a favorite of the Morozovs, the former owners of the factory, was sentenced to "the highest measure of social defense," that is, to be shot, for agitating workers against intensified labor and competition.[98]

As these instances show, the leaders of opposition to the shock movement and socialist competition, and more generally, to the rationalization of production, were invariably described as "elements alien to the working class." In the autumn of 1929 at Coal Mine No. 151 of the Kasnoluch Anthracite Trust in the Donbas, there took place a "class struggle" between "kulaks" and shock workers. Those who were called kulaks threatened and verbally and physically attacked the shock workers (who were "devils"), thwarted the mechanization of production, and succeeded in concluding an agreement with the chief engineer and members of the production commission: "Not to increase output quotas, not to create any labor communes [of workers, in which wages were equally divided among members], not to drop wage rates, not to organize shock brigades, not to introduce socialist competition, until 1935." The "class struggle"

[96] *Sputnik agitatora dlia goroda*, 1930, no. 12 (April), p. 13.

[97] Ibid., 1930, no. 8 (March), p. 48.

[98] Galin, *Perekhod*, pp. 5–27, and *Rabochaia gazeta*, 24 October 1929. When he referred to this sentence at a Moscow party meeting, K. Ia. Bauman evoked cries ("Quite right!") and applause from the audience. Bauman, *Sotsialisticheskoe nastuplenie i zadachi Moskovskoi organizatsii*, p. 59.

prompted outside intervention.[99] In the autumn of 1929, when pressure for the shock movement and socialist competition was great, the press frequently reported that the "class enemies, cut to the quick, have assumed an open offensive."[100] Evidently the political authorities sought to pin all the blame on "class aliens," alert the workers to the "danger" they posed, and close the ranks of workers against it.

Resistance to the shock movement and socialist competition, however, did appear to some managers and technical experts to threaten peace and harmony. The manager of the Vykssa Factory in Nizhegorod, for example, issued an order: "It is necessary to ban the organization of shock brigades, because they make workers nervous."[101] In Siberia, it was reported that there had emerged a "fear of the shock movement among technical specialists."[102] Some Communist engineers opposed the movements, which, they feared, disturbed workers' composure of mind in production.[103] A leading technical journal of the Donbas complained that the movements increased spoilage and the stopping of machines, because workers cared less than before about the quality of products and the proper operation of machines.[104]

Some party organizations in the factories, too, expressed concern about the ill effects of the movements. The party cell of the K. Liebknecht Factory in Dnepropetrovsk, for example, opposed the organization of shock brigades because they "disjoined" workers.[105] In the AMO Plant in Moscow the hostility of "backward" workers to shock workers was such that the plant's party committee had to stop publicizing the names of shock workers who "voluntarily reduced their wage rates," and to protect them from attacks by ordinary workers.[106]

Resistance would continue to plague the factories, but the available, though circumstantial, evidence indicates that as the leadership forcefully promoted the movements, both the older, skilled workers and new, unskilled workers found a convenient way to adapt: toward the end of 1929, they began to rush into the ranks of

[99] *Revoliutsiia i kul'tura*, 1930, no. 8, pp. 68–75.
[100] See, for example, *Komsomol'skaia pravda*, 24 September 1929.
[101] *Trud*, 27 November 1929.
[102] *Izvestiia Sibirskogo kraevogo komiteta VKP(b)*, 1930, no. 4 (25 February), p. 8.
[103] Ivushkin et al., *Sorevnovanie na "Elektrozavode,"* p. 71.
[104] *Inzhenernyi rabotnik*, 1929, no. 9, p. 10.
[105] *TPG*, 26 May 1929.
[106] *Sotsialisticheskoe sorevnovanie v promyshlennosti*, p. 181.

Table 5.1. *Skill composition of shock workers in Nizhegorod*
(in %)

	1 Oct. 1929	1 Jan. 1930	1 Apr. 1930
Skilled	60	58.5	61.5
Semiskilled	39.9	31.2	24.8
Unskilled	0.1	10.3	(13.7)

shock workers, rather than continue to resist, in hopes of sharing the benefits, honor, and privilege accorded to the shock workers.[107] By the summer of 1929 the resistance of older, skilled workers to the shock movement was said to have almost disappeared.[108] By 1930 the composition of shock workers would change dramatically: they were mainly adult, skilled workers who had a long production experience.[109] The influx of unskilled workers was much slower, but became substantial by the spring of 1930, as is indicated in Table 5.1.[110]

The political leadership expected the shock movement and socialist competition to play an important political and social role: they encouraged (or forced) the new workers to be socialized in industrial discipline and the older workers to get rid of their work culture and accommodate industrial modernization. Both groups resisted; their recalcitrance threatened to widen political fissures in the working class and was an important element of what we have called the "crisis of proletarian identity." In the Stalin group's view, this may have been part of the "unavoidable costs of revolution."

Yet through these movements emerged workers who distinguished themselves and willingly answered the call of the party. It was on these new forces that Stalin sought to rely in mobilizing resources for rapid industrialization.

The policy change in favor of the socialist offensive and class war does not seem to have been initiated with overwhelming social and

[107] See, for example, *Proizvodstvennyi zhurnal,* 1929, no. 24, p. 9. See also the Appendix.
[108] Kuz'min, *Vremia velikogo pereloma,* p. 114.
[109] Ol'khov, *Za zhivoe rukovodstvo sotsialisticheskim sorevnovaniem,* p. 45.
[110] *Politicheskii i trudovoi pod'em,* p. 373. The number of unskilled for April 1930 is corrected here. The original is simply "13."

institutional support. Its legitimacy was widely contested: the party leadership was split; the commitment of the party, government institutions, and trade unions appeared suspect to Stalin and his group, and these organizations were purged; and the working class itself was divided. Yet the legitimacy of NEP was equally widely contested: whatever its contribution to economic recovery, NEP had never been regarded by any political constituency of the party as the final settlement of the October Revolution. It was indeed a matter of timing, as Mikoyan suggested, to end the retreat of NEP and its class-conciliatory policy. The socialist offensive won support among those in the party, the Komsomol, the proletarian vigilante groups, and the working class who were dissatisfied with NEP ideologically, emotionally, and perhaps also materially.

In the course of 1928–29 the rapid industrialization drive gained the support of regional political leaders awake to their own regions' particular interests; the purge–recruitment campaigns forced institutions and organizations to be much more responsive to the class-war line; and the shock movement and socialist competition distinguished the committed workers. Within the party leadership the Rightists were defeated, and the majority of the Left Oppositionists came to terms with Stalin. There were signs of problems that would soon manifest themselves, but Stalin and his advisers perhaps saw them as the inevitable.

Part III

1930

6

Industrialization in crisis

"The apparatus of the party and [that] of proletarian dictatorship have always been reorganized depending on changes in the character of main political tasks."[1] The class-war policy led to the purges of the apparatuses, and central economic planning necessitated administrative reforms to integrate the economic apparatus. In the late 1920s the factory gained a greater autonomy in management, but this implied "no slackening of its integration into a complex system of planned production and distribution"; in fact, the factory was brought "firmly into the planning system" through "planned orders" (*nariady-zakazy*) issued by the trust.[2] The increased autonomy of the factory was complemented by increased pressures both from above in the form of administrative control and from below in the form of workers' control.

In 1930, however, three factors, including the reforms themselves, made the integration of the factories into central economic planning difficult. First, the plan targets were constantly pushed upward, aggravating an already serious disequilibrium both between demand and supply and among individual industries. Unwillingly and often after having put up strong resistance, the factory directors had to shoulder tasks that were unrealistically ambitious. Second, credit reform, which sought to integrate the financial system into the central planning of the national economy, actually left the factories out of central financial controls: the reform based on optimistic premises provided no checking mechanism of fulfillment; the reform, it turned out, helped render management all the more unaccountable. Third, the reform of industrial management sought

[1] *Voprosy torgovli*, 1930, no. 2, p. 5.
[2] Carr and Davies, *Foundations of a Planned Economy*, p. 383.

to streamline the industrial apparatus and to concentrate managerial attention on the "technical leadership" and rationalization of production; but the reform instead overcentralized the supply system and actually deprived managers of discretionary powers in this critically important sphere of management. With production frequently interrupted because of a shortage of materials, factory directors had to busy themselves at once appealing to Moscow for intervention and engaging in unofficial dealings with other factories.

The accelerated industrialization drive and the reforms thus frustrated the efforts to integrate the basic industrial unit into central planning. The planning and industrial institutions failed to predict this outcome, mainly because they were misguided in the optimistic belief that once freed of the "fetishism of value" inherent in the capitalist mode of production, the "whole process of production must become crystal clear."[3] This optimism was an inevitable consequence of the constant exhortation of the party leadership to those institutions, but the adverse outcome of the reforms called their administrative capability into question.

In the meantime, by the summer of 1930, administrative chaos and the shortage of resources plunged the economy into crisis. Not only did economic performance fall far short of the planned targets, but the production of some key industries such as ferrous metallurgy actually dropped. The crisis gave rise to a short-lived reform movement (the so-called Syrtsov-Lominadze affair) in the summer and autumn of 1930, but Stalin and his close associates shied away from any reforms and resorted to police intervention in the economy to overcome the crisis.

The acceleration of industrialization

In June 1929 an article published in the Vesenkha newspaper declared: "Time is money, Americans say. If this is correct in the capitalist, immeasurably rich USA, it is all the more suitable to us."[4] Indeed, this dictum characterized the atmosphere in which the industrialization drive accelerated at breakneck speed under the slogan "The Five-Year Plan in Four Years."

[3] *Problemy ekonomiki*, 1930, no. 10, p. 52.
[4] *TPG*, 8 June 1929 (M. G. Gurevich).

The acceleration, as in collectivization, was an inevitable consequence of the political atmosphere of the time: the party leadership constantly called for ever more rapid tempos. In June 1930 Voroshilov frankly stated: "If the Central Committee saw even the slightest possibility of squeezing a larger quantity of production out of this or that industry, it did so irrespective of circumstances."[5] At the sixteenth party congress in June–July 1930, Stalin's declaration that "people who talk about the necessity of *reducing* the rate of development of our industry are enemies of socialism, agents of our class enemies" evoked applause.[6] In January 1931, Kaganovich told the ninth Komsomol congress that for the party "the figures of the Five-Year Plan were not a fetish."[7]

Against this political setting, at least three factors combined to accelerate the drive. First, what was called regional "industrial self-consciousness" continued to grow in 1929–30. Local party and industrial leaders thronged into Moscow to grab more resources for their own regions. At a session of the All-Union Central Executive Committee in late 1929, the Ukrainian leader G. I. Petrovskii, for example, bitterly complained about the budget Moscow allotted to the Ukraine. He declared that if Moscow did not give more money, the Ukraine would be desolate, and he sought the audience's sympathy by saying that "when you drink tea, you have to remember the Ukraine because it produces eighty percent of the sugar [consumed in the USSR]."[8] Provincial leaders pressed Moscow for the exclusive development of their own industries.[9] These demands pushed the plan upward.

Second, the acceleration of the collectivization campaign from the summer of 1929 on pressed for a sharp increase in tractor

---

[5] Voroshilov, *Na istoricheskom perevale*, p. 58.

[6] Stalin, *Sochineniia*, 12:274. Emphasis in the original. Later, in 1933, Stalin stated that "the party, as it were, spurred the country on and hastened its progress" (ibid., 13:183).

[7] *IX Vsesoiuznyi s˝ezd VLKSM*, p. 8.

[8] *2 sessiia TsIK Soiuza SSR 5 sozyva*, 6:8. A delegate from the North Caucasus then criticized Petrovskii by dwelling on how difficult life was in the North Caucasus. (ibid., 9:13–14).

[9] See, for example, the speech of Anan'in of the Moscow Coal Trust in *Pervyi Moskovskii oblastnoi s˝ezd sovetov RK i KD*, pp. 54–55. From late 1929 on, the party leadership often warned against such local patriotism, but local leaders insisted on the importance of their demands for the country as a whole. See, for example, Eikhe, *Novyi etap i zadachi Sibpartorganizatsii*, p. 36. See also Khavin, *U rulia industrii*, pp. 149–50.

production, which caused a chain reaction in the economy as a whole. (This phenomenon will be discussed later in this section.)

Third, like collectivizers in the countryside, industrial planners, caught in an uncontrollable competition for accelerated industrialization, proposed ever higher plan targets. Constantly exhorted by the party leadership, Gosplan could not control these "spontaneous revisions of the Five-Year Plan."[10] In his book *SSSR cherez 10 let* (The Soviet Union in ten years), published in 1930, L. M. Sabsovich, for example, projected fantastically high industrial outputs: 38.6 times in 1937/38 and 295 times in 1942/43 the 1927/28 output; in sector A (capital goods industries) in particular, 64.6 times and 655 times in the respective years![11]

The planners went too far.[12] These targets were patently unrealistic, and invited the intervention of the party and industrial authorities. As early as October 1929 V. V. Kuibyshev warned against "unfounded projections of some industrialists": "It is necessary to object categorically to proposals for accelerating these tempos."[13] On 1 February 1930, S. I. Syrtsov, addressing the congress of planning commissions, sharply criticized those "irresponsible planners" who "seek to surpass everybody in terms of tempos . . . with no consideration of our real possibility and strength."[14] The sixteenth party congress in June–July 1930 attacked their plans as " 'Leftist' excesses of the

[10] *Planovoe khoziaistvo*, 1930, no. 2, p. 38 (V. A. Levin, "Sistema kontrol'nykh tsifr 1930/31 g.").

[11] Sabsovich, *SSSR cherez 10 let*, pp. 40–41. Of course the actual ouptut was far below the projected goals. According to Soviet statistics, the prewar high of industrial output in 1940 was 7.6 times the 1927/28 output (in 1926/27 prices). See Zaleski, *Planning for Economic Growth*, p. 306, and *Stalinist Planning for Economic Growth*, pp. 524–25. Sabsovich's figures were much higher than his earlier projections in *SSSR cherez 15 let*, p. 35, where he predicted that industrial output would increase only 99.4 times (!) from 1927/28 to 1947/48.

[12] One reason why the planners were caught by such fantastic projections was that they failed to appreciate that "the rapid industrial expansion of the late 1920s was a consequence not only of new investments, but also of the improved use of prerevolutionary capacity." See R. W. Davies's introduction to Christian Rakovskii, "The Five-Year Plan Crisis," *Critique*, no. 13 (1981), p. 11, citing A. Vainstein's obituary of G. A. Fel'dman, one of the overoptimistic planners of 1929–30, in *Ekonomika i matematicheskie metody*, 1968, no. 2, pp. 298–99.

[13] Quoted in Kuz'min, *V bor'be za sotsialisticheskuiu rekonstruktsiiu*, p. 92. Apparently this particular part of his speech was not published. See *TPG*, 13 October 1929.

[14] Syrtsov, *O nashikh uspekhakh, nedostatkakh i zadachakh*, p. 22. These planners were accused of "dizzy chirping." See, for example, *Planovoe khoziaistvo*, 1930, no. 4, pp. 9, 14.

superindustrialist type."[15] Toward the end of 1930, when the revised plans proved too ambitious, the party passed the buck to the "wrecking" of "bourgeois" specialists (the "Industrial Party" trial in November 1930). They were accused of shifting their tactics in late 1929 and early 1930 from minimalist to maximalist planning.[16]

For example, the chief defendant in the industrial party trial, L. K. Ramzin, was accused of maximalist planning (especially having increased in early 1930 the plan target of oil production for 1932/33 to forty-two million tons). Yet G. M. Krzhizhanovskii, chairman of Gosplan, proudly declared that the maximalist Ramzin did not know that the target was now set at forty-six million tons a year in 1932/33 "without any instructions on the part of Ramzin's company."[17] This may well have been an implicit defense of Ramzin, and a subtle condemnation of Stalin.

The Five-Year Plan began to be revised upward from the summer of 1929 on.[18] In August 1929 the Council of Labor and Defense worked on an upward revision of the plan for the nonferrous metallurgy industry: the annual output of smelted copper was to increase in five years to 150,000 tons instead of 85,450 as in the original plan; the annual production of aluminum was projected to skyrocket by forty times to 200,000 tons![19] In November 1929 the plans of other industries were also subjected to upward revisions.[20] From late 1929 on, the acceleration of the collectivization drive pressed the tractor industry, whose target was thus raised to 168,000 units a year in 1932/33 instead of the plan's 55,000.[21] This

---

[15] *KPSS v rezoliutsiiakh,* 4:447. A few weeks previously, the party cracked down on "semifantastic" plans for the "reconstruction of life" proposed by Sabsovich, Iu. Larin, and others. See the resolution of the Central Committee dated 16 May 1930: "O rabote po perestroike byta," *Partiinoe stroitel'stvo,* 1930, nos. 11–12. See also Starr, "Visionary Town Planning during the Cultural Revolution."

[16] *Protsess "Prompartii,"* p. 76. See also *Problemy ekonomiki,* 1930, nos. 11–12, p. 9 (N. Berezin, "Blok opportunizma").

[17] *Planovoe khoziaistvo,* 1930, nos. 10–11, p. 15 (Krzhizhanovskii, "Vreditel'stvo v energetike").

[18] It was said that it took only six months for the already ambitious optimal plan of the Five-Year Plan to become "minimal." See *TPG,* 11 October 1929.

[19] *Deiatel'nost' SNK i STO. Svodnye materialy. IV kvartal (iiun'-sentiabr') 1928/29 g.,* p. 10. The actual output of aluminum at the end of the Five-Year Plan was a mere 860 tons or 14.3% of the original plan. See Zaleski, *Planning for Economic Growth,* p. 331.

[20] Bogushevskii and Khavin, "God velikogo pereloma," p. 370.

[21] *Na planovom fronte,* 1929, no. 7 (15 December), p. 31. See also *Ekonomicheskaia zhizn',* 5, 15 September 1929.

increase in the plan for tractor production and agricultural machinery, in turn, called for upward revisions of the plans for metals, oil, etc. Thus, in a sort of chain reaction, by the beginning of 1930 "there was not a single region, not a single republic, not a single branch of the economy for which the Five-Year Plan had not been reexamined."[22] Accordingly, the entire plan of industry was revised. On 14 August 1929 the presidium of Vesenkha resolved to raise the production of industry in 1929/30 28 percent instead of the 21.5 percent called for in the plan; the November 1929 plenum of the Central Committee further pushed the target up to 32.1 percent; and industrial construction was projected to increase by 91.0 percent instead of the plan's original 52.0 percent.[23]

The chain reaction in planning aggravated economic disequilibrium. As early as August or September 1929, Gosplan, pointing out the "paradoxical situation" in which a maximum increase of industrial production still led to an aggravation of shortages of materials, ordered that Vesenkha arrive at an accurate balance of industrial production.[24] Such a balance was never successfully devised, however, because plan targets were revised constantly and without much central coordination. To borrow Naum Jasny's expression, central economic planning thus turned into "bacchanalian planning."[25] By February 1930, many targets of the Five-Year Plan doubled: pig iron from 10 to 18–20 million metric tons a year; chemical fertilizers from 8 to 16 million tons; cement from 41 to 110 million barrels; railway freight traffic from 281 to 450 million metric tons; tractors from 55,000 to 200,000–450,000 units, to name a few.[26] The "bacchanalian planning" of that time was exemplified by the fact that a new, comprehensive Five-Year Plan was not drawn up. The sixteenth party congress in June–July 1930 set the somewhat lower yet still grandiose goal of 17 million

[22] *Planovoe khoziaistvo*, 1930, no. 2, p. 38. See also Zaleski, *Planning for Economic Growth*, p. 118.

[23] Kuibysheva et al., *Valerian Vladimirovich Kuibyshev*, p. 304; *KPSS v rezoliutsiiakh*, 4:328; and *Osnovnye problemy kontrol'nykh tsifr narodnogo khoziaistva SSSR na 1929/30 g.*, pp. 24–25.

[24] *Deiatel'nost' SNK i STO. Svodnye materialy. IV kvartal (iiul'-sentiabr') 1928/29 g.*, p. 28.

[25] Jasny, *Soviet Industrialization, 1928–1952*, p. 73.

[26] *Na planovom fronte*, 1930, nos. 3–4 (28 February), p. 18 (V. Shematovskii, "Za novye tempy energeticheskoi bazy"). See also *Planovoe khoziaistvo*, 1930, no. 2, p. 38 (V. A. Levin).

tons of pig iron in 1932/33, but paid little attention to the overall balance of the economy.[27]

The grand-scale revisions of the plan had a strong impact on individual factories. For instance, the projected annual (1932/33) output of the Stalingrad Tractor Plant, which during 1928 had already doubled from 20,000 tractors to 40,000, was further raised to 50,000 tractors at the end of 1929.[28] The case of the Putilov Factory in Leningrad is no less impressive. The factory produced 1,115 tractors in 1927/28 and 3,050 in 1928/29.[29] The management of the factory proposed a plan of 3,600 tractors for 1929/30, to which Rabkrin opposed 8,000–10,000, only to be superseded by an even more ambitious plan of 12,000 put forth by Vesenkha in late 1929. The actual output (8,935) in 1929/30 fell short of the target, though the factory had nearly tripled its production. What is more, the plan for 1930/31 was further raised to 25,000 tractors.[30] Metallurgical factories were also subjected to the same pressure. The planned capacity of the Magnitogorsk Plant, for example, was raised in February 1930 from the original 656,000 to 2,500,000 tons of pig iron per year; that of the Kuznetsk Plant in Siberia more than tripled from the original 360,000 tons to 1,200,000 tons of pig iron a year. Likewise, in October 1929 planners raised the production capacity of the Southern Steel factories in 1932/33 from 6–6.5 million tons to 10–12 million a year.[31] In some cases, such as the Kuznetsk Plant, the initiative of upward revisions of plans came from the factories (construction projects), which thereby sought greater capital investment.[32] Otherwise, factory managers and engineers understandably resisted the imposition of overambitious

---

[27] *KPSS v rezoliutsiiakh*, 4:422.

[28] *Na planovom fronte*, 1929, no. 7 (15 September), p. 31. See also Dodge and Dalrymple, "The Stalingrad Tractor Plant in Early Soviet Planning," p. 166.

[29] *Istoriia Kirovskogo zavoda*, p. 296.

[30] *Izvestiia TsK VKP(b)*, no. 25 (284), 1 September 1929, p. 26; *SSSR. God raboty pravitel'stva. Materialy k otchetu za 1928/29 g.*, p. 407; *XI z'izd KP(b)U*, p. 168; *Za industrializatsiiu*, 19 February 1930; and *Industrializatsiia Severo-Zapadnogo raiona v gody pervoi piatiletki (1929–1932 gg.)*, p. 123.

[31] *Na planovom fronte*, 1929, no. 3 (15 October), pp. 24–25. For the revision of the plan of Magnitogorsk, see also Kirstein, *Die Bedeutung von Durchführungsentscheidungen in dem zentralistisch verfaßten Entscheidungssystem der Sowjetunion*, chap. 2.

[32] See Frankfurt, *Rozhdenie stali i cheloveka*, pp. 36–38, for the revision (in the autumn of 1930) of the plant's capacity by one-third.

plans, and as a result some engineers such as V. M. Sablin of the Putilov Factory were arrested as "wreckers."[33]

The continual revision of the Five-Year Plan, moreover, made it difficult for factories and construction projects to have any final plans at all. As a matter of fact, the original plan itself did not include detailed plans for the reconstruction of factories and for new construction projects. In other words, the plan was like a skeleton without flesh. The dire shortage of planning specialists was one reason for the inadequate plan, and the haste with which it was drawn up was another. In 1929 it was reported from the Urals, a major industrial center, that "the labor of planners, designers, tellers, and even draftsmen has come to be thought literally worth their weight in gold."[34] Because of the shortage of specialists, in "Moscow, Leningrad, Kharkov, Sverdlovsk, and in all cities there emerged a new 'cottage' industry – planning": skilled and experienced engineers hired beginning draftsmen for a penny, and earned tens of thousands of rubles for themselves; thus an "atmosphere of speculation" (*azhiotazh*) was created about planning.[35] On one hand, plans drawn up in haste often would not do at all. On the other, even giant projects like the Kuznetsk and the Magnitogorsk plants had to start construction without clear plans, and as of May 1930 they still did not have final plans.[36] In February 1930 only fourteen of sixty-five large construction projects in Moscow had final plans.[37] As of 1 September 1930, one-third of the construction projects in the USSR still had no approved plans.[38]

Lack of approved plans demoralized the managers. As early as May 1929, a delegate from White Russia to the fifth Congress of Soviets declared: "[We] used to scream, 'Give us money, give [us] resources, and we will build'; but now some people are willing to give up the money, fearing that there will be no drafts, no plans, and

---

[33] See chap. 7, this volume.

[34] Bogushevskii and Khavin, "God velikogo pereloma," p. 336.

[35] Ibid.

[36] Rozengol'ts (ed.), *Promyshlennsot'*, p. 39. Even in September 1930 it was reported that "most elemental data with which to compose an accurate construction plan are absent." See S. Birman's report on Magnitogorsk in *Za industrializatsiiu*, 27 September 1930. For more general observations, see Ginzburg's memoirs, *O proshlom – dlia budushchego*, p. 65.

[37] Panfilova, *Formirovanie rabochego klassa SSSR v gody pervoi piatiletki*, p. 32.

[38] "Kon'iunktura, 1929/30" (see section I of the Bibliography), section "Kapital'noe stroitel'stvo," p. 3.

no designs."[39] In 1930 even the money proved scarce, and practically all managers found themselves compelled to build "present-day factories" with "future bricks."

The disorganization of industry

It was not only the acceleration of industrialization and collectivization that confused the Soviet economy in 1930. Planning principles expelled market relations from the official economy, and, to use R. W. Davies's apt expression, a "socialist moneyless, product-exchange" economy came into being.[40] Theoretical and organizational disorder was also characteristic of the year 1930, and the factories had to circumvent the official planned economy to keep production going. This practice, in turn, added confusion to the economy.

In late 1929 and early 1930 theoretical and practical optimism dominated the country. Addressing a conference of Marxist agrarian specialists on 27 December 1929, Stalin not only declared the famous policy of eliminating the kulaks as a class. Refuting "those who think that NEP is necessary as a link between town and country," Stalin also contended:

It is not just any kind of link between town and country that we need. What we need is a link that will ensure the victory of socialism. And if we support NEP, it is because it serves the cause of socialism. When it ceases to serve the cause of socialism, we shall cast it to the devil.[41]

Six weeks later, in his interview with students of the Sverdlov Communist University, Stalin answered their questions concerning this seemingly enigmatic speech:

[The speech] should be understood as meaning that we shall "cast it to the devil" when we are no longer under the necessity of permitting a certain freedom for private trade, when permitting it would yield only adverse results, and when we are in a position to establish economic relations between town and country through *product exchange without trade* with its private turnover and tolerance of a certain revival of capitalism.[42]

[39] *5 s"ezd Sovetov* [*SSSR*], 11:4 (Karklin).
[40] Davies, "Models of the Economic System in Soviet Practice," p. 18.
[41] Stalin, *Sochineniia*, 12:171.
[42] *Pravda*, 10 February 1930. Emphasis added. Note that Stalin's *Sochineniia*, 12:187, is edited: the italicized phrase reads "our trading organizations without private trade."

This still enigmatic, but evidently optimistic, view gave rise to enthusiastic arguments for the abolition of NEP, market, and trade, and for the introduction of socialist "product exchange."[43] Stalin himself may have been carried away. In fact, by June–July 1930, when the sixteenth party congress met, Stalin apparently reversed his position and attacked those who claimed that "NEP is essentially a retreat, and that since the retreat has ended, NEP must be abolished":

This is nonsense, of course. . . . In passing to the offensive along the whole front, we do not yet abolish NEP, for private trade and capitalist elements remain; *commodity turnover and a money economy* remain.[44]

Yet Stalin quickly added: "But we are certainly abolishing the initial stage of NEP, and developing its next stage, the present stage, which is the last stage of NEP."[45] Whatever the rhetoric, market and trade were being squeezed out of the official economy, and Stalin believed that a money economy, along with trade, would eventually be abolished in the Soviet Union.

A similar kind of optimistic theory prevailed in the industrial sphere as well. As planning principles forced market relations out of the economy, some economists believed, as did many economists in 1919–20, that the emerging planned economy would lead directly to a moneyless economy. These economists, convinced that "money [and] finance are obsolete categories of bourgeois society," made efforts to design "a unit of account and of remuneration which could replace money."[46] In higher economic institutes, "financial science" was eliminated from the curriculum.[47]

The credit reform undertaken in early 1930 by the State Bank and Rabkrin was at the same time a cause and a consequence of this enthusiasm for the imminence of a moneyless economy. In order to compile accurate financial plans on a nationwide scale and to keep the

---

[43] See for example, V. Bogushevskii, "O novom etape," in *Za industrializatsiiu*, 9 and 11 February 1930, and the discussions caused by the articles in *Bol'shevik*, nos. 7–8 and 9 (1930). Note that in 1925 Bogushevskii was firmly in support of NEP and was attacked for his "pro-kulak deviation." See Davies, "The Socialist Market," p. 204.

[44] *XVI s˝ezd VKP(b)*, p. 37. Emphasis added. Stalin's *Sochineniia*, 12:307, is edited: the italicized part reads " 'free' commodity turnover."

[45] *XVI s˝ezd VKP(b)*, p. 37.

[46] See G. F. Grin'ko's criticism in *3 sessiia TsIK Soiuza SSR 5 sozyva*, 4:15, and Davies, "Models of the Economic System in Soviet Practice," pp. 20–21.

[47] *Vestnik finansov*, 1929, no. 9, p. 145.

currency issue at a minimum, the credit reform abolished commercial credits, concentrated all short-term credit operations in the State Bank, and organized noncash settlements of accounts in the socialized sector.[48] Thus the reform closed "the legal gap through which resources were issued without the sanction and control of the planning authorities."[49] The head of the State Bank and chief architect of the reform, Iu. L. Piatakov (a former Trotskyist whom Lenin had characterized as a "man of outstanding will and outstanding ability, but shows too much zeal for administrating and the administrative side of the work to be relied upon in a serious political matter"),[50] revealed considerable zeal: "The magic of banks gives way to simple economic accounting and record-keeping. The credit shell falls off; the clear features of the process of production and circulation in physical terms are emerging."[51] At the sixteenth party congress in June–July 1930, Stalin still optimistically declared that the reform

transforms the State Bank into a nationwide apparatus for keeping account of the production and distribution of goods; and, second, it withdraws a large amount of currency from circulation. There cannot be the slightest doubt that these measures will lead (are already leading) to the regulation of the credit system and to the strengthening of the ruble [*chervonets*].[52]

Such pervasive optimism no doubt had hindered the authors of the reform in foreseeing both detailed effects and subsequent development of the reform; much vagueness was left in the provisions of the reform, and the reform provided no mechanism to assess fulfillment. The State Bank, moreover, showing "too much zeal for administrating," "sought to appropriate the functions of planning and regularizing all economic processes, functions unusual to the bank and beyond its strength."[53]

The credit reform was not so much an economic as an administrative measure aimed at strengthening administrative controls over

[48] See the government resolution of 30 January 1930 in *Resheniia partii i pravitel'stva po khoziaistvennym voprosma*, 2: 166–73. See also Weißenburger, *Monetärer Sektor und Industrialisierung der Sowetjunion*, pp. 149–55, and Arnold, *Banks, Credit, and Money in Soviet Russia*, pp. 345–74.
[49] Davies, *The Development of the Soviet Budgetary System*, pp. 210, 229.
[50] Lenin, *Polnoe sobranie sochinenii*, 45:345. For Piatakov's role in the reform, see *XVI s˝ezd VKP(b)*, p. 314.
[51] See Davies, "Models of the Economic System in Soviet Practice," p. 20.
[52] Stalin, *Sochineniia*, 12:330–31.
[53] *Bol'shevik*, 1931, no. 7 (15 April), p. 30 (M. Kalmanovich, "Kreditnaia reforma i khozraschet"). In October 1930 Kalmanovich replaced Piatakov as head of the bank.

the economy. Vesenkha apparently had opposed the reform on the grounds that it would lead to the State Bank's "dictatorship over industry."[54] Some economists regarded the reform as "ultracentralization" and warned against its possible ill effects on the economy.[55] Yet their concern was overridden by the optimism of the reform's authors.

The reform proved injurious to the economy. The State Bank took into its hands the current credit accounts of the factories and conducted the transactions purely formally "according to the plan" and irrespective of whether the factories actually fulfilled their production plans. Factory directors found it convenient to use "blind" credits to cover the failure to fulfill the plans, in hopes that "any lag in the industrial-financial plan of production will be covered by the bank." According to one account, the managerial responsibility for the fulfillment of the plans and the guarantee for the correct use of bank credits were thus "totally lost."[56] Moreover, the bank automatically paid the bill of the purchaser (factory) to the supplier (factory) regardless of whether the former had in its account sufficient funds for the purchase, with the result that the bank often ended up paying in excess of the purchaser's account. According to one manager, "Yesterday there were 500,000 rubles in my account current. Yet today it turned out to be gone. Yesterday I was rich, but the night passed and I have nothing in my purse. And all this was done without my knowledge."[57] Managers naturally gave up any concern with finance: "To a considerable degree the possibility of their concern with it [finance] was lost."[58]

---

[54] Morin, Piatakov, and Sher, *Reforma kredita*, p. 44.

[55] See for example, M. Birbraer, "Ocherednye zadachi ratsionalizatsii finansovogo khoziaistva tovaroprovodiashei seti," *Puti industrializatsii*, 1929, no 12; and "O finansovoi reforme," ibid., 1929, no. 15. (In 1932–33, Birbraer was to become a protagonist for a "socialist market." See Davies, "The Socialist Market.") See also Ia. Kuperman, "Vzaimootnosheniia sovetskogo banka s ego klientiroi," *Ekonoimicheskoe obozrenie*, 1929, no. 9, and A. Blium, "Nekotorye voprosy ekonomiki reformirovannogo kredita," ibid., 1930, no. 2. For a detailed discussion on the reform, see Weißenburger, *Monetärer Sektor und Industrialisierung der Sowjetunion*, pp. 128–48.

[56] *Finansovye problemy*, 1931, nos. 1–2, p. 15, and *Bol'shevik*, 1931, no. 7 (15 April), p. 29.

[57] *Pervaia Vsesoiuznaia konferentsiia rabotnikov sotsialisticheskoi promyshlennosti*, p. 26.

[58] *Bol'shevik*, 1931, no. 7 (15 April), pp. 29–30. For the problems of reform, see Weißenburger, *Monetärer Sektor und Industrialisierung der Sowjetunion*, pp. 157–72, and Davies, *The Development of the Soviet Budgetary System*, p. 230.

This loss, contrary to Stalin's claim, led to an inflationary currency issue. "The financial machine," according to a contemporary account, "broke out of our hands."[59] The amount of currency in circulation jumped from 2,773,000,000 rubles on 1 January 1930 to 4,264,000,000 rubles on 1 October 1930, a 53.8 percent increase.[60] This inflationary currency issue was a sure sign of the dire shortages of material resources.

Credit reform and the inflationary currency issue dramatically weakened central financial controls over the factories. As R. W. Davies has pointed out, the reform showed that "in a planned economy from which the automatic checks of a market economy are absent, a mechanism in which there are no built-in checks on fulfilment and penalties for non-fulfilment will run out of control."[61] Some managers found this freedom from control enjoyable. At a conference of industrial managers in early 1931, Ordzhonikidze sharply criticized them: "The wages have been paid without you, output has been paid irrespective of quality, they take your output from you and redistribute it." A participant interjected, "That's quite all right," to which Ordzhonikidze responded: "It seems quite all right, but if you look at it more closely, it turns out it's not all right, and very much not all right."[62] In June 1931 Stalin would attack the managers for having assumed that the State Bank "will advance the necessary money anyway."[63] It was "not a secret," according to G. F. Grin'ko (who in October 1930 would take over the People's Commissariat of Finance from L. P. Bruikhanov), that "many managerial organs have extremely weakened their financial apparatus, and the institution of commercial directors has disappeared or has been disqualified."[64]

Thus a paradoxical outcome took place in 1930. The attempt to integrate the factories into central planning actually had the opposite effect: centralization led to a loss of central control and managerial accountability.

To make matters worse, the reform of industrial management,

[59] *Problemy marksizma*, 1931, no. 2, p. 81 (G. Grin'ko).
[60] Arnold, *Banks, Credit, and Money in Soviet Russia*, pp. 412–13.
[61] Davies, *The Development of the Soviet Budgetary System*, p. 230.
[62] *Pervaia Vsesoiuznaia konferentsiia rabotnikov sotsialisticheskoi promyshlennosti*, p. 12, and Davies, "Some Soviet Economic Controllers – III," pp. 40–41, from which the English translation was taken.
[63] Stalin, *Sochineniia*, 13:75.
[64] *Finansy i sotsialisticheskoe khoziaistvo*, 1931, no. 12 (April), p. 9.

which was implemented in 1930 jointly with credit reform, brought about similar outcomes. Reversing the trend toward decentralization in 1927–28, the reform overcentralized management.[65]

As its makers – Rabkrin and Vesenkha – conceived it, the main objective of the reform was to concentrate the attention of industrial management on the "technical direction" and rationalization of factory operation rather than on the "operative-commercial" functions. This goal itself derived from the imperative of industrial modernization and the disappearance of the market. The "commercial functions" (especially supply and sale) of the trusts and the factories, deemed secondary to technical issues, were transferred to the so-called associations (*ob"edineniia*). (The associations – one for each industry, as a rule – formed from the merger of the former *glavki* [Chief Administrations] of Vesenkha and the marketing agencies, syndicates, which by that time had already taken over most of the commercial functions from the trusts.)[66] Thus factories were deprived of the right to manage their own storehouses.[67]

Before the reform the supply of industrial goods typically took the following route: from a factory to its superior trust; then from the trust to a syndicate according to a contractual arrangement; then from the syndicate to a purchaser syndicate; then from this syndicate to another trust according to a contractual arrangement; and then finally from the trust to its subordinate factory. This flow was complicated but was relatively free of the direct intervention of the center. The reform of industrial management simplified and centralized this mechanism. Now typically the goods were transferred according to planned administrative arrangements from a factory to its superior association in Moscow to another association in Moscow, and then to its subordinate factory.

On the one hand, this simplification and centralization, like that of the credit system, was widely acknowledged as desirable and neces-

[65] For the December 1929 resolution concerning the reform, see *Resheniia partii i pravitel'stva po khoziaistvennym voprosam*, 2:136–42. For a detailed account of the reform, see Lakin, *Reforma upravleniia promyshlennost'iu v 1929/30 g.*

[66] See N. Beregin and A. Gol'tsam, "Kak reorganizovat' upravlenie promyshlennosti'iu," *Biulleten' TsKK VKP(lb) i NK RKI SSSR i RSFSR*, 1929, nos. 4–5, pp. 19–20, and Gol'tsman's articles in *Pravda*, 18, 23 July, and 13 August 1929. The reform greatly reduced the authority of the trusts.

[67] See Lakin, *Reforma upravleniia promyshlennost'iu v 1929/30 g.*, pp. 56–58. See also *Sovety narodnogo khoziaistva i planovye organy v tsentre i na mestakh*, pp. 213–14.

sary for a planned economy. On the other hand, it was intended to alleviate the problem of resource constraints through effective central control of scarce materials: the party and industrial leadership optimistically believed that centralization would alleviate the shortages of raw and industrial materials by preventing the factories from hoarding materials."[68] The acute shortages of raw and industrial materials already evident since 1927–28 had prompted the factories to seek supplies through unofficial channels. In other words, centrifugal forces had strengthened in the supply system and hampered the centripetal forces required by centralized planning. Pressures for centralization thus came from below as well: the factories, while getting supplies in unofficial ways, actively demanded the central control of supplies as a means of alleviating shortages.[69]

Both theoretical and practical concerns thus justified the centralization of industrial management. Like credit reform, this reform provided convenient grounds for what was called "excessive administrative ecstasy," leading to centralization far beyond expectation.[70] Theoretical optimism hindered the working out in advance of clear channels for physical allocation and control. Because planning was assumed to be perfect and self-enforcing, legal theorists came to attack the "bourgeois" contract system, which they considered had lost much of its raison d'être as a control over material allocation. State arbitration commissions for contract cases, too, had contributed to the undermining of the NEP systems of contracts: they regarded contracts as subject to the national economic plan and modified the terms of contracts as they saw fit.[71] In 1930, according to a contemporary observer, it became "unfashionable to remember contract discipline."[72] All these factors helped the industrial and planning authorities to dismantle the system of contracts and state arbitration.[73] According to a Leningrad study, before 1930, 80 percent of the production of the socialized sector was sold on the basis of contracts; in the 1929/30 economic year this

---

[68] Lakin, *Reforma upravleniia promyshlennost'iu v 1929/30 g.*, pp. 56–57.
[69] See *Sovetskoe gosudarstvo i revoliutsiia prava*, 1930, no. 7, pp. 118–19, and *Puti industrializatsii*, 1931, no. 9, p. 4. See also Drobizhev, *Glavnyi shtab sotsialisticheskoi promyshlennosti*, p. 168. In late 1929, 10–25% of supplies to the factories were provided by "self-procurements." *Ekonomicheskoe obozrenie*, 1929, no. 11, p. 25.
[70] See, for example, *3 sessiia TsIK Soiuza SSR 5 sozyva*, 5:10.
[71] Gavze, *Razvitie sotsialisticheskogo grazhdansko-pravovogo dogovora*, pp. 84–89.
[72] Gintsburg, *O khozraschete*, p. 5.
[73] Ibid., and *Sovetskoe gosudarstvo i revoliutsiia prava*, 1931, nos. 5–6, p. 126.

could be said of only 5 percent.[74] Thus, mutual legal control between supplier and buyer almost disappeared.

Management reform could not halt the centrifugal forces in the supply system, and bureaucratism implicit in a centralized system may even have encouraged them. In fact, factory directors, anticipating short supplies as well as abrupt increases in plan targets, hoarded whatever materials were available. For example, directors of metal factories, while stockpiling available metals, screamed: "The factory is perishing because of a lack of metals." However, they suffered from shortages of other kinds of metal, which other factories stockpiled.[75] Thus, in some factories there were excessive materials and in others, shortages.[76] As a result, the reform of industrial management did not alleviate but aggravated the shortages.[77]

Industrial leaders responded to this breakdown by reducing supplies to those factories and construction projects suspected of hoarding. However, directors easily passed the buck to the center: "You say we must not stockpile stuff, [but] we don't want to adjust to bottlenecks, old man, [because] we are Bolsheviks, old man." The authorities found it difficult to rebut such claims.[78] At the same time, the factories bombarded Vesenkha and other central organizations with requests for help.[79] At the sixteenth party congress in June–July 1930, a spokesman for Rabkrin, which had often encountered managers' hostility because of its frequent intervention, complacently declared: "It is flattering . . . that many of the big, medium, and small managers even ask the Central Control Commission and Rabkrin to come to help them. This has started recently, very recently."[80] In

---

[74] Iakovleva, *Razvitie dogovornykh sviazei gosudarstvennoi promyshlennosti SSSR po snabzheniiu i sbytu*, p. 341. See also Atlas, *Kreditnaia reforma v SSSR*, p. 147, and Weißenburger, *Monetärer Sektor und Industrialisierung der Sowjetunion*, pp. 165–66.

[75] *Metall*, 1930, nos. 10–12, pp. 142–43.

[76] *Za industrializatsiiu*, 3 August, 10 September 1930, 19 March 1931.

[77] See editorial in *Bol'shevik*, 1931, no. 10 (31 May), p. 6.

[78] *Za industrializatsiiu*, 28 March 1931.

[79] See the case of the Marti Factory, which sent hundreds of telegrams to the Council of People's Commissars, Vesenkha, Vesenkha's chairman Kuibyshev himself, etc. *Za industrializatsiiu*, 27 July 1930. For other cases see *Pravda*, 4 May 1930, and *XVI s″ezd VKP(b)*, p. 346.

[80] *XVI s″ezd VKP(b)*, p. 368. Even before 1930 Rabkrin had received managers' grievances and petitions, which in 1930 became much more frequent. On 7 October 1930 Kuibyshev issued an order deploring this practice and appealed to the managers to settle conflicts within Vesenkha. See *Sbornik postanovlenii i prikazov po promyshlennosti*, 1930, 76:1159. Managers turned for help not only to Rabkrin but also to the procurators, the Council of People's Commissars, the Council of Labor and Defense, etc. See ibid., 57:743 (order of 16 July 1930).

August 1930, Vesenkha was compelled to issue an order prohibiting such requests.[81]

While supplicating Moscow, managers also resorted to unofficial channels for supplies. When the suppliers were known, "pushers" (*tolkachi*) were sent to them to expedite supplies.[82] (In many cases, however, because of overcentralization, the supplier was unknown to the purchaser, and vice versa.) Factories also remedied the defects of the system by "mutual service," or direct exchange of materials.[83] Some factories, circumventing central control, took orders from other factories and distributed products directly to them.[84] Naturally, in 1930 these unofficial dealings eroded the system of planned allocation, which in some factories accounted for only 40 percent of the total supply.[85] The supply system had thus fallen into what was called a "state of true bacchanalia."[86]

The reform of industrial management, like credit reform, thus had a paradoxical outcome: efforts to incorporate the factories into a planned economy actually weakened central controls over the factories, and efforts to alleviate the problem of resource constraints actually aggravated it.

In 1930 industrial management was further complicated by another feature of the reform: the introduction of Taylorist functionalism (*funktsionalka*), a form of management based on the division of complex administration into a number of specialized functions. Functionalism too was justified by both theoretical and practical concerns. First, the experience of advanced capitalist countries (particularly the United States and Germany) provided a theoretical rationale for functionalism. It was generally regarded as a way of improving the efficiency of increasingly complex industrial management, which the traditional hierarchical line system was no longer deemed capable of handling. Second, the influx of workers into managerial positions necessitated a division of labor so that workers with little expertise in management could "go straight to the heart of the matter and cope with the tasks entrusted [to them]";

---

[81] *Sbornik postanovlenii i prikazov po promyshlennosti*, 1930, 66:915–16 (21 August 1930).

[82] See, for example, the case of Kuznetsk in *Za industrializatsiiu*, 27 March 1931. For more general discussion, see "Tolkachi" in ibid., 27 July 1930.

[83] *Metall*, 1930, nos. 10–12, pp. 142–43.

[84] See, for example, *Pravda*, 4 May 1930.

[85] See the case of a shipbuilding yard reported in *Za industrializatsiiu*, 19 March 1931.

[86] *Biulleten' 3-ei leningradskoi oblastnoi konferentsii VKP(b)*, 5:30.

just as the conveyor system of production could be operated by semiskilled workers, so, it was believed, the functional system of management could be run by inexperienced workers and Communists.[87] The factories were thus controlled by the associations through the latter's functional departments (such as administrative-organizational, planning-economic, technical-production, cadres, supply, finance), which in turn were controlled by Vesenkha through its corresponding functional departments.[88]

The extent to which functionalism was introduced into factory management in 1930 is not clear. It is clear, however, that in this reform, too, theoretical optimism hampered the working out of practical issues, leaving much vagueness in the provisions of the reform. The institutionalization of one-man management concentrated power by forcing the party and union organizations out of the managerial domain; within management, however, functionalism resulted in a division of power. The functional departments of Vesenkha and the associations came to direct the corresponding managerial personnel of the factories over the heads of the directors. Functionalism thus brought the departments into "war" with one another from Vesenkha down to the factories: "norm setters fought with production workers, finance personnel with supply personnel, mechanics with miners."[89] Functionalism thus confused one-man management in the factories.

In 1930 the rapid disappearance of market relations caused Bolsheviks to believe optimistically that with the disappearance of the market the whole process of production would become crystal-clear. The influence of Western scientific management was evident: credit reform envisaged a "conveyor" method of credit whereby credit automatically followed the goods; management reform applied Taylorist functionalism on a nationwide scale, something not attempted even in the most advanced capitalist countries. The idea was perfect, as V. V. Sher, and author of the credit reform, defended it at the Menshevik trial in March 1931: "The idea of the reform itself did not cause any inflation."[90] It appeared as if the whole

---

[87] For an explicit discussion to this effect, see Zatonskii in *XV s˝ezd VKP(b)*, p. 470, and *Organizatsiia upravleniia*, 1934, no. 3 (May–June), p. 5, criticizing this view.

[88] For Vesenkha, see Sakharov, Chernai, and Kabakov, *Ocherki organizatsii tiazheloi promyshlennosti SSSR*, pp. 48–50. For associations, see the example of the Steel Association, in *Metall*, 1930, no. 5, p. 7.

[89] Paramonov, *Uchit'sia upravliat'*, pp. 149–50.

[90] *Protsess kontrrevoliutsionnoi organizatsii men'shevikov*, p. 314.

mechanism of production and management became simpler and clearer. It so appeared because the reforms, along with tax reform,[91] almost did away with the complexities of the elaborate control mechanisms built into market economies. Ironically, the reforms, which sought to incorporate the factories into the centrally planned economy, had the opposite effect: the control of the center weakened dramatically, and *khozraschet* in the factories was virtually eliminated without "preliminary permission."[92] To the extent that central controls weakened, managers' unofficial powers increased. Sometimes they had to use their unofficial powers dictatorially to keep the factory running, but they were helpless in relation to the centralized industrial hierarchy. In either case, police intervention could be easily justified.

The economic crisis of the summer of 1930

The disorganization of industry and the increasing shortages of material resources and skilled labor[93] plunged the Soviet economy into deep crisis: the reforms of credit and management made it impossible to maximize the utility of the already scarce resources, and the large-scale diversion of resources to new construction and production threatened the operation of old factories.

In the third quarter (April–June) of 1929/30, the economic indexes began to drop. The gross output (in constant prices) of large-scale industry decreased by 4.9 percent from the second to the third quarter. Although capital goods industries registered an increase of 4.1 percent over the second quarter, the output of consumer goods industries dropped sharply by 12.7 percent.[94] This was a clear sign of crisis. At first, however, it appeared

---

[91] The tax reform undertaken in 1930 by Rabkrin and the People's Commissariat of Finance simplified and "automatized" the taxation of factories on the basis of planned gross sales. This reform, like the credit reform, confused the financial management of factories and contributed to the virtual elimination of *khozraschet*. See Holzman, *Soviet Taxation*, pp. 105–26. See also Ordzhonikidze's speech in *XV s"ezd VKP(b)*, pp. 312–13.

[92] *Puti industrializatsii*, 1931, no. 8, p. 6 (S. Birman).

[93] The problem of labor will be discussed in chap. 8, this volume.

[94] *Za tri mesiatsa. Deiatel'nost' SNK i STO. III kvartal (aprel'-iiun') 1929/30 g.*, p. 67.

to be seasonal fluctuations: with the exception of the year 1928/
29, the third quarter usually had registered a seasonal drop due
largely to the outflow of industrial workers to the countryside.
There were other signs of crisis such as the decline in real wages of
industrial workers and the deterioriation of the quality of products. Yet there were considerable achievements as well: substantial
increases in labor productivity and a solid decline in industrial
costs; the industrial output of the third quarter of 1929/30 was,
according to official statistics, still 23.8 percent above that of the
same period of 1928/29.[95] Thus, optimistic prospects for the economy prevailed at the sixteenth party congress in June–July 1930,
which revised upward the targets of the Five-Year Plan, especially
that of pig iron to seventeen million tons a year. The crisis became
evident soon thereafter, however. Contrary to seasonal upturns in
the previous years, the industrial output in the fourth quarter
(July–September) declined by 4 percent from the previous quarter,
and increased only 12.3 percent from the same period of the previous year.[96]

As a result, the plan targets of census (large-scale) industry were
far from achieved. According to official claims, gross output of
1929/30 as a whole was up 24.6 percent over 1928/29, falling short
of the projected goal of 32 percent. The failure was due primarily to
the underfulfillment of the plan in the consumer goods industries,
the output of which rose not by 21.9 percent as planned, but only
9.6 percent from 1928/29. The capital goods industries, according
to official data, increased production by 42.7 percent over 1928/29,
coming closer to achieving the target of 45 percent.[97] However,
industrial costs declined only 7 percent, well below the planned 11
percent drop; labor productivity was up only 10.4 percent, less than
half the planned 25 percent; in the fourth quarter of 1929/30, labor
productivity was even below the level of the same period of 1928/
29.[98] Even capital construction in industry achieved only 78 percent

[95] *Industrializatsiia SSSR, 1929–1932*, p. 230.
[96] Ibid. For a detailed contemporary analysis of the crisis by the Trotskyist in exile, K.
    G. Rakovskii, see "Na sʺedze i v strane," *Biulleten' Oppozitsii* (Paris), nos. 25–26
    (1931), pp. 9–32. (The article was written in July 1930.) An English translation of
    this article is in *Critique*, no. 13 (1981), pp. 13–53. See also R. W. Davies's
    introduction to the article, pp. 7–12.
[97] *Industrializatsiia SSSR, 1929–1932*, p. 221.
[98] "Konʺiunktura, 1929/30," section "Otsenka," p. 3, and "Trud," p. 4.

of the plan target.[99] Present-day factories could not have been built with future bricks.

Production in individual industries dropped to alarming levels. Coal production in particular decreased precipitously from 12,991,600 tons in the second quarter to 11,969,400 tons and 9,160,800 tons in the third and fourth quarters, respectively, falling far short of plans (77.8, 68.2, and 66.1 percent for July, August, and September, respectively); the output in the fourth quarter was even below the level of the same period of the previous year (down 3.4 percent).[100] Moreover, the costs rose by as much as 19.4 percent over the 1928/29 level, while almost all other industries were reported to have reduced production costs; and during 1929/30 the stock of coal reserves decreased by more than half.[101] The coal crisis had a direct impact on another key industry, iron and steel. The shortages and declining quality of coke contributed to the decreased output of pig iron in the fourth quarter, a 20 percent underfulfillment of the planned target.[102]

This state of the economy gravely aggravated the shortages of materials, which in the summer of 1930 stopped the operation of many factories. Lack of metal, for example, halted factories in Leningrad and Nizhegorod.[103] In the South and the Urals, shortages of metal forced construction projects to a standstill.[104] Shortages of raw agricultural products, particularly cotton, closed textile factories "for 75 days."[105] Train tracks could not be repaired because of a lack of rails.[106]

[99] *Planovoe khoziaistvo*, 1930, no. 9, p. 9. According to the unpublished data of Gosplan, during the eleven months (October 1929–August 1930), capital construction in industry planned by Vesenkha reached only 61.3% of the set level. "Kon"iunktura, 1929/30," section "Kaptal'noe stroitel'stvo," p. 1. For a vivid description of the summer crisis on the Magnitogorsk construction site, see Kirstein, *Die Bedeutung von Durchführungsentscheidungen in dem zentralistisch verfaßten Entscheidungssystem der Sowjetunion*, pp. 58–79.

[100] "Kon"iuktura 1929/30," Table 4.

[101] *Industrializatsiia SSSR, 1929–1932*, pp. 231, 233, 239.

[102] Ibid., p. 234. This caused a sharp increase in the importation of metals from 376,800 tons in 1929 to 762,100 tons in 1930. Mishustin, *Vneshniaia torgovlia i industrializatsiia SSSR*, p. 185. The Stalingrad Tractor Plant, faced with shortages of metals, demanded increased importations. See N. Osinskii's report in *Pravada*, 31 July 1930.

[103] *Kommunist* (Nizhegorod), 1930, nos. 8–9, p. 8, and *Industrializatsiia Severo-Zapadnogo raiona v gody pervoi piatiletki*, pp. 123, 204, 205.

[104] *Metall*, 1930, nos. 8–9, p. 198.

[105] See *XVI s"ezd VKP(b)*, p. 135, and *Za tri mesiatsa. Deiatel'nost' SNK i STO. III kvartal (aprel'–iiun') 1929/30 g.*, p. 67.

[106] See editorial in *Za industrializatsiiu*, 3 August 1930.

A vicious circle emerged at this time: the overwhelming pressure for the fulfillment of plan targets inevitably led to a sharp decline in the quality of products; the lower quality of goods forced factories to consume them in greater quantity, thereby increasing demands for quantity.

The same kind of emphasis on quantity manifested itself in an inflationary currency issue that also contributed to the aggravation of shortages. In 1929/30, despite Stalin's optimistic prediction at the sixteenth party congress, "a large amount of currency" was not withdrawn from circulation. On the contrary, the planned goal of 415 million rubles was far surpassed by the actual issue of 1,626,400,000 rubles. The financial difficulties caused by the failure of industry to fulfill the plans of output, costs, and labor productivity were solved by issuing more currency than planned.[107]

Another important reason for the shortages was that industrial performance, despite substantial increases in output, lagged far behind needs. The number of Soviet-made tractors supplied to agriculture, for example, almost quadrupled from 2,800 units in 1928/29 to 10,050 units in 1929/30; simultaneously, the import of tractors more than tripled from 6,666 units in 1928/29 to 23,017 units in 1929/30.[108] Even this dramatic increase, however, could not compensate for the decline in animal draft power caused by the massive slaughter in the winter of 1929–30.[109] The production of machinery increased by 76 percent (in the constant 1926/27 prices) from 1929 to 1930, almost reaching a level six times the 1913 production. In 1930 the import of machinery nevertheless increased by 81.5 percent over the level of 1929, accounting for 51.2 percent of the total sum spent on import.[110] The forced import of metals and machinery left little money for the import of raw materials. Cotton imports, for instance, plunged from 115,000 tons in 1929 to 57,900 tons in 1930. Accordingly, the domestic production of cotton cloth sharply dropped;

[107] "Kon'iunktura, 1929/30," section "Finansy."

[108] *Sotsialistischeskoe stroitel'stvo SSSR* (1935), p. 303, and Mishustin, *Vneshniaia torgovlia i industrializatsiia SSSR,* p. 169. The Soviet Union purchased 40.8% and 90.5% (in value terms) of all the tractors in the world market in 1930 and 1931, respectively.

[109] Davies, *The Socialist Offensive,* p. 448.

[110] Mishustin, *Vneshniaia torgovlia i industrializatsiia SSSR,* pp. 29 and 59. For a fuller discussion of import in this period, see Dohan, "The Economic Origins of Soviet Autarchy, 1927/28–1934."

especially in the fourth quarter of 1929/30, it was only 40.8 percent of the output in the same period of the previous year.[111]

In the summer of 1930 railway tranport also fell into crisis. Because the railways, like consumer goods industries, suffered from the concentration of investment in heavy industry, they could not accommodate the expansion of industry. Between 1928 and 1930 railway passenger traffic more than doubled, fulfilling the Five-Year Plan in two and a half years; freight traffic increased 43.4 percent, but the number of freight locomotives increased only 9.4 percent, and freight cars 26.8 percent. (The length of the rail network increased only 0.2 percent during the same period.)[112] The industrial slump in the summer of 1930 mitigated the critical state of railway transport, but as industry somewhat recovered from the crisis in the autumn, transport was pushed beyond its capacity and entered a prolonged crisis.[113]

This summer economic crisis succeeded the "crisis in the party" in the wake of wholesale collectivization in the winter of 1929–30.[114] The political impact of the summer crisis appeared to be stronger than that of the spring crisis: by the autumn, criticism of party policy was voiced from within Stalin's camp (the so-called Syrtsov-Lominadze affair).[115] S. I. Syrtsov and V. V. Lominadze, from different wings of opinion within the Stalinist leadership, proposed at least three measures to overcome the crisis: first, the curbing of excessive centralization, the revamping of industrial management, and a partial introduction of market incentives; second, the "narrowing of the front of capital construction," in other words, a shift in emphasis from quantity to quality; and third, improvement in the living conditions of workers.[116]

The significance of the affair lay in the fact that in 1931–33 some

---

[111] Mishustin, *Vneshniaia torgovlia i industrializatsiia SSSR,* pp. 67 and 202, and "Kon″iunktura, 1929/30," Table 5.

[112] Hunter, *Soviet Transportation Policy,* p. 316. The official estimates have to be dealt with cautiously, however. In 1930 the railway authorities reported: "How much has actually been transported is quite unknown. . . . It has to be acknowledged with all candor that we don't know what kind of economy we are directing." Seliunin and Khanin, "Lukavaia tsifra," p. 189.

[113] "Kon″iunktura, 1929/30," section "Transport," pp. 1–5. See also *Zheleznodorozhnyi transport v gody industrializatsii SSSR (1926–1941),* pp. 88–102.

[114] Davies, *The Socialist Offensive,* chap. 7.

[115] For this, see Davies, "The Syrtsov-Lominadze Affair."

[116] This last issue will be discussed in chap. 9.

of these proposals, with necessary corrections, would be put into practice by the party leadership. In the autumn of 1930, however, Stalin and his close associates attacked this dissent as a "Left–Right bloc." On 3 September 1930 the Central Committee issued an appeal that, admitting a "shameful reduction in rates" of growth, called for the overcoming of the crisis by the further promotion of the shock movement and socialist competition and stricter controls over labor discipline.[117] As R. W. Davies has correctly pointed out, this appeal was "a repeat dose of the prescription that all troubles could be cured by better organization, exhortation and greater exertion."[118] The party continued to press hard for overambitious plan targets: in the so-called special quarter (October–December 1930) gross industrial output was projected to increase by 46.9 percent over the previous quarter; coal production in particular was to reach 21,270,000 tons, a 124.4 percent increase![119]

There were grounds for both optimism and pessimism. The ideas of the reforms aimed at creating a centrally planned economy were believed to be perfect; the administrative framework of a new economy had been set up; and everything looked fine when seen from Moscow.[120] In reality, the center had little but illusory control over the actual working of the economy, the confusion and disorganization of which, along with the dire shortage of resources, led to the summer crisis. Syrtsov and Lominadze appeared to Stalin and his close associates to have failed to appreciate the achievements, surrendering to the difficulties in un-Bolshevik fashion. It was politically expedient to assume that all the problems lay with the economic and planning institutions and that there was "counterrevolutionary wrecking" afoot in them. It was an assumption, however, that imposed great human and material costs by refusing to appreciate the real causes of the economic difficulties.

The drive against the economic administration

The reinforcement in 1930 of Bolshevik voluntarism and optimism was an inevitable consequence of the constant exhortation of the

[117] *Pravda*, 3 September 1930.
[118] Davies, "The Syrtsov-Lominadze Affair," p. 38.
[119] *Planovoe khoziaistvo*, 1930, nos. 10–11, pp. 324, 344.
[120] See, for example, the account of the Union Agricultural Machinery Association in *Ekonomicheskaia zhizn'*, 11 June 1930.

party leadership to enhance the "fighting ability" of the apparatus: the leadership believed that in a revolutionary situation moderation was more dangerous than excess. It is not surprising, then, that the apparatus, guided mainly by urgent appeal, fell into "excessive administrative ecstasy." While the ecstasy may have reflected the responsiveness of the apparatus to the leadership's command, the apparatus could not cope with the economic crisis that had resulted from the administrative chaos.

At the third Leningrad *oblast'* conference in June 1930, one delegate, criticizing the disorganization caused by the reform of industrial management, declared with impatience and despair: "We cannot solve any questions in earnest."[121] In his speech of 30 August 1930, for which he was soon to be attacked, S. I. Syrtsov contended:

It was expected, you see, that the quality of the work of bureaucracies [*vedomstva*] would become better over the year. We have worked in the course of the year on improving the bureaucratic apparatus [*apparaty vedomstv*] by conducting purges and creating a number of organizations. Yet it has turned out as if the apparatus had come to work worse.[122]

Stalin and his associates regarded Syrtsov's contention as a criticism of the party line under the guise of an attack on the bureaucracy, always a convenient target.[123] Yet the summer crisis made the apparatus appear to them, too, to be faltering. Indeed, the summer and autumn of 1930 were a period of intense criticism of the economic administration, particularly Vesenkha and Gosplan.

In the summer of 1930 Vesenkha came under sharp attack by Rabkrin. At the sixteenth party congress, G. K. Ordzhonikidze, with the aid of the GPU, singled out Vesenkha as a target. His report, in marked contrast with the optimistic tone of other speeches, appears not to have been cleared with the Politbureau, because V. V. Kuibyshev, chairman of Vesenkha and member of the Politbureau, was taken off guard and devastated at the congress. Ordzhonikidze's intent to denounce Vesenkha and Kuibyshev also surprised S. M. Kirov, a candidate member of the Politbureau. Ordzhonikidze may well have cleared the attack with Stalin, but

---

[121] *Biulleten' 3-ei leningradskoi oblastnoi konferentsii VKP(b)*, 5:31.
[122] Syrtsov, *K novomu khoziaistvennomu godu*, p. 3.
[123] See, for example, *Za industrializatsiiu*, 31 October 1930 (V. S., "Novyi etap opportunizma").

apparently he took the initiative.[124] Ordzhonikidze adopted the line of criticism set by the Shakhty trial, alleging that it was the inadequate technical expertise and administrative incompetence of Communist managers that fostered "wrecking" by "bourgeois" specialists. He supported his condemnation of Vesenkha's industrial leadership by circulating to congress members materials prepared by the GPU in which arrested "bourgeois" specialists maintained one after another how inept Communist managers were as administrators.[125] If these contentions should not be taken at face value, clearly Rabkrin and the GPU succeeded in politically discrediting the Vesenkha leadership.

Gosplan too came under attack at the congress. Stalin, for example, rather proudly disparaged Gosplan:

It may be said that in altering the estimates of the Five-Year Plan so radically the Central Committee is violating the principle of planning and is discrediting the planning organizations. But only hopeless bureaucrats can talk like that. . . . For us the Five-Year Plan, like any other, is merely a plan adopted as a first approximation, which has to be made more precise, altered, and perfected in conformity with the experience gained in the localities, with the experience gained in carrying out the plan.[126]

Curiously enough, at the congress G. M. Krzhizhanovskii, then head of Gosplan, lavishly praised Ordzhonikidze for his criticism of managers as if to deflect blame from Gosplan: "And he [Ordzhonikidze] did well, because when the Bolshevik meets resistance, he can be guided by only one principle: unless you press, you won't get [anything]."[127]

In 1930 Rabkrin constantly intervened in the economic administration. One delegate aptly declared that the Central Control Commission and Rabkrin had "recently become more a punitive-planning organ [*bichuiushchii planovyi organ*] than a Rabkrin."[128] At the eleventh congress of the Ukrainian Communist Party held

---

[124] Fazin, *Tovarishch Sergo*, pp. 91–105; Kuibysheva et al., *Valerian Vladimirovich Kuibyshev*, pp. 300–2; Khavin, *U rulia industrii*, pp. 82–84. See also Fitzpatrick, "Ordzhonikidze's Takeover of Vesenkha," pp. 161–62.

[125] *Materialy k otchetu TsKK VKP(b)*. See also *XVI s˘ezd VKP(b)*, pp. 319–22, 377, 405, and Fitzpatrick, "Stalin and the Making of a New Elite," pp. 387–89.

[126] Stalin, *Sochineniia*, 12:346–47. Note that Syrtsov consistently criticized the planning agency for its failure to signal problems of planning. See his *O nashikh uspekhakh, nedostatkakh i zadachakh*, pp. 16–24, and *K novomu khoziaistvennomu godu*, pp. 3, 7, 10.

[127] *XVI s˘ezd VKP(b)*, p. 557.

[128] Ibid., p. 368.

shortly before the sixteenth (All-Union) party congress, M. M. Maiorov of the Ukraine's Rabkrin bluntly stated:

We don't want to substitute the leadership of the industrial organizations; we don't intend to replace Vesenkha's work at all. But now the nature of Rabkrin's work is such that we have sometimes to substitute for the leadership of this or that institution, for they are lagging behind, for they themselves are not in a position to cope with the tasks entrusted to them.[129]

The attack led in the summer and autumn to mass arrests of "bourgeois" and Menshevik specialists associated with Vesenkha, Gosplan, the State Bank, and the People's Commissariat of Trade. To name just a few prominent experts, on 13 July, V. G. Groman, an ex-Menshevik specialist at Gosplan who had played a central role in the compilation of the Five-Year Plan, was arrested; in mid-August, L. K. Ramzin, director of Vesenkha's Thermal Engineering Institute, and N. F. Charnovskii, deputy chairman of Vesenkha's Scientific Council of Engineering, both "bourgeois" experts, were arrested; on 20 August, L. B. Zalkind, an ex-Menshevik and director of the Statistics and Market Data Sector of the People's Commissariat of Trade; on 13 September, V. V. Sher, an ex-Menshevik and a member of the board of the State Bank, who, along with Piatakov, had drafted the credit reform; and 16 September, A. M. Ginzburg, an ex-Menshevik and a planning specialist at Vesenkha who, like Groman, played a promient role in the compilation of the Five-Year Plan.[130] This was a serious blow to those institutions responsible for industrialization. At a meeting with Gosplan officials on 6 October 1930, a former shock worker promoted to a position of responsibility enthusiastically urged the GPU to "help" Gosplan:

Wreckers have been sitting in the old Gosplan, and [even now] the leading staff of Gosplan is perhaps not very strong. Can Gosplan work by itself? I definitely think that it cannot work alone in any case; it needs to be helped by the GPU.[131]

[129] *XI z'izd KP(b)U*, p. 206.
[130] *Protsess "Prompartii,"* pp. 163, 206, and *Protsess kontrrevoliutsionnoi organizatsii men'shevikov*, p. 323. On 3 September 1930 the Soviet press reported the arrests of "leaders of counterrevolutionary organizations" including Kondrat'ev, Groman, A. K. Chaianov, N. N. Sukhanov, Ramzin, and V. A. Bazarov. For Kondrat'ev and Groman, see also "The Purge of Government Institutions," chap. 2, this volume. The careers of these economists are discussed in Jasny, *Soviet Economists of the Twenties*.
[131] *Planovoe khoziaistvo*, 1930, no. 9, p. 49.

Figure 6.1. The lightning spelling out GPU is striking a counterrevolutionary wrecker; at the bottom is Dem'ian Bednyi's poem praising the strike. From *Pravda*, 27 September 1930.

Until early 1931 the opinion reportedly persisted in the party leadership that there were more chances of the Five-Year Plan's being fulfilled with the GPU's tutelage than with the "present staff of Vesenkha."[132]

The GPU's "help" and "tutelage" culminated on 27 October 1930 with the press announcement that the GPU had discovered a "counterrevolutionary organization" aimed at the overthrow of Soviet power.[133] This so-called Industrial Party affair involved "bourgeois" experts in "almost all sections of USSR Gosplan and directorates of USSR Vesenkha."[134] In recent years the trial has attracted the attention of Western scholars,[135] but like other affairs, it is still shrouded in secrecy despite having been conducted openly. It is clear, however, that the defendants were held responsible for the summer economic crisis: they were accused of intentionally creating economic troubles such as shortages of metals and the disorganization of the supply system; moreover, they allegedly conspired with foreign powers, especially France, for military intervention that would have coincided with the economic crisis and helped them to topple the Bolshevik government.[136]

The trial reflected the highly charged political atmosphere of that time as much as the political leadership's temptation to find scapegoats. As economic problems mounted in 1929–30, the concept of "wrecking" ("economic counterrevolution") expanded uncontrollably. In November 1929 Krzhizhanovskii declared with emphasis: "*The state of managerial morass is already wrecking.*"[137] In February 1930 Kuibyshev maintained that there was a "direct link be-

---

[132] *Sotsialisticheskii vestnik,* 1931, no. 3 (9 February), p. 13.

[133] *Pravda,* 27 October 1930. The arrested Menshevik specialists were tried separately in March 1931. See *Protsess kontrrevoliutsionnoi organizatsii men'shevikov.*

[134] *Protsess "Prompartii,"* p. 10. The defendants included L. K. Ramzin, I. A. Kalinnikov (deputy chairman of Gosplan's production sector), N. F. Charnovskii, and S. V. Kupriianov (a textile specialist at Vesenkha).

[135] See, for example, Bailes, *Technology and Society under Lenin and Stalin,* chap. 4.

[136] *Protsess "Prompartii,"* passim, particularly pp. 31, 69, 78, 84, 105, 340–41, and 377. Interestingly enough, the defendants were accused of both "minimalist" and "maximalist" planning. Their technical and economic knowledge did favor lower plan targets than those of the ambitious Five-Year Plan. Yet they allegedly shifted their tactics in late 1929 and early 1930 from minimalism to maximalism. They found themselves committed to the fantastic tempos of some planners in Gosplan. Clearly that feeling was widespread among specialists: "I would rather stand for high tempos than sit [in jail] for slow tempos." (Quoted by Syrtsov in *Pervyi Moskovskii oblastnoi s˝ezd RK i KD,* p. 33.)

[137] *2 sessiia TsIK Soiuza SSR 5 sozyva,* 2:7.

Figure 6.2. Caricature of the Industrial Party: the claws of the Soviet Union are cutting off puppet wreckers from the French hand. From *Pravda*, 25 November 1930.

tween wrecking and the underfulfillment of plans."[138] Rabkrin resolved to consider "any opposition to the socialist rationalization [of production] wrecking."[139] In the summer and autumn of 1930 it was frequently declared that there "is almost no corner and no branch in the economy in which we have not found organized wrecking."[140] Ironically for Kuibyshev and Krzhizhanovskii, in the autumn of 1930 Vesenkha and Gosplan were attacked as centers of "wrecking."

---

[138] *Za industrializatsiiu,* 18 February 1930.
[139] *Rabota NK RKI SSSR ot V k VI Vsesoiuznomu s″ezdu Sovetov,* p. 15.
[140] XI z″izd KP(*b*)U, p. 301 (Lavrentii); Note also Kirov's similar statement in *Biulleten' 3-ei leningradskoi oblastnoi konferentsii VKP(b),* 6:12, and Krylenko's in *Sovetskaia iustitsiia,* no. 31 (20 November 1930), pp. 1–2. See also *Vrediteli piatiletki.*

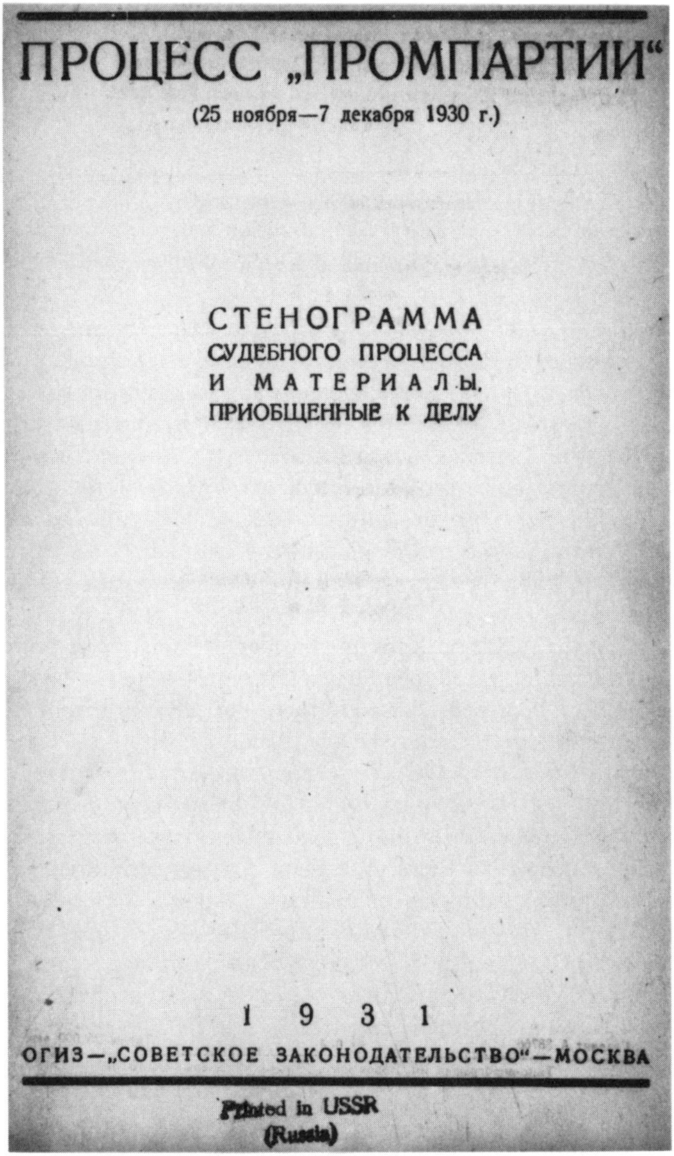

ПРОЦЕСС „ПРОМПАРТИИ"

(25 ноября—7 декабря 1930 г.)

СТЕНОГРАММА
СУДЕБНОГО ПРОЦЕССА
И МАТЕРИАЛ Ы,
ПРИОБЩЕННЫЕ К ДЕЛУ

1 9 3 1

ОГИЗ—„СОВЕТСКОЕ ЗАКОНОДАТЕЛЬСТВО"—МОСКВА

Printed in USSR
(Russia)

Figure 6.3. Title page of the court proceedings of the Industrial Party trial published shortly after the trial. From *Protsess "Prompartii," 25 noiabria– 7 dekabria 1930 g. Stenogramma sudebnogo protsessa i materialov, priob- shchennye k delu* (Moscow, 1930). Courtesy of the Library of Congress.

The announcement of the discovery of the Industrial Party made it difficult for Krzhizhanovskii to stay in Gosplan as its chairman. He wrote to the GPU chairman, V. R. Menzhinskii: "We are not supposed to tender a resignation. What to do then?" Menzhinskii responded:

All institutions are in the same situation – the People's Commissariats of Finance, Trade, Agriculture, Transport, etc., in a word, all the institutions, including the Central Statistical Administration and others, that give you figures. It is necessary to clench our teeth, select honest cadres, and keep working.

Nevertheless Krzhizhanovskii decided to leave Gosplan and reported to Stalin, who said: "In my opinion, you need not leave. But if you have decided to, don't leave altogether – at least keep your hat on the hanger in Gosplan."[141] On 10 November 1930 Krzhizhanovskii was removed from Gosplan, which Kuibyshev, relieved of Vesenkha's chairmanship, took over.[142] In December 1930 Molotov declared that the "former Gosplan" with its old specialists "now no longer exists" and that "we are creating a new Gosplan."[143] A new Vesenkha, too, was to be created. With Kuibyshev's departure, Ordzhonikidze moved over from Rabkrin.[144]

In 1930 the GPU and Rabkrin considered almost all institutions far from reliable, placed them under constant surveillance and pressure, and frequently intervened in their work. Rabkrin came close to substituting for the industrial and planning institutions. "Wrecking" may or may not have taken place. It appeared to the GPU and Rabkrin that irrespective of "wrecking" these institutions, if left alone, were unable to live up to their tasks. Hence in the summer and autumn of 1930 there took place a major reshuffling of the economic administration: In addition to that of Gosplan and Vesenkha, on 11 June M. L. Rukhimovich took over the People's Commissariat of Transport from Ia. E. Rudzutak; on 3 August A. S. Tsikhon succeeded the Rightist N. A. Uglanov as head of the Commissariat of Labor; on 18 October G. F. Grin'ko replaced L. P. Briukhanov at the People's Commissariat of Finance, and M. Kalmanovich succeeded Iu. L. Piatakov as president of the State

[141] Kartsev, *Krzhizhanovskii*, p. 339. Actually, the Central Statistical Administration had been closed down in late 1929. See chap. 2, note 30, this volume.

[142] *Za industrializatsiiu,* 11 November 1930.

[143] Molotov, *V bor'be za sotsializm,* p. 75.

[144] *Za industrializatsiiu,* 11 November 1930.

Bank; and on 19 December the chairman of the Council of People's Commissars, A. I. Rykov was replaced by Stalin's right hand, V. M. Molotov.[145]

The massive intervention of the GPU and Rabkrin in the economic administration resulted from the systematic chaos of the economy. The overambitious plans had already caused enormous strains in the economy as a whole. Theoretical optimism and actual difficulty, and the spontaneous upward revisions of the plans and economic disequilibrium, reinforced each other. The econony ran out of the control of the central economic administration. From 1928 on, administrative controls had replaced much of the spontaneous control of the market; in 1930 the market was almost eliminated. Ironically, however, the reforms of credit and industrial management, which were designed to strengthen central administrative control so as to replace fully the control of the market, resulted in the loss of central controls. In despair the political leadership resorted to massive police intervention.

The class-war policy of that time also mobilized workers' control from below by constantly keeping workers on the alert for "wrecking." The disorganization of industry, like many other problems, was seen by vigilant observers as a result of "wrecking."[146] Clearly, political manipulations were commonplace, as was understood by "some party members" in Eastern Siberia, one of whom was reported to contend: "In the transition to NEP we had created wrecking [charges], and after the elimination of NEP, wrecking again got to rear its head."[147] Police intervention, however, gained implicit support even from those who were the least likely to be manipulated. Stalin's political archenemies, Trotsky and his still irreconcilable supporters, accepted all the charges against the defendants in the Industrial Party trial, or in Trotsky's as in Stalin's view, "specialist wreckers . . . hired by foreign imperialists and émigré Russian *compradores.*"[148] An underground Trotskyist in Moscow, who,

---

[145] *Izvestiia TsIK SSSR*, 12 June, 6 August, 19 October, 20 December 1930.

[146] See, for example, the speech of a delegate named Kobrisev in *3 sessiia TsIK Soiuza SSR 5 sozyva*, 6:47.

[147] *I kraevaia konferentsiia VKP(b) Vostochno-sibirskogo kraia*, p. 221.

[148] *Biulleten' Oppozitsii*, nos. 17–18 (November–December 1930), p. 21. Those Trotskyists who had returned to the party in 1928–29 also accepted all the charges. See, for example, Radek, *Portraits and Pamphlets*, pp. 217–29. For Western accounts of the trial, see Lyons, *Assignment in Utopia*, pp. 37–79, and Mosley, "1930–1932," pp. 54–55.

like Trotsky himself, believed the charges against the Industrial Party, wrote to the Oppositionist journal published abroad that angry Soviet workers had demanded that the "wreckers" be sentenced to death, and that when the death sentences announced at the trials for the chief defendants were subsequently commuted to ten years' imprisonment, the workers could not understand the "pardon." Deeply impressed by their reaction to the "wreckers," this Oppositionist reported with excitement that "in the working class as a whole there still is genuine revolutionary enthusiasm."[149] Even forty years after the trial, V. V. Ermilov, who in 1930 was a worker at the Red Proletarian Factory in Moscow, recalled: "The anger and indignation of the workers [at the factory] condemning the traitors' acts have remained in my memory for life."[150]

The class-war concept almost a priori inclined Bolsheviks to attribute the economic problems to the "wrecking" of "class enemies." Moreover, Bolsheviks were more political fighters than economists, and therefore were more adroit in politics than in economics. They utilized workers' prejudice against the previously privileged groups at the expense of careful economic analysis of the problems.

[149] *Biulleten' Oppozitsii,* no. 19 (March 1931), p. 18.
[150] Ermilov, *Schast'e trudnykh dorog,* p. 133.

7

The troika and mass politics

The concept of one-man management fitted well into those of the credit and management reforms. These reforms relieved the factory of its "operative-commercial" functions and concentrated managerial attention on the "technical direction" and rationalization of production. The factory was now expected to work like a cog in the machine of a centrally planned economy, and its operation to become simpler and more routinized, making it unnecessary for outsiders to intervene in management. The new regime in the factory characterized by the peculiar combination of single managerial command and multiple controls over management was expected to ensure the orderly and harmonious functioning of the factory with the economic machine.

In 1930, however, the factory became a place "where all the defects of higher organs cross and meet one another in action."[1] The machine was creaking because the tempo had accelerated beyond its capacity, but the cog was expected to keep up with or even outpace the machine, an impossible task. More often than not, however, the cog managed to work rather at its own rate and independently of that of the machine, because the machine could not impose its pace: the administrative control of the center weakened and the unofficial power of the factory increased. Under these circumstances, managers found themselves alternating between two extremes of dictatorial and collective management. The GPU, the Procuracy, Rabkrin, the local party organ, and the party and trade union organizations in the factory, for their part, were compelled to intervene in management. One-man management was virtually abrogated. According to an acute American observer,

[1] *Problemy ekonomiki*, 1931, no. 3, p. 120.

There is plenty of authority and an abundance of responsibility, but at each and every industrial unit this authority is divided among four or five heads – the Party chief, labor-union chief, local plant director, Russian technical chief, Foreign technical chief, and the OGPU representative – each supreme in his own corner of the picture. Furthermore, for good measure, there is always the power of the Workers, in conference assembled, to approve or veto any particular local move on which they may wish to express their pleasure. All this is extremely democratic, but very damaging to industrial progress. No amount of earnest well-meant advice from the outside engineer to the effect that rapid industrial advance requires the same one-man leadership that functions in their army and their military affairs has yet registered, as far as one can discern. One-man authority is of course imcompatible with Soviet precept.[2]

It was not a military regime, as discussed in Chapter 3, that the party leadership sought to create in the factories. Single managerial command and multiple controls over command were assumed to be compatible. In the critical year of 1930, however, the managers appeared to the party leadership not to be in a position to mobilize all the resources available in the factories.

At the second Moscow *oblast'* conference of the party in June 1930, L. M. Kaganovich warned against the factory troika of the director, the party secretary, and the factory trade union committee chairman: " 'We [the troika] are the splendor and pride of the party and the revolution, but you [constantly] criticize us. . . .' Comrades, if we remain conceited, we won't get out of the difficulties for a long time." Appealing for the establishment of one-man management, he went on to say:

We know that now it's very hard to work, indeed very hard. We must not underestimate the difficulty. Every day *Pravda* lashes out at some director or other, some factory or other. The trade unions are also put under pressure, so are the party organizations. It's difficult for the director to work; it's difficult for the [party] cell to work; it's difficult for the factory committee to work; and it's difficult for the workers to work in production. . . . [People say:] "I stand for the general line [of the party]; I stand for the Central Committee; I am against the Right; but it's difficult to fulfill the industrial-financial plan; it's very hard to work, [because] I'm criticized on all sides," and whatnot. But it has to be understood, comrades, that capitalism has its own stimuli: it is lashed by competition and by the tides of capital from one branch to another. We don't have such stimuli. Our stimuli are socialist construction, aspirations for advance, the proletarian public, socialist competition, and self-criticism. And if you are true Leninist

---

[2] The Guy C. Riddle file in "American Engineers in Russia" (see Section I of the Bibliography).

Bolsheviks, then, however difficult it may be, don't retreat. Plans are taut, no doubt about it. But history has given us no exits but taut plans.[3]

Kaganovich, following Stalin, maintained that these artificial stimuli, in place of the built-in stimuli of capitalism, had to become "permanently operating forces" in the Soviet Union. Just as the capitalist economy with its anarchic competition in the market was seen by the Bolsheviks as costly and irrational, so the planned economy with its artificial stimuli appeared to the capitalists to be costly and irrational. As market relations disappeared and the planned economy plunged into crisis in 1930, the political leadership used these artificial stimuli, along with the violent attack on nonparty specialists, as a means to overcome the economic crisis. The leadership appeared to insist that the problem of resource constraints could be solved by deploying mass politics.

The manager

In 1930, as Kaganovich emphasized, it was very difficult for managers to work. Indeed, they had every reason to chafe at unrealistically ambitious plan targets and chaotic administrative arrangements. To them, one-man management meant one-man responsibility without one-man control.

As the plans were constantly revised upward, managers understandably put up considerable resistance. At the sixth plenum of Vesenkha in October 1929, almost all managers declared that the plans devised by Gosplan were far beyond their means and demanded more resources.[4] This attitude made the party leadership, Rabkrin, and the planners suspect all the more that the managers hid the real capacities of their plants.

The case of the Putilov Factory in Leningrad is illustrative. The government eventually succeeded in raising the factory's plan target of tractor production dramatically from 3,050 for 1928/29 to 12,000 for 1929/30 and 25,000 for 1930/31, but only after overcoming persistent resistance on the part of the factory. At a July 1928 session of Vesenkha, the director, V. F. Grachev, an old Bol-

[3] *Pravda,* 8 June 1930.
[4] *TPG,* 11 and 12 October 1929. Note especially the speech of G. Lomov, head of the Donbas Coal Trust.

shevik who during the civil war had led the food detachments in the Ukraine and Siberia, and the technical director, V. M. Sablin, openly opposed the plan of 2,500 Fordson tractors for 1928/29.[5] Rabkrin, however, pushed the target to 3,000, which met "colossal resistance" from the factory; Rabkrin therefore stationed its "detachment' in the factory to "show management how to work."[6] The factory managed to fulfill the plan by turning out 3,050 tractors.

In July 1929 a government commission headed by I. Kossior of Vesenkha set the 1929/30 plan target of the factory at 10,000, which both Grachev and Sablin opposed again. In November 1929 Kuibyshev went to the factory to give a speech at a production conference in the tractor shop, and raised the target to 12,000.[7] At about the same time, S. M. Kirov, head of the Leningrad party organizations, visited the factory and pressed for the same target:

Let's assume that Vasilii Fedorovich Grachev is wrong, although he is the director. He was promoted from among ordinary Putilov workers. And the following is what Viktor Matveevich Sablin, an experienced engineer who is respected in the factory, and Ivanov, an engineer and the shop manager of the tractor department, say: [the plan] is technically impossible.

Kirov went on to say: "What if we approach the issue in a Communist way?" Awkward silence ensued. Then, to the surprise of management, some workers declared with one voice: "Yes, we have to. Let's produce [12,000]."[8] One is tempted to think that this drama had been prearranged. Whatever the case, management was compelled to shoulder the ambitious target.

In the meantime, Vesenkha's Chief Engineering Administration sent Letter No. 768/3143 to the Putilov Factory. The letter stated that despite the rumor of a decision taken by the factory concerning the target of 12,000 tractors, the Chief Engineering Administration, in view of the acute shortages of spare parts, ordered a plan of 10,000 tractors and spare parts amounting in value to 2,500 tractors. On 3 January 1930 Grachev, encouraged by the letter, categori-

[5] *Istoriia Kirovskogo zavoda*, pp. 245 and 287.
[6] See the report of Ia. Kh. Peters (a Rabkrin representative) to the sixth Transcaucasian party congress in *Zaria Vostoka*, 8 June 1930.
[7] *Leningradskaia pravda*, 21 January 1930. According to Ordzhonikidze's report of 31 December 1929, the target of 12,000 was decided by the Politbureau. See *Deiatel'nost' organov partiino-gosudarstvennogo kontrolia po sovershenstvovaniiu gosudarstvennogo apparata*, p. 65.
[8] Krasnikov, *S. M. Kirov v Leningrade*, p. 62.

cally stated to the government commission and to the factory trade union committee that no decision had been made on the plan of 12,000 tractors and that the factory was working to produce the planned 10,000. Six days later, Kuibyshev responded by sending a telegram ordering the production of 12,000 tractors for 1929/30.[9]

According to a press report, Grachev then "appealed over the head of the factory party organization to the masses of workers" against the "tempos beyond the strength" of the factory: on 31 January a production meeting was held in the factory; the party secretary and the party organizer of agitation and propaganda were not notified of the meeting. There the government commission gave a detailed report, but Grachev, Arkhipov (chairman of the factory trade union committee), Borkov (chairman of the production commission led by the factory trade union committee), and others opposed the plan of 12,000 tractors; only Lysakov (secretary of the Komsomol committee) and Vukolov (secretary of the party cell of the tractor shop) did not oppose it. Of 400 workers present at the meeting, only 18 voted for the proposal of the government commission (12,000 tractors).[10] This opposition invited the intervention of the alarmed Central Committee.[11] A production meeting was reconvened shortly thereafter to approve the government proposal.[12]

Production lagged behind the unrealistically high target. In July 1930 the Putilov Factory fulfilled only 57.7 percent of the monthly plan; in August, a time of overall economic crisis, the factory reportedly produced only fifteen tractors.[13] As early as June 1930 the technical director, Sablin, was arrested by the GPU as a "wrecker"; Grachev was accused of having fallen under the "influence of the wrecker," and on 1 October, at the beginning of a new economic year, he was removed from his post.[14] Summing up the party leader-

[9] *Leningradskaia pravda,* 6 January 1931 (V. Grachev, "Pis'mo v redaktsiiu") and 21 January 1930.
[10] *Za industrializatsiiu,* 19 February 1930.
[11] See Kirov's speech in *Biulleten' 3-ei leningradskoi oblastnoi konferentsii VKP(b),* 6:13. According to Ordzhonikidze, Stalin personally intervened in the matter. See *XVI s˝ezd VKP(b),* p. 320.
[12] *Za industrializatsiiu,* 19 February 1930.
[13] See the report in *Za industrializatsiiu,* 26 August 1930, which obviously provides incomplete data.
[14] *Biulleten' 3-ei leningradskoi oblastnoi konferentsii VKP(b),* 6:13, 16, and 10:58; Krasnikov, *Sergei Mironovich Kirov,* p. 151; and *XVI s˝ezd VKP(b),* pp. 320, 332–33. See also *Protsess "Prompartii,"* p. 337.

ship's struggle with the managers, Kirov declared at the third Leningrad *oblast'* conference of the party in June 1930: "In a number of factories we had to impose by force [ambitious] programs, against which stood up not only technical personnel but also Communist managers, and, in some factories, the factory committee and the party bureau."[15]

In 1930 the managerial inclination toward lower plan targets led the party leadership to launch the so-called counterplan campaign, a campaign for mass mobilization to push upward the plan targets of the factories. Rabkrin aptly characterized the campaign whose aim it was to remove those managers "who suffer from tempophobia, from the inclination to retreat in face of difficulties, and from talks about 'objective conditions.' "[16]

The acceleration of the construction plan of the Stalingrad Tractor Plant is a good example of a counterplan. During his business trip to the United States in the spring of 1930, the director of the plant, V. I. Ivanov, was surprised to read in the Soviet press that the plant was rescheduled to start operations three months earlier (i.e., in June 1930) than previously planned. He wrote a "very strong letter" to the plant to obtain "[even] a few weeks of grace." His attempt failed. In the barely equipped foundry shop, for example, one "enthusiast" solemnly promised in the name of workers and employees that the plant could be completed on time. Management had to give way silently to the "maelstrom."[17]

Some managers and engineers like Grachev and Sablin did resist the maelstrom, however. They even mobilized workers against the pressure of the center; others feared that workers' participation in planning encroached on managerial authority, and also that the constant upward revisions of plan targets would only add chaos to the already chaotic administrative arrangements. In the Sickle and Hammer Factory, for example, an engineer named Shtein opposed workers' participation in the discussion of control figures because, he was quoted as saying, the workers "will mess them up."[18] A shop manager in the Kuznetsk Plant named Oleinikov opposed

[15] *Biulleten' 3-ei leningradskoi oblastnoi konferentsii VKP(b)*, 6:12.
[16] See editorial in *Za ratsionalizatsiiu*, 1930, nos. 8–9, p. 7. For attacks on managers' inclination toward easy plans, see also the editorial in *Za industrializatsiiu*, 17 September 1930.
[17] Galin, *Vsegda za mechtoi*, pp. 61–62.
[18] *Bol'shevik*, 1930, nos. 15–16, p. 22 (A. Kapustin, "Za vstrechnyi promfinplan").

workers' counterplans and was expelled from the party.[19] Even the higher industrial authorities showed considerable dismay at the movement. On 26 June 1930 the Russian Republic's Vesenkha issued an order signed by its vice-chairman Ivanov directing the managers not to put preliminary plans forward for discussion in the factories because, the order stated, it could bring confusion into planning. On 2 July the Moscow *oblast'* council of national economy suggested that "at this stage the control figures not be subjected to wide discussions of workers."[20]

Managers, convinced though they were of the impossibility of fulfilling the unrealistic plans, were often forced to admit that the plans were realistic and feasible. They publicly stated that they would fulfill the plans, while privately they complained that they would not be able to cope with the tasks. They therefore were seen by the center as "double-dealers."[21] In his speech on 30 August 1930, S. I. Syrtsov warned against the counterplan movement: managers allowed impossible plans to be imposed upon themselves because of their "tail-endism" and "lack of a significant grain of civil courage." This, according to Syrtsov, only led to "social depravity" and "hypocrisy."[22]

Not only did the counterplan movement exert pressure on managers; socialist competition and the shock movement continued to exert pressure on managers on a daily basis. (In fact, the counterplan movement was said to be a new form of socialist competition, a competition for higher plan targets.) The hectic tempos imposed upon the factories and the chaotic administrative arrangements caused by the credit and management reforms combined to aggravate managerial disorganization. Management became increasingly vulnerable to workers' criticism of shortages of raw materials, fuel, and other prerequisites of production, stoppages of electricity, sloppy norm setting, and a host of other managerial shortcomings.

From late 1929 on, the managerial chaos and disorganization often pushed some shock workers to eliminate managerial authority on the shop floor. Convinced that they could not expect help from management, they sought to manage the shop floor on their own.

[19] *Kuznetskstroi*, p. 95.
[20] *Pravda*, 30 July, 16 August 1930.
[21] See, for example, *I-oe mezhkraevoe soveshchanie Obl. KK-RKI Urala, Sibiri, Bashkirii i Kazakhstana po Uralo-Kuzbassu*, p. 86.
[22] Syrtsov, *K novomu khoziaistvennomu godu*, p. 9.

Thus, they came to take on what was called unconditionally abnormal production autonomy (*proizvodstvennyi avtonomizm*), constituting a "state within a state," an "autonomous, self-management production unit."[23] The majority of shock workers elected their brigadier (elder) or even a collective leadership (soviet) in explicit challenge to one-man management. In 1930 as many as 61 percent of Leningrad shock brigades elected their "managerial organ."[24] Shock workers were often said to be "more managers than managers themselves were."[25] In the Donbas and the Urals, managers' inability to meet workers' demands gave rise to what was called "production syndicalism," which was described as "a by-product of competition."[26] The press attacked those workers who were allegedly "illiterate" enough to justify the elimination of one-man management in shock brigades by referring to the "withering away of the state."[27]

The impact of one-man management was hardly ever felt on the shop floor. The problem was compounded by the fact that managers lost much control over the dynamics of wages. In 1929–30, the collective agreements underwent a fundamental transformation from unilateral obligations imposed upon management to bilateral obligations for both labor and management; and the most important article, wage setting, taken out of the collective agreements, was centrally planned.[28] This measure, leaving little room for bargaining, was expected to strengthen mangerial power with relation to labor. Yet on the shop floor wage-leveling trends strengthened spontaneously and out of managerial control.[29] Money wages did

---

[23] *Trud*, 16 November 1929.

[24] *Statistika i narodnoe khoziaistvo*, vyp. 4–5 (1930), p. 11 (Ia. Maletskii, "Sotssorev-novanie i udarnichestvo leningradskikh proletariev"). For a slightly different figure (62.1%), see *Na fronte industrializatsii*, 1930, no. 11 (7 June), p. 9.

[25] See, for example, Bakhtamov, *Kuznetskstroi*, p. 20.

[26] *Trud*, 16 November 1929. See also *Partiinoe stroitel'stvo*, 1929, no. 2 (December), p. 19.

[27] *Vecherniaia Moskva*, 6 March 1930. In a similar vein, M. Gegechkori, a member of the central committee of the Soviet employees' union, contended that the power of the director "dissolved" in the new attitude of workers (i.e., the shock movement), and that one-man management would become unnecessary. He came under sharp attack and criticized himself. *Nasha gazeta*, 21, 28 September, 2, 4, 8, 16 October 1929.

[28] See particularly the model collective agreement worked out by Vesenkha and the All-Union Central Council of Trade Unions for 1931 in *Trud*, 13 November 1930.

[29] See "Egalitarianism and the Exodus of Skilled Workers," chap. 9, this book.

not provide strong incentives, in any case, and rationing was out of managerial jurisdiction.[30]

Faced with the collapse of authority, managers often went, unwittingly or not, to extremes of dictatorial and collective management.[31] Often the two were found amalgamated in the same manager. The director of the Stalingrad Tractor Plant, V. I. Ivanov, for example, at times found himself behaving like a dictator:

The conveyor had run out of parts. Fitters started smoking. . . . As usual, Ivanov appeared abruptly.
—Where's the brigadier? Why are you smoking?
—But what can we do if there are no parts?
Ivanov flared up, started swearing rudely at them, and in the heat of the argument declared to the brigadier that only counterrevolutionaries could act as he did. The workers were strongly offended and, in turn, shouted at Ivanov. At the end of the argument, Ivanov declared to the brigadier:
—You're fired. Report to the personnel office.[32]

At other times Ivanov would take refuge in the factory trade union committee. At a Komsomol meeting in the factory, he was asked:

When are we going to work properly? When will parts be available? When will food supplies and diet improve? Ivanov wouldn't answer.
—Here is Plotnikov, the secretary of the factory committee. He will convey these questions to me.
He declared thus and left the meeting, saying that he had no time [to answer the questions].[33]

As the discussion between Ia. A. Iakovlev and S. P. Birman analyzed in Chapter 2 showed, the party leadership had all along apprehended the two extreme forms of management. Concerned though it was about the collapse of managerial authority on the shop floor,

[30] Ration books were issued by cooperatives until 1931, when the local Soviet executive committees took over (Neiman, *Vnutrenniaia torgovlia SSSR*, p. 176). In late 1932, workers' closed cooperatives were placed under managerial jurisdiction in an attempt to strengthen managerial control over workers.

[31] See numerous reports on this in *Pravda*, 12 September 1929; *Inzhenernyi rabotnik*, 1930, nos. 5–6, p. 4; *Rabochaia gazeta*, 27 February and 26 March 1930; *XI z'izd KP(b)U*, pp. 432, 667, 706; *Izvestiia Stalingradskogo okrkoma VKP(b)*, 1930, nos. 7–8, p. 19; *Izvestiia Nizhegorodskogo kraevogo komiteta VKP(b)*, 1930, nos. 14–15, pp. 4–5.

[32] *Liudi Stalingradskogo traktornogo*, p. 86. For Ivanov, see Tepliakov, *Operatsiiu nachnem na rassvete*. Similarly, in February 1930 Syrtsov condemned managers' indiscriminate "repression." In a workshop employing 2,000 workers, for example, 1,800 received reprimands in one month. Syrtsov, *O nashikh uspekhakh, nedostatkakh i zadachakh*, pp. 11–12.

[33] *Liudi Stalingradskogo traktornogo*, pp. 197–98.

the party leadership did not tolerate these forms of management. Again, the case of the Stalingrad Tractor Plant may illustrate the issue of managerial accountability. The director Ivanov and the party and union organizations, driven as they were by the counter-plan movement, felt obliged to put the new factory into operation by June 1930 when the sixteenth party congress was to convene, in order to celebrate the congress. In June 1930 the factory was far from ready to start operating the conveyors: much of the equipment needed had not yet arrived. The head of the mechanical-assembly shop declared that it could not produce tractor frames, so it was decided to manufacture by hand one frame a day. The factory thus embarked on production before it was ready. On the first day, 17 June 1930, it produced only one tractor. The machine, dedicated to the congress and widley proclaimed as the first tractor assembled on a Soviet conveyor, was actually a handmade "dummy."[34] Naturally, the factory was immediately in deep trouble. In his candid speech on 30 August 1930, Syrtsov openly attacked the plant for "eyewash"(*ochkovtiratel'stvo*) and "deception" (*obman*), calling the fake tractor a "Potemkin village."[35] Syrtsov was shortly to be condemned for his frank criticism. Yet before the open attack on Syrtsov began, the factory's director, Ivanov, was dismissed in October 1930.[36]

This story concerning Ivanov is very indicative of the difficult conditions under which managers had to work. Ivanov was shocked by the acceleration of the construction plan forced from below (perhaps from above as well). Thus he felt obliged to start operations hastily. Once the plant got under way, moreover, a host of problems led him at times to behave like a dictator and at other times to seek refuge in the troika. His management appeared to the party leadership to be poor indeed.

Poor management often invited police intervention. In the tense political environment of the time, accidental errors and technical failures were judged by the police to be deliberate "wrecking." The GPU and its agents closely watched the factories.[37] At the Kharkov

[34] See Peshkin, *Dve zhizni Stalingradskogo traktornogo*, p. 30, and *Liudi Stalingradskogo traktornogo*, pp. 323–35.

[35] Syrtsov, *K novomu khoziaistvennomu godu*, p. 12.

[36] *Istoriia zavodov*, p. 113.

[37] See, for example, WKP 150, which contains numerous GPU reports on factories in Smolensk.

Figure 7.1. The first tractor produced at the Stalingrad Tractor Plant. From Iu. Zhukov, *Liudi 30-kh godov* (Moscow, 1966).

Locomotive Plant, for instance, the head of the factory GPU (known to us only as Aleksandrov) "constantly attended the *partkom* [party committee] conferences, the workshop meetings, and also dropped in at the editorial office [of the factory newspaper]." On such occasions, Aleksandrov asked the young editor and the wrecker hunter Kopelev "pointed questions" and gave "pointed advice":

Now, take your article "Knuckleheads or Wreckers?" A bit too sharp-toothed, brother. You haven't figured out the situation, boys. The master craftsman hasn't been there long; he was appointed foreman less than a month ago. But you jump on him right away – wham! "Knuckleheaded wrecker!" You ought to be giving him some encouragement. As regards waste and defects in the foundry – that's a more serious matter. You have to look into it a bit closer. Who are the worker reporters there? Are they reliable? The cracks in the chrome nickel casts might not be accidental. Maybe somebody is playing tricks with the composition or the casting or the method of pouring. . . . Find out all the details. . . . Every Communist, every Komsomolets, should be a Chekist.[38]

[38] Kopelev, *The Education of a True Believer*, p. 201. GPU agents were often referred to as "Chekists," after the Cheka, the predecessor of the GPU.

In the Southern Steel Trust technical failures prompted vigilant workers to tip off the GPU.[39] In the Glukhovka Textile Factory near Moscow, which in 1930 employed 11,000 workers (of whom 1,000 were party members), "wrecking" was reported to occur constantly:

In July [1929] a wire attached to the brush of a chuck by some "experienced hand" caused a short circuit in a 175-horsepower motor. In August there occurred an accident with a 250-horsepower motor because of unskilled treatment and bad maintenance. In September a 48-horsepower motor caught fire; when the motor was cleansed of burning dust, two military cartridges were found. They were put in on purpose. . . . On 16 September a transformer broke down after working for only a month after repair. . . . In November there were three fires. Metal plates and plugs had been put into fire hydrants. In the same month in the bleaching-dyeing shop, attempts were made to spoil a hoist. In December a 30-horsepower motor caught fire. In January there occurred in the spinning shop a fire that was clearly arson.[40]

These incidents may or may not have been deliberate "wrecking." Whatever the case, they often severely compromised the director's administrative and technical leadership and invited police intervention. There were instances in transport factories in which the Procuracy went so far as to dictate "recipes for making metals so that the axle would not break down."[41]

Yet some managers also sought to take advantage of "wrecking" to shift responsibility. In an organizational conference of the Central Committee in early 1930, a "responsible organizer" of the committee complained about the managers, who, claiming that it would take years to correct "wrecking," reduced every problem to "wrecking." When motors were installed in a metal factory in Tula, it turned out that they did not work at all. They had to be reinstalled at the cost of 100,000 rubles. The factory claimed that it was wrecking, but the organizer of the Central Committee stated bluntly: "Not wrecking, but simple mismanagement."[42]

This statement of the party organizer may indicate that much of "wrecking" elsewhere was also actually simple mismanagement.

[39] *Revoliutsiia i kul'tura*, 1929, no. 12, p. 9 (L. Cherniavskii, "Svet i teni sotsialisticheskogo sorevnovaniia").
[40] *Sputnik kommunista*, 1930, no. 2, pp. 28–29.
[41] *Organy iustitsii na novom etape*, p. 68.
[42] *Partinoe stroitel'stvo*, 1930, nos. 7–8, p. 59 ("Dnevnik orgsoveshchaaniia TsK VKP(b)").

Whatever the case, the party leadership utilized the accusation to strike home the message that Communist managers' leadership was seriously flawed. As early as August 1929 Syrtsov maintained that "the lesson of the Shakhty affair was lost on many [managers]," who could "not understand their mistakes and continued obstinately to hold their stance, assuring that everything is fine with them."[43] In his speech quoted early in the present chapter, Kaganovich bluntly declared: "[Directors] are the most honest proletarians working from morning till night. But what can you do if their [technical] knowledge is not sufficient?"[44] Again and again party leaders warned against what appeared to them to be the most honest proletarians' negligent attitudes toward technical expertise. At the sixteenth party congress in June–July 1930, Stalin emphasized that the task of reconstructing the entire technical basis of the national economy called for "new and more experienced cadres, capable of matching the new technology and of developing it further."[45]

Stalin's speech was yet another strong warning against Communist managers. "Comrade Shatunovskii,"[46] however, surprised as he was to hear Stalin say that "the new managerial cadres should be technically more experienced than the old," wrote to Stalin for clarification. Stalin responded in August 1930:

Is it not true that in our country our old managerial cadres were trained during the restoration period, the period when the old and technically backward factories were working to capacity, and consequently did not afford much technical experience? Is it not true that in the period of reconstruction, when new, modern technical equipment is being introduced, the old managerial cadres have to be retrained in the new methods, not infrequently giving way to new, more qualified technical cadres? Will you really deny that the old managerial cadres, who were trained in working the old factories to capacity or restarting them, frequently prove to be quite unable to cope not only with the new machinery but also with our new tempos?[47]

There was no shortage of evidence to support Stalin's contention. In May 1930 a commission of the Steel Association, having investi-

---

[43] *Pravda*, 5 August 1929.
[44] Ibid., 8 June 1930.
[45] Stalin, *Sochineniia*, 12:301.
[46] Comrade Shatunovskii seems to be Ia. M. Shatunovskii. In 1930 he worked in the Planning Department in the People's Commissariat of Transport and on the Standing Commission on Standardization in Gosplan. He had belonged to the Right Opposition. I owe this information to William Chase. See also Stalin, *Sochineniia*, 11:270, 281.
[47] Ibid., 13:18–19.

gated the metallurgical factories in the Urals, reported with a mix-
ture of surprise and despair that it had "discovered no America. . . .
We had to teach factory personnel the most elemental truths."[48]
Looking back at the so-called Industral Party trial in the aftermath
of the summer economic crisis, Stalin maintained in February 1931
that the trial had been a "second warning" (following the Shakhty
trial) to Communist managers and that "we shall not get it [one-
man management] until we have mastered technology."[49] In the
meantime, police intervention and mass politics seemed all the more
attractive to the party leadership.

The party and trade unions

At the sixteenth party congress, G. K. Ordzhonikidze repeatedly
emphasized that one-man management did not diminish the role of
the party and trade unions. He paid special tribute to the party
organizations: "Our cells in the factories and their secretaries are as
dear to us as the directors are." (This remark provoked cries from
the audience: "Quite right.") Citing a passage from the September
1929 Central Committee resolution on one-man management to
the effect that the troika must facilitate the "exposition of all production capacities of the factory in order to establish the higher
tasks of a production program," Ordzhonikidze went on to say:

> What did comrade Semichkin, secretary of the cell of the Stalin Metal
> Factory in Leningrad, do? He carried out precisely this part of the Central
> Committee's resolution on one-man management. As soon as we showed
> up in the factory, he came up to us and announced: in the factory there are
> such and such [production] potentials, and if such and such obstacles are
> removed, we will be able to double the program. . . . It is necessary to
> encourage in every possible way such an initiative of our party cells.[50]

Ordzhonikidze quoted Semichkin's initiative as an example of
checking managerial bureaucratism and conservatism in order to
mobilize all the available resources. A triple bloc would have made
such an initiative impossible. Ordzhonikidze suggested that this
kind of control over management was an indispensable mechanism

---

[48] *Za industrializatsiiu*, 20 May 1930.
[49] Stalin, *Sochineniia*, 13:37–38.
[50] *XVI s˵ezd VKP(b)*, p. 405. For P. P. Semichkin (Semiachkin)'s account, see
Neizvedannymi putiami, pp. 187–91.

of a system devoid of the spontaneous control of the market. Yet if Semichkin had removed (or sought to remove) the obstacles independently rather than mobilize the workers to press management for their removal, he would have abrogated one-man management and rendered management unaccountable.

Many did annul or reject one-man management, however. Numerous incidents were reported in which the party and union organizations, regarding one-man management as a "disgrace," constantly intervened in management, especially in the selection of personnel and the transfer of workers from one job to another in accordance with production needs.[51] At a Zamoskvorech'e *raion* party meeting in Moscow in October 1929, the party secretary, Riabov, assured the audience that the party cells would not "lose face" (*obezlichen*) because of one-man management. Nonetheless cries of "They will!" rang out.[52] Prozherenkov, chairman of the factory committee of the K. Marx Factory in Leningrad, appealed to the general meeting of workers to vote against one-man management.[53] Some workers regarded one-man management as a return to the old regime and a capitulation to the specialists in managerial positions.[54] Workers in the Tomskii Factory in Stalino considered one-man management the "enslavement of the working class," even after as many as 118 meetings were held to discuss it.[55]

The reaction against one-man management may have been due in part to the emphasis the party leadership laid on workers' participation in management. In fact, the September 1929 resolution on one-man management recommended that the chairman of the production conference be appointed, on an experimental basis, assistant to

[51] *Leningradskaia pravda*, 15 March 1930; *Za industrializatsiiu Sibiri*. 1930, no. 2, p. 6; *Izvestiia Nizhegorodskogo Kraevogo komiteta VKP(b)*, 1930, nos. 4–5, p. 18, nos. 14–15, pp. 5–6.

[52] *Pravda*, 31 October 1929. For similar cases, ibid., 2 November 1929. In October 1929 in factory meetings in Moscow, D. I. Matveev, the Rightist and former secretary of the Komsomol Central Committee, criticized one-man management as "belittling the meaning and the role" of the party and union organizations and as "enslaving the working class." *Rabochaia Moskva*, 5, 15 October, and *Pravda*, 31 October 1929.

[53] Etchin, *O edinonachalii*, p. 15.

[54] See, for example, *Rabochaia gazeta*, 16 November 1929; *Sputnik kommunista*, 1929, no. 20, p. 36; *Partiinoe stroitel'stvo*, 1930, no. 2, p. 57; *Izvestiia Severo-Kavkazskogo Kraevogo komiteta VKP(b)*, 1930, no. 6, pp. 10–11, nos. 11–12, p. 7; *Izvestiia Stalingradskogo okrkoma VKP(b)*, 1930, nos. 7–8, pp. 16–17. See also Lampert, *The Technical Intelligentsia and the Soviet State*, pp. 113–14.

[55] *Za industrializatsiiu*, 7 February 1930.

the director exclusively in charge of realizing the resolutions of the production conference as well as workers' suggestions.[56] At the sixteenth party congress, both Kuibyshev of Vesenkha and Shvernik of the All-Union Central Council of Trade Unions maintained that this experiment had succeeded in encouraging workers' production initiative, socialist competition, and the shock movement.[57]

No doubt, however, this experiment caused confusion among the troika. In the Glukhovka Textile Factory near Moscow, for example, there developed a serious controversy about a trivial question: where the newly appointed assistant to the director should sit in a meeting – next to the director or with the factory trade union committee.[58] On 3 January 1931, Vesenkha's presidium under the new chairman, Ordzhonikidze, issued an order against using workers' participation in management as a way of buck-passing:

It has to be considered an absolutely wrong understanding of the task of drawing workers to participate in the management of production that many managers seek to hide behind workers' brigades and to shift the responsibility for production and construction from themselves. Vesenkha considers absolutely abnormal the situation in which [workers'] brigades travel around the country as solicitors and pushers and in which, worse still, managers report to leading [party and government] agencies [for help], accompanied by brigades, instead of taking necessary measures for securing production and answering for their own actions.[59]

This sort of relationship may well have provided the workers with a sense of power, but to Ordzhonikidze it was little more than a usurpation of managerial responsibility. Certainly this order may well have reflected Ordzhonikidze's new position as chairman of Vesenkha, which must have inclined him to emphasize managerial authority rather than control over management. Yet it appears that he was equally concerned with managerial accountability.

The relationship within the troika was further complicated by the weak authority of foremen on the shop floor. They had since the revolution been stripped of some vital discretionary powers. For instance, before 1933 they had no final say in setting output quotas and wage rates on the grounds that, pressed by workers, the fore-

[56] *KPSS v rezoliutsiiakh*, 4:315.

[57] *XVI s˝ezd VKP(b)*, pp. 503, 654–55.

[58] *Sputnik kommunista*, 1930, no. 2, p. 30. For a similar case, see, for example, *Za industrializatsiiu*, 9 February 1930.

[59] Cited in Ginzburg, *O proshlom – dlia buduschego*, p. 150. For the use of shock brigades as pushers, see "Tolkachi" in *Za industrializatsiiu*, 27 July 1930.

men "might have changed them in the workplace."[60] This problem was also part of a larger "crisis of foremen": when production became modernized and managerial-technical functions accordingly specialized, it was increasingly difficult for the still traditional, "universalistic" foreman to manage the shop floor.[61] The shock movement and socialist competition, as discussed earlier, often deprived foremen of their authority, giving rise to "production syndicalism." In early 1931 it was reported from the Donbas coal mines that there was "not a trace of one-man management underground": the *desiatniki* (roughly the equivalent of assistant foremen) could not enforce discipline on those workers who had "grown up with them."[62] In fact, many foremen were said not to want one-man management.[63] Nor did the party leadership grant unconditional one-man management to foremen.[64] The hierarchy of sole managerial command hardly ever existed on the shop floor. The authority of the foreman was therefore constantly undermined by the party and union organizations.

This configuration of the troika on the shop floor perplexed American engineers who worked in the Soviet Union at the time. According to L. D. Anderson, who from 1930 to 1933 worked in Leningrad, Moscow, the Urals, Kharkov, and other parts of the Soviet Union,

the most outstanding aspects of our relationship with administrative officials lay in the difficulty in finding any one who had really authoritative power. Almost invariably it was necessary to deal with several individuals to get the simplest matter settled. Rarely would any one person seem to have any authority. All questions were settled by conference of several persons, even to the simplest of technical details. There appeared to be quite obvious effort to avoid any personal responsibility, giving the impression that most persons feared to assume any such.[65]

[60] Ordzhonikidze, *Stat'i i rechi*, pp. 29–30, and *XVII konferentsiia VKP(b)*, p. 29.
[61] *Sputnik agitatora dlia goroda*, 1928, no. 18 (September), pp. 39–40, and *Za povyshenie kvalifikatsii tekhnicheskikh i khoziaistvennykh kadrov promyshlennosti*, 1930, no. 1, p. 42. This crisis was not confined to Soviet industry, but was seen in American industry as well. See Granick, *Red Executive*, pp. 7 and 277–83.
[62] *Za industrializatsiiu*, 25 January 1931. According to one survey, as of 1 October 1929, 72.1% of the foremen were former workers or children of workers (but only 33.5% were party members). *Inzhenerno-tekhnicheskie kadry promyshlennosti*, p. 9, and Beilin, *Kadry spetsialistov v SSSR*, pp. 122 and 130.
[63] See, for example, *Pervaia Vsesoiuznaia konferentsiia rabotnikov sotsialisticheskoi promyshlennosti*, pp. 29, 81–82, 156, 223.
[64] At that time, the party leadership did not emphasize foremen's one-man management, although it was quite aware of their lack of authority.
[65] The L. D. A. Anderson file in "American Engineers in Russia."

Leon M. Banks, who had worked in the Ridder mines in Kazakhstan from June 1930 to June 1931, reported:

> No one of these [the troika's three bodies] had complete authority and any one could countermand the orders or instructions of the others. . . .
>
> As far as control went it was noticeable by its absence. No one had any control. Orders were given from many sources, too many, but any workman could comply or refuse as he chose.[66]

Management appeared neither authoritative nor accountable.

In the summer economic crisis the party and union organizations, like the GPU, Rabkrin, and the Procuracy, found themselves compelled to "aid" management. The case of the Red Sormovo Factory in Nizhegorod, which in August 1930 was widely publicized in *Pravda,* is illustrative.[67] In the summer of 1930, Red Sormovo, like many other factories, fell far short of the plan targets for locomotives, wagons, and other commodities. The Central Committee, the Central Control Commission, and Rabkrin sent their representatives to "aid" the factory; they found that the shock movement had lost momentum and that managerial personnel did their best to "evade one-man management." To catch up with the plan, on 12 June the party faction of the factory trade union committee adopted a resolution in violation of one-man management: "To create an authoritative, provisional extraordinary commission of five persons" (representatives of the bureau of the *raion* committee of the party, factory management, the factory trade union committee, technical personnel, etc.). It was reported that this "theory of the elimination of one-man management" was widespread on the shop floor, where the troika adopted "protocol decisions binding for all." On 27 July the local newspaper, *Krasnyi Sormovich,* published an article that charged by their real names those responsible for an accident that had occurred in the forge shop some time before. The secretary of the party *raion* committee, Kaigorodov, however, summoned the newspaper's editor, edited out these names, and ordered him to confiscate this particular issue, of which 4,000 copies had been printed. The day before, on 26 July, the director of the factory, Voinov, apparently accused both of the failure to fulfill the production plan and of the accident, declared in his closing remark at the

---

[66] The Leon M. Banks file in "American Engineers in Russia."
[67] The following is based on *Pravda,* 15, 18, 21, 25 August 1930; *Izvestiia Nizhegorodskogo kraevogo komiteta VKP(b),* 1930, nos. 14–15, pp. 1–9; and *Istoriia "Krasnogo Sormova,"* pp. 328–33.

plenum of the *raion* committee: "We'd better stop criticizing and get back to business." Both Voinov and Kaigorodov were attacked by the central press as suppressors of self-criticism.

The Sormovo affair became a convenient point of attack for the Moscow center, which reshuffled the local party leadership and removed the factory committee's chairman, Naugol'nyi. Voinov remained temporarily, but the factory management was charged with "bureaucratism," "formalism," and "sympathy with the wreckers removed from the factory" (this suggests that some engineers were arrested as wreckers in connection with the accident). Voinov was forced out by early October.[68]

The "extraordinary commission" of Red Sormovo was not an isolated case: similar commissions (or so-called headquarters) were set up in the Stalingrad Tractor Plant, the Kuznetsk Iron and Steel Plant construction project, and others, whose management was described as "helpless."[69] From a formalistic point of view, these commissions were a blatant violation of one-man management, for which Red Sormovo was in fact criticized. Yet when the party (or Rabkrin or the GPU) judged management to be incapable of mobilizing the factory to fulfill the plan targets, one-man management was virtually abolished. The party secretary of the Stalingrad Tractor Plant, I. B. Lapidus, justified such headquarters because "there was no other way out."[70] In fact, Kaganovich, in addressing the Moscow *oblast'* party committee plenum in February 1931, warned against the supplanting of management by the party, but added quickly: "Only if the Soviet managerial organizations absolutely cannot raise the question will we raise and solve it."[71] Such an emergency measure, however, was usually condemned ex post facto and the troika disbanded, as was the case with Red Sormovo.

The Sormovo affair also raises another important question, namely, the relationship of the local party leader to the factory director. Again the Sormovo case was not an isolated instance. The secretary of the *raion* committee of the party often intervened in the management of the factories under its territory. For instance, in late

[68] See Syrtsov, *K novomu khoziaistvennomu godu*, p. 29, and *Za industrializatsiiu*, 26 October 1930. According to Syrtsov, a similar incident took place in the Kizel *raion* in the Urals, whose party, managerial, and union leaderships were all removed.
[69] *Liudi Stalingradskogo traktornogo*, p. 85 (October 1930); *Kuznetskstroi*, p. 180 (October 1931), etc.
[70] *Liudi Stalingradskogo traktornogo*, p. 85.
[71] *Rabochaia Moskva*, 1 March 1931.

1929 in the Donbas Central and Red Army coal mines, the secretary of the party *raion* committee, Chugunov, and the director of the committee's labor department, Fomenko, asked the militia for help in rounding up "shirkers" in the mine barracks and the surrounding villages.[72] In 1930 or 1931, the director of the AMO Factory in Moscow, I. A. Likhachev, came into conflict with the party committee of the factory concerning the transfer of I. F. Antonov from management to the factory committee. The case went to the secretary of the party *raion* committee for solution.[73] In 1930, the new director of the Kuznetsk Plant construction project, S. M. Frankfurt, found the *raion* committee of the party eager to direct every matter on the construction site.[74] Frankfurt, however, often had problems because the construction materials and the work force were insufficient and food supplies very poor. In 1935 he recalled those days: "There was not a single day when we did not turn to him [R. I. Eikhe, the secretary of the Siberian party committee] for support."[75]

The September 1929 resolution on one-man management did not clarify the relationship between the managers and the local party organ. The unrealistic tempos of industrialization constantly forced managers to run to the local party organ for help; the emerging planned economy, nullifying the automatic market mechanism to coordinate the local economy, required in its stead some kind of system of priorities. The local party organ regarded the troubles of the factories in its territory as far more than routine issues, and was compelled to constantly coordinate priorities. It was this role that the leader of the Nizhegorod party committee, A. A. Zhdanov, defended as legitimate. He stressed that the local pride, the Nizhegorod Automobile Plant, had been given priority over all other factories and construction projects: "There were both insult to and blaming of the Automobile Plant, which overshadowed a whole series of other construction projects. I think you approve of the policy of the *krai* com-

---

[72] *Visnyk profrukhu Ukrainy*, 1929, no. 23 (170), p. 30. This incident led to a scandal because the militia rounded up workers indiscriminately, including those who after the night shift were sleeping in the barracks and elsewhere.

[73] *Direktor I. A. Likhachev v vospominaniiakh sovremennikov*, p. 55. According to I. V. Paramonov, who at that time worked in the Urals, "all everyday managerial activity of trusts" was conducted in direct consultation with the leaders of the city and *raion* organizations of the party. See Paramonov, *Uchit'sia upravliat'*, pp. 135–36.

[74] Frankfurt, *Rozhdenie stali i cheloveka*, pp. 43–53.

[75] Ibid., p. 260.

mittee of the party: we neither could nor should have spared anything for the Automobile Plant."[76] A number of issues such as the
supply and sale of materials and the recruitment of the work force,
which in capitalist societies were usually solved spontaneously in the
market, had to be solved artificially under Soviet conditions. This
mechanism allowed for greater room for the politicization of conflict
of interests and therefore for a greater role of the political organ in
conflict solution. The term "prefects," which Jerry Hough has used
with regard to postwar local party leaders,[77] may also apply to the
local party leaders in the early Stalin years.

An overall picture thus emerges of the local party organs as well
as the factory's party and union organizations constantly intervening in management, a picture precisely contrary to the one associated with one-man management. It was reported from the Donbas
in early 1931: "Here in our mines the secretary of the [party] cell,
the chairman of the mine [trade-union] committee, the procurator,
the chairman of the *raion* trade union council, in other words,
everyone . . . but the mine managers is in command."[78]

Was this a foreseeable and inevitable consequence of the ambiguities and contradictions implicit in the concepts of one-man management and control?[79] Or was it an unforeseeable consequence of the
exigencies of the situation, which was to be eliminated in the course
of the 1930s?[80] To be sure, each of these views contains elements of
truth. Yet both seem to oversimplify the complex issue.

First, it is hard to believe that the party leadership intended or
even foresaw constant outside intervention in management: the
leadership meant for one-man management to eliminate the constant intervention that had jeopardized the troika's political authority. The exclusion of the party and union organizations from
the domain of "routine" questions was further justified by the

---

[76] *Nizhegorodskaia kommuna*, 11 February 1932, quoted in Khavin, *Kratkii ocherk istorii industrializatsii SSSR*, p. 123.

[77] Hough, *The Soviet Prefects*.

[78] *Za industrializatsiiu*, 25 January 1931 (A. Khavin).

[79] Both Granick and Bendix, whose research has been limited to the late 1930s and after, maintain that these concepts were "irreconcilable." Granick, *Management of the Industrial Firm in the USSR*, pp. 228–30, and Bendix, *Work and Authority in Industry*, pp. 193–7, 364–66, 381–83.

[80] Lewin suggests that as their power became consolidated in the 1930s, managers became "little Stalins." Lewin, "Society and the Stalinist State in the Period of the Five-Year Plans," pp. 160–61, 172–73. See also Lewin, *The Making of the Soviet System*, p. 252.

optimistic view that the management of the factory in a centrally planned economy would be considerably simplified and routinized. If the party leadership had not provided a new framework for the troika, the management of the factory would have fallen into total chaos.

It is also hard to believe that the party leadership anticipated no practical contradictions between one-man management and all sorts of control. As the debate between Ia. A. Iakovlev and S. P. Birman at the sixteenth party conference vividly demonstrated, the simultaneous promotion of one-man management and workers' control had in fact caused frictions. Yet the party leadership resolutely insisted on the need for constant control, because however routinized managment became, it believed, management free of control would easily become despotic or collude with the party and union organizations. If the manager proved incapable of coping with routine questions, intervention would be inevitable. Indeed, this was what actually happened in 1930 on a scale much more extensive than had been expected (although it should be emphasized that the routinization of management proved far more difficult than had been expected). Moreover, the political environment of the time, which politicized even routine questions, made the distinction between control and intervention tenuous.

By 1930 industrial management had become chaotic at both the national and the factory levels; the magnitude of the chaos far surpassed all expectations of the leadership; and the resultant economic crisis made management all the more difficult by inviting a host of organizations to intervene. Much despair was observed in the leadership, and much disorientation in the factories. The leadership did not yet see a clear way out of the situation except to apply further pressure in its economic administration.

The troika and the shock workers

As Kaganovich aptly put it, in 1930 the party and union organizations, like management, found it very difficult to work under pressure, and pressures came not only from above but also from below. Among the shock workers in the Dnepropetrovsk factories, it was reported that "spontaneous opposition" to the unions' "bureaucratic methods" of work was growing.[81] In February 1930 one union leader complained that the trade unions suffered from what he called "worker phobia" (*massoboiazn'*).[82] N. P. Glebov-Avilov, then director of the Rostov Agricultural Machinery Plant and former head of the Leningrad trade union organizations who in 1925 belonged to the New Opposition, maintained at the sixteenth party congress that the lack of one-man management jarred the nerves of shock workers: "Shock workers are nervous when the 'troika' confers and specialists hide behind the 'troika.' . . . This ['parliamentarism'] has to be eliminated."[83] This remark may well have reflected his new managerial position, but evidently there was a good deal of truth to it. In the course of 1930, these nervous shock workers came to play a critical role in mass politics.

In recruiting workers into the party, the party leadership laid special emphasis on the shock workers. In its February 1930 resolution concerning recruitment, for example, the Central Committee declared that the "most important criterion of acceptance to the party is the worker's active participation in the shock movement and socialist competition and his truly vanguard role in production."[84] The mass recruitment of workers at that time far outstripped the simultaneously organized purges: the overall membership of the party (including candidates) increased from 1,305,854 in 1928 to 1,535,362 in 1929, 1,677,910 in 1930, 2,212,225 in 1931, and 3,117,250 in 1932.[85] The recruitments increased the ratio of those who were workers by social origin (i.e., those whose father was a worker) from 56.8 percent in 1928 to 65.3 in 1930, and the ratio of those who were workers by occupation from 40.8 percent to 46.3 percent during the same period.[86] Shock workers accounted for the majority of the new recruits: 73 percent in the third quarter of 1930, 78.5 percent in the fourth quarter of 1931, and 82.4 percent in the first half of 1932.[87] Because these figures applied to

---

[81] *Revoliutsiia i kul'tura,* 1929, no. 12, p. 17 (A. Cherniavskii, "Svet i teni sotsialisticheskogo sorevnovaniia").

[82] *Trud,* 2 February 1930 (V. I. Polonskii).

[83] *XVI s'ezd VKP(b),* p. 672.

[84] *Spravochnik partiinogo rabotnika,* vol. 7, part 2, p. 116.

[85] See Rigby, *Communist Party Membership,* p. 52.

[86] Ibid., p. 116.

[87] *Partiinoe stroitel'stvo,* 1931, no. 23, p. 37, 1932, no. 15, pp. 51–52, no. 21, p. 46. Ibid., 1932, no. 6, p. 31, and *Sostav VKP(b) v tsifrakh,* p. 15, give 56.2% for the fourth quarter of 1930.

workers by social origin, perhaps almost all workers recruited directly from the factory bench were shock workers.

The trade union organizations too were inundated by shock workers. In May 1930 the central organ of the trade unions declared in an editorial that the task of the reelection of the factory committees was "to renew the [trade union] organizations by promoting vanguard shock workers."[88] At the sixteenth party congress, L. M. Kaganovich likewise maintained that "the shock movement is becoming the lever by means of which we reorganize the work of the trade unions, and a source of new cadres with whom to replace old cadres."[89] In the spring of 1930 the party leadership concentrated its efforts on the reorganization of the most important trade union: the metal workers' union. According to Kaganovich, this campaign was a "brilliant example": some 80 percent of factory trade union committee members were replaced, with the result that shock workers accounted for 51 percent of new factory committee members in Moscow, 70.5 percent in Leningrad, 84.6 percent in Nizhegorod, 65.8 percent in the Ukraine, 95 percent in the Putilov Factory in Leningrad, and 72 percent in the Baltic Shipbuilding Plant in Leningrad.[90] So drastic was the renewal that some factories, having lost all incumbent members, were said to be paralyzed.[91] Again in 1931, an additional 41.6 percent of factory committee members were replaced by shock workers.[92]

By late 1930 the reorganization of the trade unions had achieved tangible results, although the purges continued into 1931. The party wrought a break with "trade unionism," which meant, in Bolshevik parlance, relative political autonomy and the promotion of wages rather than production. In late December 1930 Kaganovich rather complacently declared to Moscow party activists:

[88] *Trud*, 15 May 1930.

[89] *XVI s"ezd VKP(b)*, p. 64.

[90] Ibid. and *Trud*, 5, 6, 10, 12, 13 May 1930. A very different figure for Moscow (80%) is in *Materialy o rabote profsoiuzov moskovskoi oblasti*, p. 92. The renewal rate of the factory committee members was lower in the previous years: 62.4% in 1928 and 65.7% in 1929. *Professional'nye soiuzy SSSR, 1926–1928*, p. 43, and *Trud*, 30 August 1929. Party "saturation" in the factory committees also increased from an overall 29.2% in 1928 to 47% in Moscow, 63% in Leningrad, and 52% in the Urals. See *Trud*, 5 May 1930.

[91] *XVI s"ezd VKP(b)*, p. 667.

[92] *Trud*, 11 April 1932. By 1932, approximately 90% of the committee members were shock workers. See the case of engineering workers' union in *IX Vsesoiuznyi s"ezd professional'nykh soiuzov SSSR*, p. 143.

"Good or bad – the party better, the trade unions worse, they nevertheless have reorganized themselves. . . . The trade unions are still far from having completed their reorganization, which they had to do under great pressure from the party. Yet a great job has been done here too."[93]

The reorientation of the trade unions away from "trade unionism" was seen in the reorganization of the budget structure as well: the budget, to use an expression often seen in the Soviet press at that time, "turned its face to production." In 1928, out of a total budget of 135,000,000 rubles for cultural activities, 42,000,000 and 16,000,000 went to films, plays, and concerts, and to physical education, respectively, while only 1,564,000, 1,428,000, and 632,000 rubles were expended on promoting literacy, technical education, and "production enlightenment," respectively. In 1930, out of a total budget of 270,000,000 rubles for cultural activities, 54,000,000 was allocated to technical education and 17,300,000 to "production enlightenment."[94] The new budget was clearly in line with the immediate aspirations of the shock workers.

The takeover of the trade unions by shock workers was much less successful in establishing a stable relationship in the troika. Even though the shock workers appreciated one-man management, upon takeover they found themselves compelled to intervene in management, if not because of power struggles, then because they saw management as too weak and irresponsible. On the shop floor, shock workers were inclined for the same reason to what was called "production autonomy" and "syndicalism."

The purge-recruitment operations were also economically costly because many workers, particularly shock workers, were mobilized away from the shop floor. For the election campaign of the metal workers' union alone, 300 brigades of workers were organized in major factories.[95] The costs of these campaigns evoked considerable resistance from the troika. At the sixteenth party congress in the summer of 1930, I. M. Gordienko of Moscow, almost certainly representing the view of the Stalin group, harshly attacked those "opportunists" who, he contended, claimed that

---

[93] Kaganovich, *Ob itogakh dekabr'skogo ob″edinennogo plenuma TsK i TsKK VKP(b)*, p. 38.
[94] *XVI s″ezd VKP(b)*, pp. 76 and 662–63. The 1930 budget was 225 million rubles according to ibid., p. 76.
[95] *Metall*, 1930, no. 19 (10 June), p. 51.

of course there are achievements in the reelection of the metal workers' union, but how much did it cost? How many brigades did you send [to the factories]? How many people did you remove from production? And how much did all this cost in monetary terms?. . . . we simply did not want to spend that much money and hinder production; we approached [the issue] from the point of view of maintaining [human] power.

Gordienko indignantly charged that these "opportunists" mistook politics for economics and that they

do not understand the essence of the political content of the work deployed. They do not understand that without developing new methods and forms of trade union work we would not be able to cope with the colossal tasks [of fulfilling and overfulfilling the plans]. . . . Without mobilizing the attention of the workers we won't manage to compose properly the control figures for the next year.[96]

The purge-recruitment campaigns brought the trade unions under stricter control of the party, and the takeover by shock workers reoriented them along more productivist lines. This was a major political achievement for Stalin and his group.

Many other mass campaigns swept the country in 1930. Each campaign mobilized away from the shop floor the best shock workers and organizers so much needed for production. At the sixteenth party congress, A. S. Enukidze, secretary of the presidium of the All-Union Central Executive Committee, sounded an alarm: The system of dispatching plenipotentiaries [to the countryside] is many times more expensive than maintaining permanent members of the Soviets and executive committees in the provinces. This year alone we have spent many million rubles on temporary plenipotentiaries sent to the countryside."[97] Within the confines of the factory too, many campaigns and meetings invaded the working day and distracted the workers from production. According to official data that apparently did not cover the lost working time, in 1930 the average male worker in Moscow was "spending over half an hour a day attending meetings, generally at his place of work." More generally, male workers were spending 27 hours and female workers 12 hours a month on "public affairs," a sharp increase from 9.0 and 5.5 hours, respectively, in 1923/24.[98] To those concerned with

[96] *XVI s˝ezd VKP(b)*, p. 678.
[97] Ibid., p. 335.
[98] Barber, "Notes on the Soviet Working-Class Family, 1928–1941," pp. 7–8 and Table 4. See also Gimpel'son and Shmarov, "Ispol'zovanie vnerabochego vremeni trudiashchikhsia Moskvy," p. 116.

production, mass mobilizations were costly to an economically irrational degree.

Yet the Soviet political leaders, considering the problem of resource constraints not so much in economic as in political terms, paid the costs. The type of the economy they sought to create in 1930 required mass campaigns as a substitute for the "stimuli" inherent in a capitalist, market economy. At the sixteenth party congress, M. M. Kaganovich of the party Central Control Commission characterized *New York Times* correspondent Walter Duranty's report about Soviet mass politics as a "bourgeois" interpretation, but evidently quoted it with some pride: "The Bolsheviks are remarkable people. When something goes wrong somewhere, they make a fuss. This fuss mobilizes public opinion, which helps them get out of a difficult situation."[99]

In 1930, however, the economic costs of mass mobilization surpassed all expectations, at least in part because, as Gordienko suggested, the party leadership cared little about the costs. Mass politics was caught in a vicious circle. The leadership saw the factory organizations as too weak to fulfill the plan targets, so that it increasingly resorted, without regard for losses incurred, to mass mobilizations to apply pressure to the factory organizations. This undoubtedly contributed to the summer economic crisis, which invited more mass mobilizations, thereby further raising the costs. The more successful the mass mobilizations, the greater the price to the economy.

[99] *XVI s˘ezd VKP(b)*, pp. 521–22.

8

The transformation of the labor market

The economic disorder was compounded in 1930 by a rather abrupt transformation of the labor market from mass unemployment to labor shortages. This transformation was a mixed blessing. On the one hand, it unexpectedly solved one of the most vexing problems: mass unemployment, which during NEP amounted to well over 10 percent of the employed population of the country, was a source of a host of social evils as well as a great political embarrassment to the country of proletarian dictatorship. From late 1929 on, the rapid expansion of industry and construction eased mass unemployment and came to provide much hope to millions of people. On the other hand, the transformation of the labor market was a result not only of an accelerated industrialization drive but also of a "wager on quantity" – a desperate attempt to compensate for the dire shortage of skilled workers by using much larger numbers of workers than planned. This practice induced new, unskilled workers into industry on an unprecedented scale and aggravated the already difficult problem of socialization. More important, the wager adversely affected the economy in its qualitative performance (particularly the productivity of labor and the costs of production), thereby further aggravating the problem of resource constraints.

Moreover, this transformation of the labor market, not envisaged by the Five-Year Plan, posed a very serious problem to the emerging planned economy: a planned recruitment and allocation of labor. Oddly enough, the planned economy turned out to have no mechanism for labor planning, and Vesenkha and the People's Commissariat of Labor appeared to be caught off guard and at the mercy of market spontaneity. In the autumn of 1930 an article in Vasenkha's journal declared with determination: "It is self-evident that a planned economy cannot reconcile itself to the spontaneous ebb and flow of the labor force, because such spontaneity brings to nought the very principle of planning."[1] The summer economic crisis challenged the administrative capability of the People's Commissariat of Labor (and that of other institutions) whose primary task was the regulation and planning of the labor market. The commissariat failed, in the view of the party leadership, to live up to the challenge after all. This failure would doom it.[2]

From mass unemployment to labor shortages

Although even the original ambitious optimum variant of the Five-Year Plan foresaw as many as half a million unemployed in 1932/ 33, the number of unemployed declined sharply in 1930: from 1,741,000 in April 1929 to 1,316,000 in January 1930, 1,079,100 in April 1930, 236,000 in January 1931, and a negligible 18,000 in August 1931.[3] This drastic reduction caused a panic among those responsible for labor allocation, which had been predicated upon the assumption that half a million unemployed was "about the size of the free labor reserve necessary in the system of the Soviet economy for a normal turnover of the labor force."[4] As early as the summer of 1929, when almost one and a half million unemployed were still registered, not only skilled construction workers but, in many places, even unskilled workers were reported to be already scarce.[5] In 1930 the situation deteriorated and spread to industry as a whole.

This peculiar coexistence of unemployment and labor shortages reflected both the influx of an unskilled urban and rural population into the labor market and the shortages of skilled labor. Stalin, irritated by the peculiar phenomenon, ascribed it to "considerable confusion" that reigned "both at the People's Commissariat of Labor and the All-Union Central Council of Trade Unions." He declared at the sixteenth party congress in June–July 1930:

[1] *Puti industrializatsii*, 1930, nos. 15–16, p. 32.
[2] It was to be abolished in 1933. See chap. 11, note 86, this volume.
[3] Rogachevskaia, *Likvidatsiia bezrabotitsy v SSSR*, p. 161; *Voprosy truda v tsifrakh*, p. 43; and *Trud v SSSR* (1932), p. 9. There are slight differences between the last two sources.
[4] *Piatiletnii plan narodno-khoziaistvennogo stroitel'stva SSSR*, vol. 2, part 2, p. 178.
[5] "Iz istorii sozdaniia stroitel'noi industrii v SSSR," p. 38. See also Uglanov (ed.), *Trud v SSSR*, p. 38, and *2 sessiia TsIK Soiuza SSR 5 sozyva*, 16:18.

On the one hand, according to the data of these institutions we have about a million unemployed, of whom those to any degree skilled constitute only 14.3 percent, while about 73 percent are those engaged in so-called intellectual labor and unskilled workers; the vast majority of the latter are women and minors [*podrostki*] not connected with industrial production.

On the other hand, according to the same data, we are suffering from a frightful shortage of skilled labor; the labor exchanges are unable to meet about 80 percent of the demands for labor by our factories and thus we are obliged hurriedly, literally as we go along, to train absolutely unskilled people and make skilled workers out of them in order to satisfy at least the minimum requirements of our factories.

Just try to find your way out of this confusion. It is clear, at all events, that these unemployed do not constitute a *reserve* and still less a *permanent* army of unemployed workers of our industry.[6]

This was an attack on the People's Commissariat of Labor whose head was the Rightist N. A. Uglanov. In August 1930 the Politbureau reviewed the work of the labor exchanges and maintained that the majority of unemployed were "connected with agricultural farming and handicraft and interested only in getting a little extra." The Politbureau then concluded that it was necessary to cope not so much with unemployment as with industry's demands for the work force.[7] In early August the People's Commissariat of Labor was reshuffled: A. S. Tsikhon (former chairman of the construction workers' union) replaced Uglanov as commissar, and I. A. Kraval' (former director of the labor section of Vesenkha) was appointed deputy commissar.[8] Some prominent labor economists, including L. E. Mints, were arrested or purged as "wreckers" and "counterrevolutionaries."[9] In its appeal of 3 September 1930, the Central Committee accused the old People's Commissariat of Labor of having squandered tens of millions of rubles on unemployment benefits.[10] Under the pressure, on 9 October 1930, when over 300,000 unemployed were still registered, the commissariat prematurely declared that unemployment had been eliminated, and terminated the payment of unemployment benefits.[11]

[6] Stalin, *Sochineniia*, 12:292–93. Emphasis in the original.
[7] Suvorov, *Istoricheskii opyt KPSS po likvidatsii bezrabotitsy*, p. 218.
[8] *Trud*, 6 August 1930, and Rogachevskaia, *Likvidatsiia bezrabotitsy v SSSR*, p. 275.
[9] See *Protsess kontrrevoliutsionnoi organizatsii men'shevikov*, pp. 20, 25, and *Voprosy profdvizheniia*, 1933, no. 3, p. 42.
[10] *Pravda*, 3 September 1930.
[11] *Izvestiia N.K. Truda SSSR*, 1930, no. 28, pp. 610–11. See also Davies, "The Ending of Mass Unemployment in the USSR."

Premature though it was, the declaration did reflect the rapid transformation of the labor market, from mass unemployment to labor shortages, to which both the People's Commissariat of Labor and the industrial managers had to adapt. It was an abrupt and formidable challenge: neither was ready to cope with it because the assumption of labor surpluses, on which the Five-Year Plan had been based, became suddenly problematic in 1930. The commissariat frankly admitted in the summer of 1930 that the labor exchanges were not in a position to meet industry's demands.[12] It was therefore accused of taking "passive, contemplative attitudes" toward the spontaneity of the labor market.[13] The managers were also attacked for their habit of regarding labor as abundant and of relying exclusively on the labor exchanges for labor supply. The managers' attitude was often characterized as follows: "The worker will come [in any case]. . . , or the labor exchanges will secure the work force."[14] In September 1930, M. I. Kalinin declared that the surpluses of labor had "habituated" managers to paying little attention to the question of the work force.[15] At any rate, the new challenge to the commissariat and managers consisted of two major tasks: the acceleration of the training of skilled workers, and a planned recruitment and distribution of the work force.

With the acceleration of industrialization, the network of technical education expanded enormously and far surpassed the original plans. For example, the number of pupils in industrial and other apprenticeship schools, which were projected to provide the core of skilled workers, increased from 178,300 in 1928 to 754,100 in 1932, a nearly sixfold increase.[16] However, these schools hurriedly set up in 1929 and 1930 were not expected to produce a substantial number of skilled workers until 1932.[17] In the meantime, managers had to resort to the short-term courses of the Central Institute of Labor and on-the-job training. This practice, however, only invited

---

[12] Uglanov (ed.), *Trud v SSSR*, p. 30.

[13] Mordukhovich (Mokhov), *Na bor'bu s tekuchest'iu rabochei sily*, pp. 89–91, and *Za industrializatsiiu*, 8 April 1930.

[14] *Izvestiia Nizhegorodskogo kraevogo komiteta VKP(b)*, 1930, nos. 11–13, p. 19. See also *Voprosy truda*, 1930, nos. 10–11, p. 69, no. 12, p. 75.

[15] *Pravda*, 7 September 1930.

[16] *Sotsialisticheskoe stroitel'stvo SSSR* (1936), p. 572. For slightly different figures, see Fitzpatrick, *Education and Social Mobility in the Soviet Union*, pp. 199–200, 238.

[17] See *Voprosy truda*, 1931, nos. 8–9, p. 54.

the old complaint of the Komsomol, whose official report to the sixteenth party congress stated:

Hoping to obtain immediately the labor force from the labor exchanges or to train workers in the courses of the Central Institute of Labor in a short period, the managers have not taken timely measures to organize an effective training of skilled workers in factory apprenticeship schools and evening schools. At a time of need they were forced to train workers *hurriedly* or to take workers *without any training* and teach them on the job. As a result both old and, especially, new factories now experience an acute shortage of cultured, technically developed workers. Because of this the fulfillment of production programs is often thwarted and qualitative indexes decline.[18]

Pressed by the dire need for skilled labor, managers resorted to a palliative: they compensated for poor quality (low skills of workers) with quantity (an additional labor force). In the spring of 1930 the Putilov Factory, for example, pressed hard by the need to fulfill the plan, hurriedly employed about 2,000 workers, the majority of whom had no previous experience of industrial labor and were unskilled. The factory had to train them on the job; despite its efforts, the factory failed to fulfill the plan in the summer of 1930.[19] The new factories such as the Stalingrad Tractor Plant had devoted their efforts to the completion of construction and then found themselves at a loss for workers capable of operating new technology.[20] Resort to quantity naturally resulted in holding an "excessive" number of workers in factories.[21] This practice, in turn, not only adversely affected their economic performance but also aggravated labor shortages.

The second task, a planned recruitment and distribution of the labor force, was equally formidable and had enormous implications for the establishment of a planned economy. Just as the Soviet industrial leadership lost control over industrial supplies, so it lost control over the industrial labor force. The difference was that the work force, unlike industrial materials, was mobile, making planned recruitment and distribution all the more difficult.

Soviet labor market policy in the second half of the 1920s was

[18] *Komsomol k XVI parts'ezdu*, p. 44. Emphasis in the original.
[19] *Istoriia Kirovskogo zavoda*, p. 338, and Mordukhovich (Mokhov), *Na bor'bu s tekuchest'iu rabochei sily*, p. 36.
[20] See, for example, Ginzburg, *O proshlom – dlia budushchego*, pp. 81–82. See also *Za promyshlennye kadry*, 1931, no. 4, p. 19.
[21] *KPSS v rezoliutsiiakh*, 4:370 and 374 (December 1929), and *3 sessiia TsIK Soiuza SSR 5 sozyva*, 15:35–36.

aimed at alleviating mass unemployment. The Soviet labor force, like its counterpart in capitalist societies, was cited in the market, a reflection of the lack of the state monopoly characteristic of NEP. In 1925/26 the state labor exchanges (under the jurisdiction of the People's Commissariat of Labor) handled only 37.9 percent of the total hirings in census industry.[22] From 1927 on, however, the state increasingly tightened entitlement to unemployment benefits and strengthened its hold on the labor market in accordance with the progress of economic planning.[23] Moreover, the trade unions, in collaboration with the labor exchanges, sought to restrict employment to their members, thereby establishing a virtual compulsory employment through the labor exchanges (this measure was called "state protectionism").[24] As a result, the grip of the labor exchanges on the market tightened: they handled 73.3 percent of the total hirings in census industry in 1926/27 and 85.6 percent in 1927/28.[25] As industrialization accelerated, however, "state protectionism" proved powerless in the face of the spontaneity of the labor market: the rate of hirings through the labor exchanges slightly decreased to 84.6 percent in 1928/29 and then dropped sharply from 80.2 percent in the first quarter of 1929/30 to 73.0 percent in the third quarter, and 60.5 percent in the fourth quarter.[26] In the Donbas coal mines, for example, 63.0 percent of the new workers, who had first entered mining labor in 1930, were employed "in unorganized ways" (*samotekom*).[27] The problem was more serious on construction sites. The Kuznetsk Iron and Steel Plant construction project, for example, hired 74.2 percent of the work force *samotekom* between January and September 1930.[28] The conference of labor organs held on 15 June 1930 frankly admitted their inability to control the labor market: "The construction worker gets a job by himself in spite of our every attempt at planned mobilization, and jeopardizes our giant projects of socialist construction."[29]

---

[22] *Voprosy truda v tsifrakh*, p. 57.

[23] Schwarz, *Labor in the Soviet Union*, pp. 42–43, and Panfilova, *Formirovanie rabochego klassa SSSR v gody pervoi piatiletki*, pp. 19–20.

[24] *Bol'shevik*, 1929, no. 7, pp. 77–78.

[25] *Voprosy truda v tsifrakh*, p. 57.

[26] *Industrializatsiia SSSR, 1929–1932*, p. 385; Mordukhovich (Mokhov), *Na bor'bu s tekuchest'iu rabochei sily*, p. 90; and *Voprosy truda*, 1931, no. 5, p. 40.

[27] *Trud v SSSR* (1932), p. 95.

[28] *Za promyshlennye kadry*, 1931, no. 1, p. 16.

[29] Quoted in Eliseeva "O sposobakh privlecheniia rabochei sily v promyshlennost' i stroitel'stvo v period sotsialisticheskoi industrializatsii SSSR (1926–1937 gg.)," p. 58.

Another factor that contributed to the loss of central control over the work force was the collectivization drive in the countryside. The impact of the drive was particularly great in the mining and construction industries, whose work force had stronger ties to the countryside. In early 1930, when the drive intensified, there was a movement of workers to the countryside, where they sought to "participate in this or that question of collectivization."[30] In the critical summer of 1930 there was a further exodus of workers who were concerned with the distribution of the harvest (a bumper crop, as it turned out).[31] As a result, the number of coal miners steadily declined from 256,934 in March to 253,649 in April, 249,107 in May, 235,765 in June, 202,267 in July, and 187,440 in August, a 26 percent decline in five months. The numbers of miners in June, July, and August 1930 were even lower than in the same months of 1929.[32] The number of construction workers also declined in the peak months of the building season, a phenomenon that had never been seen in the 1920s: the number reached a peak of 1,968,357 in July, then dropped to 1,781,363 in August and 1,754,647 in September, to pick up to 1,793,245 in October.[33]

In urgent need of workers, the state labor organs came to resort to blind recruitments: the Leningrad organ of the People's Commissariat of Labor reportedly characterized its own work as follows: "Scream around the city and the suburbs: 'Whoever wants a job, come and get one.' "[34]

In the meantime, managers were forced to hire workers by their own methods, or "from the gate" (*ot vorot*). The construction project of the First Ball Bearing Factory in Moscow, for example, had by June 1930 suffered enormously from labor shortages and desperately searched for workers:

The director of the future factory and [former] fitter of the Putilov Factory, Andrei Bordov, and the secretary of the party committee and [former] turner from Kiev, Nikolai Tikhonov, found out that there was a gypsy camp not far from the site, headed there, and soon came back with a group of people dressed in parti-colored clothes, who also dragged draft animals.

[30] See, for example, *Planovoe khoziaistvo*, 1930, no. 2, p. 27, and *XVI s'ezd VKP(b)*, p. 499 (Kuibyshev).
[31] *3 sessiia TsIK Soiuza SSR 5 sozyva*, 17:18; *Bol'shevik*, 1930, no. 17, p. 25; *Planovoe khoziaistvo*, 1930, no. 12, p. 28.
[32] *Ezhemesiachnyi statisticheskii biulleten'*, no. 10 (July 1930), pp. 2–3.
[33] *Industrializatsiia SSSR, 1929–1932*, p. 387.
[34] Mordukhovich (Mokhov), *Na bor'bu s tekuchest'iu rabochei sily*, p. 91.

They settled the gypsies in the barracks still redolent of shavings, provided them with food and [ration] cards, and set about teaching them how to read and write.[35]

Cries for the work force mounted in 1930. The Ural Heavy Engineering Plant construction project, for example, bitterly complained in the summer that it had received only eight of the five hundred carpenters for whom it had concluded an agreement with the local labor organ and had paid 18,000 rubles.[36] When it started operations in June 1930, the Stalingrad Tractor Plant was bombarded by "threatening telegrams" requesting transfers of its construction workers to Magnitogorsk and Kuznetsk. Yet the plant, too, far from completed, suffered from labor shortages. The Vesenkha commission sent to the plant in July instructed that no construction workers be removed from the plant.[37] New factories such as the Stalingrad Tractor Plant were in urgent need of skilled workers, a considerable portion of whom had to be provided by old factories. Yet the latter, also in need of skilled workers, resisted their transfer.[38]

The dire need of skilled workers often prompted managers to "pirate" (*peremanivat'*) them from other factories and construction projects. The luring away of specialists was not at all new,[39] but in 1930 the enticement of skilled workers was reported to have become an "everyday phenomenon."[40] Recruiters traveled from one factory to another, went to workers' lodgings, "penetrated factories under the guise of excursion," and "engaged in the ugliest forms of hiring."[41] It was reported from the Putilov Factory, for example, that the factory, particularly its tractor shop, suffered from the desertion of workers: "People come ostensibly as excursionists, but [in fact] ask workers around if they would not like to come over to another factory"; these "anarchic" methods of employment only "disorganized the situation with the labor force."[42] The legal au-

---

[35] *Byli industrial'nye*, p. 168.

[36] *Za industrializatsiiu*, 22 August 1930.

[37] *Pravda*, 30 July 1930 (N. Osinskii).

[38] *Za promyshlennye kadry*, 1931, no. 4, p. 20, and *3 sessiia TsIK Soiuza SSR 5 sozyva*, 17:6.

[39] See, for example, *Vestnik Donuglia*, no. 71 (1 November 1929), p. 3.

[40] *Voprosy truda*, 1930, no. 9, p. 21.

[41] Ibid. See also *Trud*, 21 March 1930 (editorial); Uglanov (ed.), *Trud v SSSR*, p. 30; and Mordukhovich (Mokhov), *Na bor'bu s tekuchest'iu rabochei sily*, pp. 95, 128–31.

[42] *Voprosy truda*, 1931, no. 9, p. 21.

thorities therefore repeatedly warned that the piracy of "workers of scarce professions," highly skilled workers, and specialists from state and cooperative factories, especially from capital construction projects, was a "socially dangerous act" to be punished according to the criminal code.[43]

The industrial authorities sought to cope with this chaotic state of affairs by centralized transfers of skilled workers. For example, in early 1930 Vesenkha issued an order to transfer 1,000 skilled workers to the Stalingrad Tractor Plant from Baku, Odessa, Lugansk, and other industrial centers, while Moscow and Leningrad were to provide 291 highly skilled workers. Yet as of 16 April 1930, only 635 of the "thousanders" and 1 of the 291 recruits had actually arrived at the plant. Moreover, it was reported that the factories had retained "good workers" and instead sent "shirkers, flitterers, and alcoholics." In April the plant was forced to dismiss 115 "rowdies, drunkards, and shirkers"; three "hooligans" who caused a fight in the cadre department were put on trial. As a result, only 142 thousanders remained in the plant.[44] By the spring of 1931, the Komsomol too had mobilized 12,500 young workers to the plant, only 2,262 of whom remained, however.[45]

Thus, even though they were fortunate enough to recruit workers, the factories and construction projects often found it difficult to keep them. Workers knew how things were elsewhere – what meals were served in Stalingrad, what goods were available in the Dnepro Hydroelectric Dam construction project, how much money people got in Magnitogorsk, and so on.[46] In September 1930 the forthright industrial manager Birman, then in charge of the metallurgical industry in the East, reported on the Magnitogorsk Iron and Steel Plant construction project:

They [recruitment agents] promise them [recruitees] heaven in Magnitogorsk. The recruits therefore head there barefoot and ragged in hopes of getting shoes, overalls, and a trade-union membership card. Having come

---

[43] See the resolutions of 28 March and 6 November 1930 of the Supreme Court of the Russian Republic in *Sud i prokuratura litsom k proizvodstvu*, p. 154, and *Sud i prokuratura na okhrane proizvodstva i truda*, 1:197–98.

[44] *Byli industrial'nye*, pp. 52–53 (memoirs by the former deputy director of the cadre department of the plant, M. A. Vodolagin), and *Vestnik Kommunisticheskoi Akademii*, 1931, no. 7, p. 52.

[45] *Pravda*, 9 May 1931.

[46] Eliseeva, "O sposobakh privlecheniia rabochei sily," p. 58.

to the site and received all these and also advances, they run away in most cases.[47]

The American engineer C. R. Olberg, who worked in the Soviet Union in 1929–33, aptly remarked on the subjective side of mobile labor:

The Russian peasant, who constitutes the average worker, "doesn't know what it's all about." Present conditions are hard and he either has an exaggerated idea of his own importance under the new regime and is searching for some place where his ability will be appreciated, or he remembers the old days and he hopes to find some place where conditions are better.[48]

Certainly Russian workers had never been a stable group. In the mid- and late 1920s, labor turnover in census industry had been very high: the annual rate of discharges to the average number of employed remained around 100 percent. In other words, on average every worker changed jobs once a year. Of course, this did not mean that all the workers did so. In fact, there were vast sectorial differences: the rate of discharges ranged from the highest of almost 200 percent in the mining industry to the lowest of 30–40 percent in the cotton industry.[49] Significant proportions of the high turnover in the 1920s were due to mass temporary hirings followed by dismissals. The skilled workers tended to be more stable than the unskilled, and among the former there were workers who had remained in the same factory for an extended period.[50]

Yet in 1930 labor turnover sharply increased: while temporary hirings became insignificant, the overall rate of discharges in all industries rose from 115.2 percent in 1929 to 152.4 percent in 1930, and, in the producer goods industries in particular, from 140.4 percent to 177.6 percent. In the coal industry the turnover jumped from 192.0 percent to 295.2 percent, and even in the traditionally relatively stable cotton industry it increased from 37.2 percent to 62.4 percent in the respective years.[51] The workers

---

[47] *Za Industrializatsiiu*, 27 September 1930.

[48] The C. R. Olberg file in "American Engineers in Russia."

[49] *Sotsialisticheskoe stroitel'stvo SSSR* (1936), p. 531. Labor turnover in the seasonal industries was naturally much higher, ranging from 300% to 500–600%. See Mordukhovich (Mokhov), *Na bor'bu s tekuchest'iu rabochei sily*, p. 26.

[50] See *Moskovskii proletarii*, 1928, no. 6, pp. 4–6; TPG, 11 April 1928; *Statisticheskoe obozrenie*, 1928, no. 5, pp. 58–59.

[51] *Sotsialisticheskoe stroitel'stvo SSSR* (1936), p. 531.

were literally in flux. So mobile were they that in the Stalingrad Tractor Plant, for example, nobody knew the exact number of workers.[52]

Many factors were responsible for this upsurge: various mobilizations (such as the dispatch of workers to the countryside), the massive promotion of workers to full-time administrative work and higher education, the transfer of workers from old factories to new ones, the exodus of workers to the countryside due to the collectivization drive, the piracy of skilled workers, intersectorial mobility (specifically from the textile industry to the metal industry where wages were generally higher),[53] and the departure of skilled workers from the factories in which bad living conditions and poor wages reigned.

In the last analysis, it was the transformation of the labor market from a buyers' market to a sellers' market that had a decisive impact. In fact, as labor shortages became less acute toward the mid-1930s, labor turnover (the discharge rate) declined to below 100 percent.[54]

Because of the high labor turnover, factories lost many more skilled workers than they received from elsewhere. The Klimovsk Engineering Factory near Moscow was a typical case in point. It discharged 282 workers and hired 361 between October 1929 and March 1930. Yet the factory lost many skilled workers, as shown in Table 8.1.

The problem was not as simple as the "law of conservation of matter" reportedly prevalent at that time among the labor organs and managers:

Well then, if individual factories or even individual [industrial] branches *lose* their skilled workers, then evidently other factories or branches *gain* these skilled workers. What's wrong here? This is a quite natural phenomenon, from which neither industry nor the national economy as a whole loses.[55]

---

[52] See the report of a Vesenkha commission sent to the plant in *Avtotraktornoe proizvodstvo*, 1931, no. 1, p. 6.

[53] Eliseeva, "O sposobakh privlecheniia rabochei sily," p. 71; *Voprosy truda*, 1930, no. 6, p. 23; *Za industrializatsiiu*, 15 May 1930. See also Granick, *Soviet Metal-Fabricating and Economic Development*, p. 34.

[54] *Sotsialisticheskoe stroitel'stvo SSSR* (1936), p. 531. The impact of the harsh measures against turnover was also important, however.

[55] *Voprosy truda*, 1930, no. 6, p. 24.

Table 8.1. *Discharges and hirings in the Klimovsk Factory*
(October 1929–March 1930)

Wage-scale rank[a]	Discharges	Hirings	Rise(+) or fall(−)
1	80	219	+139
2	75	79	+4
3	71	31	−40
4	31	19	−12
5	11	11	0
6	4	0	−4
7	5	2	−3
Unknown	5	0	−5

[a]Ranks run from 1 to 7 in ascending order of skill.

Source: Statistika i narodnoe khoziaistvo, vols. 6–7 (15–16), 1930, p. 99.

In a rapidly expanding economy, skilled workers were increasingly scattered, and the jobs left by skilled workers had to be taken over by the less skilled workers. The mobile skilled workers needed time and effort to adjust to new jobs, and accordingly their "skill value" declined at least temporarily. As a result, in 1930 high labor turnover led to a "deterioration of the qualitative composition of the labor force," a process of "deskilling."[56]

Labor shortages contributed considerably to the weakening of managerial authority on the shop floor because the manager feared that the enforcement of strict labor discipline would lead workers to leave for other factories. The assistant director of the Red October Factory, in Leningrad, for example, opposed the trade union's disciplinary measure against "rolling stones" and uttered a "historic phrase": "I'd rather be tried in court for [pardoning] rolling stones than for the underfulfillment of the plan."[57] In late 1930 the Leningrad party organ complained that during the first half of 1930, of 164,300 workers surveyed, as many as 86,400, or almost 53 percent, had received administrative reprimands for lack of labor disci-

---

[56] Mordukhovich (Mokhov), *Na bor'bu s tekuchest'iu rabochei sily,* pp. 35–37, 98–102.

[57] Ibid., p. 129.

pline, but that those actually fired were only less than 10 percent of those surveyed.[58]

The disorganization of the labor market also made an important contribution to the economic crisis in the summer of 1930: the lack of central control over the labor force stymied every effort to organize its planned recruitment and distribution in accordance with industry's needs. On 20 October 1930 the Central Committee adopted a resolution entitled "On Measures for a Planned Supply of the National Economy with Labor Power and for Combating Labor Turnover," in which the committee sharply attacked the People's Commissariat of Labor and ordered a reorganization of the labor exchanges along the lines of a planned training and distribution of the labor force.[59] At the All-Union conference on problems of labor in November 1930, the deputy people's commissar of labor, I. A. Kraval', declared:

It is necessary to lay the former labor exchanges to rest. *The words "labor exchange" and "labor market" should be removed once and for all from the* [Soviet] *lexicon because it is entirely inappropriate to the socialist state that the labor force should be quoted on some "market."*[60]

In December 1930 this attempt at central planning led to the compulsory employment of labor through the state labor organs. (Certain exceptions were permitted, however.) In the same month the labor exchanges were reorganized into "cadre administrations" whose task it was to organize "a planned supply of the national economy with labor force and the planning and control of training worker cadres."[61]

To declare the removal of the terms "labor exchange" and "labor market" from the Soviet vocabulary was one thing; actually to remove them by establishing a planned economy was quite another. In 1930 the spontaneous ebb and flow of the labor force in fact went out of control.

---

[58] *Partiinoe stroitel'stvo*, 1930, nos. 29–30 (77–78), p. 27.

[59] Ibid., 1930, nos. 19–20, pp. 61–63.

[60] *Za industrializatsiiu*, 17 November 1930. Emphasis in the original. In late November, an editorial in the industrial newspaper declared: "The labor exchanges have disappeared naturally." Ibid., 23 November 1930.

[61] *Sobranie zakonov*, 1930, I, 60–641, and *Izvestiia N.K. Truda SSSR*, 1931, nos. 1–2, pp. 4–7.

The rapid movement of new workers into the factories

The number of workers in census industry rose from 2,921,200 in 1929 to 3,675,000 in 1930, a 25.8 percent increase.[62] Some industrial centers underwent a more rapid influx of workers. In Leningrad, for example, between 1 January 1930 and 1 January 1931 the number of workers in census industry grew from 285,553 to 415,089, a 46.8 percent growth; the number of metal workers increased even more rapidly: from 108,122 to 181,353, a 73.5 percent increase.[63] The influx of workers into some individual factories was even more striking. The Nevsky Engineering Factory increased its work force by 82.7 percent in 1930.[64] On the Kuznetsk Iron and Steel Plant construction site, there were 445 workers in May 1929, 4,100 in September 1929, and 14,925 in September 1930.[65] The AMO Factory in Moscow is one of the most striking cases: in five years the number of workers in the automobile factory increased from 1,000 in 1927 to 3,500 in 1929, 12,000 in 1931, and 14,000 in 1932.[66]

The rapid influx of new workers necessarily "diluted" the ranks of "older" workers. As discussed in Chapter 4, in the spring of 1929 those who had first entered industrial labor before 1918 accounted for 50.7 percent of the total industrial work force. By the spring of 1931, the corresponding figure dropped below 30 percent. (No exact data are available for industry as a whole.) According to a Gosplan survey of the spring of 1931, those "old" workers accounted for 31.0 percent of the metal workers in Leningrad, 30.5 percent in the Ukrainian metallurgical industry, and only 19.6 percent in the Donbas coal mines; new workers who had first entered industrial labor in 1930 and the first quarter of 1931 accounted for

---

[62] *Trud v SSSR* (1932), pp. 16 and 61 (average annual number of workers including factory apprentices). For a slightly different figure, see M. Avdienko, "Sdvig v strukture proletariata v pervoi piatiletke," *Planovoe khoziaistvo*, 1932, nos. 6–7, p. 147.

[63] *Ekonomiko-statisticheskii spravochnik Leningradskoi oblasti*, p. 414.

[64] *Na putiakh stroitel'stva sotsializma*, p. 17.

[65] *Istoriia Kuznetskogo metallurgicheskogo kombinata im. V. I. Lenina*, p. 34.

[66] *Partiinoe stroitel'stvo*, 1931, no. 8 (April), p. 41, and *Moskovskii avtozavod im. I.A. Likhacheva*, p. 189.

21.6, 19.6, and 33.0 percent in the respective industries.[67] Simultaneously, the rate of those of proletarian origin among the new recruits decreased, and that of those of peasant origin increased. In the Leningrad engineering industry, for example, children of workers accounted for 38.8 percent of the new recruits during 1930 and the first quarter of 1931, a substantial drop from the corresponding ratios of 46.9 percent for 1929, 52.0 percent for 1928, and 55.6 percent for 1926–27. Accordingly, the ratio of workers of peasant origin (excluding "kulak" origin) increased to 48.5 percent for the 1930–31 cohort from 40.7 percent for 1929, 34.7 percent for 1928, and 34.0 percent for 1926–27.[68] The Urals metallurgical industry underwent a more drastic change: the ratio of workers of proletarian origin decreased from 43.7 percent for the 1926–27 cohort to 38.6 percent for 1928, 33.6 percent for 1929, and 29.0 percent for 1930–31; that of peasant workers rose accordingly from 54.2 percent to 59.9, 62.6, and 69.9 percent for the respective cohorts.[69] The Donbas coal mines were literally flooded with new arrivals from the countryside: the ratio of workers of proletarian origin decreased from 27.2 percent for the 1926–28 cohort to 23.6 for 1929 and 17.8 for 1930; that of peasant workers accordingly increased from 70.3 percent to 73.2 and 79.4 for the respective cohorts.[70] Warnings were voiced again and again at that time: "The factory is threatened by the danger of the dilution of proletarian composition by the peasants and the petty bourgeoisie."[71]

---

[67] *Narodnoe khoziaistvo SSSR*, 1932, nos. 1–2 (March–April), pp. 127–28. The data concerning the Donbas workers are as of December 1930.

[68] Ibid., pp. 128–29.

[69] Ibid.

[70] Ibid. In contrast to this "peasantization," the "feminization" of the working class still had not taken place by 1930–31. Certainly the number of female industrial workers rose from 725,900 in 1928 to 804,000 in 1929, 881,500 in 1930, and to 1,273,600 in 1931, or a 75.5% increase in four years. (*Planovoe khoziaistvo*, 1932, nos. 6–7, p. 160. The figures are average annual numbers in census industry, apprentices included.) And again individual factories underwent a rapid influx of women: the Putilov Factory in Leningrad, for example, increased its female labor force from 286 in early 1929 to 2,391 in early 1931; its ratio to the total work force rose from 2.8% to 11.1% during the same period (*Na putiakh stroitel'stva sotsializma*, pp. 19–20). However, while the total work force in census industry increased by 36.6% from 1928 to 1930 and 72.5% from 1928 to 1931, the female labor force rose by 21.4% and 75.7% in the respective periods. *Planovoe khoziaistvo*, 1932, nos. 6–7, pp. 147 and 160. According to another source, the ratio of female workers rose slightly from 28.4% on 1 January 1930 to 30.7% on 1 January 1931. *Udarnik*, 1932, no. 10, p. 24.

[71] *Pravda*, 13 July 1930, concerning the Moscow Electric Factory.

The age composition of the workers also changed considerably. In 1926–29 those workers younger than twenty-three years of age accounted for about 30 percent of the new recruits. From 1930 on, the ratio of those young workers to the new recruits as a whole (including apprentices) jumped to about 70 percent.[72] In the Leningrad engineering industry, for example, those young workers accounted for 66.4 percent of the new workers who had first entered industrial labor in 1930 and the first quarter of 1931; in the Donbas coal mines the corresponding figure was as high as 75.9 percent.[73] M. I. Kalinin, reporting to a party conference in the Middle Volga in June 1930, warned that in some factories, particularly in those requiring high skills, 70–80 percent of the workers were less than twenty years of age and had little work experience.[74]

The inevitable consequence of this rapid influx of new workers was a rapid deterioration of the skill composition of the working class. Its average years of industrial work experience fell from 11.9 years in 1929 to 6.8 years in 1933.[75] The ratio of the illiterate among the new recruits constantly rose from 1928/29 to 1932 in all industries.[76] It is difficult to pinpoint the degree of decline in the skill composition of the workers. Many contemporary accounts, including official government reports, state that in 1930 the average skill of the work force declined.[77] No comprehensive data are available, but there is some interesting information. In the metal and electric industries in Leningrad, for example, the ratio of skilled workers and semiskilled workers dropped from 23.2 percent and 43.2 percent in 1929 to 18.6 percent and 40 percent, respectively, in 1931; that of unskilled workers rose from 33.6 percent to 41.4 percent during the same period.[78] According to another report, the

---

[72] Vdovin and Drobizhev, *Rost rabochego klassa SSSR*, p. 133.

[73] *Narodnoe khoziaistvo SSSR*, 1932, nos. 1–2 (March–April), p. 134.

[74] Kalinin, *Izbrannye proizvedeniia*, 2:418.

[75] *Profsoiuznaia perepis' 1932–33 g.*, p. 74. No data are available for 1930–31.

[76] Ibid., p. 44. The only exception was the electrotechnical industry, of whose 1930 cohort only 2.3% were illiterate, down by 0.4% from the 1928/29 cohort. Yet the ratio rose to 3.9% for the 1931 cohort and 7.0% for the 1932 cohort.

[77] *Za tri mesiatsa. Deiatel'nost' SNK i STO. III kvartal (aprel'–iiun') 1929–30 g.*, p. 68; *Industrializatsiia SSSR, 1929–1932*, p. 378 (Gosplan material); *Na fronte industrializatsii*, 1930, no. 20 (November), p. 42, and *Partrabotnik*, 1930, nos. 29–30 (December), p. 25. According to *Kommunisty Leningrada v bor'be za vypolnenie reshenii partii po industrializatsii strany (1926–1929 gg.)*, p. 413, in some raions of Leningrad the decline started as early as 1927–28.

[78] *XV let diktatury proletariata*, Table 90. (These data do not include the apprentices.) The only industry in which skill composition improved was the textile

Figure 8.1.   An army of young Komsomol workers arriving at the Kuznetsk construction site (c. 1930). From Iu. Zhukov, *Liudi 30-kh godov* (Moscow, 1966).

ratio of highly skilled workers in the Dinamo Electric Factory in Moscow declined from 10.7 percent in 1927 to 6.6 percent in 1928, 4.8 percent in 1929, 3.8 percent in 1930, 3.3 percent in March 1931, and 2.7 percent in September 1931. The ratio of skilled workers similarly dropped from 26.5 percent in 1927 to 11.6 percent in September 1931, whereas the ratio of unskilled workers and auxiliary workers sharply increased from 26.2 percent to 49.8 percent during the same period. The average wage-rate index declined from 3.19 to 2.73 from January to March 1931.[79] The official average wage-rate index of the workers in the Boiler-Turbine Association dropped from 1.56 as of 1 January 1930 to 1.48 as of 1 January 1931 and 1.47 as of July 1931. The actual index was said

industry, because, according to a Soviet account, the overall number of workers declined and the less skilled workers drifted to other expanding industries. *Leningradskie rabochie v bor'be za sotsializm, 1926–1937 gg.*, p. 153.

[79] *Za promyshlennye kadry*, 1932, nos. 7–8, pp. 26 and 30. In the aviation industry, in 1929 those workers whose wage ranks belonged to the lowest three (out of eight) accounted for 44%, but in the first quarter of 1931 the ratio increased to 66%. *Trud*, 30 June 1931.

to be lower than this.[80] In the Urals metallurgical industry unskilled workers accounted for 22.9 percent in 1929, but in 1932 the ratio rose to 34.7 percent, as a result of which the average wage-rate index dropped from 5.2 to 3.6.[81] All this happened despite a massive unwarranted transfer of unskilled workers to skilled labor.

Many new workers naturally had never seen machines and lacked elementary skills. Peasant workers "looked mistrustfully at the machines; when a lever would not work they grew angry and treated it like a baulking horse, often damaging the machine."[82] A miner who in 1930 left a Donbas mine for a Moscow metal factory later recalled how afraid he was of machines because he had never seen any before and did not know how to handle them.[83] The majority of those 7,000 young workers recruited in 1930 to the Stalingrad Tractor Plant had "never had a nut in their hands before."[84] A journalist who visited the plant found a young Komsomol woman weeping beside a broken machine:

She had worked for a publishing house in Nizhni [Novgorod]. She had not the slightest idea about production before, but was mobilized to Stalingrad. She observed for a day how people worked with a machine, and then was assigned to this machine. Even now, after having stayed in the plant for several months, she knows neither the names of the parts she makes with the machine nor what role the parts play in the tractor.[85]

Technical education lagged far behind the rapid expansion of the labor force.

Low skills were responsible at least in part for the trouble that caught the plant in 1930. The machine operator Petrov of the assembly workshop, for example, tried to drive an automobile, though he was totally ignorant of its mechanism. The automobile crashed into the wall at full speed; the machine was taken to a repair shop, and Petrov to a hospital.[86] The mobilized young workers had to

learn not just to oil the machines but also how to carry oil. It was all right to use not absolutely pure oil in machines whose bearings were large and whose revolution was slow, but mud in oil was inadmissible for small

[80] *Voprosy truda*, 1931, nos. 8–9, p. 52.
[81] Shcherbakova, "Kvalifikatsionnye izmeneniia v sostave rabochikh metallurgicheskoi promyshlennosti Urala v 1929–1937 godakh," pp. 363–64.
[82] Ehrenburg, *Memoirs: 1921–1941*, p. 222.
[83] *Slovo masterov*, p. 265 (Nikolai Zadorezhenko).
[84] Galin, *Vsegda za mechtoi*, p. 70.
[85] Gershberg, *Rabota u nas takaia*, pp. 45–46.
[86] *Istoriia zavodov*, p. 113.

Figure 8.2. Workers at the Stalingrad Tractor Plant (1930). From Ernst Glaeser and F. C. Weiskopf, *Der Staat ohne Arbeitslose. Drei Jahre "Fünfjahresplan"* (Berlin, 1931).

bearings whose revolution is fast. But we thought that it was all right, and poured dirty oil. It was necessary to convince and teach [the young workers] for a long time – how to keep and carry oil so as not to take dust in, how not to put oil cans on the dirty floor, and thousands of other production "trivialities."[87]

Nevertheless, machines broke down: in the first four months (June–September 1930), there were 2,788 such incidents.[88] In Kuznetsk, many workers (as well as horses) were panicked to see automobiles, which they had never seen before, move around.[89] In the fourth quarter of 1929/30, only 19 percent of the brickwork plan in the construction of a blast furnace in Kuznetsk was fulfilled, mainly because of the low skills of bricklayers, whose productivity was merely "a quarter of the normal level."[90]

A perceptive observer in Siberia, noting the rapid influx in 1930 of unskilled peasants into the factories, could not but strike a pessimistic chord: "The very structure of workers' composition is a factor of their reduced utility in production. . . . such workers cannot provide a high coefficient of utility."[91] He came under severe attack for his "Menshevik deviation," that is, for allegedly reducing all the evil to the working class. Yet the low skills of workers were indeed responsible at least in part for the reduced "utility" (productivity) of labor. This fact was abundantly clear to managers, who compensated for the qualitative deterioration of labor with quan-

---

[87] Galin, *Vsegda za mechtoi*, pp. 70–71. See also *Liudi Stalingrdaskogo traktornogo*, p. 64. In 1930 more than half of the machine operators in the plant did not know how to oil the machines properly. This situation prompted the factory newspaper to launch a campaign: "Learn how to use oil cans." See Gudov, *Besedy o kul'ture na proizvodstve*, p. 34. (Gudov had mistakenly referred to 1931.)

[88] See editorial in *Pravda*, 18 April 1931. According to another source, there were 6,000 incidents in the first eight months. See Ginzburg, *O proshlom - dlia budushchego*, p. 90.

[89] *Kuznetskstroi*, p. 88.

[90] *Za promyshlennye kadry*, 1931, no. 1, p. 16.

[91] The author is "Riasentsev," who is quoted in "Sibirskaia gromanovshchina," *Zhizn' Sibiri*, 1931, no. 4, p. 7. The American engineer H. H. Angst, who worked in Moscow, Leningrad, and elsewhere from May 1930 to February 1932, remarked even more harshly: "Russia has a long way to go industrially, economically, and mentally. Starting at zero, they can never hope by their Five-Year Plans to attain equality with other modern nations in the next 50 years. First, they must be educated mentally, physically, and morally. Then they must have experience and training in the use of tools and machinery. Then they must develop industrial leaders who know how to handle men and machine and make them operate." The H. H. Angst file in "American Engineers in Russia."

tity: they recruited more workers than planned, causing a rapid influx of new workers even in the spring and summer of 1930, when the "productive work of industry" declined.[92]

This "wager on quantity" not only exacerbated the labor shortages but also had a strong adverse impact on the qualitative performance of the economy. In the economic year 1929/30, the average number of workers (including apprentices) in census industry increased by 17.2 percent, far exceeding the planned target of 6.0 percent,[93] whereas almost all other economic indexes fell short of the plan targets: according to the official report, which almost certainly overstated economic performance, gross industrial output increased 24.6 percent instead of 32 percent; productivity rose a mere 9.5 percent instead of the planned 25 percent increase; and the costs of industrial production declined by 6.9 percent, far short of the planned 11 percent.[94] The American engineer Leon M. Banks, who had worked in the Ridder mines from June 1930 to June 1931, aptly remarked: "The greater output was accomplished by [the] addition of more workers as places were ready for work."[95]

Much confusion was evident. Industry desperately needed skilled labor, but the Taylorist theory of deskilling was not repudiated. Rather, the shortage of a skilled work force practically necessitated the division of complex work processes into simpler, specialized tasks, thereby validating the theory of deskilling. The massive addition of human resources to industry threatened to consume already scarce material resources and to make the accumulation of capital impossible without further squeezing national consumption.

Administrative control over labor

The transformation of the labor market and the rapid influx of new workers posed many social problems, some of which will be discussed in the following chapter. The transformation also raised at least two issues with important political implications.

[92] "Kon″iunktura, 1929–30," section "Trud," pp. 1–2. The mines and construction sites, which lost large numbers of workers, were exceptions.

[93] *Kontrol'nye tsifry narodnogo khoziaistva SSSR na 1929/30 g.*, p. 155, and *Planovoe khoziaistvo*, 1930, nos. 10–11, p. 343. The difference between this and note 62 is due to the difference between the economic and the calendar years.

[94] *Industrializatsiia SSSR, 1929–1932*, p. 221; "Kon″iunktura, 1929–30," section "Trud," p. 5; and Malafeev, *Istoriia tsenoobrazovaniia v SSSR*, pp. 157 and 406.

[95] The Leon M. Banks file in "American Engineers in Russia."

First, the political and industrial authorities came to assume that strong central control on free labor had to be established to incorporate the "labor market" into the centrally planned economy.[96] The labor market turned out to be the weakest link of a centrally planned economy that emerged in 1929–30: when other market relations were being squeezed out of the official economy, the spontaneity of the labor market actually strengthened. Labor shortages increased the workers' bargaining power in the market. They appeared to be able to behave as they pleased, as seen in the following informed advice:

> If you want to move to another place of work, just leave your work. If they don't let you leave, violate the factory regulations and get dismissed for violation of labor discipline. Then you'll be registered with a labor exchange, which in good order will send you to an appropriate place. If you find a suitable place for yourself, you'll be lucky.[97]

Yet the People's Commissariat of Labor under Uglanov insisted that some degree of labor fluidity was inevitable. In May 1930 Uglanov expressed serious doubts about harsh administrative measures against mobile workers that apparently were being discussed in the political leadership: it was necessary to regard labor fluidity as "an enduring phenomenon"; the problem of turnover should not be dealt with by "fire-fighting measures" that would alleviate the problem for only a short period; the People's Commissariat of Labor should "not embrace the unembraceable [task]."[98] The party leadership saw this as slavish cringing before the spontaneity of the labor market.

The removal of the term "labor market" from the Soviet lexicon actually implied an increase in administrative control over the movement of the labor force. At a meeting of the board of the People's Commissariat of Labor in November 1930, the new deputy commissar, I. A. Kraval', who had been sent by the Central Committee to inspect the Donbas, made it clear that harsh administrative coercion was needed to regulate the labor market. Referring to the "usual phenomenon" that 10–12 percent of Donbas workers did not show

---

[96] It is noteworthy here that reliance on convict labor instead of free labor (especially in the timber industry) became an attractive economic enterprise during the Five-Year Plan. See Solomon, "Soviet Penal Policy," and *II sessiia VTsIK XIV sozyva*, 11:32 (Ianson).

[97] Mordukhovich (Mokhov), *Na bor'bu s tekuchest'iu rabochei sily*, p. 89.

[98] Quoted in *Problemy ekonomiki*, 1930, nos. 4–5, p. 49.

up for work every day, Kraval' declared that it was "impossible to work when 12 percent of workers don't show up," and proposed the following measures: if absent three days, a worker should be immediately "removed from production," evicted from factory, or mine, housing, and expelled from the party, the Komsomol, and the trade unions. Kraval' went on to say that if the commissariat was to organize the distribution of the labor force, it would be necessary to introduce work books so that the commissariat would know whom to hire, who actually worked how many days, and what bonuses had been given to the worker. The commissariat board adopted his proposal on work books.[99] These measures were not realized at the time,[100] probably because the commissariat appeared insufficiently capable to the party leadership of regimenting the workers.[101] But harsh administrative restrictions on workers' movements were gradually introduced from late 1930 on.[102] Noteworthy is the 20 October 1930 resolution of the Central Committee referred to earlier, which attempted to combine coercive measures with special privileges (preferential allocation of living quarters and scarce goods) to shock workers and those with exemplary work records. The resolution stipulated that any registrants refusing a job were to be immediately removed from the rolls of the labor exchange, and that "deserters and rolling stones" (i.e., those who quit their jobs) were to be deprived of the right to be sent for industrial labor for six months.[103] A series of decrees and regulations defining the implementation of these measures ensued.[104]

It was difficult, however, to fight against high labor turnover under the conditions of labor shortages. Moreover, to enforce these measures and the state monopoly of hiring, it was necessary to have a powerful administrative apparatus. In fact, the 20 October 1930 resolution expressed a serious concern about the administrative capability of the People's Commissariat of Labor: in light of its "ex-

---

[99] *Za industrializatsiiu*, 12 November 1930.

[100] The eviction of workers from factory housing for violation of labor discipline was not imposed until November 1932. The work book was not introduced until 1938.

[101] The plan to introduce work books was submitted in February 1931 to the All-Union Central Executive Committee for ratification, and then quietly forgotten. Filtzer, *Soviet Workers and Stalinist Industrialization*, p. 111.

[102] Schwartz, *Labor in the Soviet Union*, pp. 96–98.

[103] *Partiinoe stroitel'stvo*, 1930, nos. 19–20, pp. 62–63.

[104] See Schwarz, *Labor in the Soviet Union*, pp. 353–54.

tremely unsatisfactory composition of qualified party cadres," the resolution entrusted the Secretariat of the Central Committee to take measures to strengthen the commissariat with qualified party cadres.[105] Yet the problem was that the party was running out of "qualified cadres."

The "proletarianization" of the party, state, and other apparatuses had taken a great number of workers away from the shop floor. Workers not only replaced those who were purged but also staffed the rapidly expanding bureaucracies. At the third Leningrad *oblast'* party conference in June 1930, a Leningrad party leader complained that Leningrad

had to part with the best proletarians for the sake of the country. [Applause.] This is painful for me, because during the [past] year we have sent more than two thousand outstanding workers to the command of the Central Committee, but like it or not, we have to do so even further.

Comrade Molotov: That's good.

This is good for the Central Committee, but for us it's a little painful and bad. [Laughter.][106]

By the end of the year, the massive mobilization of workers was no longer a laughing matter. Hard pressed by the dire shortage of skilled workers in production, the Central Committee ordered in its 20 October 1930 resolution a two-year ban on the promotion of workers from the bench to any kind of administrative institutions "with a view to keeping skilled cadres of workers in production."[107]

In the meantime, between 1929 and 1931 the People's Commissariat of Labor, like other commissariats, underwent extensive purges that removed its old cadres almost completely, i.e., 100 percent of its top staff and department heads; yet the Commissariat of Labor, unlike most other commissariats, increased in size.[108] This means that a considerable number of new cadres were brought in. The proletarianization of the commissariat undoubtedly made it more militant, as may have been reflected in the adoption by its board of Kraval's proposals on work books and other draconian measures. Nevertheless, the party leadership saw the commissariat as too weak administratively.

[105] *Partiinoe stroitel'stvo*, 1930, nos. 19–20, p. 63.
[106] *Biulleten' 3-ei leningradskoi oblastnoi konferentsii VKP(b)*, 2:45 (B. P. Pozern).
[107] *Partiinoe stroitel'stvo*, 1930, nos. 19–20, p. 62. Promotions within industrial and trade union institutions were not banned.
[108] I owe this to Getty, "Soviet City Directories."

The People's Commissariat of Labor had its own complaint that it lacked a stong apparatus and able cadres. The discussion at an All-Union Central Executive Committee session in early January 1931 vividly illustrated this issue. V. P. Zatonskii, apparently a watchdog for Rabkrin over the commissariat, emphasized that the commissariat had to become the leading center for a planned training, recruitment, and distribution of the labor force, but that it was not such a leading center through its own fault. In the commissariat, he contended that there was "incredible routine," which would persist until the Commissar Tsikhon would drive out "more than half of its own organs," and that the "entire old experience of work" hindered the commissariat from reorganizing itself.[109] The deputy commissar of labor, Kraval', responded resentfully. People constantly criticized the bureaucratism and stagnation of the commissariat, but, he contended, they would not see why the commissariat had difficulties:

When a grain procurement campaign takes place, the best people are mobilized from the party, administrative organs, and other apparatuses, for grain procurements. Now our best organizers are taken and sent for meat procurements. Any of these campaigns takes away people, and [even] the mobilization of people's commissars is not excluded. But when it comes to the question of our recruiting 3.3 million people for the seasonal industries for the next economic year, who out of the big people is sent to help us? When it comes to the question of training 2 million people and recruiting about 1.5 million women into production, people needed for this task are not given to the labor organs.

Kraval' went on to refute Zatonskii's criticism of bureaucratism in the commissariat. Kraval' contended that the chief problem was that the commissariat simply did not have enough people: one labor inspector, for example, had to engage in all sorts of duties (from labor protection to the regulation of wages) in many *raion*s. He had to challenge the unsympathetic audience:

Can one person cope with all these problems in ten to fifteen *raion*s or fifteen to twenty factories? Of course not.

A voice: Difficult.

No, not difficult but, it's necessary to say openly, impossible because he can hardly visit these twenty factories when some complication or [labor] accident occurs somewhere. . . . There is not enough time.

[109] *3 sessiia TsIK Soiuza SSR 5 sozyva,* 17:16–17.

Here at the session we have to emphasize this question because it is necessary to help us with people, to help us to pose the question of great significance for the entire cause of socialist construction; otherwise the labor organs will not be in a position to cope with the task facing us.

Kraval' further discussed how difficult it was to contain labor turnover and declared:

It is impossible to cope, by administrative measures alone, with those enormous tasks anticipated in supplying the national economy with the work force for this coming year.

A voice from the floor: If you can't cope, you'll have to be replaced.

The point is not replacement. Of course, if we can't cope, we have to be replaced, but the main task is to *cope at all costs.*[110]

In November 1930 Kraval' was wrapped up in "administrative ecstasy"; by January 1931 he had come to insist that administrative measures alone were inadequate, but felt obliged to promise to "cope at all costs." His desperate plea for aid won little sympathy from the audience, if only because, as GPU chairman Menzhinskii suggested, all institutions were in the same situation.[111]

The transformation of the labor market presented a formidable obstacle to the industrialization drive. It deprived the People's Commissariat of Labor of control over the labor market, and the commissariat found itself faced with the "unembraceable" task of fighting against the spontaneity of a free labor market. In the course of 1931 the party leadership would judge that the commissariat was unable to cope with the task, and would abandon the state monopoly of hiring in tune with the general shift away from "administrative ecstasy."[112]

The transformation, on the one hand, was an unexpected success in solving one of the most vexing problems of NEP, urban mass unemployment, and created enormous opportunities for, to use Stalin's expression, "millions of people who were formerly oppressed and downtrodden."[113] Young women and men found not only opportunities but also a "romantic appeal" in going out to work in the factories and on the construction sites.[114] Moreover, the trans-

---

[110] Ibid., 17:46–49 (emphasis in the original). For the same point, see *Voprosy truda,* 1930, nos. 11–12, pp. 67, 70 (M. Romanov).

[111] See chap. 6, note 141.

[112] See "The Correction of the Planned Economy," chap. 10, this volume.

[113] See chap. 5, note 2.

[114] Ermilov, *Schast'e trudnykh dorog,* pp. 112–13.

formation removed the very cause of such conflicts as took place in 1929 between "permanent" and "temporary" workers at the Lenin Tea-Weighing Factory.[115]

On the other hand, this success was bought dearly. The Five-Year Plan did not foresee the elimination of mass unemployment because it was based on the assumption that "a vast increase in the productivity of labor" would make it unnecessary to increase the labor force to the point of fully absorbing unemployment.[116] To some extent, success in eliminating mass unemployment was a failure in disguise in the achievement of "a vast increase in the productivity of labor."

This failure seriously aggravated the problem of resource constraints. The wager on quantity was a spontaneous managerial response to the acceleration of industrialization and the dearth of skilled labor. This response was economically disruptive, and the loss of central control over the labor market led the desperate government to accuse nonparty labor economists of "wrecking" and to intervene directly in the labor market (the compulsory employment of labor through the state labor organs). Much despair was evident when the state labor organs proved unable to subject the labor market to central planning. Yet the political gains of the wager on quantity were also evident, and condemnation of it became lukewarm. The leadership turned misguided managerial behavior to its political advantage by cheerfully declaring that the country of proletarian dictatorship was a country of full employment in sharp contrast to capitalist societies in the agonies of mass unemployment caused by the Great Depression. The problem of resources was politically covered up.

[115] See "From Resistance to Adaptation," chap. 5, this volume.
[116] *Piatiletnii plan narodno-khoziaistvennogo stroitel'stva SSSR*, vol. 1, p. 94, and vol. 2, part 2, p. 12.

9

Conflict and cohesion among the workers

In the Soviet Union, as in other societies, vast social dislocation was an inevitable accompaniment of rapid industrialization. In 1930 the country was, as it were, "a society in flux," "a society unhinged and temporarily amorphous."[1] The spontaneous movement was compounded by violent political attacks on previously privileged groups in the town and the countryside, many of whom were uprooted and sent to labor camps. The flux was further intensified by the massive promotion of industrial workers, particularly shock workers, away from the shop floor and into full-time administration and higher technical education. The country was undergoing what might be called a "revolution of status."[2]

Consequently, the Soviet working class of 1930, as the Ukrainian Communist Party leader S. Kosior perceptively noted in June 1930, no longer resembled the working class that "had endured the famine during the civil war . . . beaten the class enemy, and raised our economy from the verge of ruin."[3] This transformation, however, caused mixed feelings in the leadership. The very rapid addition of new workers was nothing new historically, but in 1930–31 it was so rapid as to end mass unemployment. On the other hand, the influx rapidly "peasantized" the working class and adversely affected economic performance.[4] The mass promotion of shock workers deprived the factories of many of the most productive forces, but

---

[1] Lewin, "Society and the Stalinist State in the Period of the Five-Year Plans," pp. 139–40.
[2] This concept of "revolution of status" is found in Schoenbaum, *Hitler's Social Revolution*.
[3] *XI z'izd KP(b)U*, p. 251.
[4] The phrase "peasantization" is used by Arutiunian in "Kollektivizatsiia sel'skogo khoziaistva i vysvobozhdenie rabochei sily dlia promyshlennosti," p. 116.

it meant that the government and higher education institutions were being rapidly proletarianized.

Indeed, it was difficult at the time for the leadership to assess the positive against the negative impact that various policies and events exerted on the working class. The influx of new workers and "class aliens," the shock movement and socialist competition, and industrial modernization combined to create turmoil on the shop floor, threatening the old order and intensifying both conflict and cohesion among the workers. On the one hand, the conflict led to tremendous labor turnover within the factory. On the other hand, there was a wave of "spontaneous collectivization" of workers into shock brigades and egalitarian production communes. Similarly, wage-leveling trends had the political utility of maintaining among the workers a certain measure of "economic homogeneity" as a "fence" against the surrounding "nonproletarian" milieus and thus as a safeguard against political differentiation; but the trends caused an exodus of skilled workers from production. The declining standard of living continued to pose serious social and political problems. Even this issue, however, helped the political leadership evoke a war atmosphere in society and mobilize the workers for attack on the bureaucratic apparatus.

Further declines in the standard of living

In February 1930 a Gosplan official declared to the All-Union conference of planning and statistical organs: "It would be absurd to build high tempos of industrialization of the country upon a declining consumption of the great bulk of the toilers of the country."[5] Indeed, absurd tempos were imposed on society. Willis B. Clemmitt, an American engineer who was in Leningrad in late 1929, wrote:

There was a sharp decline in available goods in the autumn of 1929 when the large number of private shops remaining from the NEP period were closed. After that there was a gradual diminishing of supply of all kinds of goods. . . . Before the autumn of 1929 it was possible to get a fair variety of food and a reasonable assortment of other things in private shops. . . . After 1929 these things, except the strictly rationed staples, were almost non-existent in everyday trade.[6]

[5] *Planovoe khoziaistvo*, 1930, no. 2, p. 30 (V. A. Levin).
[6] The Willis B. Clemmitt file in "American Engineers in Russia."

Another American engineer, John D. Littlepage, found that in Siberia

during the few months [in the winter of 1929–30] I was gone [back to the United States], prices had gotten completely out of hand. Butter, which had been fifty kopecks, or half a ruble, per kilogram, was now eight rubles. . . . Eggs, which had been a ruble a hundred, were now a ruble apiece. A few months before we had been able to buy a whole wagonload of potatoes for fifteen rubles, but now we had to pay twenty rubles for a small pailful.[7]

Soviet diplomat Alexander Barmine, who after four years of service abroad returned to Moscow in the summer of 1930 to attend the sixteenth party congress, was struck by economic hardships not seen before:

After the improvements of 1922–28, Moscow showed appalling changes. Every face and every house front was eloquent of misery, exhaustion, and apathy. There were scarcely any stores, and the rare display windows still existing had an air of desolation. Nothing was to be seen in them but cardboard boxes and food tins, upon which the shopkeepers, in a mood of despair rather than rashness, had pasted stickers reading "empty." Everyone's clothes were worn out, and the quality of the stuff was unspeakable. My Paris suit made me feel embarrassed in the streets. There was a shortage of everything – especially of soap, boots, vegetables, meat, butter, and all fatty foodstuffs.

I was much astonished to see crowds waiting in front of the candy stores. Fellow travellers after a hasty trip through Russia would return home and tell glowing tales of the socialist paradise where crowds waited in long lines, not for bread, but for candy. The truth was quite different. Famished people sought anything to fill their empty stomachs. Even the revolting sweets made of saccharine and soya beans were gladly consumed, because they were almost the only edible things that could be bought – and even then one pound of them cost an average day's wages.[8]

Soviet political leaders, like fellow travelers, gave similarly glowing reports of the "socialist paradise." At the sixteenth party congress, Stalin declared that "real wages in our country are steadily rising from year to year."[9] In June 1930 S. M. Kirov insisted that the overall "well-being of the working class is growing."[10] In the same month, Rudzutak vehemently rejected the "assertion of some comrades that in the past years we have had a decline in real

---

[7] Littlepage and Bess, *In Search of Soviet Gold*, p. 62.
[8] Barmine, *One Who Survived*, pp. 196–97. Note that Barmine wrote this passage nearly fifteen years later in exile. One may have to be careful of his bias.
[9] Stalin, *Sochineniia*, 12:297.
[10] *Biulleten' 3-ei leningradskoi oblastnoi konferentsii VKP(b)*, 6:38.

wages."[11] Molotov also contended that claims about the decline of real wages were "Cadet-Menshevik conclusions."[12]

The leaders' claims to the contrary notwithstanding, the contemporary press implicitly (and sometimes explicitly) admitted the declining standard of living. The organ of the Central Committee reported in early 1930 that real wages in Tula had declined by 6 percent from 1929.[13] In May 1930 the Central Union of Consumer Societies self-critically repudiated the contention concerning the favorable effects of the expanding socialized sector of trade: *"The level of real wages rose slightly, but even this slight increase was more than offset by workers' purchases from private traders because of inadequate supplies by the consumer cooperatives."*[14]

In the summer and autumn of 1930 some influential party figures implicitly challenged the official myth of rising real wages. In early June 1930, V. V. Lominadze, the new secretary of the party's Transcaucasian Committee, stated that in Georgia "real wages do not have a tendency to increase" and that not to see the "significance and seriousness" of the problem of real wages would be an "inadmissible mistake."[15] In his speech of 30 August 1930, S. I. Syrtsov declared:

I won't argue about the methodology [of calculating real wages]. I think that the feelings of the main strata of the working class on this question are much more faultless than many indexes; and they show that in this sphere there is great trouble [*neblagopoluchie*], and above all [it is] growing.[16]

In September 1930, a declaration of the Transcaucasian Committee drafted by Lominadze condemned the "lordly feudal attitudes to

[11] *XI z'izd KP(b)U*, p. 23.

[12] Molotov, *Stroitel'stvo sotsializma i protivorechiia rosta*, p. 105. The Cadets were former Constitutional Democrats, a political opponent of the Bolshevik party. For the same contention, see Kaganovich, *Ob itogakh dekabr'skogo ob"edinennogo plenuma TsK i TsKK VKP(b)*, p. 22. "A comrade from the Institute of the Monopoly of Foreign Trade" openly came out at a Krasnaia Presnia party conference in Moscow against the official statement of rising real wages. See Voroshilov, *Na istoricheskom perevale*, p. 73.

[13] *Partiinoe stroitel'stvo*, 1930, nos. 7–8, p. 61 ("Dnevnik orgsoveshchaniia TsK VKP[b]").

[14] See *Informatsionnyi biulleten' Tsentrosoiuza SSSR i RSFSR*, 1930, no. 17 (185) (10 June), p. 519. Emphasis in the original.

[15] *Zaria Vostoka*, 2 June 1930. For a similar speech of his, see *XVI s"ezd VKP(b)*, p. 197.

[16] Syrtsov, *K novomu khoziaistvennomu godu*, p. 19. In September 1929 Syrtsov spoke of the "growth of the well-being of the bulk of workers." See *Pervyi Moskovskii oblastnoi s"ezd sovetov RK i KD*, p. 18.

the needs and interests of the workers and peasants" prevalent in the Transcaucasian government, trade, and cooperative institutions.[17] This implicit but candid discussion of declining real wages got Syrtsov and Lominadze into trouble with Stalin. Yet six years later, in 1936, in his conversation with an American, Roy Howard, Stalin rather proudly, and frankly, admitted that a reduction in consumption had been needed to promote rapid industrialization:

If one wants to build a new house, one saves up money and cuts down consumption for a while. Otherwise the house would not be built. This is all the truer when it is a matter of building an entirely new human society. We had to cut down consumption for a time, collect the necessary resources, and strain every nerve. This is precisely what we did and we built a socialist society.[18]

It is not easy, however, to ascertain the extent of the decline in real wages. According to data compiled by Gosplan, in the period of 1928–32 the nominal wages of workers and employees rose 126 percent. The price index of the state and cooperative trade, however, rose 155 percent during the same period. Therefore, "real" wages in 1932 were 88.6 percent of the 1928 level.[19] Yet these data do not take into account the effects of purchases in the free and the black markets, where prices were much higher than those in the socialized sector of trade.[20] Nor do they take into account the sharp decline in services available to the population: the number of private shops and stalls in the cities, for example, dropped from 124,283 in 1928/29 to 37,765 in January 1930 and to a mere 9,500 in January 1931.[21] Furthermore, private businesses and artisan activities (restaurants, cafés, clinics, barbers', cobblers' and other repair shops, etc.) were harassed and taxed out of business.[22] The

---

[17] Quoted in *Bol'shevik*, 1930, no. 21 (15 November), p. 40, and Gaisinskii, *Bor'ba s uklonami ot general'noi linii partii*, p. 280.

[18] Stalin, *Sochineniia*, 1(14):127. See also Rudzutak's speech to a similar effect in *I kraevaia konferentsiia VKP(b) Vostochno-sibirskogo kraia*, p. 185. In fact, the rationing of food and other goods also meant the "rationing" (i.e., artificial reduction) of demands on the part of the population. See *Planovoe khoziaistvo*, 1930, no. 2, pp. 114–15. For similar views, see Bolotin, *Voprosy prodovol'stvennogo snabzheniia*, p. 57.

[19] Malafeev, *Istoriia tsenoobrazovaniia v SSSR*, p. 174.

[20] The prices in the private sector of trade were 60.4% in 1928/29, 176.0% in 1930, 238.8% in 1931, and 478.0% in the first half of 1932, above those in the socialized sector. Malafeev, *Istoriia tsenoobrazovaniia v SSSR*, p. 173.

[21] Gromyko and Riauzov, *Sovetskaia torgovlia za 15 let*, pp. 22–23, 29, 189.

[22] For an interesting account of the decline in urban services in 1930, see Mosely, "1930–1932," p. 53.

housing situation deteriorated precipitously because housing construction was given lower priority in investment at a time of massive in-migration.[23]

As far as food consumption was concerned, there was a "significant deterioration of the consumption pattern of the workers."[24] Specifically, from late 1929 to early 1930 there was a "sharp decline in the consumption of highly nourishing foods (meat, wheat, bread, sugar, and butter)."[25] In August 1930, workers' average consumption of meat and other animal products was only 72.9 percent of the August 1929 level.[26] The changes in annual food consumption in workers' families from 1927/28 to 1929/30 are shown in Table 9.1. As is clear from Table 9.1, workers ate more rye bread (as Molotov correctly predicted in July 1928),[27] potatoes, and fish, and less meat, eggs, butter, milk, and sugar. In other words, the consumption pattern was forced to become increasingly "vegetarian."

In 1929/30, however, the consumption by industrial workers did not drop as rapidly as their real wages thanks both to the increase in the number of gainfully employed members of workers' families and to the restructuring and adaptation of expenditure. Rapid industrialization nearly eliminated unemployment and induced more labor power out of workers' families.[28] The average working-class family's expenditure on foodstuffs rose from 48.9 percent of its monthly budget in the first quarter to 57.9 percent in the last quarter of 1929/30.[29] These changes cushioned the ill effects of declining real wages on consumption.

---

[23] Barber, "The Standard of Living of Soviet Industrial Workers, 1928–1941," pp. 113–16.

[24] _Na planovom fronte,_ 1930, no. 7 (15 April), p. 24.

[25] _Na novom etape sotsialisticheskogo stroitel'stva,_ 1:283 (E. O. Kabo). For this allegedly "Menshevik" finding, Kabo came under fierce attack. (See _Bor'ba na dva fronta v oblasti ekonomiki truda,_ passim.) The official report on the first year (1928/29) of the Five-Year Plan suggested a "tendency to a declining per capita consumption." See Mendel'son (ed.), _Vypolnenie plana pervogo goda piatiletki,_ p. 37.

[26] "Kon'iunktura, 1929–30," section "Obmen i raspredelenie," p. 9.

[27] See chap. 4, note 24, this volume.

[28] See _Na novom etape sotsialisticheskogo stroitel'stva,_ 1:285. The number of gainfully employed per family unit increased from 1.28 in the fourth quarter of 1928 to 1.45 in the first quarter of 1931. The number of dependents for each provider (including the provider) fell from 3.25 to 2.70 during the same period. _Planovoe khoziaistvo,_ 1931, nos. 5–6, p. 66.

[29] _Trud v SSSR_ (1932), p. 151.

Table 9.1. *Annual food consumption in worker families (kg per capita)*

	1927/28 (1)	1928/29 (2)	1929/30 (3)	Increase(+)/ decrease(−) (3:1)
Rye flour	21.4	21.2	26.1	+22.0
Wheat flour	66.6	38.8	24.6	−63.1
Other flour	2.1	2.4	3.5	+66.6
Rye bread[a]	21.4	36.0	52.7	+146.3
Wheat bread[a]	46.6	54.3	49.3	+5.8
Cereals	12.8	15.7	16.7	+30.5
Potatoes	94.9	114.7	154.1	+62.4
Vegetables	43.2	53.6	62.0	+43.5
Meat and fats	52.8	51.0	40.7	−22.9
Fish	9.3	11.0	16.8	+80.6
Milk	83.8	77.7	79.5	−5.1
Butter	2.3	2.4	2.2	−4.3
Other dairy products	3.4	4.0	4.2	+23.5
Eggs	4.5	4.3	3.4	−24.4
Vegetable oil	3.3	3.8	3.4	+3.0
Sugar	16.1	15.6	12.8	−20.5
Confectionery	1.6	2.2	3.0	+87.5
Daily calories	2,331	2,324	2,348	+0.7
of which animal substance	16.5%	16.4%	15.1%	

[a]In terms of flour content.

Source: Planovoe khoziaistvo, 1931, nos. 5–6, pp. 76–77.

In spite of its public claim that the Soviet Union was a "socialist paradise," the party leadership actually dealt with the practical problems of a declining standard of living. As Molotov declared in July 1928, the official prices of scarce goods were artificially kept at lower levels than at the private market level. In February 1930 prices of some consumer goods had been reduced despite growing shortages.[30] At the second All-Union congress of consumer cooperatives in July 1930, Mikoyan, people's commissar of trade, attacked the pro-

[30] *Zadonodatel'stvo i rasporiazheniia po torgovle,* 1930, no. 10 (20 February), p. 8, and *Informatsionnyi biulleten' Tsentrosoiuza SSSR i RSFSR,* 1930, no. 6 (174) (28 February), p. 156. See also Malafeev, *Istoriia tsenoobrazovaniia v SSSR,* pp. 153, 166, 422.

posal of some industrial managers to increase substantially the prices of food and other goods to alleviate the "goods famine," because, he contended, the proposal "ignored the interests of workers."[31] Although it was economically unsound, the price policy had a symbolic political significance: the introduction of rationing was aimed at shielding industrial workers from the consumption squeeze. Food and other scarce items were explicitly distributed in favor of the workers. An article in Gosplan's organ, *Planovoe khoziaistvo*, declared in 1930: "Can we increase the level of workers' consumption at the costs of other strata of the urban population? Of course we can and must."[32] The Siberian party leader, R. I. Eikhe, declared in mid-1930: "We provide what [little] we have first of all to the workers."[33] From the summer of 1930 on, when food shortages became increasingly acute, "closed shops" were set up for industrial workers.[34]

Indeed, workers' consumption compared favorably with that of other segments of the urban population. For instance, in 1930 workers accounted for 34 percent of Moscow's population, but they consumed more than their share of basic foodstuffs: 47 percent of bread, 56 percent of cereals, 47 percent of meat, 55 percent of herring, 43 percent of butter, and 45 percent of vegetable oil.[35] In the period of October 1929–August 1930 the food consumption by workers surpassed that of white-collar employees by 15.7 percent.[36]

S. M. Kirov was perhaps right when he declared to his Leningrad constituency in June 1930 that to alleviate the food problem, "basically everything has been done that could have been done."[37] Yet in 1930 the press often reported workers' bitter complaints about their hard lives: "Feed the hungry workers first, and then propose to adopt [ambitious] control figures."[38] In the Red Sormovo Fac-

---

[31] *Pravda*, 30 July 1930.

[32] *Planovoe khoziaistvo*, 1930, no. 2, p. 30.

[33] Eikhe, *Novyi etap i zadachi Sibpartorganizatsii*, p. 87.

[34] *Pravda*, 16, 20, 23, 26, 31 August 1930. See also Rubinshtein, *Razvitie vnutrennei torgovli v SSSR*, pp. 290–91, and Bulgakov and Ponomarev, *Za perestroiku potrebitel'skoi kooperatsii*, p. 6.

[35] Neiman, *Vnutrenniaia torgovlia SSSR*, p. 177.

[36] "Kon"iunktura, 1929–30," section "Obmen i raspredelenie," p. 9. However, according to this source, workers' consumption of meat and animal products, whose procurements were not yet firmly under state control, was 90.5% of that of white-collar employees.

[37] *Biulleten' 3-ei leningradskoi oblastnoi konferentsii VKP(b)*, 6:37.

[38] Textile workers' complaint quoted in *Sputnik kommunista*, 1930, no. 2, p. 33. According to the Menshevik journal published abroad, in the summer of 1930 food shortages caused unrest among workers in the Donbas, Moscow, and

tory in Nizhegorod, some workers and even party members declared: "Feed us first, and then talk about the Five-Year Plan."[39] At the fifteenth All-Russian Soviet Congress in early 1931, a shock worker delegate from the Ural Engineering Factory complained in the same vein: "A hungry man won't work. . . . [Factory canteens] serve only cabbage soup and pearl barley kasha. Nothing else. This disgrace arouses discontent among the workers and badly affects production. After all, unless one eats, one cannot work."[40] At a session of the All-Union Central Executive Committee in January 1931, a delegate from the Trekhgorka Textile Factory in Moscow openly declared: "It is necessary to feed the workers first and then to demand from them." Molotov sharply attacked the delegate by charging that her speech was "not the voice of the workers." She was forced to criticize herself.[41]

Molotov's threat was apparent. Yet he apparently feared that the "voice of the workers" no longer readily echoed the voice of the party leadership. The voice of skilled workers must have sounded particularly dissonant to sensitive ears: in addition to the overall declining standard of living, social turmoil and wage leveling in the factories most adversely affected skilled workers.

Social turmoil on the shop floor

The influx of new workers into the factories became even more rapid in 1930 than in 1928–29. The movement intensified conflict between new and old workers and caused a multitude of problems, particularly the political and social integration of new workers. The accelerated change, moreover, strengthened the vigilance against "class aliens" already evident in the late 1920s. Propaganda literature and the press constantly alerted the workers to "class aliens" who allegedly infiltrated the factories and agitated against Soviet power.[42] From late 1929 on, some factories resorted to massive

Odessa. See *Sotsialisticheskii vestnik,* 1930, no. 16 (230) (30 August), p. 11, nos. 17–18 (231–32) (27 September), p. 22, and no. 19 (233) (11 October), p. 14.

[39] *Izvestiia Nizhegorodskogo kraevogo komiteta VKP(b),* 1930, no. 16 (18 October), p. 8. For similar reports from the Donbas, see *Partiinoe stroitel'stvo,* 1930, no. 2, p. 48.

[40] *XV Vserossiiskii s˝ezd sovetov,* 17:6 (M. I. Utkin).

[41] *3 sessiia TsIK Soiuza SSR 5 sozyva,* 10:12, 15:4, 16:20.

[42] See, for example, Ermilov, *Byt rabochei kazarmy.*

purges of the working class, which affected not only so-called class aliens but also new workers whose political loyalty was suspected. The party leadership condemned this disruptive operation, but it constantly struck a watchful chord.[43]

In late 1929, the presidium of the central committee of the textile workers' union, faced with stiff worker resistance to the shock movement and socialist competition, resolved to "purge the factories of has-beens, kulaks, and other alien elements."[44] Spontaneous purges persisted in the workplace. On the Kuznetsk Iron and Steel Plant construction site, for example, poor peasant women attacked as kulaks those who had a fair number of skirts, clothes, tablecloths, and towels.[45] In a Donbas coal mine, a general meeting of miners adopted a decision proposed by its manager concerning the arrest of those collective farm workers who tried to "desert" the mine.[46] At a session of the All-Union Central Executive Committee in early 1931, a delegate, declaring that the kulak elements, having lost the battle with Soviet power in the countryside, now infiltrated the factories and engaged in "wrecking," appealed for a check on the new workers in order to "paralyze the disorganizing influence of the kulak elements."[47]

The vigilant spirit strengthened by the growing numbers of new workers may well have promoted the solidarity of older workers on the shop floor. In the autumn of 1930 the canteens in the Donbas coal mines were closed to peasants who came to eat while the miners were working. This measure was "unanimously supported" by "all cadre workers."[48]

The shock movement and socialist competition also advanced

[43] See, for example, *KPSS v rezoliutsiiakh*, 4:376 (resolution of 5 December 1929), and *Partiinoe stroitel'stvo*, 1930, nos. 19–20, p. 63 (resolution of 20 October). According to S. Kheinman, "Problemy truda v plane sotsialisticheskogo nastuplelniia," *Planovoe khoziaistvo*, 1930, no. 12, p. 228, there was a directive of the Central Committee concerning "purging the factories of socially alien elements."

[44] *Golos tekstilei*, 26 October 1929. See also ibid., 9 October 1929, and *Trud*, 30 October 1929.

[45] *Kuznetskstroi*, pp. 167–68. In the spring of 1931, several thousand "dekulakized" people actually arrived in the construction site. See Frankfurt, *Rozhdenie stali i cheloveka*, p. 167. For the "not very sound relations" in the Nizhni Tagil iron ore mines between native miners and "newcomers" (among whom were "dekulakized" people), see Krupianskaia et al., *Kul'tura i byt gorniakov i metallurgov Nizhnego Tagila*, p. 46.

[46] *Pravda*, 17 January 1931.

[47] *3 sessiia TsIK Soiuza SSR 5 sozyva*, 17:9.

[48] *Za industrializatsiiu*, 12 November 1930.

collective solidarity *within* each brigade. Indeed, these movements allowed the workers to act as a brigade. V. P. Zatonskii, a Rabkrin leader, observing this new configuration of workers, declared in late 1929: "A wave of spontaneous collectivization [of workers] is rising."[49] The shock movement helped workers to gain collective interests in improving brigade discipline and productivity. They exercised mutual aid and control, and created joint responsibility for the brigade's work.

On the other hand, these movements also sowed the seeds of bitter conflict among the workers, thereby fragmenting them into quarreling camps. E. Mikulina, who was quoted in Chapter 5, relates the following story about the Trekhgorka Textile Factory in Moscow:

We [young Komsomol workers] wanted to organize a shock brigade of the youth in the winding department and do 50 spools instead of 40. The director said yes and we'd got everything ready, when suddenly the foreman put some old women in our brigade, so old they ought to be drawing the old age pension. How can they intensify the work, they've got one foot in the grave already? And we were so enthusiastic about our plan![50]

Some shock brigades thus became "aristocratic" and "castlike" organizations, to quote expressions frequently used in the press. They ridiculed new arrivals from the countryside and workers keeping aloof from the shock movement, denied women and the physically frail the right to join the brigade, and demanded privileges and special favors from management.[51] Moreover, shock workers often drove "shirkers" and "loafers" out of the brigades and demanded their dismissal.[52]

Some shock brigades called production communes and collectives were often subterfuges for the defense of the particular interests of members. Naturally the communards evoked spiteful reactions

---

[49] *Visti VUTsVK*, 27 November 1929.

[50] Mikulina, *Socialist Competition of the Masses*, p. 32. For a similar discussion of conflict in the factory, see *Sputnik kommunista*, 1929, no. 23, p. 26.

[51] *Trud*, 16 November 1929. See also *Ratsionalizatsiia proizvodstva*, 1929, no. 12, p. 4, and *Bol'shevik*, 1929, no. 15, p. 32.

[52] Ol'khov, *Za zhivoe rukovodstvo sotsialisticheskim sorevnovaniem*, p. 39; Skobtsov, *Partiinaia organizatsiia Donbassa v bor'be za osushchestvlenie Leninskogo plana industrializatsii strany, 1926–1929 gg.*, p. 100. See also *Pervaia Vsesoiuznaia konferentsiia rabotnikov sotsialisticheskoi promyshlennosti*, pp. 114 and 182. This spontaneous practice caused a legal controversy. See *Sovetskaia iustitsiia*, 1931, no. 2, pp. 22–23, no. 15, p. 9.

from other workers.[53] Certainly the shock movement generated "new, revolutionary forces," who, however, were soon promoted away from the shop floor. So by the summer of 1930 the shock movement seems to have lost much of its initial momentum.[54] At the sixteenth party congress in June–July 1930, Kaganovich declared with a shade of indignation: "In a number of factories, the more workers involved in shock brigades, the less true shock work in the brigades, . . . and their militancy is lost."[55]

It was not only the shock movement and socialist competition that promoted conflict and cohesion among the workers. Industrial rationalization and modernization, particularly the introduction of *nepreryvka* (continuous production) from mid-1929 on, made the labor force very mobile on the shop floor, and cohesion strengthened as a reaction to this mobility.

Continuous production (or a continuous working week from the workers' point of view) was introduced to maximize plant use by minimizing idle machinery. The traditional seven-day week was transformed into a "five-day week" (four days on and one day off) with rotation of day schedules to guarantee continuous operation seven days a week.[56] The continuous working week expanded rapidly, and as of 1 January 1931, 68.5 percent of industrial workers (79.1 percent and 49.4 percent in the capital goods and consumer goods industries, respectively) worked on continuous schedules.[57]

In economic terms, the continuous working week made a substantial contribution to the increase in industrial output by intensifying equipment use.[58] Yet in social terms the new system had a destructive impact on workers' life. To religious workers, it signified a blatant affront to Holy Sunday and the traditionally numerous Russian holidays, and many workers did in fact not show up for work

[53] *Na novom etape sotsialisticheskogo stroitel'stva*, 1:223, and *Sotsialisticheskoe sorevnovanie v promyshlennosti v SSSR*, pp. 54 and 74. Some communards justified their brigades by calling themselves *kolkhozniki* (collective farmers) and others "kulaks." *Na novom etape sotsialisticheskogo stroitel'stva*, 1:179, and *Proizvodsvennyi zhurnal*, 1931, no. 23 (20 April), p. 13.

[54] Vorobei, *Odin – za vsekh, vse – za odnogo*, pp. 136–37.

[55] *XVI s'ezd VKP(b)*, p. 61.

[56] For continuous production, see Schwarz, *Labor in the Soviet Union*, pp. 268–77.

[57] *Trud v SSSR* (1932), p. 129.

[58] *Puti industrializatsii*, 1931, nos. 19–20 (5 November), p. 8, where the continuous week was credited for an 8–9% increase in the industrial output of the economic year 1929/30.

on Sundays.[59] Often family members were not able to have days off together.[60]

More important, the continuous working week made the labor force mobile on the shop floor. In the traditional order of production, many workers, particularly skilled workers, used "their own" machines, that is, machines assigned exclusively to themselves, with only the shift partners, usually of comparable skills, sharing the machines. So workers had taken good care of their own machines. The introduction of continuous production, however, made it difficult to maintain this traditional order because the machines were assigned to other workers when the "master" workers were off. The scheduling of shifts and the assignment of workers became an intricate business. Moreover, rotation schedules and time charts had to be adjusted every morning depending on who actually showed up for work, and the confusion was thus compounded. Workers were no longer attached to their own machines but migrated, as it were, from one machine to another.[61] At the Sickle and Hammer Engineering Factory in Kharkov, the foreman (and other supervisory personnel) "feverishly" assigned workers to jobs day by day on an ad hoc basis.[62] Every morning at the Red Triangle Rubber Factory in Leningrad, peculiar labor exchanges formed around the conveyor, and "dealing" took place as to who would take which job.[63] As a result, the whole factory was extremely mobile. Even the very high interfactory labor turnover shrank compared with intrafactory turnover, which in 1930 was said to be "over 10,000 percent [a year?]."[64] Workers roamed both in and out of the factories.

The continuous working week had a particularly adverse effect on skilled workers. The old regime was in jeopardy. According to various reports, the enormous labor turnover within the factory

---

[59] See, for example, Taskaev, *Pervyi traktornyi*, pp. 20, 23, 32.

[60] Schwarz, *Labor in the Soviet Union*, p. 273. See also the firsthand account by Mosley, "1930–1932," pp. 60–61. The confusion was such that a public bath near the Arbat in Moscow posted on its door a hilarious sign: "Closed on the former Sundays" (Mosley, "1930–1932," p. 60).

[61] *Na fronte industrializatsii*, 1930, no. 2 (31 January), p. 52, no. 23 (15 December), p. 49, and 1931, nos. 13–14 (31 July), pp. 6, 19.

[62] *Metall*, 1930, no. 5, p. 69.

[63] *Na trudovom fronte*, 1931, nos. 4–5 (February), p. 16. For more general discussion of "everyday, spontaneous exchanges," see *Predpriiatie*, 1930, nos. 17–18 (95–96) (September), pp. 10–11.

[64] *Predpriiatie*, 1930, nos. 17–18 (September), p. 9.

disorganized production and broke down "the production regime."[65] Frequent transfers from one machine (job) to another almost invariably meant lower wages for skilled workers because they had to engage in jobs with lower wage scales. In 1930–31 in the Nevsky Engineering Factory in Leningrad, for instance, skilled workers largely performed work that required low skills: as much as 80 percent of the work done by those relatively skilled (whose wage rank was 5) was ranked below 5. (By contrast, unskilled workers performed work that required higher skills and were paid accordingly.)[66] At the Stalingrad Tractor Plant, young workers expressed mistrust in narrow specialization, regarding "despecialization" (i.e., rotation of jobs) as a "socialist revision of the Ford system."[67]

Thus the continuous working week had paradoxical consequences: at a time when the skilled labor force was in short supply, it was utilized very inefficiently. Moreover, as Stalin contended, continuous production created a regime of disorder and irresponsibility.[68] Frequent transfers often resulted in the collapse of workers' brigades.[69]

Even when workers did not migrate from one machine to another and their brigade held together, the skilled workers felt victimized:

When continuous production was introduced, a fifth worker was attached to every four workers to replace whoever was off. Every day he has to work with different machines. The four workers work always with the same machines; each of them takes a day off every five days; and the fifth worker replaces the off-duty worker and works with his machine. And this [shuttle] worker . . . has to be more skilled and experienced . . . Because every day he has to move and adapt to another machine, his wages . . . usually turn out lower than those of the workers he replaces. . . . Thus frictions occur within each five-men group: "I am the best worker; I tend your machines, but I earn less than you."[70]

[65] *Rezoliutsiia shestogo Vserossiiskogo soveshchaniia po trudu,* p. 17, and *Predpriiatie,* 1930, nos. 17–18 (95–96) (September), p. 10. For an increase in the breakdown of machinery due to continuous production, see *Ratsionalizatsiia proizvodstva,* 1930, nos. 15–16, p. 6.

[66] *Na fronte industrializatsii,* 1931, nos. 13–14 (31 July), p. 29. The highest rank was 8, the lowest (least skilled), 1. For the same argument, see also *3 sessiia TsIK Soiuza SSR 5 sozyva,* 6:3–4.

[67] *Liudi Stalingradskogo traktornogo,* p. 195. See also *Revoliutsionnyi derzhite shag,* p. 199.

[68] Stalin, *Sochineniia,* 13:61–62.

[69] See, for example, *Ratsionalizatsiia proizvodstva,* 1930, nos. 15–16, p. 6.

[70] Larin, *Stroitel'stvo sotsializma i kollektivizatsiia byta,* p. 14.

To avoid such frictions, these workers often "united" themselves and formed a "production commune," dividing wages equally.[71] In February 1930, *Pravda* reported that in many factories the continuous working week "has pushed workers to '*artel* work' . . . in the form of collective responsibility for work and collective interest of the entire brigade in the best organization of production processes."[72]

Thus we see on one hand the intensification of conflict in the form of high labor turnover within the factory, and on the other the cohesion of workers into small production units as a response to conflict. Conflict and cohesion as a consequence of continuous production were observed in one form or another in industry as a whole. Yet they assumed peculiar twists in individual industrial branches in response to peculiar forms of industrial modernization and rationalization.

In the coal-mining industry, for example, the mechanization of production threatened the traditional collective organization of labor (*artel*). The *artel* formed an organic whole in which the "will and conduct of all members were directed toward maintaining order" underground. So with the dissolution of *artel*s the old order itself was disappearing: miners' collaboration and solidarity declined; labor turnover increased; conflict of individual miners with management rose; the edifying influence of senior on junior members disappeared; and labor accidents, which were said in some cases to be "indistinguishable from wrecking," became more frequent.[73]

In 1930 there was also reaction to this crisis of the old order. Experienced miners concerned with the underground order were willing to enter *artel*s still in existence.[74] In the Kuzbas coal mines, workers were reported to raise "artisan rebellions against ma-

---

[71] Ibid.

[72] *Pravda*, 25 February 1930, and *Puti industrializatsii*, 1930, nos. 11–12, p. 33.

[73] *Inzhenernyi trud*, 1930, no. 10, pp. 17–26. For the *artel*s, see Kuromiya, "The *Artel* and Social Relations in Soviet Industry in the 1920s." The *artel*s of construction workers came under similar attack at that time. Note *Sobranie zakonov*, 1930, I, 2–22 (1 January 1930), which ordered the reorganization of the *artel*s into "brigades" – gangs of workers that were to be organized on the basis of individualized labor and to be placed directly under managerial control. (See, for example, *Govoriat stroiteli sotsializma*, pp. 111–13, 149–53.) Yet in many cases, *artel*s were simply renamed brigades. See *Voprosy truda*, 1931, no. 5, p. 8, and *Nashe stroitel'stvo*, 1931, no. 15 (August), 612. See also *Organizatsiia truda*, 1936, no. 3, p. 15.

[74] *Inzhenernyi rabotnik*, 1930, no. 10, p. 22.

chines,"[75] and moved "from individual shift work and small *artels* to large *artels*."[76] The Donbas coal mines witnessed a revival of what was called "petty bourgeois utilitarianism (a reversion to the old contract-type *artels*)."[77]

Yet the old order appeared to the old workers to be doomed. It was openly claimed that the traditionally highly regarded trade of coal hewers (*zaboishchiki*) would be liquidated by mechanization.[78] Miners with ten to fifteen years of experience left mines in search of better living and working conditions.[79] Many coal hewers were either "dispersed" or reassigned as pack-horse drivers as a result of mechanization. Thus the "old cadres of hewers, timberers [*krepil'-shchiki*], and other major manual trades were partially scattered and lost."[80]

In the textile industry, the introduction of the functional organization of labor, a division of skilled labor into simpler and more specialized tasks, met strong resistance on the part of skilled workers and assistant foremen who feared the destruction of the old order. The press reported in early 1931 that their resistance had created a "combat situation in production."[81] On the one hand, the new

---

[75] Eikhe, *Novyi etap i zadachi Sibpartorganizatsii*, p. 42. See also *6 s˝ezd Sovetov* [*SSSR*], 9:4, for workers' resistance to mechanization in the Donbas. According to a typical account, even the new machine operators were hardly capable of handling the machines properly: "[In 1930 there were] tens and hundreds of small and minute troubles, damages, and breakages. Here a bolt fell out, there—a plug, and in yet another place some part of a machine failed to work. The qualification of the great majority of machine operators was limited to the most elemental skills: the ability to turn on a machine, set it in motion, and stop it. On the first occasion of the smallest trouble, which an experienced operator would have fixed while the machine was in motion, an inexperienced operator (which the overwhelming majority were) would turn the machine off" (Khavin, *Kratkii ocherk istorii industrializatsii SSSR*, p. 178). Naturally in 1930 and 1931 as mechanization progressed, the productivity of labor decreased in the coal-mining industry. See *Na ugol'nom fronte*, 1931, nos. 30–31 (130–31) (30 November), p. 15, and *6 s˝ezd Sovetov* [*SSSR*], 9:10–11.

[76] *Za industrializatsiiu Sibiri*, 1930, no. 1 (14) (January), p. 41.

[77] See the resolution of the Central Committee of the Ukrainian Communist Party in *Pravda*, 5 October 1930.

[78] *Na ugol'nom fronte*, 1931, no. 15 (115) (30 March), p. 16.

[79] *6 s˝ezd Sovetov* [*SSSR*], 9:2. See also *3 sessiia TsIK Soiuza SSR 5 sozyva*, 17:5.

[80] *Na ugol'nom fronte*, 1931, nos. 16–17 (116–17) (30 April), pp. 4 and 12–13, and *Visti VUTsVK*, 29 March, 12 April 1931.

[81] *Za industrializatsiiu*, 24 January, 19 April 1931. On 13 February 1931 the board of the All-Union Textile Association resolved to expand the functional organization of labor to the entire industry. See Ranevskii, *Za bol'shevistkii pokhod za kachestvo*, pp. 26–27.

method of labor was said to promote the "collectivization" of workers engaged in functional labor because it, as in conveyor labor, required their maximum harmony and collaboration in work.[82] On the other hand, the functional organization of labor caused a mass movement of skilled workers (who felt that their skills and status in production were no longer appreciated) either to factories where the new method was not yet employed, or to unknown places.[83]

In the railways, the so-called depersonalized drive system (*obezlichennaia ezda*) had been introduced to maximize locomotive use by assigning engine drivers to locomotives on a planned basis. Just like continuous production in industry, this system (commonly called "American drive") forced drivers to shuttle from one locomotive to another, and threatened the old order (master drive [*khoziaiskaia ezda*]) in which each engine driver was attached to "his own locomotive." Naturally, the engine drivers resisted the innovation.[84] The American system, along with the wage-leveling trends, resulted in an exodus of skilled engine drivers. As of 1 January 1930 there were 28,439 engine drivers in the country. But by 1931, thousands, and possibly more, of engine drivers had walked out of locomotive operation in protest: as many as 7,000 skilled engine drivers switched to work in the depots, not to count those who moved elsewhere permanently.[85] Their leaving aggravated the transportation crisis.

In 1930 the social turmoil on the shop floor thus promoted both conflict and cohesion among workers. The overall outcome was an additional depletion of skilled workers: industrial rationalization and modernization caused confusion in the trade hierarchies of

---

[82] See, for example, *Trud*, 26 January 1931; *Voprosy truda*, 1930, no. 4, p. 24.

[83] *Proizvodstvennyi zhurnal*, 1931, no. 25 (5 May), p. 14; *Voprosy truda*, 1933, no. 1, pp. 18–25; *Plan*, 1933, no. 2, p. 8; *Za rekonstruktsiiu tekstil'noi promyshlennosti*, 1933, no. 7, p. 5; *XVII konferentsiia VKP(b)*, p. 66; *XVII s"ezd VKP(b)*, pp. 165 and 534. In 1937 Molotov attributed the introduction of functionalism to the "peculiar union of wreckers and stupid bunglers." See *Pravda*, 21 April 1937.

[84] See *Zheleznodorozhnoe delo*, 1927, no. 2, 1931, no. 5, p. 4, and *Otchet IX s"ezda profsoiuza rabotnikov zheleznodorozhnogo transporta SSSR*, pp. 225–26, 248, 264.

[85] *Zheleznodorozhnoe delo*, 1931, nos. 7–8, p. 19. See also *Partiia i X s"ezd zheleznodorozhnikov o zh.-d. transporte*, p. 37. The overall number of engine drivers increased from 1930 to 1931. This means an influx of less skilled drivers. According to the people's commissar of transport, Rukhimovich, in early 1931 new, young engine drivers accounted for about 40% of the profession; the "majority" of those young drivers "cannot handle locomotives properly." *Ekonomicheskaia zhizn'*, 28 January 1931.

workers and threatened the traditional status of skilled workers,[86] thereby provoking a departure of skilled workers from the factories.

Egalitarianism and the exodus of skilled workers

The exodus, moreover, was compounded by the egalitarian trends that gained momentum in the factories in 1929–30.

Social inequality had been inherent in the social diversity and market relations that characterized NEP. Throughout NEP popular demands persisted for social equality.[87] In 1926 (or 1927) some workers in Tver proposed the "equalization of wages of workers and white-collar employees in all spheres of industry."[88] The anti-expert atmosphere in the wake of the Shakhty affair strengthened such demands. A report of 21 June 1928 by the Smolensk party committee characterized the mood of workers: "You [Communists] can live well off. You have apartments, but we live under bad conditions. Give us such apartments or one like Maksim Gorky's."[89] In the spring or summer of 1928, the Verkhne-Grod district party organization in Smolensk reported:

Antispecialist feelings are extremely widespread: "Down with engineers, bookkeepers. . . ."

Genuine demands for egalitarianism [*uravnilovka*] are observed. Those who demand this maintain that the entire evil lies in unequal pay [and that] a man receiving a high salary can afford more than all the rest: drinking, sexual licentiousness, etc. These people break away from the workers and degenerate; thus there come into being the upper and the lower [*verkhi i nizy*].[90]

The party leadership never supported this kind of demand, but nor did it repudiate a certain degree of leveling of workers' wages.

[86] In January 1931, Lenin's widow, N. Krupskaya, spoke of the "bitter feeling" of skilled workers toward industrial modernization: "I've learned for years, but here now some worker comes and does the work that previously only I, a skilled worker, could do." See *3 sessiia TsIK Soiuza SSR 5 sozyva*, 17:24.

[87] The Smolensk Archive is full of information on workers' demands for egalitarianism (*uravnilovka*). See, for example, WKP 33, pp. 468 and 477; WKP 294, pp. 105–106, 115, 336.

[88] Finarov, *Kommunisticheskaia partiia – organizator i vdokhnovitel' velikogo trudovogo pod"ema rabochego klassa SSSR v 1926–1929 gg.*, p. 83.

[89] WKP 33, p. 473.

[90] Ibid., p. 405. For similar reports, see *Izvestiia Severo-Kavkazskogo kraevogo komiteta VKP(b)*, 1930, no. 22 (30 November), p. 16.

On the one hand, the party leadership feared that social differentiation might develop into political differentiation. In 1930 the party leader of Red Sormovo in Nizhegorod proudly responded to workers' complaints about food shortages: "You see, all workers in Sormovo receive approximately the same [amount of wages] and live under roughly identical conditions."[91] On the other hand, it was widely believed among the Bolsheviks that modern technological developments represented by conveyor labor and the Ford system would lead to and were actually leading to "dequalification" of labor and that, therefore, individual piecework would be unnecessary.[92] Reflecting this belief, the eighth trade union congress in 1928 advocated a transition from individual piecework to "collective bonuses."[93] Some economists enthusiastically hailed the collectivization of wages.[94] While overall piecework declined in 1930,[95] collective (as opposed to individual) piecework spread. For instance, one out of every six delegates to the congress of shock brigades in December 1929 worked on collective piece rates at the time of its convocation.[96] Indeed, wage differentiation in terms of

[91] *Izvestiia Nizhegorodskogo kraevogo komiteta VKP(b)*, 1930, no. 16 (18 October), p. 8.

[92] See the retrospective accounts in *Pravda*, 28 July 1931; *Za industrializatsiiu*, 16 October 1931; *Bor'ba na dva fronta v oblasti ekonomiki truda*, pp. 99–101; *Liudi Stalingradskogo traktornogo*, passim, especially pp. 199, 211, 340; *XVII s''ezd VKP(b)*, p. 138. At the Stalingrad Tractor Plant, for example, the norm-setting bureau was in fact abolished in late 1930. *Udarnik*, 1931, nos. 2–3, p. 65. See also *Liudi Stalingradskogo traktornogo*, p. 211.

[93] *VIII s''ezd professional'nykh soiuzov SSSR*, pp. 522 and 666. In Leningrad, as industrial modernization progressed in the late 1920s, collective work and "*artel* work" did in fact increase in some factories, but decreased in others. See *Zavershenie vosstanovleniia promyshlennosti i nachalo industrializatsii Severo-Zapadongo raiona (1925–1928 gg.)*, p. 342.

[94] See, for example, S. G. Strumilin in *Na novom etape sotsialisticheskogo stroitel'-stva*, 1:44–54.

[95] The rate of piecework hours in industry declined from 59.3% in 1929 to 57.2% in 1930 (*Narodnoe khoziaistvo SSSR* [1932], p. 108). In July 1931, only 21.1% of the work done at the Stalingrad Tractor Plant was piecework. (*Avtotraktornoe delo*, 1931, no. 12, p. 5). Piecework in the railways was "virtually abolished" at that time (*Sotsialisticheskii transport*, 1932, no. 7, p. 122). In January 1931, piecework in fact accounted for only 12.2% of railway work (*Zheleznodorozhnyi transport v gody industrializatsii SSSR*, p. 139).

[96] *Politicheskii i trudovoi pod''em rabochego klassa SSSR*, p. 360. According to the People's Commissariat of Labor material of October 1931, in 1930–31 piecework had been done "mainly" on a collective basis. See *Industrializatsiia SSSR, 1929–1932*, p. 267.

decile ratio of highest to lowest wages narrowed from 3.60 in 1927 to 3.33 in 1930.[97]

It is more difficult to ascertain the extent of the wage-leveling trends in more detailed statistical terms. Certainly the leveling trends in this period did not come close to the downright leveling that had taken place during the years of war communism (1918–20). Yet the trends were evident. Numerous cases were reported in which both skilled and unskilled workers were paid equally.[98]

The leveling trends were incomprehensible from a market point of view, because this was a time when the skilled labor force was in acute shortage and therefore, under normal market conditions, wage differentials would have widened. Apart from the political and technological aspects just discussed, several factors accounted for this paradoxical phenomenon.

First, the wage-scale reform of 1927–29 contributed to the leveling trends by increasing the wages of the workers of the lowest brackets[99] and by increasing the base wages in piecework.[100] It was clear at that time that the reform designed to narrow differentials would "decrease the stimulus for workers to increase the productivity of labor"; the party leadership therefore emphasized the need to "raise the consciousness of our workers and to raise their will to labor."[101]

The impact of the reform is important statistically. The second factor is also important statistically, but more so sociologically. While the skilled work force became increasingly depleted, the un- and semiskilled work force expanded enormously because of the massive growth of new, unskilled workers. This rapid change in the composition of workers decreased piecework, which generally required certain skills, and leveled the average wages of the workers.[102]

---

[97] See note 43 of chap. 4. See also Mozhina, "Ekonomiko-statisticheskii analiz riadov raspredeleniia rabochikh po razmeram zarabotnoi platy to periodam razvitiia narodnogo khoziaistva SSSR," pp. 199–201. For the leveling trends, see also Strievskii, *Material'noe i kul'turnoe polozhenie moskovskikh rabochikh*, p. 16, and Uglanov (ed.), *Trud v SSSR*, p. 51.

[98] See, for example, the case of the Glass Trust factories in the Western *oblast'* in *Za industrializatsiiu*, 2 April 1931.

[99] Rabkina and Rimashevskaia, "Raspredelitel'nye otnosheniia i sotsial'noe razvitie," p. 21.

[100] This measure was intended to facilitate the incorporation of wages into overall economic planning.

[101] See Rudzutak's speech in *Otchet IX s"ezda profsoiuza rabotnikov zheleznodorozhnogo transpota SSSR*, p. 234.

[102] *Koldogovor tret'ego goda piatiletki*, p. 27, and *Na fronte industrializatsii*, 1930, no. 6 (31 March), p. 67.

Third, as in the years of war communism, rationing, which was introduced owing to the acute shortages of goods, produced egalitarian trends. "All work was based on revolutionary enthusiasm and mutual aid," according to a worker at the Red Proletarian Factory in Moscow, so that payments for labor were replaced by the sharing of modest material goods.[103] Moreover, at that time there were strong social pressures for egalitarianism. The sixth Komsomol conference in June 1929, for example, explicitly advocated "facilitating by all means the transition of the shock brigades to an even distribution of wages."[104] At the sixteenth party congress in the summer of 1930, Kaganovich spoke of "moral pressures for drawing [people] into [egalitarian] production communes."[105] At a meeting of norm setters and labor economists in May 1931, a man named only Nevol'skii, of the Armatrest Trust in Leningrad, allegedly "without sufficient analysis" of the reasons for the "confusions" in the wages of skilled workers, warned against bending to the "will of the market": "I think it is necessary to overcome the market, not to be tied down by it."[106] The wage-leveling trends had a heroic tone of fighting against the spontaneity of the market.

Fourth and finally, the social turmoil on the shop floor discussed in the previous section strengthened egalitarian trends (as was evident in the formation of communes and *artels*), thereby making it difficult for management to have tight control over the dynamics of wages. High labor turnover within the factory greatly confused the precise application of wage scales to individual workers and made record keeping difficult. The wage ranks thus came to "lose their meaning as indexes of skills."[107] Moreover, management had good reason to shy away from the complex task of norm setting for numerous individual jobs.[108] It was much less complicated to divide wages mechanically and equally than to keep precise records for

---

[103] Ermilov, *Schast'e trudnykh dorog*, p. 130.
[104] *VI Vsesoiuznaia konferentsiia VLKSM*, p. 459.
[105] *XVI s˝ezd VKP(b)*, p. 62. For moral pressures for egalitarianism, see also Stoklitskii, *Postup'iu millionov*, p. 75, and *Liudi Stalingradskogo traktornogo*, p. 209.
[106] *Trud*, 8 May 1931. For the tendency of management to raise wages for skilled workers to the "market" level by lowering the output quota (wage rates were decided centrally, so it was illegal to raise them), see *Na planovom fronte*, 1931, no. 2 (January), p. 24.
[107] *Voprosy truda*, 1931, nos. 3–4, p. 78.
[108] For this, see Siegelbaum, "Soviet Norm Determination in Theory and Practice, 1917–1941."

individual workers. Managers thus felt easier with collective piece-work, fixed time wages, and uniform bonuses for all workers than with individual piecework; workers, in turn, gained some security against wage fluctuations inherent in individual piecework.[109]

Thus a number of factors contributed to the wage-leveling trends. Yet this was a time of rationing, and what mattered to workers was not so much how much money they earned as how much they could actually buy with it. "Many workers" in the Donbas, for example, were reported to be uninterested in money wages because "they cannot obtain anything with the earned money."[110] The American engineer, R. W. Stuck, who worked in Magnitogorsk in 1930–32, reported:

Regardless of how hard they [workers] work they will only get about a certain amount of money each day or month and . . . for some reason the amount of money that he gets is commensurate with the available things that he is allowed to buy, so he adjusts himself to that condition and does just enough to see that he breaks even.[111]

Before 1931 there were in fact only narrow differentials among workers: rations were to a large extent leveled.[112] One can see clearly how this occurred by comparing the consumption of the poorest and the richest groups of Moscow workers. According to available statistics, in November 1928, that is, before full-scale rationing was introduced, there were considerable differentials in consumption among Moscow workers: the highest paid workers (group VI) consumed eight times as much veal, four times as many eggs, three times as much fish (except herring), milk, and nonrationed grain, and two and half times as much pork and butter, as did the lowest paid workers (groups I and II).[113] The introduction of rationing, however, entitled every worker who was a cooperative member (whether he was a skilled metal worker or a beginning worker fresh from the factory apprentice school) to the same

[109] *Na fronte industrializatsii*, 1930, no. 6 (31 March), p. 61, 1931, nos. 13–14 (31 July), p. 5, nos. 15–16, pp. 42–43; *Koldogovor tret'ego goda piatiletki*, p. 12. For a reduction of conflicts in consequence of collective piecework, see *Predpriiatie*, 1928, no. 12 (64) (December), p. 45.

[110] *Na ugol'nom fronte*, 1931, nos. 16–17 (30 April), pp. 9–10.

[111] The R. W. Stuck file, "Russia as I Saw It," p. 99, in "American Engineers in Russia."

[112] *Voprosy torgovli*, 1929, no. 14 (November), p. 19.

[113] Ibid., 1930, no. 5, p. 18, and Bolotin, *Voprosy prodovol'stvennogo snabzheniia*, p. 85.

amount of scarce foodstuffs.[114] Thus, by November 1929, when many items of food had been rationed, the differentials were almost eliminated. Respective per capita monthly rations for groups VI and I–II were as follows: 17.0 and 15.0 kilograms of grain, 1.54 and 1.25 kilograms of cereals, 466 and 437 grams of butter, 3.5 and 3.2 kilograms of meat, 11.6 and 8.8 eggs, 490 and 410 grams of vegetable oil, 570 and 504 grams of herring, 0.35 and 0.30 kilograms of macaroni, 1.5 and 1.5 kilograms of sugar, and 30 and 30 grams of tea.[115]

This was a definite leveling trend. Certainly, the preceding data did not indicate the actual consumption by workers: the rations were often more than groups I and II could afford, and less than group VI could afford; and group VI could afford more nonrationed food and consumer goods than groups I and II.[116] Yet the prices of nonrationed food and consumer goods available in the free and black markets were prohibitively expensive; the purchasing power of the ruble dropped precipitously.[117] Therefore, the overall effect was a leveling in workers' consumption of the most needed and scarce foodstuffs.[118] In January 1930 K. Ia. Bauman, head of the Moscow party organization, admitted that under rationing, the highly skilled workers received only as much food as the unskilled. The former received the same (or even less) amount of foodstuffs as before, but the latter received somewhat more than before.[119] As rationing expanded to cover more items of foodstuffs and consumer goods in 1930, overall egalitarian tendencies were strengthened.[120]

The central authorities sent conflicting signals concerning egalitarianism, and did not seriously challenge it. In October 1930 the Central Union of Consumer Societies, for instance, simultaneously

---

[114] *Voprosy torgovli*, 1930, no. 5, p. 18.

[115] Bolotin, *Voprosy prodovol'stvennogo snabzheniia*, p. 86.

[116] Ibid., and *Voprosy torgovli*, 1930, no. 5, pp. 20–21.

[117] See the acute observation of an American scholar who lived in the Soviet Union in 1929–30: Hoover, *The Economic Life of Soviet Russia*, pp. 254–55. In 1930 the role of the free market in the provisioning of workers rose in value terms: 46% in August 1930 up from 32% in August 1929 for agricultural produce; and 12% up from 2% in the respective months for industrial goods. Yet in natural terms the role of the free market *declined* for the majority of items despite its growth in value terms ("Kon'iunktura, 1929–30," section "Obmen i raspredelenie," pp. 8–9).

[118] *Voprosy torgovli*, 1930, no. 5, p. 22.

[119] Bauman, *Sotsialisticheskoe nastuplenie i zadachi Moskovskoi organizatsii*, pp. 52–53.

[120] *Bol'shevik*, 1931, no. 11 (15 June), p. 40 (L. Gatovskii).

warned against the "egalitarian division of premium funds for shock workers" and the "division of all scarce industrial goods exclusively among cadre workers, which leads to oversupply of one group and inadmissible undersupply of another."[121] This instruction was far from practical and was ignored in the localities.

As food shortages became more acute and shopping more time-consuming and frustrating, skilled workers and unskilled peasant workers came to rub elbows in factory canteens. This was a symbolic feature of the leveling trends. In the Stalingrad Tractor Plant, for example, many new workers from collective farms worked in the foundry shop, and highly skilled workers were concentrated in the toolmaking shop. The toolmakers, dissatisfied with eating in the canteen with the unskilled peasant workers, came out with a proposal for "opening up a separate canteen" that would serve them "better food."[122] Certainly, from 1929 on, so-called commercial stores were set up to give "highly skilled workers and specialists" the chance to obtain otherwise rationed products at market prices. Yet at that time the operation of these shops was very limited and sales were virtually rationed, thereby effectively restricting preferential access of those people to scarce goods.[123]

As K. Ia. Bauman suggested, the leveling trends were strengthened at the expense of the skilled workers. Naturally they were strongly offended and resorted to self-defense. One important form of such self-defense was the formation of production communes and collectives, which served as peculiar security organizations against the fluctuations of wages.[124] Specifically in the textile industry, where skilled workers were hardest hit by industrial rationalization, production communes were composed mainly of skilled work-

[121] *Informatsionnyi biulleten' Tsentrosoiuza SSSR i RSFSR*, 1930, nos. 28–29 (196–97) (30 October), p. 771.

[122] *Liudi Stalingradskogo traktornogo*, p. 434.

[123] Gromyko and Riauzov, *Sovetskaia torgovlia za 15 let*, p. 28, and *Itogi razvitiia sovetskoi torgovli*, p. 55. The set-up of commercial shops was also intended to absorb some of the surplus money in circulation that caused inflation.

[124] See the characterization of communes by I. A. Kraval' of Vesenkha in *Trud*, 10 November 1929. See also *Sotsialisticheskoe sorevnovanie v promyshlennosti SSSR*, pp. 52 and 160. As a matter of fact, this kind of informal mutual aid had long existed. One weaver of the Yartsevo Factory in Smolensk, for example, declared in August 1929: "We have been working collectively for a long time . . . but it has not been visible [to outsiders] that we work collectively" (WKP, 35, p. 35). Communes were formed on the basis of these mutual-aid collectives.

ers with high wage ranks (*vysokorazriadniki*.)[125] This does not mean at all that there was no grass-roots enthusiasm for egalitarianism or revolutionary romanticism, which evidently some communes embodied.[126] Indeed, it appears that skilled workers took advantage of the widespread enthusiasm to safeguard their own particular interests.

Unskilled workers, for their part, made every effort to join the communes, "not for the sake of [proletarian] consciousness," but because they sought to cash in on the egalitarianism of the communes.[127] In some cases, unskilled workers took the initiative to organize communes. In the Sickle and Hammer Factory (perhaps the one in Kharkov), there was a worker brigade: one-third of its members were highly skilled and earned 280 rubles; the remainder were unskilled and earned 90–100 rubles. The unskilled workers proposed to form a commune, to which the skilled were opposed. The former accused the latter of politically "backward spirits."[128] In fact, communes and collectives in the metal industry were swamped by un- and semiskilled workers.[129] Old, skilled workers therefore had to exclaim: "In the collective we are depended upon by the little peasant [*muzhichok*]."[130] Many communes, like some shock brigades, often assumed "castlike exclusivism" and expelled the idle and the frail.[131] At the sixteenth party congress, Kaganovich declared that the communes had "very interesting – but surely also

---

[125] See my article written in Japanese, "Production Communes, Production Collectives, and the Labor Movement, 1929–1931," p. 35. The same was true of the sewing industry. See *Shveinik*, 1930, nos. 6–7, pp. 1, 3; no. 9 (April), p. 1. The most important data concerning the communes and collectives were provided by the spring 1930 Gosplan survey, the results of which were published in *Sotsialisticheskoe sorevnovanie v promyshlennnosti SSSR*. In 1930, 7–9% of the industrial workers were in communes and collectives.

[126] At a Leningrad party conference in June 1930, a delegate extolled the communes. See *Biulleten' 3-ei leningradskoi konferentsii VKP(b)*, 7:7–8. Siegelbaum, "Production Collectives and Communes and the 'Imperatives' of Soviet Industrialization, 1929–1931," seems to overstate this point.

[127] *Rabochaia gazeta*, 15 March 1930.

[128] See Drobizhev and Vdovin, *Rost rabochego klassa SSSR*, p. 225. For similar cases see, for example, *Za industrializatsiiu*, 9 April 1930.

[129] See my article, "Production Communes, Production Collectives, and the Labor Movement, 1929–1931," p. 38.

[130] Quoted in *Bol'shevik*, 1931, no. 12 (30 June), p. 15.

[131] *Sotsialisticheskoe sorevnovanie v promyshlennnosti SSSR*, p. 85, and *Na novom etape sotsialisticheskogo stroitel'stva*, 1:221–23.

very negative – dependent, equalitarian tendencies [*izhdivencheskie, uravnitel'nye tendentsii*]."[132]

In spite of their ostensibly "vanguard"appellation, the communes resembled the old *artels* (traditional collective organizations of labor and mutual aid) in many respects: the election of an elder as a representative for negotiation with management, an egalitarian division of wages, and joint responsibility for work.[133] Reports abounded that the communes took shape "spontaneously and without any participation" in their formation by the factory troika, often assuming "syndicalist" tendencies by replacing one-man management with "self-management."[134] In the Donbas coal mines, it was reported that old *artels* had reemerged "under the guise of communes."[135] The press and workers often referred to communes simply as *artels*.[136] In a coal mine near Moscow, there was a commune whose slogan was "Not to Admit Communists."[137] This collectivization, as it were, on the shop floor has yet to be studied in detail. But it can be said that the traditional mode of mutual aid apparently influenced the way old, skilled workers sought to protect their status and authority from outside encroachments.

The egalitarian trends also strengthened another traditional mode of Russian popular resistance already encouraged by the social turmoil discussed earlier, the movement of skilled workers away from the factories and mines in much the same way Russian peasants had fled from exploitation for centuries. As soon as wages were divided evenly, it was reported from the Liubertsy Engineering Factory in Moscow that the skilled workers started talking about leaving for factories where there were no communes.[138] From Leningrad it was reported in May 1930 that "a massive loss of skilled workers" was beginning because of communes.[139] In his speech of

---

[132] *XVI s"ezd VKP(b)*, p. 62.

[133] For this, see my article, "Production Communes, Production Collectives, and the Labor Movement, 1929–1931."

[134] *Sotsialisticheskoe sorevnovanie v promyshlennosti SSSR*, p. 46, 51, 84, 160. See also *Na fronte industrializatsii*, 1930, nos. 10–11 (7 June), p. 7, and *Golos tekstilei*, 30 July 1930.

[135] *Na novom etape sotsialisticheskogo stroitel'stva*, 1:224, and *Gornorabochii*, 1930, no. 15 (24 April), p. 18.

[136] See the cases in Leningrad reported in *Partrabotnik*, 1930, nos. 19–20 (67–68) (July–August), p. 46, and 1931, no. 2 (80) (January), p. 121.

[137] *Sputnik kommunista*, 1930, no. 3, p. 42.

[138] *Rabochaia gazeta*, 15 March 1930.

[139] *Partrabotnik*, 1930, no. 12 (60), p. 50.

30 August 1930, which doomed his political career, S. I. Syrtsov expressed grave concern:

Some leveling is taking place in the everyday life of skilled and unskilled workers. The recent outflow of skilled workers is connected with this. The fact that coal hewers are running away from the Donbas, the Kuzbas, and the Urals is extremely alarming. It shows that the process of leveling in real wages [and] some decrease in the well-being of certain groups of workers very important to the economy cause a correspondent spontaneous outflow. . . . Concern with the welfare of the working class is the topmost obligation of the Soviet government, the party, and the organs of proletarian dictatorship.[140]

According to incomplete data, the number of coal hewers in the Donbas fell constantly from 9,057 in March 1930 to 8,735 in May, 8,624 in June, and 7,721 in July. This last figure was even lower than that of July 1929 (7,748).[141] The actual decline was much sharper because a considerable number of new, less skilled workers were hired to replace those who had left the coal mines. In early September 1930 S. Kosior, leader of the Ukrainian Communist Party, declared that in the past two months "nearly ten thousand coal hewers" had left the Donbas.[142] In the railways, egalitarian trends, coupled with the "American drive" system, caused an exodus of skilled workers, who were said to have been "scattered" in railway depots and other industries.[143] It was reported in early 1931 from the Dvina Factory in Vitebsk, White Russia, that "recently" as many as 900 skilled workers had left the factory.[144]

Certainly the egalitarian trends were not the sole reason for the movement of skilled workers, and it is difficult to ascertain the

---

[140] Syrtsov, *K novomu khoziaistvennomu godu*, p. 19.

[141] *Inzhenernyi rabotnik*, 1930, no. 9, p. 46. No data for August have been located. For the exodus of skilled workers, see also *3 sessiia TsIK Soiuza SSSR 5 sozyva*, 6:28.

[142] Kosior, *Vybrani statti i promovy*, p. 389.

[143] *Partiia i X s″ezd zheleznodorozhnikov o zh.-d. transporte*, p. 37 (A. A. Andreev). There was a case in which a skilled engine driver with ten years' experience worked as a yard keeper (see *Ekonomicheskaia zhizn'*, 12 February 1931). (For the exodus of skilled railway workers to industrial factories where wages were higher, see *3 sessiia TsIK Soiuza SSR 5 sozyva*, 6:5.) For similar reactions of elite engine drivers to wage equalization in 1917, see Rosenberg, "The Democratization of Russia's Railroads in 1917," pp. 999 and 1004.

[144] *3 sessiia TsIK Soiuza SSR 5 sozyva*, 7:33. For the exodus of skilled workers from the Red Sormovo Factory, see *Za industrializatsiiu*, 20 October 1930, and *Izvestiia Nizhegorodskogo kraevogo komiteta VKP(b)*, 1930, no. 16 (18 October), p. 8.

Figure 9.1. A Donbas coal miner (c. 1930). Courtesy of the David King Collection, London.

extent to which the egalitarian trends were responsible for the abrupt upsurge in labor turnover in 1930. Undoubtedly the transformation of the labor market, along with the introduction of new work methods, also caused the exodus. Moreover, not all skilled workers deserted production: some did return to the countryside, if only temporarily, but others drifted to other factories, mines, and construction sites where higher wages and better working and living conditions were expected. The exodus of skilled workers of course did not mean that there were not stable workers in production. Comparatively speaking, they may well have been more stable than young, unskilled workers. Yet the rapid expansion of industry made it difficult for individual factories to make up for lost skilled workers, and high labor turnover contributed to the decrease in the overall skill level of the labor force.

Thus by late 1930 the ill effects of the egalitarian trends on the skilled labor force were alarming enough not to be overlooked. In the autumn of 1930 Molotov inspected the troubled Donbas coal mines and prompted the Central Committee of the Ukrainian Communist Party to attack both "petty bourgeois utilitarianism (a reversion to the old contract-type *artel*s)" and " 'Leftist' phrasemongering (the implantation of artificial production communes)."[145]

The political implications

In the heady year of 1930 the social and political configuration of workers was in a state of change so complex and confusing that even political leaders appeared to be dismayed. One could have readily agreed with Syrtsov, who contended in the autumn that "the party overestimates the strength of the working class."[146] At the same time, one could have found convenient relief and comfort in the "glowing tales of the socialist paradise."

Yet even the optimistically minded were haunted by the declining standard of living that underlay all the complications of workers'

---

[145] *Pravda*, 5 October 1930. The disorder caused by the dissolution of *artel*s had given rise to a heated controversy among coal-mining specialists concerning their utility. In September 1930 the Coal Association, to cope with the crisis, issued an order to organize "production *artel*s" and to lend wide support to the communes and shock brigades (*Za industrializatsiiu*, 20 September 1930). The resolution was apparently directed against this order.

[146] Quoted in *Bol'shevik*, 1930, no. 21 (15 November), p. 3 (editorial).

lives. In June 1930 an editorial in an organ of the People's Commissariat of Trade warned that food difficulties had become "an object of political speculation."[147]

This problem of everyday life, like those social and economic problems discussed in previous chapters, brought into question the administrative capability of all bureaucratic apparatuses concerned. In this case the trade and supply organizations in particular came under sharp attack.

Many consumers' cooperatives took advantage of the drastic curtailment of private traders and arbitrarily increased the prices of goods fixed much lower than those in the private market. At the sixteenth party congress, Stalin harshly attacked the "commercial deviation" and "NEPman spirit" in the cooperatives, and contended that no one would need such cooperatives as "do not carry out the function of seriously raising the workers' real wages."[148] Many cooperatives also appeared to the political leadership to lack the administrative capability of carrying out the "class principle" in trade, namely, discrimination in favor of the workers. "A considerable portion of the cooperative shops" thus allegedly became "channels through which scarce goods were pumped over to the private market by means of the criminal maneuvers of sales people." In Moscow there was a case in which a resourceful person managed to obtain 6,500 ration books from cooperatives using false documents.[149] In despair, Syrtsov characterized the activity of the cooperatives and trade organizations as "self-dekulakization."[150]

In 1930 the cooperatives and their central organ, the Central Union of Consumer Societies, were extensively purged. Workers were easily mobilized for the purge. In April 1930, for instance, five senior officials were purged from the Central Union on charges of "having lowered workers' wages." The specialist Sitnikov in particular outraged workers, according to the press report:

This miserable tradesman had the insolence to seek at a workers' meeting to convince the [purge] commission that the unserviceable fish buried in the earth by a resolution of the sanitation commission could have been put on sale after it had been in the ground for three days.
—Nothing special here. It was edible!

---

[147] *Voprosy torgovli*, 1930, no. 6 (June), p. 5.
[148] Stalin, *Sochineniia*, 12:297.
[149] *Pravda*, 1 September 1930.
[150] Syrtsov, *K novomu khoziaistvennomu godu*, p. 23.

—But would you [*ty*] eat it? – one of the workers asked him.
—I don't know what quality the fish was. It may or may not have become [rotten] – spoke Sitnikov without blushing.[151]

The mobilized workers knew that not all the blame for the food problem could not be heaped upon the Central Union, but they were angered by its ineptitude and expelled the officials in any case.[152] By June 1930, the staff of the Central Union declined sharply from 4,236 to 2,150; among those 600 officials who were purged, it was reported, were 136 who had formerly belonged to other political parties than the Bolshevik party, 109 former merchants, 82 former officers of the Imperial Army, 34 officers of the White Army, and 11 ministers of various former governments, mayors, and members of the *zemstvo* council.[153] By August, more than 800 personnel of storehouses and shops in "major industrial regions" had been put on trial.[154]

In 1930 the supply of food and other consumer goods, like the supply of industrial materials, was increasingly centralized to cope with growing shortages. As the shortages became acute, the "regulating activity of the state was strengthened" to protect the industrial centers.[155] The expansion of centralized rationing, like credit reform, was promoted by the theory of the withering away of money and the emergence of nonmonetary transactions (product exchange).[156] The overcentralization and "naturalization" caused a host of bureaucratic blunderings. For example, Union Meat, the People's Commissariat of Trade department responsible for meat supplies, had in the first quarter of 1929/30 delivered 177,600 tons of meat products, or nearly half the annual plan of 358,000 tons. The delivery of meat products therefore had to be reduced to 86,600 tons and to a mere 38,200 tons in the second and third quarters respectively, to rise slightly to 54,900 in the fourth quarter.[157] At the sixteenth party congress the chairman of the commis-

---

[151] *Obshchestvo potrebitelei,* 4 April 1930.
[152] See *XVI s˝ezd VKP(b),* p. 373.
[153] Ibid., pp. 316, 350, and 373.
[154] *Pravda,* 5 August 1930. For concrete cases see, for example, *Sud i prokuratura na okhrane proizvodtstva i truda,* 2:157–59. In the provinces, livestock on the way to the capitals was often "hijacked" for local consumption. See, for example, *Ekonomicheskaia zhizn',* 5 October 1930.
[155] "Kon˝iunktura, 1929–30," section "Obmen i raspredelenie," p. 7.
[156] See, for example, *Na novom etape sotsialisticheskogo stroitel'stva,* 2:36–37.
[157] "Kon˝iunktura, 1929–30," section "Obmen i raspredelenie," p. 6.

sion for the purge of the commissariat, B. A. Roizenman of Rabkrin and the Central Control Commission, declared that the commissariat, as it stood, was "too weak" to cope with its task of supplying food.[158] The supply system was so disorganized, according to vigilant observers, that it was "very difficult to find out where stupid bungling ends and wrecking starts."[159]

Food supply was a matter of extreme political sensitivity. As early as October 1929 the chairman of the Donbas Coal Trust, G. Lomov, declared with the impatience typical of that time:

The main difficulty in the Donbas is food supply. The situation is worsening from day to day. *There are no potatoes, no tomatoes, no vegetables.* Supply of butter is fulfilled only by 60 percent. Industry must speak in a much louder voice of *wreckers who frustrate the supply plan of industrial regions.*[160]

As in industry the summer economic crisis led to trials of "wreckers" and "counterrevolutionary organizations" in trade. On 9 September 1930 it was announced that the GPU had discovered an "organized group of wreckers and embezzlers" in a Moscow consumer cooperative. Six "wreckers," D. I. Valuev, P. K. Akimov, and others had been accused of embezzlings scarce foodstuffs with tens of thousands of false ration books and were sentenced "to the supreme measure of social protection – death by shooting." The sentence, it was reported, had been carried out.[161] This affair was followed by a press announcement on 22 September that the GPU had uncovered another "counterrevolutionary" organization, and that forty-eight high officials of the People's Commissariat of Trade associated with food trade (among them the head of Union Meat, Levankovskii) had been indicted for sabotaging food supplies. An editorial in *Pravda* on the same day accused the officials under arrest of attempts to "disorganize the supplying of cities . . . and organize famine." The editorial contended that the "enemy" had chosen food trade to "wreck [the plan to increase] real wages" because it was "one of the most delicate and sensitive issues." Three days later, all forty-eight accused were reported to have been shot.[162]

[158] *XVI s″ezd VKP(b)*, p. 400.
[159] Bulgakov and Ponomarev, *Za perestroiku potrebitel'skoi kooperatsii*, p. 17.
[160] *TPG*, 12 October 1929. Emphasis in the original.
[161] *Golos tekstilei*, 9 September 1930.
[162] *Pravda*, 22, 25 September 1930. For a Western account of this case, see Lyons, *Assignment in Utopia*, pp. 356–59. See also Davies, *The Socialist Offensive*, p. 374.

Trade and supply officials had their own complaints about chaotic administrative arrangements and, above all, the rapidly widening gap between official and free market prices because of the drastic shortage of foodstuffs themselves. From within the party, Syrtsov attacked the "excessive centralization" of trade and circulated an appeal for a partial reinstatement of market relations into the supply system. In operational terms, Syrtsov's proposal meant a price increase. Molotov dismissed this proposal as a "wager on the free market."[163] Symbolically, when the People's Commissariat of Trade was divided in November 1930, its domestic activities were placed under a "Commissariat of 'Supplies,' avoiding the tainted word 'trade.' "[164] An editorial in *Ekonomicheskaia zhizn'*, explaining the reorganization, declared that "more and more supplies of the working class" would be provided, "not on the basis of 'free sale,' but through organized rationing."[165]

Firmly resisting the market forces, the political leadership sought to prod trade and supply organizations into action by police intervention and purges, a method used for almost all other bureaucratic apparatuses. In December 1930 L. M. Kaganovich declared that "no less than half of the old cooperative workers" had to be expelled and replaced by "new, strong cadres connected with the masses of workers."[166] Kaganovich's appeal met more than ready echoes. At a session of the All-Union Central Executive Committee in January 1931 one frustrated delegate exclaimed: "We have to purge, purge, and purge [the cooperatives]."[167] On 9 February the chairman of the Central Union of Consumer Societies board, A. E. Badaev was replaced by I. A. Zelenskii.[168] At the fifteenth All-Russian Soviet congress held shortly thereafter, Zelenskii suggested in a very subtle way that "wrecking" in the cooperatives was actually mere bungling. But a shock worker delegate from Ivanovo indignantly responded by maintaining that "it is clear to us that wrecking exists." Zelenskii met dissent from within as well: an

---

[163] Molotov, *V bor'be za sotsializm*, pp. 61–62. See also Gaisinskii, *Bor'ba s uklonami ot general'noi linii partii*, p. 274.

[164] Nove, *An Economic History of the USSR*, p. 202.

[165] *Ekonomicheskaia zhizn'*, 23 November 1930.

[166] Kaganovich, *Ob itogakh dekabr'skogo ob"edinennogo plenuma TsK i TsKK VKP(b)*, p. 33.

[167] *3 sessiia TsIK Soiuza SSR 5 sozyva*, 5:47 (Kobrisev).

[168] *Informatsionnyi biuelleten' Tsentrosoiuza SSSR i RSFSR*, 1931, no. 9 (25 March), 98.

official of the Central Union named Radchenko urged the delegates to "purge the cooperatives of wreckers and SR and Menshevik elements" upon returning from the session. Radchenko was followed by another shock worker delegate from Krasnoyarsk, who declared that "leading positions in our cooperatives are often occupied by alien people, beginning with Kolchak supporters and merchants and ending with an entire Menshevik gang."[169]

In 1930 the declining standard of living and the exodus of skilled workers caused some prominent Bolsheviks like Syrtsov to apprehend that the workers would not be able to bear the burden of industrialization. Indeed, cries for food were heard all over the country. The party leadership also underestimated the ill effects of egalitarianism on skilled workers. Yet the leadership blatantly discriminated in favor of the working class as a whole in the distribution of scarce foodstuffs and other consumer goods, and attributed all the problems to the activities of "class enemies" in the trade network. Workers' discontent and anger seem to have been easily mobilized against the perceived enemies. Here, as in other respects, the real problem of resources was at least partially covered up.

[169] *XV Vserossiiskii s"ezd Sovetov,* 15:21, 16:31–32, 36, 43. Kolchak was Admiral Aleksandr Kolchak, the former commander of the Black Sea Fleet who had fought against the Bolshevik government during the civil war.

Part IV

1931–1934

10

Toward the restoration of order

In spite of a miserable economic performance in the so-called special quarter of October–December 1930, the December 1930 joint plenum of the Central Committee and the Central Control Commission adopted the most ambitious annual program in the history of Soviet industrial planning, projecting for 1931 a 45 percent increase in output.[1] This overambitious plan naturally caused great anxiety in all parties concerned. According to the journalist Iu. Zhukov, the morale of industrial managers tended to fall:

The tempos were beyond reach [*sverkhudarnye*]. People were getting tired. Far from everything planned was successful. Inexperienced workers broke machines. What was to be done?

The conference of managers [in January–February 1931] took place under the banner of sharp self-criticism: in the previous year the plan targets were not successfully fulfilled; there was not enough strength to use all the resources; there was not enough skill to direct the factories properly. Some managers posed such a question as this: maybe, in the third year of the Five-Year Plan, 1931, is there any sense in somewhat holding the tempo, making up for what is lost, and later on advancing with new force?

Everybody waited for a decisive voice from the party.[2]

It was Stalin who provided the decisive voice, at the conclusion of the conference:

It is sometimes asked whether it is not possible to slow the tempo somewhat, to put a check on the movement. No, comrades, it is not possible! The tempo must not be reduced! On the contrary, we must increase it as much as it is within our powers and possibilities. . . . To slacken the tempo

---

[1] *KPSS v rezoliutsiiakh*, 4:493. In the special quarter, the actual industrial output was only 88.2% of the plan targets; the performance of the coal-mining industry was particularly poor, fulfilling only 62.5% of the plan. See *Industrializatsiia SSSR, 1929–1932*, pp. 240 and 242.

[2] Zhukov, *Krutye stupeni*, p. 12.

263

would mean falling behind. And those who fall behind get beaten. But we do not want to be beaten. No, we refuse to be beaten!

Stalin went on to speak of the "continual beatings" Russia had suffered because of its backwardness, and declared: "We are fifty to one hundred years behind the advanced countries. We must cover this distance in ten years. Either we do this, or they will crush us."[3]

The economic crisis of the summer of 1930 and the emergence of the Syrtsov-Lominadze faction within the Stalinist camp thus could not force Stalin and his close associates to slacken the pace they had set. While pushing for rapid industrialization, the party leadership responded to the crisis by massive police intervention in the economic administration. The GPU, the Procuracy, Rabkrin, and the Central Committee all involved themselves deeply in economic affairs.

On the one hand, this wholesale intervention could not have continued unabated. At the joint plenum of the Central Committee and the Central Control Commission in December 1930, Molotov made this point clear:

Lately the Central Committee has more and more involved itself in concrete economic problems. In some instances the Central Committee had not only to direct central state organs [such as Vesenkha and Gosplan] but also to almost replace them. In a number of cases, the work of the central state organs lagged so much behind life that the Central Committee was obliged to perform individual tasks by nine-tenths for them, carrying out these measures under its direct leadership. Of course this is abnormal.[4]

On the other hand, the party leadership appeared to be willing to consider the summer crisis, grave though it was, as one of the "unavoidable costs of revolution," or as a by-product of a successful industrialization drive that far outpaced the Five-Year Plan: the elimination of private trade and industry, which aggravated the shortages of foodstuffs and consumer goods, signified the dominance of the socialized sector;[5] the disappearance of the market, with all the confusion it caused, meant the emergence of a planned economy; the declining standard of living was an undesirable but unavoidable (as Stalin admitted in 1936) result of the successful

[3] Stalin, *Sochineniia*, 13:38–39.

[4] Molotov, *V bor'be za sotsializm*, p. 60.

[5] Note that at the sixteenth party congress in June–July 1930, Stalin maintained that the country had "already entered the period of socialism." See Stalin, *Sochineniia*, 13:5–6.

allocation of resources to the capital goods industries;[6] the labor shortage reflected the disappearance of one of NEP's most vexing problems, unemployment; and the acute shortage of the skilled labor force was at least in part a result of an extensive "proletarianization" of governmental and educational institutions. In the collectivization campaign too, the crisis of the spring of 1930 had been overcome by a temporary retreat in the spring and a good harvest in the summer and autumn, and a careful but forceful campaign was resumed thereafter.[7] The leadership regarded all these as major political achievements, which, however, blinded them to the real causes of the economic difficulties.

It was a serious challenge for the party leadership whether to advance or retreat from this crisis-ridden campaign. Both in the minds of all political leaders and among the top leaders there must have been intensified discussion. The leadership appeared to hold firm to the rapid pace of industrialization, but in early 1931 it began to imply that a breakthrough had been wrought in the industrialization campaign. In February 1931 L. M. Kaganovich, addressing a plenum of the Moscow *oblast'* committee of the party, spoke of the revolutionary campaign as if it were a stage that had been gone through: "What factories have we specifically built during the time of the revolution?" He enumerated the new factories and then declared that "even more factories have been reconstructed during the time of the revolution."[8] In April V. M. Molotov was more explicit: speaking to the All-Union conference on the planning of scientific research, he declared that "the Soviet government by now has in the main solved the most difficult tasks of the revolution that had faced the government in all their magnitudes in the past two or three years."[9] In his famous speech to a conference of industrial managers on 23 June 1931, Stalin clinched the argument in favor of what might be called a "restoration of order" in industry – a new series of policies that had been discussed in the press as well as in the leadership for the preceding six months or so. Stalin declared that

lately the conditions of development of industry have radically changed; new conditions demanding new methods of management have arisen; but

---

[6] See chap. 9, note 18.
[7] Davies, *The Socialist Offensive*, chaps. 8 and 9.
[8] Kaganovich, *Kontrol'nye tsifry tret'ego goda piatiletki i zadachi moskovskoi organizatsii*, p. 9.
[9] Molotov, *V bor'be za sotsializm*, p. 198.

some of our industrial managers, instead of changing their methods, are continuing in the old way. The point, therefore, is that the new conditions of development of industry require new work methods, but some of our managers do not understand this and do not see that they must now adopt new methods of management.[10]

Stalin's speech was suggestively entitled "New Conditions – New Tasks in Economic Construction." While emphasizing that the production program for 1931 was "most certainly" realistic, Stalin proposed six new tasks: an organized recruitment of the labor force; an end to wage leveling; an end to the confusion caused by the continuous working week; the making of "a working-class industrial and technical intelligentsia"; the rehabilitation of the old industrial and technical intelligentsia; and the reinstatement of *khozraschet* in industrial management. Some of these were merely practical, but others, especially antiegalitarianism and the rehabilitation of "bourgeois" specialists, implied a profound rethinking of the political situation. The Stalinist leadership came to conclude that the class-war policy and ideology that had propelled the rapid industrialization drive had achieved its immediate goals.[11]

As a matter of fact, by the summer of 1931 a consensus had emerged in party and government institutions (including the GPU) in favor of four general policies: the introduction of "correctives" into the planned economy; the rehabilitation of "bourgeois" specialists; the cessation of the massive promotion and mobilization of workers; and the widening of wage differentiation among industrial workers. Stalin's six tasks were actually ramifications of these policies.

The correction of the planned economy

From late 1930 on, the party leadership sought to correct the dysfunctional aspects of a newly created planned economy, especially the decline in financial controls and the disorganization of industrial supplies. Vesenkha's new chairman, Ordzhonikidze, almost certainly came under political pressure for taking the responsibility for the economic disorder. As Rabkrin's chairman, he had supervised both the credit and management reforms. Keen though it was to

---

[10] Stalin, *Sochineniia*, 13:51–52.
[11] For the same phenomenon in culture, see Fitzpatrick, *Education and Social Mobility in the Soviet Union,* chap. 10.

watch factories closely, Rabkrin displayed remarkable enthusiasm and optimism for reforms that created an economic structure with little central control over the finances and management of factories. Rabkrin therefore had to take over, de facto, the industrial and planning institutions. The summer economic crisis led to the Syrtsov-Lominadze affair, and Ordzhonikidze's expertise in handling factional struggle was much appreciated. When the affair was settled in the autumn, Ordzhonikidze took over Vesenkha. At a session of the Vesenkha presidium in March 1931, Ordzhonikidze declared that "the planning principle in the Soviet economy is our greatest achievement and we of course have to strengthen it in every possible way," but that "life requires us to introduce, in the course of this year, these or other corrective steps."[12] Indeed, the few years following the summer of 1930 were marked by the party leadership's efforts to keep the planned economy running by introducing corrective measures and without constant police intervention.

The first measure concerned the financial issue. Loss of central control over the financial situation and the inflationary currency issue, which in 1930 were mutually reinforcing, caused cost inflation and aggravated the problem of resource constraints. In October 1930 the people's commissar of finance, L. P. Briukhanov, and the chairman of the State Bank, Iu. L. Piatakov, were held responsible for the currency inflation and were replaced by G. F. Grin'ko and M. Kalmanovich, respectively.[13] In fact, in the special quarter of 1930 further currency issues were ruled out to strengthen financial controls; and the December 1930 joint plenum of the Central Committee and the Central Control Commission resolved to wage "a decisive struggle against the underestimation of the role and the significance of the financial system" by introducing "the strictest financial discipline and a regime of economy."[14] In early 1931, corrective measures were introduced into the flawed credit reform that had contributed enormously to inflation during 1930. According to new rules, all transactions were to take place, not automatically according to production and supply plans, but on the basis of contracts and orders; the supplier (factory) was to receive pay-

[12] *Za industrializatsiiu,* 19 March 1931.
[13] See chap. 6, note 145.
[14] *KPSS v rezoliusiiakh,* 4:496. Kaganovich called the special quarter a "nonemission quarter." See his *Ob itogakh dekabr'skogo ob″edinennogo plenuma TsK i TsKK VKP(b),* p. 11.

ments only when it met the obligations it had taken on according to the contract; the purchaser (factory) was to receive the product only when it transferred through the State Bank an appropriate sum of money (which had to be within the limit of its account) to the supplier's account.[15] The "decisive struggle" for financial discipline did halt increases in currency issues: between 1 October 1930 and 1 June 1931 currency in circulation rose only 1.2 percent in sharp contrast to a 54 percent increase in the previous ten months.[16]

These measures meant, in a word, the restoration of "control by the ruble." Kalmanovich epitomized this in a phrase familiar to everyone: "If the purchaser doesn't have money, he won't get products."[17] The rehabilitation of the ruble in turn meant the reinstatement of *khozraschet* principles. At the conference of industrial managers in January–February 1931, Molotov emphasized the critical importance of cost accounting to industrial management at all stages: "It is impossible to manage not only industrial associations and factories but even individual workshops within a factory without the ability to count money for each credit and debit item."[18]

The restoration of the ruble and of *khozraschet* reflected a profound reappraisal of the planned economy by the party leadership. It came to conclude by early 1931 that it was impossible to run the economy by administrative controls and police intervention alone. Certainly, police intervention continued. In the course of 1931, 2,700 officials were "expelled" from the financial apparatus as "class aliens" and "corrupt and inept" elements; and 2,460 more officials, whose presence in the apparatus was said to be "inexpedient," were removed.[19] By reinstating control by the ruble, however, the leadership sought to introduce a semiautomatic control mechanism. However incomplete this mechanism may have been in a

---

[15] *Sobranie zakonov*, 1931, I, 4–52 (14 January), 18–166 (20 March), 40–282 (16 June). See also the directive of 12 April of the Central Committee in *Resheniia partii i pravitel'stva po khoziaistvennym voprosam*, 2: 297–300. See also Weißenburger, *Monetärer Sektor und Industrialisierung der Sowjetunion*, pp. 173–88.

[16] See Davies, "Models of the Economic System in Soviet Practice," pp. 22, 28.

[17] Quoted by Vyshinsky in *Sud i prokuratura na okhrane proizvodstva i truda*, 1:168 (May 1931).

[18] *Pervaia Vsesoiuznaia konferentsiia rabotnikov sotsialisticheskoi promyshlennosti*, p. 166.

[19] *Finansy SSSR mezhdu VI i VII s˝ezdami Sovetov*, p. 51. See also *XVII s˝ezd VKP(b)*, p. 486 (G. F. Grin'ko).

centrally planned economy, the leadership came to consider it more cost efficient than direct administrative control.

A similar reevaluation took place in relation to other aspects of the planned economy as well. At the aforementioned conference of managers in early 1931, Molotov attacked the proposal made by managers that the industrial supply system be further centralized, because, he contended, it would be an "overbureaucratic" and, moreover, "absolutely unrealizable" venture.[20] At a session of the Vesenkha presidium in March 1931, Ordzhonikidze condemned the practice of direct product exchange and appealed to the factories to fight for timely supplies without asking associations and Vesenkha to intervene. For, Ordzhonikidze emphasized, "Vesenkha cannot intervene directly in the operative work of a thousand factories under its jurisdiction."[21] Here too, some kind of decentralized control mechanism was deemed necessary to keep the planned economy functioning. Hence contractual arrangements between factories for the supply of goods were reintroduced, and the state arbitration system was reinstated to effect them.[22] Financial pressures based on *khozraschet* principles were expected to solve supply problems and do away with constant central intervention.

The attempts to reinforce control over the economy by these corrective measures posed new work methods to administrative organs. In February 1931 Rabkrin and the Central Control Commission condemned the arbitrary investigations of factories by various institutions.[23] In May, the new procurator of the Russian Republic, A. Ia. Vyshinsky, clearly indicated new methods for the judiciary: "In certain cases we are obliged to intervene actively [in the economic administration], but this has to be the exception, not the norm."[24] In his article *"Khozraschet* and the Tasks of the Judiciary,"* published on 18 June, Vyshinsky again condemned the "administrative ecstasy" of the judiciary organs that "did not see any

[20] Ibid., pp. 48–49 and 167–68. For similar criticism, see Ordzhonikidze in *Za industrializatsiiu*, 13 February 1931.

[21] *Za industrializatsiiu*, 19 March 1931. By 1931 bulky associations began to be disbanded, and the prereform chief administrations came to be reinstated in Vesenkha.

[22] *Sobranie zakonov*, 1931, I, 10–109 (18 February), 26–210 (21 April), 26–203 (3 May), and 31–239 (20 May).

[23] *Za industrializatsiiu*, 4 February 1931. In May 1931, a government resolution signed by Molotov and I. Mezhlauk called for the elimination of "excessive" investigations of factories. See *Sobranie zakonov*, 1931, I, 29–228.

[24] *Sud i prokuratura na okhrane proizvodstva i truda*, 1:167.

limits to their intervention in the work of managers."[25] Thus before Stalin's speech of 23 June, the judiciary organs began to turn away from the "active intervention" in the economy that had characterized their work during the previous few years.[26]

The new course would have meant much less police intervention and administrative pressure and a much freer managerial rein. Yet apparently industrial managers did not find it easy to adapt to the new course immediately. The "administrative ecstasy" of the judiciary organs, Vyshinsky complained, was "everywhere nurtured by the tendencies of managers who preferred to solve the problem with contract partners by turning to the judiciary organs for intervention."[27] Moreover, the new course imposed legal and financial sanctions on managers. At the conference of managers in January–February 1931, Ordzhonikidze, proud of the sanctions to be introduced, declared: "If you don't meet the obligations you have taken on yourself, I won't pay you, the bank won't pay on my behalf any more, and you, dear comrade, will have to think very hard how to pay your wages, how to carry on the work of your factory. The contract must be legally binding. If you don't meet it, you answer to a Soviet court."[28] In fact, some factories ran out of money and were unable to pay wages to workers. Ordzhonihidze

---

[25] Ibid., 1:179. The article was published in *Izvestiia TsIK SSSR*, 18 June 1931. The 20–25 June 1931 plenum of the Ukrainian Communist Party ordered the party organizations to eliminate immediately any intervention of the administrative and judiciary organs in the "production life of the factories." See *Komunistychna Partiia Ukrainy v rezoliutsiiakh*, pp. 733–34.

[26] It appears that there was discontent among the judiciary with the new course. When Vyshinsky declared at a meeting of "leading judiciary workers" in June 1931 that it would be wrong to establish a mechanical link between the efficacy of the work of the Procuracy and the frequency of accidents in the railways, he evoked a cry from the audience: "There is a link!" See *Organy iustitsii na novom etape*, p. 67.

[27] *Sud i prokuratura na okhrane proizvodstva i truda*, 1:179. The Electric Power Factory in Leningrad, for example, unable to get the Putilov Factory to accept its order for thirty-five tons of plugs, apparently turned to Rabkrin and the Procuracy for intervention. See *Biulleten' 3-go Leningradskogo oblastnogo s"ezda sovetov*, 4:2.

[28] *Pervaia Vsesoiuznaia konferentsiia rabotnikov sotsialisticheskoi promyshlennosti*, pp. 12–13. See also Davies, "Some Economic Controllers – III," p. 41, from which the English translation is taken. Later at the conference, Ordzhonikidze contended that "if you violate the contract I will take you to the Soviet court, and you, young man, will be put in jail for it" (*Pervaia Vsesoiuznaia konferentsiia rabotnikov sotsialisticheskoi promyshlennosti*, p. 180). For legal sanctions, see *Sud i prokuratura na okhrane proizvodstva i truda*, 1: 198–208.

therefore had to issue an order to eliminate delays in payments.[29] These factories were singled out for criticism as examples of poor management.

The legal and financial sanctions were not strictly enforced, however. Certainly upon taking over Vesenkha, Ordzhonikidze imposed much harsher administrative sanctions on factory directors than did his predecessor, Kuibyshev, often removing directors from their posts for violations of labor, financial, or managerial discipline.[30] Yet this discipline was always treated by the party leadership and the managers alike as secondary to the fulfillment of plan targets. On 2 February 1931 the new commissar of finance, Grin'ko, bitterly complained about managers' negligent attitude toward financial matters, and warned: "Managers must realize that a strict financial regime awaits them. They must accustom themselves to stern financial discipline."[31]

Here again we see one of the central contradictions of the Soviet planned economy as it had emerged in 1929–30: the control and punishment of the market were not effectively replaced. Two months later, on 13 April 1931, Grin'ko, addressing a meeting of party activists in Nizhegorod made this point very clear:

It is necessary to thrash the psychology that unfortunately is widespread among our managers. This psychology could be characterized thus: "We are state enterprises; we cannot be sold by auction, why [do we have to] worry?" Of course, the Sormovo Factory and the [Nizhegorod] Automobile Plant won't be sold by auction. But the party and the government have many other, no less effective methods of teaching the leaders both of factories such as Sormovo and of construction [projects] such as the Automobile Plant to implement *khozraschet* unflinchingly. There will be show trials and much more that will force them to get cracking and carry out the directives of the party.[32]

Grin'ko's threat was not very effective. The real problem was perhaps not so much psychological as systemic.

The rethinking about the working of the planned economy involved similar rethinking concerning trade and labor supply. In trade, in the course of 1931 rationing was abolished for certain

[29] *Za industrializatsiiu*, 30 January 1931. For instances of delays in payment see, for example, *Finansy i sotsialisticheskoe khoziaistvo*, 1931, no. 10 (10 April), pp. 5 and 23.

[30] For this, see Ginzburg's memoirs, *O proshlom – dlia budushchego*, pp. 174–80.

[31] *Finansy i sotsialisticheskoe khoziaistvo*, 1931, no. 5 (20 February), p. 4.

[32] Ibid., 1931, no. 12 (30 April), p. 9.

items of industrial consumer goods.[33] For, it was believed, "setting up from above a considerable number of differentiated categories of supply means introducing into rationing even more bureaucratization."[34] The abolition practically meant an increase in the retail prices – a partial adjustment to market prices. This adjustment reminded people of the proposal Syrtsov had made several months before, so the chairman of the Central Union of Consumer Societies, Zelenskii, found it expedient to attack Syrtsov anew for having advocated a "wholesale increase in prices" – an "alignment with the private trader."[35] However, this rethinking surely provided an important backdrop to the legalization of the "kolkhoz market" in trade in 1932 and the abolition of food rationing in 1934.

In the labor market too, in the course of 1931 the state monopoly was abolished in favor of direct, organized hirings by factories.[36] This was not so much a radical reform as a practical response to the virtual dismantlement of the state monopoly that had taken place in 1930: because the People's Commissariat of Labor lacked a recruitment apparatus, the actual recruitment of labor was conducted by the plenipotentiaries of industrial organizations; therefore the commissariat and industry were passing the buck to each other.[37] Had it possessed a powerful administrative apparatus, the party leadership might have adhered to the state monopoly. But the commissariat appeared to the leadership to be too weak to control the labor market, and further centralization would have added to bureaucratism and organic paralysis. Here, as elsewhere, institutional constraints led the leadership to reappraise labor policies.

The rehabilitation of "bourgeois" specialists

Rethinking about the planned economy necessarily involved reassessing the apparatus and the people that ran the economy. The problem of creating a "proletarian technical intelligentsia" continued to plague the party leadership. Addressing the conference of

---

[33] *Direktivy KPSS i sovetskogo pravitel'stva khoziaistvennym voprosam*, 2:273–78.
[34] *Bol'shevik*, 1931, no. 11 (15 June), p. 40 (L. Gatovskii).
[35] *Problemy marksizma*, 1931, nos. 5–6, p. 22.
[36] *Sobranie zakonov*, 1931, I, 60–385 (13 September).
[37] Platunov, *Pereselencheskaia politika sovetskogo gosudarstva i ee osushchestvlenie v SSSR*, pp. 139–40, and *Industrializatsiia SSSR, 1929–1932*, p. 425.

managers in January–February 1931, Stalin vented his impatience with their lack of technical expertise: "We must ourselves become experts, masters of the business; we must turn to technical science – such was the lesson life itself was teaching us. But neither the first warning [the Shakhty trial] nor even the second [the "Industrial Party" trial] brought about the necessary change."[38]

By 1931, however, the leadership had wrought a fundamental transformation of the educational system, and hundreds of thousands of Communists, workers, and peasants were being trained in higher technical education. In spite of Stalin's cautious assessment, this breakthrough was an important political achievement, and made the political utility of attacking the "bourgeois" specialists much less appealing than before.[39] Moreover, in no way was specialist baiting economically sound. The shortage of specialists was progressively aggravated as more and more new factories were put into operation. The ill effects of specialist baiting on labor discipline more than offset the impact of the introduction of one-man management. Furthermore, the morale and production initiative of specialists were seriously undermined by specialist baiting. Such a state of affairs could not have been perpetuated.

The move toward the rehabilitation of "bourgeois" specialists emerged gradually in late 1930. On 6 November, shortly after the GPU announced the uncovering of the "Industrial Party," M. I. Kalinin, addressing the Moscow Soviets, declared that "a definite differentiation within the specialists has already taken place."[40] This assessment that the specialists had split into "socialist" and "capitalist" camps antedated Stalin's speech of 23 June by seven months, and sharply contrasted with Molotov's statement in February 1930 that "the work on stratifying the intelligentsia . . . up to now has been extremely unsatisfactorily done."[41] Ordzhonikidze's takeover of Vesenkha in November 1930 (which coincided with the Industrial Party trial) appears to have militated in favor of the specialists. It is not clear whether his takeover reflected a new course within the party leadership or whether he quickly came to

[38] Stalin, *Sochineniia*, 13:37. For similar assessments, see Molotov, *V bor'be za sotsializm*, p. 63 (December 1930); *Bol'shevik*, 1931, no. 1 (15 January), pp. 14–15 (A. Mikoyan).

[39] Fitzpatrick, *Education and Social Mobility in the Soviet Union*, p. 205.

[40] *Pravda*, 13 November 1930.

[41] *Bol'shevik*, 1930, no. 5 (15 March), p. 14 (25 February 1930 speech).

represent institutional self-interests upon the takeover. Whatever the case, as a sign of rapprochment between the government and the scientific community, Ordzhonikidze invited to his first meeting at Vesenkha some prominent scientists, including A. P. Karpinskii, the president of a supremely "bourgeois" organization–the Soviet Academy of Sciences.[42] At the January–February 1931 conference of managers, Ordzhonikidze emphasized that "a careful approach has to be taken" toward specialists who "work honestly."[43] He also received letters from engineers in camps and in exile asking for reinstatement, and Vesenkha began to review their cases.[44] By April, shortly after the so-called Menshevik trial in March,[45] Molotov, who had always taken a tough stance toward the specialists, showed signs of change. In his speech of 11 April, quoted earlier in this chapter,[46] he maintained that the political vacillation of the scientific researchers was coming to an end, and appealed for an improvement in their working conditions.[47]

Pressure for rehabilitation mounted in the spring of 1931. On 30 April the Vesenkha newspaper *Za industrializatsiiu* published an article dispatched from the Kuznetsk Iron and Steel Plant construction project, which reported that the "industrial prosecutor" of the project, Pozdniakov, had been accused of indiscriminately harassing, arresting, and sentencing its engineering and managerial personnel. Between 1 October 1930 and 1 April 1931 he was said to have prosecuted forty-eight specialists, thereby depleting the construction project of specialists. The article stated that the methods of the prosecutor were inscrutable: "People are arrested, tried, and sentenced to several years of imprisonment, but it is not even considered necessary to notify management of this."[48] A week later it was

[42] *Byli industrial'nye*, p. 9 (A. V. Ziskind's memoirs). In December 1930 the émigré (Menshevik) journal *Sotsialisticheskii vestnik* reported a rumor then in circulation in Moscow that Kalinin, Ordzhonikidze, and Voroshilov had convinced Stalin to make concessions. See 1930, no. 24 (238) (20 December), p. 15.

[43] *Pervaia Vsesoiuznaia konferentsiia rabotnikov sotsialisticheskoi promyshlennosti*, p. 178.

[44] *Byli industrial'nye*, p. 189 (I. S. Peshkin's memoirs).

[45] The trial received far less press coverage than the Shakhty and the Industrial Party trials. It might have been a compromise between different lines in the leadership.

[46] See note 9 of this chapter.

[47] Molotov, *V bor'be za sotsializm*, p. 198.

[48] *Za industrializatsiiu*, 30 April 1931 (N. Starov). See also *Sud i prokuratura na okhrane proizvodstva i truda*, 1:179, 199.

reported that Pozdniakov was dismissed from his post.[49] According to the memoirs of the project's director, S. M. Frankfurt, published in 1935, both Pozdniakov and the *raion* party committee secretary, Stankin, would put engineers on trial or fire them for simple mistakes and defects, attacking Frankfurt's protection of engineers as "playing the liberal." Meanwhile Asia Kasovskaia, a writer for *Pravda* sent by the Central Committee to Kuznetsk, was removed from the editorship of a local newspaper for opposing the harassment of the engineers. According to Frankfurt, she returned to Moscow and informed Stalin of the matter in Kuznetsk; Stalin then personally intervened and removed Stankin and Pozdniakov from their posts.[50]

On 23 May, Vesenkha's chairman, Ordzhonikidze, had taken a bolder step and published an article in *Pravda* praising four engineers who, apparently under arrest in connection with the "Industrial Party" trial, had designed and built the "first powerful Soviet blooming mill [a highly productive rolling mill]."[51] In May the Vesenkha newspaper, *Za industrializatsiiu,* began to make a clear call for the rehabilitation of the specialists: "The engineer must be the commander and the leader of production"; "Technical personnel have not yet become the commanders of production"; "Secure normal working conditions for the Soviet engineers."[52]

On 28 May the new procurator of the Russian Republic, Vyshinsky, indicated an obvious change of policy:

It is necessary and possible to fight against crimes in the form of wrecking and against wrecking not only by means of penal repression, but also by way of solving the task of mastering technology. It is necessary to wage this struggle by mastering the art of managerial leadership and becoming ourselves managers with technical expertise. The danger of wrecking will be smaller under such conditions than it is in the absence of these conditions.[53]

Thus Stalin's speech of 23 June 1931 was but a dramatization of this new orientation, which had become the concensus in the party

---

[49] *Za industrializatsiiu,* 7 May 1931.

[50] Frankfurt, *Rozhdenie stali i cheloveka,* pp. 50–53 and 270.

[51] Ordzhonikidze, *Stat'i i rechi,* pp. 308–9.

[52] See, for example, *Za industrializatsiiu,* 13, 23, 31 May 1931.

[53] *Sud i prokuratura na okhrane proizvodstva i truda,* 1:160. Vyshinsky replaced N. V. Krylenko as procurator of the Russian Republic earlier in May. See *Za industrializatsiiu,* 12 May 1931.

and state apparatus.[54] As if he had forgotten the events of the previous few years, Stalin declared: "We have always regarded and still regard 'specialist baiting' as a harmful and disgraceful phenomenon," and he called for "maximum care for those specialists, engineers, and technicians of the old school who are definitely turning to the side of the working class."[55]

Stalin's speech was followed on 20 July 1931 by a rare article by the GPU chairman, V. Menzhinskii, dedicated to the fifth anniversary of the death of his predecessor, Dzherzhinski. Menzhinskii hailed Stalin's speech and discussed how Dzerzhinski had "widely used the GPU to protect specialists from all kinds of oppression."[56] The specialist journal *Inzhenernyi trud,* welcoming this new atmosphere, exclaimed: "Specialist baiting is outlawed!"[57] On 10 July the Central Committee dispatched a secret directive entitled "On the Work of Technical Personnel in Factories and the Improvement of the Living Conditions of Engineering and Technical Workers."[58] The directive ordered, on one hand, reviews of the cases of "those specialists tried and sentenced to forced labor for defects they allowed in work and for blunders and violations of labor legislation" and, on the other, the improvement of their living conditions to a level equal to those of the industrial workers.

The cessation of massive promotion and mobilization

The correction of the centrally planned economy and the massive promotion of workers into full-time administrative work and higher education brought about changes in the political and eco-

[54] This analysis supports Fitzpatrick's criticism of Bailes's view emphasizing conflict between Stalin-Molotov and Ordzhonikidze. See Fitzpatrick, *Education and Social Mobility in the Soviet Union,* p. 211, and Bailes, *Technology and Society under Lenin and Stalin,* pp. 148–56. Ordzhonikidze took a one-month vacation on 16 May at a time when the hypothetical struggle was being fought. *Sbornik postanovlenii i prikazov po promyshlennosti,* 1930, 20:332.

[55] Stalin, *Sochineniia,* 13:72–73 and 77. The full text of his speech appeared in *Pravda,* 5 July 1931.

[56] *Pravda,* 20 July 1931.

[57] *Inzhenernyi trud,* 1931, nos. 19–20 (20 August), p. 438.

[58] WKP 162, p. 63. Note that both Fainsod and Bailes misdate this document 10 June 1931, i.e., before Stalin's speech of 23 June. See Fainsod, *Smolensk under Soviet Rule,* p. 318, and Bailes, *Technology and Society under Lenin and Stalin,* p. 151.

nomic roles to be played by workers. The introduction of correctives made workers' control from below over the economy less pressing, and the rehabilitation of "bourgeois" specialists made workers' antispecialist feelings less appealing politically and more harmful economically. The campaigns for the promotion of workers were so successful that the "pool of willing and even partially qualified workers and Communist applicants for higher education showed signs of drying up."[59]

In 1928–30 a massive promotion and mobilization of workers had been a top-priority political goal pursued without regard for the economic costs involved and in spite of explicit protests on the part of managers. A multitude of campaigns mobilized workers constantly from the shop floor. Tens and thousands of skilled workers sent to the universities for higher education and to the countryside for the collectivization drive were supported by the factories, causing a serious financial drain. The promotion of the best shock workers threatened to deplete the shop floor of able organizers.[60] Naturally, as the shortage of skilled workers became more acute, practical concern too became more pressing for a curb on the promotion and mobilization of skilled workers away from the shop floor.

By 1931, moreover, the problem of staffing some 500 new factories scheduled to be brought into operation in that year faced the party leadership, Vesenkha, Gosplan, and the People's Commissariat of Labor. According to a Vesenkha projection, 100,000 skilled workers were needed for the new factories, 12 percent of them to be transferred from existing (old) factories. Yet even this modest plan met strong resistance from the commissariat, which contended that given the dearth of skilled workers, such a mass transfer would "disorganize the work of those [old] factories," and that, moreover, the transfer itself would be difficult organizationally and cause a great finanacial strain.[61] In early 1931 the head of the Coal Association, M. A. Deich, begged the Vesenkha presidium to help the coal mines by sending over as many as 40,000–50,000 skilled workers from the metallurgical and other industries. Ordzhonikidze bluntly

[59] Fitzpatrick, *Education and Social Mobility in the Soviet Union*, p. 209.
[60] See, for example, the case of the Liubertsy Agricultural Machinery Factory in Moscow in *Sel'sko-khoziaistvennaia mashina*, 1930, no. 7, p. 38.
[61] See the People's Commissariat of Labor report of February 1931 in *Industrializatsiia SSSR, 1929–1932*, pp. 403–4.

dismissed the plea as self-serving and unrealizable.[62] At the January–February 1931 conference of managers, however, representatives of construction projects screamed one after another for the transfer of skilled workers and specialists.[63] Panicked, old factories put up stiff resistance to the proposal.[64]

Thus, after the economic crisis of the summer of 1930, the need to secure skilled workers in production gradually came to override the need to promote and mobilize them away from production. The 20 October 1930 resolution of the Central Committee (discussed in Chapter 8)[65] forbade for the next two years the promotion of workers from the bench into administrative positions "with a view to maintaining cadres of skilled workers in production."[66] In its 12 January 1931 appeal concerning the transportation crisis, the Central Committee ordered a "return to the railways of all the engine drivers and assistant drivers who left transportation in the last five years, and currently are not working in the capacity of their specialties."[67] The following day the People's Commissariat of Labor issued an order detailing the party appeal and expanding the categories of workers directed to return to the railways.[68] Five days later, Kaganovich, addressing the ninth Komsomol congress, implied an end to the massive promotion of workers from the bench. He emphasized, in anticipation of rank-and-file criticism, that those children of workers who had been educated in Soviet

[62] *Za industrializatsiiu*, 4 January 1931.
[63] *Pervaia Vsesoiuznaia konferentsiia rabotnikov sotsialisticheskoi promyshlennosti*, pp. 54, 97, 136, etc.
[64] See, for example, *Avtotraktornoe proizvodstvo*, 1931, no. 9, pp. 18–19, and *Puti industrializatsii*, 1931, nos. 23–24, p. 25. Vesenkha therefore issued a warning that it would apply "decisive measures" to those managers who resisted the transfers; indeed, it ordered the removal of Ogorodnikov, director of the Lenin Forge Engineering Factory in Kiev, and reprimanded others. See the case of the transfer of workers to the Nizhegorod Automobile Plant construction site in *Sbornik postanovlenii i prikazov po promyshlennosti*, 1931, 21:341 (order of 21 May 1931). Ogorodnikov's removal was later commuted to a reprimand (ibid., 1931, 24:396). Other managers, especially "considerable parts of the managerial organs in the Donbas," were handed over to prosecutors for their failure to observe their contracts of the training of skilled workers for other factories and construction projects. See *Industrializatsiia SSSR, 1929–1932*, p. 414.
[65] See chap 8, note 103.
[66] *Partiinoe stroitel'stvo*, 1930, nos. 19–20, p. 62. Certain exceptions were made, however.
[67] *KPSS v rezoliutsiiakh*, 4:517.
[68] *Izvestiia N.K. Truda SSSR*, 1931, 4:63. See also the 18 January order in ibid., 1931, 4:64.

schools and were being promoted into government institutions were "our people":

We cannot strengthen government institutions solely with workers from the bench, because we cannot take the best shock workers away from production. Therefore we have to go in for new people from the working class [*iz liudei rabochego klassa*]. . . . They are not alien elements; they are our people.[69]

On 14 March the Central Committee issued an order to terminate the mobilization of Communists and Komsomols in the railways to various campaigns (grain procurements, spring sowing, etc.) and to end the massive dispatch of investigative brigades to the railways; the order directed that all those mobilized Communists and Komsomols be returned to their previous places of work within three days.[70]

On 26 March the party and the government resorted to an even stronger measure by issuing a resolution entitled "On the Complete Cessation of Mobilization of Workers for the Needs of Current Campaigns by Local Party, Soviet, and Other Organizations."[71] The resolution also prohibited workers from the bench and administrative-technical personnel from being assigned to any kind of investigative work, and ordered that those who had been promoted to administrative work after the 20 October 1930 order be returned to production.[72]

As it turned out, these rather extreme measures were not strictly enforced, nor perhaps could they have been enforced given increasing demands for the politically reliable and administratively competent. In fact, Stalin emphasized in his 23 June 1931 speech that the new course in no way would limit upward social mobility: "The industrial and technical intelligentsia of the working class will be recruited not only from those who have had higher education, but

[69] *IX Vsesoiuznyi s´ezd VLKSM*, p. 213.
[70] *Spravochnik partiinogo rabotnika*, Vol. 8, p. 513.
[71] Ibid., pp. 385–86.
[72] By May, 31,000 people were returned to production, but the violation of the March decree persisted. See the warning of 26 May of the Central Committee in ibid., pp. 386–87. In other spheres too, the active policy of promoting and mobilizing workers gradually came to an end: in the autumn of 1931, the organized recruitment of workers to full-time study in the technical institutes was "quietly abandoned" (Fitzpatrick, *Education and Social Mobility in the Soviet Union*, pp. 209 and 213). The mobilization of workers to the countryside for collectivization gradually gave way to the formation of cadres from among the village population. Viola, *The Best Sons of the Fatherland*, chap. 7.

also from practical workers in our factories, from skilled workers, from the working-class cultural forces in the factories and mines."[73] Nevertheless, the massive promotion and mobilization of workers was discontinued.

Antiegalitarianism

Finally, by 1931 the political reason for maintaining a certain degree of economic homogeneity among workers had become less compelling: the "bourgeois" elements (kulaks, old specialists, NEPmen) appeared to have been removed, subdued, or co-opted; the collectivization of the countryside fundamentally transformed the "petty bourgeois world," thereby considerably undermining the bases of "political influences alien to the proletariat." A certain measure of economic homogeneity as a "fence" against the surrounding "nonproletarian" milieus became no longer politically important because the milieus themselves were thought to be disappearing. Specialist baiting too had lost much of its utility as a means to articulate and protect proletarian identity. Thus, by 1931 the party leadership no longer had any compelling political reason to hold down wage differentials (and to continue to harass specialists) at enormous costs to the economy. The differentiation of the working class, which had been highly politicized in the 1920s, was now depoliticized.

By 1931, the economic costs of the egalitarian trends had reached a critical point, becoming an overriding concern to the party leadership. Given the acute shortage of skilled workers, skilled workers were worth their weight in gold, but they tended either to "break even" with the declining standard of living or to run away from the factories and mines; the shortage of skilled workers was compensated by resorting to quantity, or hiring a great number of new, unskilled workers, with the peculiar result that the lack of skilled workers coexisted with an overall excessive labor force in industry.[74] The rapid increase in the labor force became an important factor in rising production costs in 1931.

The party leadership did not encourage the wage-leveling trends

[73] Stalin, *Sochineniia*, 13:67.
[74] See a People's Commissariat of Labor report in *Industrializatsiia SSSR, 1929–1932*, p. 438.

but tolerated them for political reasons. (Of course, technical factors also played a role here.) As early as December 1929, when production communes manifested themselves, Kuibyshev and Kraval', both of Vesenkha, attacked an even division of wages in the communes.[75] In March 1930 the trade-union leaders Shvernik and Veinberg "sharply" attacked the egalitarian communes.[76] In the summer of 1930, provincial party leaders such as Eikhe of Siberia and Zhdanov of Nizhegorod also attacked egalitarianism as "unsound."[77] Nevertheless, the party leadership neither approved nor disapproved publicly the egalitarian communes, and no serious measures against the leveling trends were taken.[78]

After the economic crisis of the summer of 1930, however, signs of reappraisal began to appear. In September 1930, an article in the Central Committee journal, *Bol'shevik,* lamented the limited application of piecework and appealed for its maximum implementation.[79] In October, as pointed out in Chapter 9,[80] Molotov (through a resolution of the Central Committee of the Ukrainian Communist Party) attacked the communes in the Donbas. Faced with the economic crisis, some managers started applying progressive piecework and premiums.[81] According to the American engineer Charles M. Harry, who worked in the Krivoi Rog iron ore mines in 1930–31,

[75] *TPG,* 10 December 1929; *Pravda,* 12 December 1929; and *Pervyi Vsesoiuznyi s"ezd udarnykh brigad,* pp. 159–61. In late 1929 the Council of People's Commissars called for the introduction of a "strict differentiation of wages of the highly skilled and unskilled" construction workers (*Za tri mesiatsa. Deiatel'nost' SNK i STO. I kvartal [okt.-dek.] 1929/30 g.,* p. 16). But no wage-scale reform seems to have ensued until the summer of 1931.

[76] *Trud,* 14 March 1930. See also the antiegalitarian articles in ibid., 21 and 30 April 1930.

[77] Eikhe, *Novyi etap i zadachi Sibpartorganizatsii,* p. 20; *Izvestiia Nizhegorodskogo Kraevogo komiteta VKP (b),* 1930, nos. 11–13, pp. 6–7.

[78] As late as March 1931 the Central Committee did order an investigation into whether the communes were justifiable as a form of socialist competition (*Partiinoe stroitel'stvo,* 1931, no. 7, p. 64). Yet this order was not carried out. See Oprishchenko, *Istoriografiia sotsialisticheskogo sorevnovaniia rabochego klassa SSSR,* p. 60.

[79] *Bol'shevik,* 1930, no. 18 (30 September), p. 95 (A. P. "Protiv pravogo opportunizma v voprosakh truda").

[80] See chap., note 145.

[81] See, for example, Frankfurt, *Rozhdenie stali i cheloveka,* p. 46; Paramonov, *Uchit'sia upravliat',* pp. 108–9, 135; and Ermilov, *Schast'e trudnykh dorog,* pp. 129–31. These measures met resistance on the part of financial personnel and bookkeepers who feared extra expenses (see also *Direktor I. A. Likhachev v vospominaniiaikh sovremennikov,* p. 18). This does not necessarily mean that the industrial managers as a whole acted as a pressure group against the leveling

during the spring of 1930 the wage scale around the mines was practically the same for all labor, skilled or unskilled. . . . The result was that no initiative was shown by the more skilled class, which was the natural thing to expect. Finally late in 1930 the wage scale was changed, giving the skilled workman more pay; also piece or contract work was introduced and consequently there was a decided upward turn in morale, quality of work, etc.[82]

On 15 January 1931 the Central Committee adopted a resolution to cope with the transport crisis. In the resolution the committee "decisively repudiated the policy of leveling the wages" of railway workers, and resolved to abolish the so-called depersonalized drive system and increase wage differentials with the aim of recalling those skilled and highly skilled workers who had fled the railways.[83] The conference of managers in January–February 1931 attacked the leveling trends and the communes, and resolved to raise wages for "leading" professions.[84] In early February 1931, the secretary of the Moscow party committee, K. V. Ryndin, faced with the rank-and-file demand for social equality, emphasized that egalitarianism would ruin the transport sector.[85] In his speech to the Moscow party committee on 19 February 1931, Kaganovich openly attacked wage equalization with reference to tram workers.[86] In March 1931, Molotov, addressing the sixth congress of Soviets, launched an assault against the leveling (*nivellirovka, uravnitel'nost'*) of the wages of the skilled and the unskilled, a phenomenon he contended was "thoroughly petty bourgeois and had noth-

trends. For example, in February 1931 the journal of the Red directors, *Predpriiatie,* published "for discussion" an article emphasizing the positive effects not of piecework but of time (fixed) wages. See E. Glikman, "Ot sdel'shchiny k fiksirovannoi oplate truda," *Predpriiatie,* February 1931. See also *Za industrializatsiiu,* 31 January 1931 (A. Mokhson).

[82] The Charles M. Harry file in "American Engineers in Russia."

[83] *KPSS v rezoliutsiiakh,* 4:513–14. In the railways, measures were taken in 1930 to raise the wages of those who played a "prominent role in the production process," but they did not produce the expected results. See *Gudok,* 15 April 1930; *Zheleznodorozhnyi transport v tret'em godu piatiletki,* p. 22; and *Sotsialisticheskii transport,* 1932, no. 7, p. 123.

[84] *Pervaia Vsesoiuznaia konferentsiia rabotnikov sotsialisticheskoi promyshlennosti,* pp. 116, 183, and 223. This was enacted in February in the coal-mining industry (*Izvestiia N.K.Truda SSSR,* 1931, 10:182). However, this order was neglected in the Donbas, and the member of the board of the Coal Association, Iu. M. Iunov, was fired. See Ginzburg, *O proshlom – dlia budushchego,* pp. 175–6, and *Sbornik postanovlenii i prikazov po promyshlennosti,* 1931, 12:192.

[85] *Rabochaia Moskva,* 9 February 1931.

[86] Ibid., 1 March 1931.

ing in common with Leninism."[87] His speech was followed by a press campaign against egalitarianism.[88]

Thus by the spring of 1931, the move against the wage-leveling trends was decisive: the Central Committee dispatched a number of brigades to factories to investigate the wage problem.[89] In April, Ordzhonikidze himself inspected the troubled Stalingrad Tractor Plant, and on 30 April he issued an order to eliminate wage egalitarianism and *obezlichka* (lack of personal responsibility caused by the continuous working week).[90] In May, a commission was set up under the chairmanship of the secretary of the Central Committee, P. P. Postyshev, to review the wage issue.[91] A plenum of the Central Committee that convened on 11–15 June advocated a "maximum application of piecework" in the railways.[92] On 19 June, Kuibyshev, reporting to the Moscow party activists on the plenum, attacked wage egalitarianism.[93]

Stalin's speech of 23 June dramatized ongoing criticism of the leveling trends by attributing them to a "Leftist" practice:

In a number of factories, wage scales are drawn up so that there is an almost total disappearance of the difference between skilled and unskilled and between heavy and light labor. Because of egalitarianism, the unskilled worker has no interest in becoming skilled; thus deprived of the prospect of advancement, he feels somewhat like a "visitor [*dachnik*]" in the factory, working only temporarily so as to "earn a little extra" and then to go elsewhere to "seek his fortune." Egalitarianism also prompts the skilled worker to migrate from factory to factory until he finds at last a place where his skill is properly appreciated. . . . We cannot tolerate a situation where a rolling mill worker in the iron and steel industry earns no more than a sweeper. We cannot tolerate a situation where a locomotive driver

---

[87] 6 *s˝ezd Sovetov [SSSR]*, 2:13–4, 27. As early as February 1931, the Kazakhstan party committee assailed egalitarianism (*uravnilovka*). See Kazakhstanskii Kraevoi komitet VKP(b), *Fevral'skii ob˝edinennyi plenum Kraikoma i KraiKK VKP(b)*, pp. 9–10. In February–April, the section of labor economy of the Communist Academy also attacked egalitarianism and the theory of "deskilling." See *Bor'ba na dva fronta v oblasti ekonomiki truda*, passim. See also *Sovetskoe trudovoe pravo na novom etape*, p. 83.

[88] See *Pravda*, 17 March 1931 (L. Mekhlis), 25 March 1931 (editorial), etc.

[89] See Markus, *Trud v sotsialisticheskom obshchestve*, p. 178.

[90] *Sbornik postanovlenii i prikazov po promyshlennosti*, 1931, 19:311–15. See also *Za industrializatsiiu*, 8 May 1931. When Ordzhonikidze visited the plant, rumor went around that "once Stalin [*sic*] has come, things will go well." *Liudi Stalingradskogo traktornogo*, p. 198.

[91] Kuz'min, *V bor'be za sotsialisticheskuiu rekonstruktsiiu*, p. 164.

[92] *KPSS v rezoliutsiiakh*, 4:543.

[93] Kuibyshev, *Stat'i i rechi*, pp. 75–76.

earns only as much as a copying clerk. . . . What, then, does it mean to promote them [skilled workers] and to raise their wage level? Where does it lead as far as unskilled workers are concerned? It means, above all others, opening up prospects for the unskilled worker, giving him an incentive to rise higher, to rise to the category of a skilled worker. You know yourselves that we need hundreds of thousands and millions of skilled workers. But in order to create cadres of skilled workers, we must provide an incentive for unskilled workers, provide for them a prospect of advancement, of rising to a higher position.[94]

In this well-conceived speech Stalin skillfully combined an attack against a "Leftist" practice with the promise of upward mobility. His characterization of leveling as "Leftist" was, of course, only partially correct and therefore incongruous with the subsequent campaign against the 1927–29 wage-scale reform (worked out by the former "Rightist" trade-union leadership and the People's Commissariat of Labor) as the main cause of leveling. Here too the party leadership could have attacked a "Left–Right" bloc.

Whatever the case, Stalin's speech clearly signified a sharp departure from the Bolshevik commitment to ultimate social equality. The new course may well have been seen by some workers as a promise of greater opportunities, but to others it was a betrayal. The new policy, for example, was interpreted by some party members in the railways as "a concession to locomotive workers" like engine drivers who traditionally had retained high professional prestige.[95] The leader of the railway workers' union, A. M. Amosov, addressing the tenth congress of the union in June 1931, somewhat apologetically advocated wider wage differentials: "It is necessary to say frankly ([though] this will not please many) that we have to widen the wage differentials between the highly skilled and the less skilled."[96] In an attempt to justify the new policy, in late 1931 Stalin attributed egalitarianism to a "petty bourgeois mentality": "Egalitarianism owes its origin to the individual peasant type of mentality, the psychology of sharing all material wealth equally, the psychology of primitive peasant 'communism.' "[97] In early 1934,

[94] Stalin, *Sochineniia*, 13:56–58.
[95] *Rabochaia Moskva*, 8 May 1931.
[96] Amosov, *Otchetnyi doklad TsK ZhD na desiatom s"ezde zheleznodorozhnikov*, p. 44.
[97] Stalin, *Sochineniia*, 13:119 (conversation with Emil Ludwig on 13 December 1931).

however, at the so-called congress of victors (the seventeenth party congress), Stalin reverted to the old theme:

[The "Leftist blockheads"] at one time idealized the agricultural communes to such an extent that they even tried to set up communes in factories, where skilled and unskilled workers, each working at his trade, had to pool their wages in a common caldron, which was then divided equally. You know what harm those infantile equalitarian exercises of the "Leftist" blockheads caused our industry.[98]

In 1931 the party leadership began to widen wage differentials in favor of skilled workers, especially those in priority industries such as metallurgy and coal mining, by introducing new wage scales.[99] The egalitarian communes began to be disbanded. To support the new policy from below, the party leadership promoted the formation of *khozraschet* brigades – brigades aimed at raising qualitative indexes of production (especially reduction in production costs) through a strict accounting of individuals' work and hence wages.[100]

Wider differentials were introduced into rationing as well: shock workers were entitled to additional meat and fat (25 percent and 50 percent, respectively, above the norm); the number of days when a dinner with meat was served in factory canteens was also to be raised for shock workers; scarce goods and housing were given first of all to them.[101]

The first six months of 1931 had been an uneasy period. The pace of industrialization was maintained or even accelerated, while signs of a new course and a new political atmosphere became increasingly perceptible. Stalin's 23 June speech apparently relieved the tension. Frankfurt, the director of the Kuznetsk Iron and Steel Plant construction project, later recalled that Stalin's speech had given him an "absolutely clear program for action."[102]

The initiative for the move toward the restoration of order, like

[98] Ibid., 13:357.

[99] See *Materialy k otchetu VTsSPS IX s'ezdu profsoiuzov*, pp. 46–48.

[100] Eskin, *Osnovnye puti razvitiia sotsialisticheskikh form truda*, pp. 72–79, and Kaplun, *Brigady na khozraschete*.

[101] Mordukhovich (Mokhov), *Na bor'bu s tekuchest'iu rabochei sily*, p. 77. It is problematic, however, how effective these measures were, if only because the majority of workers were shock workers by that time.

[102] Frankfurt, *Rozhdenie stali i cheloveka*, p. 270.

that of the revolution from above in 1928, appears to have been taken from above, probably by the new Vesenkha chairman, Ordzhonikidze. Industrial managers had many reasons to welcome the new course, but as the discussion during the first few months of 1931 revealed, many of them, having enjoyed the lack of central control and adapted to police intervention, had considerable anxiety as well about the unsettled new direction. Specialists as a whole were too intimidated and demoralized to press for a new course. And older, skilled workers, now *without* official channels of redress, were too busy fending for themselves to organize strong pressure for change. Yet the new course was accepted by managers like Frankfurt and was welcomed by specialists and skilled workers. Government institutions too soon came to appreciate the new policy, which, as the GPU and the Procuracy made it clear, promised less intervention than before.

The new course, like NEP, appeared to some rank-and-file party members and Komsomols to be a retreat from revolutionary idealism. It did contradict some elements of the revolutionary idealism that had propelled the industrialization drive. There were signs of resistance: specialist baiting did not entirely disappear, and the egalitarian ethos was not eliminated by fiat. When the need to expand piecework was emphasized as a means to reward work and service in the cooperative shops, some Communists considered it an appalling concession to a "bourgeois" practice: "You all speak against NEP, but you yourselves use the same methods as the merchants did."[103]

In 1931 the political leadership did not declare as it did in 1921 that the new course was a retreat or concession. In 1931 some leaders may still have privately intended to resume an offensive at an appropriate time. But if the war of 1918–20 devastated the economy and forced a retreat, the "war" of 1928–30 created industrial foundations. Stalin and his group had reason to believe that the new course of 1931 resulted from a "victory," however costly and rife with crisis and confusion.

[103] *Problemy marksizma*, 1931, nos. 5–6, p. 16.

11

Epilogue and conclusion

The breakthrough wrought by the revolution of 1928–31 laid the foundations of the remarkable industrial expansion in the 1930s that would sustain the country in the Second World War. By the end of 1932, when the Five-Year Plan was declared to have been completed in four years and three months, the gross industrial output, according to the official report, had more than doubled since 1928.[1] This official report is usually regarded in the West as vastly exaggerated, but as the capital projects of the First Five-Year Plan were brought into operation one after another in the mid-1930s, industrial production expanded enormously. During 1934–36, which Naum Jasny has aptly called "three 'good' years," the official index showed "a rise of 88 per cent for total gross industrial production, with the output of industries 'A' [capital goods industries] rising by 107 per cent and that of industries 'B' [consumer goods industries] by 66 percent."[2] In the decade from 1927/28 to 1937, according to Soviet data, gross industrial production leapt from 18,300 million rubles to 95,500 million; pig iron output rose from 3.3 million tons to 14.5; coal from 35.4 million metric tons to 128.0; electric power from 5.1 billion kilowatt hours to 36.2; machine tools from 2,098 units to 36,120.[3] Even discounting the exaggeration, it may be safely said that the achievements were dazzling.

The concluding years of the revolution, however, were characterized by continuous crisis. The return on investments was not easily gained: the factories, unable fully to utilize new, modern equipment, pushed up the costs of production; the high costs had to be

[1] *Itogi vypolneniia piatiletnego plana*, p. 255.
[2] Jasny, *Soviet Industrialization, 1928–1952*, p. 142.
[3] Zaleski, *Planning for Economic Growth in the Soviet Union*, pp. 306–8, and *Stalinist Planning for Economic Growth*, p. 524.

compensated for by a further inflationary currency issue. The exaction of produce from the new but unstable collective farms led to famine in 1932–33. Remarkable achievements were in evidence, but so were enormous difficulties and costs.

The continuous crisis

The correctives – money and trade – introduced in 1931–32 into the centrally planned economy were a sort of lubricant to smooth the working of the creaking machine. The machine itself was not subjected to major structural change or capital repair. Although the legalization of the collective farm free market in May 1932 brought fundamental change to trade between town and country, the state industrial sector remained centrally planned and controlled in physical terms. In the absence of a market, those correctives remained too weak and imperfect to produce the same or comparable effects as they did in a market economy. Industrial reformists' attempt at a "socialist market" in 1932–33 was not accepted by the political leadership.[4]

The reintroduction of *khozraschet* was greeted with skepticism and cynicism by industrial managers. The technical director of the Dinamo Electric Factory in Moscow, for instance, maintained that "*khozraschet* can give positive results only under the conditions of private ownership" and that under Soviet conditions "it is impossible to carry *khozraschet* to the end."[5] In the absence of the control and punishment of the market, managers knew well that their factories would not be "sold at auction" even if they went bankrupt. Managers were therefore alleged to take "lordly attitudes" toward the central authority: "I will not be punished."[6] Yet even the threats of punitive measures could not override their lordly defiance: "Beat me, strike me, reprimand me, apply this or that punishment, but still you will cover the losses."[7]

This was not so much a psychological as a systemic problem rooted in the Soviet economy. In April 1932 the people's commissar of finance, G. F. Grin'ko, addressing a meeting of "shock workers

[4] Davies, "The Socialist Market."
[5] *Za industrializatsiiu,* 25 March 1931.
[6] *VII Vsesoiuznaia konferentsiia VLKSM,* p. 100 (G. F. Grin'ko).
[7] *Finansy i sotsialisticheskoe khoziaistvo,* 1932, no. 7 (March), p. 4.

on the financial front" in the Urals, found himself rebutting those who argued for allowing unprofitable factories to go bankrupt. The capitalist road of market competition, devastation, and bankruptcy, he declared, was "not our road": "We have all the possibilities and are obliged to discipline and educate the managerial organs without closing the factories and dissolving the workers, so that on the basis of socialist consciousness and proletarian discipline, they would secure the operation of production many times more profitable than capitalist production."[8] But the appeal to consciousness and discipline proved ineffective. In early 1933 Grin'ko had to deplore the lack of discipline, which he contended allowed the "majority of managerial organs" not to fulfill their obligation to the state budget.[9] Managers found it convenient to evade, for instance, excise taxes to the state, create double accounts, and raise the centrally fixed selling prices of product.[10] The Red Triangle Rubber Factory in Leningrad, for example, had for nine months of 1932 hidden from the state a sum of one million rubles of taxable turnover.[11] This and other managerial acts were seen by the central authority as deception of the Soviet state.[12] Some managers were condemned for "petty tyranny," or "ruling like a prince" (*kniazhit' i volodet'*) and considering themselves free from punishment: "I won't be judged or treated the way the kulak is."[13]

The economy was plagued not only by systemic but by "subjective" problems as well. In spite of the on-the-job training of managers and the promotion of well-educated Communists to the managerial ranks, the managerial cadres as a whole seem to have had enormous difficulties mastering new, modern technology. Soviet industry was "jumping from manual to machine labor, from the shovel to the technology of the twentieth century, from the psychology of the digger to industrial culture."[14] The modern factories appeared to the leadership to have "outgrown" the managers.[15]

---

[8] *Izvestiia TsIK SSSR*, 19 April 1932. Note also Stalin's similar point in January 1933 in his *Sochineniia*, 13:192–93.

[9] *3 sessiia TsIK Soiuza SSR 6 sozyva*, 11:16.

[10] See, for example, *Finansy i sotsialisticheskoe khoziaistvo*, 1933, nos. 1–2 (January), pp. 24–26.

[11] *3 sessiia TsIK Soiuza SSR 6 sozyva*, 11:14–15.

[12] Ibid., 3:22.

[13] Ibid., 11:16, 14:15, 15:8–9.

[14] Lel'chuk, *Industrializatsiia SSSR*, p. 190.

[15] Ordzhonikidze, *Stat'i i rechi*, 2:452 (January 1933).

The expanding labor force too seemed ill trained for modern equipment. The dire shortage of skilled workers led the leadership to treat them with preference. Some of the new, Taylorist methods of labor introduced in 1928–30 were abandoned. In rail transport the "depersonalized drive" system was abolished in favor of the traditional master drive; by late 1932 the "functional organization of labor" in the textile industry was also canceled as having "disoriented" skilled workers; and as traditional methods of labor were partially reinstated, dispersed skilled workers began to return to production.[16] Yet the shortage forced industry to continue to wager on quantity.

The year 1931 witnessed the most rapid influx of new workers into industrial labor in the history of Soviet industrialization. The annual average number of workers including factory apprentices increased by 26.5 percent from 1930 to 1931.[17] The influx abated slightly in the following year, but by the end of 1932 the industrial labor force doubled from 1928 to more than six million.[18] The increase offset the impact of the remarkable expansion of professional and technical training: the average schooling of industrial workers in 1932–33 remained at the same level as in 1929 – only three and half years.[19] The great majority of the newcomers were arrivals from the countryside who had little or no experience of industrial labor. According to a typical (and prejudiced) observation, they "looked mistrustfully at the machines; when a lever would not work they grew angry and treated it like a baulking horse, often damaging the machine."[20] Inspecting the troubled Red October Factory in Stalingrad in the summer of 1932, Voroshilov found out why the factory was in trouble: "Those who had to produce machines by machines had had no idea about machines one or two months, or, at least, a year before. These were peasants . . . an entirely unskilled force." A large number of workers, Voroshilov noted, were unnecessary; there was no unemployment, but "needs for workers everywhere." However, he went on to say: "Confidentially I can tell you that the needs are very often caused

---

[16] *Plan*, 1933, no. 2, pp. 8–9; *Voprosy truda*, 1933, no. 1, pp. 18–25; *Za rekonstruktsiiu tekstil'noi promyshlennosti*, 1933, no. 7, p. 5.
[17] *Planovoe khoziaistvo*, 1932, nos. 6–7, p. 147.
[18] *Itogi vypolneniia piatiletnego plana*, p. 173.
[19] *Profsoiuznaia perepis'*, pp. 49–50.
[20] Ehrenburg, *Memoirs: 1921–1941*, p. 222.

by the inability of production leaders to assign people properly." He therefore removed 3,000 workers as superfluous.[21]

The wager on quantity, along with the introduction of progressive piece rates in 1931, aggravated the financial situation by inflating the wage bill. The annual wage fund of workers and employees in large-scale industry far outpaced the large increase in the labor force, and more than doubled from 4,413,000,000 to 9,548,000,000 rubles between 1930 and 1932.[22] This inflation prompted state and industrial leaders to warn managers that overexpenditures on wages would be treated as criminal offenses.[23]

The economy remained extremely unstable and critical. The gross output of census industry, according to the official report, increased by 23.3 percent in 1931, an impressive growth but far below the target of 45 percent. In 1932 the growth rate further slowed down to 13.5 percent, against the target of 36 percent.[24] In 1931 the pig iron industry, for instance, on which critical importance had been placed by the Five-Year Plan, fulfilled only 61.5 percent (in physical terms) of the plan; the 1931 output absolutely declined by 2.5 percent from 1930 because of a sharp decline in the quality of raw materials.[25] The pig iron industry continued to fare poorly, with the result that it ended up producing only 36.5 percent of the revised goal of the Five-Year Plan and 62 percent of the original plan.[26] What was more disturbing was that the costs of industrial production rose in 1931 by 6.8 percent instead of falling 10 percent according to the plan, and continued to rise the following year by 8.1 percent instead of a planned 7 percent fall.[27] Furthermore, the productivity of labor (output per man-year) in large-scale industry fell far short of the targets: in 1931 it rose only 7.6 percent as against the goal of 28 percent, and in 1932 a mere 2.6 percent instead of 22

---

[21] Voroshilov, *Stat'i i rechi,* pp. 498, 509–10, and Ordzhonikidze, *Stat'i i rechi,* 2:512.

[22] *Trud v SSSR* (1936), p. 21.

[23] *Sobranie zakonov,* 1932, I, 81–493 (3 December 1932), and *Za industrializatsiiu,* 15 December 1932.

[24] *Sotsialisticheskoe stroitel'stvo SSSR* (1935), p. 3.

[25] *Industrializatsiia SSSR, 1929–1932,* p. 289.

[26] *Itogi vypolneniia piatiletnego plana,* p. 106.

[27] Malafeev, *Istoriia tsenoobrazovaniia v SSSR,* pp. 157 and 406. In 1931 the cost of coal in the Donbas rose as much as 27.5%, and monthly productivity declined. *Narodnoe khoziaistvo SSSR,* 1932, nos. 3–4 (May–June), pp. 77–78. In the ferrous metallurgy industry costs increased by 38% from 1928 to 1932. Kuz'min, *V bor'be za sotsialisticheskuiu rekonstruktsiiu,* p. 175.

percent.[28] The growth in industrial output at this time was mainly due to the vast expansion of the labor force.[29]

The gross underfulfillment of the plans in qualitative terms made the accumulation of resources difficult. The State Bank was compelled to bail industry out: in 1931 alone it expended 1,200,000,000 rubles to cover the losses.[30] From mid-1931 on, an inflationary currency issue resumed, almost doubling the total currency in circulation from 4,355,000,000 rubles on 1 January 1931 to 8,413,000,000 on 1 January 1933.[31] In the process, national consumption was further squeezed.[32]

Agriculture, like industry, plunged into crisis at this time. In 1931 agricultural production declined from the 1930 bumper crop, but the state procurements increased: in 1930, 28.2 percent of grain production was procured by the state, in 1931 – 32.8 percent. In 1932 the procurement rate was projected to rise to 40–50 percent.[33] This policy demoralized the collective farmers, and the sown area declined. In the Kuban, North Caucasus, the "kulaks" were said to have organized sabotage of sowing and procurement and succeeded in mobilizing "a part of collective farmers" against Soviet power.[34] The brutal policy took a heavy toll. In 1932–33 the country came to suffer from a "severe shortage of food": "There were mass instances of swelling from starvation, and death."[35]

This crisis invited an attack on the party, state, and economic institutions. At the January 1933 joint plenum of the Central Committee and the Central Control Commission, Stalin subjected to

---

[28] *Sotsialisticheskoe stroitel'stvo SSSR* (1936), p. xxxv. According to Molotov, in 1932 productivity rose only 1% in the industries of major industrial commissariats. *Materialy ob"edinennogo plenuma TsK i TsKK VKP(b)*, p. 51.

[29] Lel'chuk, *Industrializatsiia SSSR*, p. 205.

[30] *XVII s"ezd VKP(b)*, p. 485 (Grin'ko).

[31] Davies, "Models of the Economic System in Soviet Practice," p. 28.

[32] See note 97 of this chapter.

[33] Moshkov, *Zernovaia problema v gody sploshnoi kollektivizatsii sel'skogo khoziaistva SSSR*, p. 226, and Kuz'min, *V bor'be za sotsialisticheskuiu rekonstruktsiiu*, p. 165.

[34] *III sessiia VTsIK XV sozyva*, 10:5. For this see Shimotomai, "A Note on the Kuban Affair (1932–1933)," and Khrushchev, *Khrushchev Remembers*, p. 73. In 1932–33 similar incidents occurred in the Ukraine, Belorussia, Central Asia, Siberia, and elsewhere. *XVII s"ezd VKP(b)*, pp. 67, 71–72, 105, 408, and 442; *IV sessiia VTsIK XV sozyva*, 4:2. See also Brower, "Collectivized Agriculture in Smolensk."

[35] Kuz'min, *Istoricheskii opyt sovetskoi industrializatsii*, p. 146, and *V bor'be za sotsialisticheskuiu rekonstruktsiiu*, p. 165; Lel'chuk, *Industrializatsiia SSSR*, p. 222; and Zelenin, "Politotdely MTS (1933–1934 gg.)," p. 47.

"harsh criticism" some party *obkoms*, *kraikoms*, and the Central Committees of the national minorities Communist parties.[36] The 1932 purge of the North Caucasus and Ukrainian party organizations led in 1933 to a general purge of the entire party. This purge applied a new and especially heavy pressure on the members. At the January 1933 plenum Stalin contended that some of the "has-beens" had "even managed to worm their way into the party."[37] Molotov and Kaganovich too attacked them as class aliens "with party membership cards in their pockets."[38] The class aliens, hostile elements, and "double-dealers" were listed as the prime targets of the purge.[39] In 1933–34, 18 percent of those expelled fell into these categories.[40]

Industrial managers came under particularly harsh attack. In January 1933 Ordzhonikidze condemned them for their defiant attitude toward the party and the government. He bitterly complained that "reprimands do not work now" and singled out for attack Smokin, the director of the troubled Stalino Metallurgical Factory, who, Ordzhonikidze declared, should have been arrested and put in jail to learn how to work.[41] A week later the Central Control Commission of the Ukrainian Communist Party removed Smokin and expelled him from the party for a year for his alleged "antiparty" acts and "double-dealing": while he told the superior organs that the factory's plan was feasible, Smokin allegedly complained privately that it was impracticable because of "objective conditions."[42] In 1933 a large number of managers in the Donbas coal mines were removed, and massive (unworkable!) reprimands were imposed.[43] The Ukranian Rabkrin therefore had to report that the "massive replacements and repressions" had taken "inadmissible forms" in the Donbas.[44] In the electricity industry (where breakdowns were particularly frequent),[45] there was staged the so-called

---

[36] See *XVII s˝ezd VKP(b)*, p. 561 (L. M. Kaganovich).

[37] Stalin, *Sochineniia*, 13:207.

[38] *Materialy ob˝edinennogo plenuma TsK i TsKK VKP(b)*, pp. 67 and 145.

[39] *KPSS v rezoliutsiiakh*, 5:98–103.

[40] See the case of Leningrad cited in Rigby, *Communist Party Membership in the USSR*, p. 204.

[41] Ordzhonikidze, *Stat'i i rechi*, 2:443, 453, 450.

[42] *Pravda*, 10 February 1933.

[43] See, for instance, *Molot*, 21 July and 9 August 1933.

[44] *Promyshlennost' i rabochii klass Ukrainskoi SSR*, 1:33.

[45] One out of every two was due to operational errors by power station personnel. Lel'chuk, *Sotsialisticheskaia industrializatsiia SSSR i ee osveshchenie v sovetskoi istoriografii*, p. 148.

Metro-Vickers trial in April 1933, in which British and Russian engineers were indicted for sabotage and wrecking.[46] In the railways a large number of managers were removed. When he took over the People's Commissariat of Transport in October 1931, A. A. Andreev was shocked to find the apparatus so disorganized, and he reported that "in spite of the purge carried out of the apparatus, it is again obstructed by unfit personnel."[47] Andreev removed "more than half of the [railway] directors" in the first six months of 1933 alone, and resolved to eliminate the "practice of irreplaceability of this or that official."[48]

The financial institutions too were subjected to purges. The People's Commissariat of Finance repeatedly issued directives to purge "class aliens, hostile and degenerated elements," and applied a variety of "repressive measures."[49] In 1933, 9,350 employees (about a quarter of the commissariat's staff) were checked out, and 1,075 were removed.[50]

In the countryside, particularly the North Caucasus and the Ukraine, coercive measures were extensively applied. An August 1932 law imposed the death penalty for theft of "socialist property" (which included collective farm grain and harvest in the field);[51] whole villages were deported to remote northern areas to eliminate opposition to state grain procurements; and party and Komsomol organizations were purged and disbanded.[52] In 1933 political departments were set up and attached to the Machine-Tractor Stations; a GPU representative joined the staff of each department as assistant to the director; although "repression" was said to have become the "decisive method" of work in "many party organizations," GPU activity tended to "grow out of the control of the party."[53] In March 1933, thirty-five officials of the People's Commissariats of Agriculture and State Farms were shot on charges

[46] See *Wrecking Activities at Power Stations in the Soviet Union.*
[47] Quoted in Molotov, *V bor'be za sotsializm,* p. 259.
[48] *Sotsialisticheskii transport,* 1933, nos. 5–6, p. 31.
[49] *Finansy i sotsialisticheskoe khoziaistvo,* 1933, nos. 4–5 (February), p. 13, no. 12 (August), p. 11; *3 sessiia TsIK Soiuza SSR 6 sozyva,* 16:36; *4 sessiia TsIK Soiuza SSR 6 sozyva,* 13:29, 30, 18:7.
[50] *Finansy SSSR mezhdu VI i VII s"ezdami Sovetov,* p. 52.
[51] *Sobranie zakonov,* 1932, I, 62–360.
[52] Danilov and Ivnitskii, "Leninskii kooperativnyi plan i ego osushchestvlenie v SSSR," p. 55.
[53] Zelenin, "Politotdely MTS (1933–1934 gg.)," pp. 45, 53–54; *XVII s"ezd VKP(b),* p. 67.

of wrecking agriculture with a view to "creating famine in the country."[54]

By mid-1933, however, the crisis appeared to have been overcome with the aid of extensive coercion. The famine abated. The performance of industry improved in qualitative as well as quantitative terms, as the number of workers slightly declined in 1933 and as a substantial amount of currency was withdrawn from circulation.[55] In 1933, according to official data, the productivity of labor increased 8.7 percent, and the costs of industrial production increased only 0.7 percent.[56] Second Five-Year Plan drafts became increasingly realistic in 1933–34; the final plan for pig iron, for instance, was settled at sixteen million tons for 1937, which was even lower than the revised target of the First Five-Year Plan (seventeen million).[57] The economy was gradually "normalized," to use the expression of a Soviet historian.[58] This recovery provided the immediate background to the "three 'good' years."

Repressive measures were not the only means used to overcome the crisis. The workers were constantly mobilized to monitor management. To implement a regime of economy, the shock movement, socialist competition, and counterplans were employed on the "financial front."[59] Tens of thousands of urban workers were dispatched to the countryside.

Yet it was the GPU and the Procuracy that came to play increasingly important and prominent roles in crisis management. Whenever the economic administration appeared too weak to cope, the GPU and the Procuracy found intervention irresistible.[60] After

[54] *Pravda*, 12 March 1933.
[55] The amount of currency in circulation declined sharply from 8,413,000,000 rubles on January 1933 to 6,825,000,000 on 1 June 1933. Davies, "Models of the Economic System in Soviet Practice," p. 28.
[56] *Sotsialisticheskoe stroitel'stvo SSSR* (1936), p. xxxv; Malafeev, *Istoriia tsenoobrazovaniia v SSSR*, p. 406.
[57] See Zaleski, *Stalinist Planning for Economic Growth*, p. 108 (Table 8).
[58] Kuz'min, *V bor'be za sotsialisticheskuiu rekonstruktsiiu*, pp. 201–34.
[59] These methods used in industry were experimented with by the financial authorities as early as 1931. See *2 sessiia TsIK Soiuza SSR 6 sozyva*, 14:12–14, 15:9.
[60] See, for example, Fitzpatrick, "Ordzhonikidze's Takeover of Vesenkha," p. 166. In 1934 in the Prokopyevsk coal field in the Kuzbas, half of the engineer-technical staff were on trial. One was given a year of forced labor for some reason; another, two years in prison for another reason, and so on. Even Sysoev, director of the Eikhe mine and a former member of the Cheka (predecessor of the GPU) with a "25 year [record] of revolutionary service," was confined to the Kuzbas on charges of exceeding the legal limit of ash content of coal. The prosecutor, Mal'tsev, was proud of helping mines stand on their own feet by the force of the Procuracy. *Za industrializatsiiu*, 16 May 1934.

Ordzhonikidze's departure, Rabkrin rapidly declined in authority and prestige, and in 1931–33 it found itself being purged. During the first nine months of 1933, for example, 30 percent of the chairmen of the local control commissions were purged for alleged "distortions of the party line" and other "compromising acts" or the inability to "cope with their work."[61]

Similarly, Communist managers fell into a politically vulnerable position. In 1928–31 they had been under constant attack both from above and from below, but they were able to shift much of the brunt to the "bourgeois" specialists. In 1932–33, however, the managers found themselves threatened with removal from their posts, purge from the party, and arrest and imprisonment as "tyrants," "double-dealers," and, more suggestively, "class aliens with a party card in the pocket." In 1934 the rhetoric became even further inflated, though with fewer class-war overtones. At the so-called congress of victors (the seventeenth party congress) in early 1934, Stalin attacked those "bigwigs" (*vel'mozhi*) who, he maintained, considered that party decisions and Soviet laws were written not for them but for fools and that because they were irreplaceable they could violate decisions and laws with impunity.[62] Such appellations as "feudal lords," "boyars," and "enemies of the Soviet government" also came to be employed.[63] At that time the labels appeared to be scarcely more than rhetoric. Yet the inflation of the rhetoric and the expansion of the concept "enemy" indicated future troubles to the Communist managers.

The troika

In the course of 1931 the factory came to acquire the status of a virtual legal entity: it was granted the right to have its own working capital and to conclude contracts on its own behalf, a right considered essential to the establishment of *khozraschet*.[64] The reform of the supply system also placed the supply department and the storehouses of the factory under the jurisdiction of the director.[65] In the

[61] *Za tempy, kachestvo, proverku*, 1934, no.2, p. 14.
[62] Stalin, *Sochineniia*, 13:370.
[63] Kuromiya, "*Edinonachalie* and the Soviet Industrial Manager," pp. 196 and 203.
[64] Venediktov, *Organizatsiia gosudarstvennoi promyshlennosti v SSSR*, pp. 620–21.
[65] *Za industrializatsiiu*, 27 March 1931.

absence of the control and punishment of the market, *khozraschet* proved inefficacious, and actual managerial authority failed to keep up with the increase in nominal managerial power.

At the July 1931 plenum of the Central Control Commission, Andreev maintained that one-man management was difficult to realize, not so much because the trade union or other organizations hampered the director, as because directors themselves did not want one-man management, fearing to answer for the entrusted business.[66] The case of V. F. Grachev, director of the Stalingrad Tractor Plant and former director of the Putilov Factory, may be illustrative. After Ordzhonikidze's order of 30 April 1931 against egalitarianism,[67] a session of the bureau of the party committee met:

Grachev came to the bureau with a whole pile of documents, protocols, diagrams, etc. People told him that there was no piecework in the plant. He got agitated and answered:
— Here is piecework for you!
and pointed to his papers and protocols. Of course there was laughter all around. Grachev took offense and declared:
— Then do as you please, vote what you want, I won't interfere with that.[68]

Grachev was thus said to have abandoned one-man management. He was removed from his post on 21 July.[69] Managers often proved less authoritative than the party organizations even in managerial-technical matters. At the Mariupol Metallurgical Plant in the Donbas, for example, technical disputes would be turned over to the party meetings for adjudication. This practice impressed the importance of the party on the worker Il'ia Zlochevskii: "Here I felt particularly strongly what the support of the party meant: without it we would not succeed in achieving anything."[70]

The burden of the task was such that managers seemed too weak to shoulder it. Just as the police and judiciary authorities were tempted to intervene in management, so the party organizations (factory cells or committees, local committees, and others) often

---

[66] *III plenum TsKK VKP(b)*, p. 23.
[67] See chap. 10, note 90.
[68] *Liudi Stalingradskogo traktornogo*, p. 452.
[69] *Istoriia zavodov*, p. 117. On 18 August he was appointed director of the construction of a motor factory in Bashkir, a clear demotion. *Sbornik postanovlenii i prikazov po promyshlennosti*, 1931, 37:624.
[70] *Rasskazy o sotsialisticheskom masterstve*, pp. 89–91. This story refers to 1932–34.

found themselves replacing management.[71] Just as the manager appeared to the party leadership to be sometimes a despot or lord who freely wielded his illegitimate power, and at other times to be an incompetent shirker who scrambled helter-skelter for help, so he was forced to behave in the factory sometimes like a dictator who exercised power that was legitimate but rather unsubstantial, and at other times like a weak and irresponsible leader who could not use his legitimate power properly but succumbed to outside inteventions.[72] Management remained far from accountable.

Part of the problem certainly stemmed from the type of economy that had emerged. The problem persists even today. An American economist who visited the Soviet Union in 1983 conveys the complaint of a Soviet economist:

> You western economists are lucky. You can count on the discipline of the market. Managers know their business will fail if they don't manage better, make better products. Workers know they will lose their jobs if they don't produce or if their employers fail.[73]

In any case, to the extent that some corrective measures were introduced into the economy, controls from above and from below were expected to become less compelling. Yet to the extent that the economy remained centrally planned in physical terms, controls remained "forces permanently operating" in some form or another.

Paradoxical though it may appear, a peculiar form of mass participation in economic management thus became part and parcel of an authoritarian political regime. Kaganovich declared in late 1929 that in the Soviet Union, "unlike in bourgeois states, people participate in the administration of the state not by means of formal voting for some delegate or other, but by means of real, everyday, and active participation in the administration of the country."[74] This statement was more than rhetorical. Kaganovich appeared to mean that the

---

[71] See for example the case of the Nizhegorod Tractor Plant in *Avtotraktornoe delo*, 1932, no. 6, p. 154, and the Central Committee's resolution of 2 April 1932 in *Spravochnik partiinogo rabotnika*, vol. 8, p. 475.

[72] See Kuromiya, "*Edinonachalie* and the Soviet Industrial Manager," p. 197. The oft-quoted remark of M. M. Kaganovich to the effect that "the director is the sole sovereign . . . in the factory. . . . The earth should tremble when the director walks around the factory" (*Soveshchanie khoziaistvennikov, inzhenerov, tekhnikov, partiinykh i profsoiuznykh rabotnikov tiazheloi promyshlennosti*, pp. 212–13) reflected partly a reality and partly a hope for strong management.

[73] Silk, "Andropov's Economic Dilemma," p. 98.

[74] *Sovetskoe gosudarstvo i revoliutsiia prava*, 1930, no. 1, p. 41.

Soviet political leadership was little interested in a Western type of democracy, but that it was serious about some form of mass partici-pation in administration. Mass participation sometimes took dra-matic forms and proportions as in the shock movement, the Stak-hanovite movement in the mid- and late 1930s, and the movement for Communist labor under Nikita Khrushchev. Yet when mass par-ticipation proved extremely costly, uncontrollable, or ineffective, the other form of control – control from above – loomed more appeal-ing. Interestingly enough, the state prosecutor at the political trials of 1936–38, Vyshinsky, justified massive police intervention by refer-ring to the ineffectiveness of control from below: "The old talk about the mobilization of social activists and groups of assistants must vanish somewhere. Now something else is needed."[75]

In the 1930s, however, a significant part of the problem was be-lieved to lie in human material. Sometimes the leadership appeared optimistic. In March 1932 Kaganovich, for instance, declared that responsibilty inherent in power would train the managers:

People grow up only under the burden of responsibility. . . . Put responsibil-ity on him [a cadre], and he will rise under the burden of responsibility; he will be compelled to rise.[76]

Yet Ordzhonikidze declared in January 1933 that the factories had "outgrown" the managers.[77] In 1933, in fact, the party leadership began to attack Taylorist functional management by contending that it rationalized and perpetuated managers' lack of technical expertise.[78] Managerial power was no longer supposed to be di-vided among various functional departments, but was concentrated in the hands of the director. This concentration appeared to lead to more traditional, hierarchical management, but the burden of power and responsibility weighed heavily upon him.

Many directors thus appeared to the leadership to be unable to "rise under the burden of responsibility." Condemning the lack of one-man management in the factories, a February 1934 editorial in *Pravda* declared impatiently: "Out of the inept director [*direktor-*

---

[75] Zhogin, "Ob izvrashcheniiakh Vyshinskogo," p. 30, and Gladkov and Smirnov, *Menzhinskii*, p. 326.

[76] *Rabochaia Moskva*, 17 March 1932. Although this remark referred to party cad-res in general, its implication for managerial cadres was apparent.

[77] Ordzhonikidze, *Stat'i i rechi*, 2:452.

[78] The first move was the Central Committee resolution of 8 April 1933 about the Donbas coal mines. *KPSS v rezoliutsiiakh*, 5:91–97.

shliapa] – whatever rights we give him and however we support him – all the same nothing comes out of him."[79] At a meeting of industrial managers in May 1935, F. F. Shefer, the director of the Central Bookkeeping Department of the People's Commissariat of Heavy Industry,[80] severely attacked factory directors for persecuting chief bookkeepers (watchdogs over the financial matters of the factories) by bringing action against them, expelling them from their apartments, attempting to get them fired. Yet, curiously, Shefer insisted that the directors subordinate bookkeeping directly to themselves. Some directors opposed doing so because, evidently, they regarded bookkeeping primarily as a burden they wanted to avoid.[81] The directors thus appeared to the leadership to wish neither to be under the control of bookkeepers nor to take the responsibility of bookkeeping. To the extent that the leadership considered managerial authority and accountability from the point of view of human material, these and other managers appeared "unfit," and the language the leadership used to attack them became increasingly harsh.

In contrast with the party organization, which apparently retained an identity of its own and remained a contender for power, the trade unions had lost much of their traditional identity. The influx of shock workers into factory committees forced the unions to "turn their faces to production," and their reorientation was a notable achievement of the Stalinist leaders, as Kaganovich proudly declared at the seventeenth party congress in early 1934:

The factory committees have considerably reorganized their work, and the overwhelming majority of them consist of real shock workers. These people do not suffer from trade union diseases: they work stubbornly and persistently to carry out the tasks of developing socialist competition and the shock movement and increasing output.[82]

The new style of work was not free of problems, however. To the extent that the unions saw management as weak, they, like other organizations, were compelled to intervene in the managerial do-

---

[79] *Pravda*, 25 February 1934.
[80] This commissariat took over the bulk of the old Vesenkha apparatus in early 1932 when the latter was split into three commissariats of heavy industry, light industry, and lumber industry.
[81] *Sovet pri Narodnom komissare tiazheloi promyshlennosti SSSR*, pp. 103 and 192. From 1932 on, the factory chief bookkeeper had been granted greater powers and rights to tighten financial control. See, for example, *Sobranie zakonov*, 1932, I, 72–440 (29 September).
[82] *XVII s´ezd VKP(b)*, p. 549.

main. After 1931, however, when the food situation deteriorated and the enormous pressure for rapid industrialization lessened slightly, there emerged among party, industrial, and union leaders a certain reappraisal of union activity. In January 1933, in the midst of the famine, Ordzhonikidze found it necessary to criticize the trade unions. He contended that in the troubled Donbas,

one cannot understand what they [trade union organizations] are doing in the factory. The trade unions must concern themselves with feeding the workers, with their living conditions, and so on. We've completed the Five-Year Plan, are building socialism, have built large-scale industry, but one cannot say this to a worker who is sitting in cold barracks—he'll throw every curse at you.[83]

The issue that drew particular attention was wages.

By 1931 the wage fund had been centrally determined and allocated according to central economic plans. The wage scales too were determined centrally and taken out of the collective agreements. Yet the union organizations at the factory or shop level retained a certain formal control over factors (particularly output quotas and piece rates) that affected the amount of actual wages. The quotas and rates were decided by management but had to be cleared with the factory Assessment-Conflict Commission, half the staff of which were union representatives. In 1932 the union leadership voiced strong concern that even the commission had lost authority among workers and that they therefore turned directly to management for the solution of wage conflicts.[84]

This issue was settled in a peculiar manner. In January 1933 the unions renounced the commission's right: management acquired the right to determine the norms and piece rates without clearing them with the Assessment-Conflict Commission.[85] This solution seems not to have strengthened the union's authority, but it did dissociate the unions from the politically subtle issue. Management had to shoulder the full burden of the constant pressure from above to raise output quotas.

What strengthened the unions' authority among the workers was the unions' assumption of social service functions. In June 1933 the

[83] Ordzhonikidze, *Stat'i i rechi*, 2:458.
[84] See, for example, *Trud*, 28 November 1932 (Shvernik). See also Markovich, *RKK na novom etape.*
[85] This was first announced in *Trud*, 9 May 1933. See also Schwarz, *Labor in the Soviet Union*, pp. 184–85.

People's Commissariat of Labor was abolished and its functions (the administration of social security, sanatoriums, and rest homes, the enforcement of safety regulations, and the registration of collective agreements, to name just a few) were transferred to the trade unions and their All-Union Central Council.[86] In 1934, in connection with the reorganization of Rabkrin and the Central Control Commission, the unions took over "all the rights of the lower-level organs of Rabkrin in the factories" and provided guidance to the control organs of consumer goods supply organizations.[87] John Scott, an American who worked at Magnitogorsk from 1933 to 1938, reported that when he started work there the authority of the trade unions was "at a low ebb," but that

later, in 1934 and 1935, the trade unions reorganized their work and began to carry on activities which won back the respect and support of some of the workers. They did this by building rest homes, insisting on the observance of labor laws, even if it meant that the jobs suffered for the time being, giving out theater tickets, organizing schools and courses of all kinds, and sending workers and their wives and children to sanitariums.[88]

This transformation of the trade unions from bargaining into social service organs shaped the framework of union activity that remains even today.[89]

A new configuration of workers

The rapid expansion of the industrial labor force made certain sociopolitical differentiations among the workers inevitable. According to the future Stakhanovite hero, A. Busygin, who worked at the Nizhegorod (later Gorky) Automobile Plant, there were "people embittered against the Soviet government, dekulakized, has-beens," but such people did not speak out but just worked. Some workers

[86] *Sobranie zakonov*, 1933, I, 40–238. Details were worked out in ibid., 57–333 (10 September).

[87] *KPSS v rezoliutsiiakh*, 5:159.

[88] Scott, *Behind the Urals*, p. 36. In May 1935 Stalin would note a "peculiar crisis of the trade unions," but this appears to have been an attempt to clinch their transformation into civil service organs. See Evreinov, *O sboeobraznom krizise profsoiuzov i ob ikh novykh zadachakh.*

[89] This was perhaps a peculiar blend of a "totalitarian" transformation and the "European socialist trade union tradition of, at least theoretically, pursuing the common interests of all workers and not solely those of the union membership." Granick, *The Red Executive*, p. 224.

spoke of their success, others complained about housing shortages, still others sought to arouse discontent among the workers: "They demand a lot from us, but as to providing us they provide nothing. . . . See how the bosses live, but how about us?" Certainly there were enormous difficulties and defects, Busygin has recalled, but "people spoke about them in different ways – some with pain in their hearts, with the wish to correct [defects] and overcome [the difficulties], others with hatred and malicious pleasure."[90]

There was noticeable concern in the party leadership about the infiltration of "class enemies" into the working class.[91] Life on the shop floor was hardly peaceful. Inexperienced workers and engineers often damaged machines, and the accidents were alleged to be "indistinguishable" from wrecking.[92] Impatient voices were raised about "class enemies" who allegedly threw bolts into machines, shut ventilators in mines, and set fire to buildings.[93] The highhanded reaction of political leaders contributed to the inflation of the concept "enemy." A December 1931 law stipulated that if production was halted through the workers' fault, no payment was to be made for the duration of the stoppage, and that similarly, no payment was to be made for the products flawed through the workers' fault.[94] When a Moscow worker with thirty-five years' industrial work experience (who was reported to have "never been against the Soviet government") came out against the law at the factory, he was declared a "class enemy." This episode prompted Kaganovich's intervention.[95] The inflation of the concept "enemy" and the expansion of the power and activity of the security organs reinforced each other; and workers' vigilant spirit continued to be inflamed by accidents and blunders.[96]

As A. Busygin stated clearly, the declining standard of living continued to plague the workers as a whole. In 1931 and 1932, capital investments grew further at the expense of consumption.

[90] Busygin, *Sversheniia*, pp. 11–12.
[91] See, for example, *Materialy ob"edinennogo plenuma TsK i TsKK VKP(b)*, p. 114 (Ia. E. Rudzutak).
[92] *4 sessiia TsIK Soiuza SSR 6 sozyva*, 8:26.
[93] Ibid., 11:21; *III sessia VTsIK XV sozyva*, 9:1, 10:11–12, 11:20, 15:10–11; Izotov, *Moia zhizn'-moia rabota*, p. 58; Busygin, *Sversheniia*, p. 11–12.
[94] *Sobranie zakonov*, 1932, I, 2–11.
[95] Quoted in *Rabochaia Moskva*, 6 April 1932.
[96] See my article "Soviet Memoirs as a Historical Source." John Scott reported that "there unquestionably was wrecking going on in Magnitogorsk." Scott, *Behind the Urals*, pp. 182 and 186–87.

According to a Soviet study, the "entire increase in the national income went into accumulation," reducing the consumption fund absolutely from 23,177,200,000 rubles (measured in 1928 prices) in 1930 to 22,705,200,000 rubles in 1931, and 22,375,800,000 rubles in 1932. As a result, the accumulation fund sharply increased from 3,697,400,000 rubles, or 14.3 percent of the national income in 1928, to 17,724,200,000 rubles, or 44.2 percent of the national income in 1932. In absolute terms, the consumption fund barely increased during the same period: from 21,305,700,000 rubles to 22,375,800,000 rubles; in relative terms, the consumption fund plummeted from 85.7 percent of the national income in 1928 to 55.8 percent in 1932. Evidently, national consumption was severely squeezed.[97]

The rapid increase in nominal wages in the cities under the conditions of goods shortages accelerated the inflation of consumer goods prices. In 1932 the retail prices in the private market reached an apex of 578 percent of those in the socialized sector.[98] The consumption of the urban population naturally continued to decline. In 1932 the per capita annual consumption of meat, fat, and poultry reached an all-time low of 16.9 kilograms, or a mere 32.7 percent of 1928 levels. Even the consumption of potatoes, which had risen to 144.22 kilograms in 1931 from 87.60 kilograms in 1928 to compensate for other scarce foodstuffs, declined to 110.00 kilograms in 1932.[99] In the summer of 1932 the supplying of meat stopped in Moscow, Leningrad, and the Donbas.[100] In the southern regions the food shortages caused workers to desert production; morale declined, and so did labor productivity.[101] In Magnitogorsk, during the entire winter of 1932–33 "the riggers got no meat, no butter, and almost no sugar and milk. They received only bread and a little cereal grain."[102]

The serious shortages of consumer goods prompted the Politbureau to set up a special commission chaired by Stalin and composed of "almost all Politbureau members and a number of people's commissars." The commission increased the circulation of nonration

[97] Barsov, *Balans stoimostnykh obmenov mezhdu gorodom i derevnei*, pp. 89–93.
[98] Malafeev, *Istoriia tsenoobrazovaniia v SSSR*, p. 173.
[99] Moshkov, *Zernovaia problema v gody sploshnoi kollektivizatsii*, p. 136.
[100] *Materialy ob'edinennogo plenuma TsK i TsKK VKP(b)*, p. 63.
[101] Volodin, *Po sledam istorii*, p. 207, and *Molot*, 23 January 1934 (B. P. Sheboldaev), referring to the 1933 difficulties.
[102] Scott, *Behind the Urals*, p. 78.

goods to encourage competition between the cooperatives and the free market, that is, to lower the overall prices of consumer goods.[103] (No doubt, it was also intended to absorb the inflated currency in circulation.) Nevertheless, market prices continued to rise in 1932.

"In all probability," as a Soviet economist has put it, the level of accumulation in 1931 and 1932 was too high to create the "optimal conditions for resolving the task of the most rapid industrialization of the country."[104] The real wages of Moscow industrial workers in 1932 were only 53 percent of the 1928 level.[105] Naturally these years witnessed strikes in factories.[106]

Paradoxical as it may appear, the forced accumulation was a source not only of privation and unrest but also of Soviet heroism. Stalin's industrialization was a drive not for "cotton" but for "steel," a symbol of modernity and power. In January 1932 Kaganovich addressed a Moscow party conference and found it convenient to argue against the steel bias:

Today one hears on all sides: "Let us have an AMO Auto Plant"; "Let us have a new ball bearing plant"; "Let us have a new electric factory," and so on. When we answer: "Let us have a textile mill . . . ."

Voice: Anything you like but no textile mills!

There you have it—"No textile mills! Can't we have something else, something in heavy industry?"[107]

But the appeal of "cotton" hardly overtook the appeal of "steel." In the same vein, Soviet youth in the 1930s found heroism in working

---

[103] Kaganovich, *Ot XVI k XVII s˝ezdu partii,* p. 32. For the competition, see Stalin, *Sochineniia,* 13:343–44, and *XVII s˝ezd VKP(b),* p. 181 (Mikoyan).

[104] Barsov, *Balans stoimostnykh obmenov mezhdu gorodom i derevnei,* p. 96.

[105] Barber, "The Standard of Living of Soviet Industrial Workers," p. 116, citing A. A. Tverdokhleb, "Material'noe blagosostoianie rabochego klassa Moskvy v 1917–1937 gg." (Moscow, 1970), p. 335.

[106] The Central Committee noted in 1932 that in Ivanovo-Voznesensk, where grave "errors" with food supply were committed, "fragments of the counterrevolutionary SR and Menshevik parties, and also counterrevolutionary Trotskyists expelled from our Bolshevik party and former members of the 'Worker Opposition' sought to build a nest for themselves and organize opposition to the party and government." Quoted in *XVII s˝ezd VKP(b),* p. 165. This apparently refers to the May 1932 strikes reported in *Sotsialisticheskii vestnik,* 1932, no. 22 (283) (26 November), p. 16, and *Biulleten' Oppozitsii,* no. 29/30 (1932), p. 13. These émigré journals reported a number of strikes in Moscow, Leningrad, the Donbas, and elsewhere.

[107] Kaganovich, *Moskovskie bol'sheviki v bor'be za pobedu piatiletki,* p. 9.

in factories and on construction sites like Magnitogorsk and Kuznetsk, whereas working in the service sector as barbers, tailors, shoemakers, etc., did not attract them at all.[108]

The theme of "steel" in the works by F. V. Gladkov, V. V. Mayakovski, M. S. Shaginian, M. Il'in, and other contemporary Soviet writers, according to a Soviet historian, was "the leitmotif of real life itself"; and Soviet popular heroism has been so closely associated with "steel" that even today it is difficult to achieve a "psychological transformation" in favor of consumer goods industries.[109]

The disappearance of mass urban unemployment provided much hope to the population. In 1928–32, according to an official estimate, 12.5 million people joined the urban labor force, both industrial and nonindustrial, and 8.5 million of them were new arrivals from the countryside; the remainder were recruited from the urban labor reserves.[110] On one hand, the transformation of the labor market from a buyers' into a sellers' market adversely affected labor discipline and turnover, and this invited high-handed reactions from the center.[111] On the other, the new workers no longer appeared to the political leadership to be as politically and socially "disoriented" as in 1928–29. In October 1930 the twenty-two-year-old illiterate A. Busygin, for instance, left the countryside (in which he saw "no hope") to seek his fortune. He found work on the Nizhegorod Automobile Plant construction site. Unsure of the future, however, he left his wife in the village and sent money back home. In a year or so he quickly adjusted to a new life, called her to the city for settlement, and in 1935 became a Stakhanovite hero.[112] Another future Stakanovite, I. Gudov, also left the countryside sometime in the 1920s to "find a new life," but only made unsuc-

---

[108] Gugel', "Vospominaniia o Magnitke," p. 320.

[109] Lel'chuk, *Industrializatsiia SSSR*, pp. 245–46.

[110] *Itogi vypolneniia piatiletnego plana*, p. 174.

[111] A draconian decree of November 1932 empowered management to dismiss workers for even a single day's unjustified absence. In December all closed workers' cooperatives were transferred to management, which thus took charge of issuing ration books. Another decree of the same month obliged urban citizens to carry an internal passport (*Sobranie zakonov*, 1932, I, 78–475, 80–489, 84–516 and 517. For these and subsequent harsh labor laws, see Filtzer, *Soviet Workers and Stalinist Industrialization*, chaps. 3, 5, and 9). This last decree not only restricted the movement of the urban population, but by fiat relegated the rural population to second-class citizenship. The introduction of an internal passport, however, helped the authorities partially shield the cities from the famine by restricting the movement of rural residents into the cities.

[112] See Busygin, *Zhizn' moia i moikh druzei* and *Sversheniia*.

cessful attempts to find a secure industrial job. During the First Five-Year Plan years he worked as a Komsomol teacher at an orphans' colony, but he felt as if "all these grandiose events had passed him by" and he decided to quit. In 1934 he found work in a Moscow factory to "start life all over again." He was now much more confident in himself than when he had left the countryside, because unemployment had long disappeared and so, he thought, he would not starve in any event.[113] These were but typical cases experienced by rural Soviet youth in the 1930s. In January 1933 Kaganovich proudly declared that it was "not long ago" that he had received thousands of similarly worded notes at factories: "What is to be done? I have a growing son. He is 15–16 years old, but behaves like a hooligan in the street. Give him work." He no longer received such notes.[114]

If the transformation of the labor market benefited the former unemployed, peasants, and other less privileged groups, antiegalitarianism benefited the shock workers and skilled workers. The Soviet labor market in the 1930s remained free in the sense that, with some exceptions and restrictions, labor was free to move. It differed from a free capitalist labor market in that the price of labor was not freely quoted, but was regulated by the central authorities. Antiegalitarianism meant to the shock workers and other skilled workers a belated adjustment by the central authorities to the market value of their labor that had been artificially depressed.

According to Stalin, egalitarianism displayed "rather considerable tenacity" in the party.[115] The leader of the trade unions, N. M. Shvernik, found it necessary to emphasize that antiegalitarianism was not a betrayal of socialism. "*By the introduction of a new wage-scale reform the working class not only does not betray socialism but turns wages into a powerful lever for the organization of labor and for the improvement of the material conditions of working-class life.*"[116] Despite the persistence of egalitarianism among some Bolsheviks, it appears that antiegalitarianism, once released from moral

---

[113] Gudov, *Put' stakhanovtsa,* pp. 3–19, and *Sud'ba rabochego,* pp. 3–4 and 111.
[114] Kaganovich, *Ob itogakh ob"edinennogo plenuma TsK i TsKK VKP(b),* p. 19.
[115] Stalin, *Sochineniia,* 13:357. "The revolutionary equalitarianism of manners was not discarded; going unshaven and tie-less was a mark of proletarian sympathies even if not of proletarian origin." Mosley, "1930–1932," p. 63.
[116] *IX Vsesoiuznyi s"ezd professional'nykh soiuzov SSSR,* p. 89. Emphasis in the original.

and ideological constraints, came to be quickly accepted by skilled workers and engineers. In late 1932 a German visitor was surprised to find a former communard opposed to the egalitarian commune in which he had lived in 1930. This communard, named only Vassya, told the German that because he had worked hard, become an engineer, and made a great contribution to the country, "it's only right and just that I should be allotted a provision shop that has preference in the matter of supply, that I have the prospect of getting a flat of my own with three rooms and kitchen in a new building."[117] In 1931, explicitly preferential treatment began to be given to the engineers and technicians: better housing, special retail shops, separate eating places in the factories.[118]

Among workers, however, egalitarianism did not immediately give way. According to some Soviet studies, the wage differentiation of workers in terms of decile ratio of highest-to-lowest tenth wages rose by only 0.02 from 1929 to 1934.[119] According to a recent Soviet study, the differentials even dropped by 0.17 between 1930 and 1934.[120] Whatever the case, at least two factors accounted for the persistent leveling trends. The first was the massive influx of new, unskilled workers and the relative scarcity of skilled workers. For example, in 1934 the most skilled workers (ranked 8) accounted for only 0.7 percent and 0.9 percent in the ferrous metallurgy and the machine-fabricating (metal-working and engineering) industries, respectively.[121] Second, food rationing continued to militate against wage differentiation, because money wages were less important than the size of the ration delivered at low fixed prices. In 1932–33 at the Chelyabinsk Ferro-Alloy Plant, for instance, skilled workers earned two to three times more than the less skilled. Yet the difference little affected workers' budgets, because rationed food was given without regard to their skills. Skilled shock workers could afford to buy extra food in the market for speculative prices,

---

[117] Mehnert, *Youth in Soviet Russia*, p. 253.

[118] Lampert, *The Technical Intelligentsia and the Soviet State*, pp. 135–48, and Fitzpatrick, *Education and Social Mobility in the Soviet Union*, pp. 215–17.

[119] See Mozhina, "Ekonomiko-statisticheskii analiz," p. 203. See also Yanowitch, "The Soviet Income Revolution," p. 686.

[120] Rabkina and Rimashevskaia, "Raspredelitel'nye otnosheniia i sotsial'noe razvitie," p. 20.

[121] Mozhina, "Ekonomiko-statisticheskii analiz," p. 203. In Leningrad, for example, those highly skilled metal workers with wage rank 8 were so few that they were called "kings." See Danilov, *Zhizn'–poisk*, p. 40.

but what they could get was at most "two loaves of bread," which was said to be "all the difference."[122]

As private market prices began to decline in mid-1933 (which was a clear sign of economic improvement),[123] however, the standard of living began to rise and wage differentials appeared to widen gradually. Shock workers were lavishly rewarded. For instance, in 1934 I. Zhukov, a shock coal miner and a party member in the Donbas, received higher rations, than other workers, of bread, groats, meat, fish, and cream butter. Moreover, he got bonus coupons for purchasing consumer goods otherwise unobtainable. When he was awarded a light motor vehicle for his shock work, he felt he had "become a 'bourgeois.'"[124] If Zhukov felt that he had become a bourgeois at all, those workers and Communists promoted out of manual occupations into white-collar and administrative positions and higher technical schools[125] were even more likely to have felt that they had become "bourgeois." Proletarian identity and class coherence faded. If the revolution promised workers (and peasants) that they would someday "become the new masters," Stalin's revolution from above fulfilled this particular promise, if not others.[126] Stalin and his close associates had some reason to believe that they had come out of the revolutionary upheaval politically mightier.

As in society in general, the move toward order and normalization became evident on the shop floor. Those upwardly mobile individuals quickly came to assume a traditional notion of status and hierarchy. The American engineer J. S. Ferguson, who worked in Kuznetsk for eighteen months beginning in July 1931, reported:

A shift engineer . . . will not turn his hand to give assistance to a workman, no matter how great the emergency may be; such a thing being beneath the dignity of the position. The Russian officials and engineers could not understand why sometimes in cases of emergency the American engineers would pitch in and help to get a certain job done, even though the delay was very costly.

[122] Gusarov, *Nezabyvaemye gody*, p. 48.
[123] Malafeev, *Istoriia tsenoobrazovaniia v SSSR*, pp. 194–95.
[124] *Vsegda vosemnadtsat'*, pp. 73 and 76. The abolition of food rationing in 1934–35 and the onset of the Stakhanovite movement in 1935 contributed to further differentiation.
[125] The number of these people is estimated at 1.5 million for the 1930–33 period. Fitzpatrick, "Stalin and the Making of a Soviet Elite," p. 387.
[126] Fitzpatrick, "The Russian Revolution and Social Mobility," p. 138.

These young engineers, many of whom are children of peasants, feel very keenly the dignity of their position and rank. On the other hand, the foreman and workers are envious of the Russian engineers and do about as they please, paying little attention to orders from the engineers, the latter having no means of enforcing discipline.[127]

This quote also suggests another aspect of the new relation between the regime (as represented by management and engineers) and the workers. Those workers who felt passed over appeared to be staging passive strikes on the shop floor by "paying little attention to orders from the engineers," much in the same way as new collective farmers resorted to passive resistance to a new rural order by neglecting work on the collective farm and tending their own tiny private plots instead.

Class war

Summing up the revolutionary years 1928–31, I. M. Vareikis, secretary of the Central Black Earth *oblast'* committee of the party, declared in February 1932:

We Marxist-Leninists build it [socialism] on the basis of scientific communism, on the basis of the teachings of Marx and Lenin. But the experience of our revolution shows that . . . even the founders of scientific communism . . . like Marx, Engels, and Lenin, could not have foreseen all the concrete details and conditions of the construction of socialist society.

One may sense in his speech both a pride in what had been achieved and a defense of the way the achievement had been gained. Indeed, Vareikis went on to urge the party to "follow through the achievements to move forward and to correct the errors committed."[128]

However, much uncertainty remained about how the revolution would be settled. In January 1933, in the midst of the famine, L. M. Kaganovich, for instance, declared:

Much as we wish and try to assess the grandiosity of these victories of the Five-Year Plan, probably we are still for the time being, I think, not in a position to fully comprehend all the grandeur of the victories of the Five-Year plan. Probably, in a few years the whole grand scale of these victories

[127] The J. S. Ferguson file in "American Engineers in Russia."
[128] Vareikis, *Osnovnye zadachi vtoroi piatiletki*, pp. 3–4.

Figure 11.1. Stalinist leaders at the "congress of victors" (January–February 1934). *Back row, left to right:* Enukidze, Voroshilov, L. M. Kaganovich, Kuibyshev; *front row, left to right:* Ordzhonikidze, Stalin, Molotov, Kirov.

will become clearer to us, just as now the extent of the victories of the October [Revolution] is becoming clearer to us.[129]

It turned out that the fight in 1932–33 to overcome the crisis and consolidate the achievement of the revolution was also character-ized by trial and error, wild exhortation and relentless coercion, hopes for victory amid desperate difficulties.

When the immediate crisis had been overcome by 1934, as dis-cussed earlier, there emerged a general feeling of elation in the party. On 29 December 1933, V. P. Zatonskii, a Ukrainian political leader, plainly stated that the Ukraine had undergone a serious crisis and triumphantly maintained that he could say so because it had already been overcome: "Even now they [Western countries] scream a lot about the famine in the Ukraine, about the devastation of collective farms, and the like. Late! We can now appear with head raised high because the Ukrainian Soviet Republic has come out of the disrup-

[129] Kaganovich, *Ob itogakh ob"edinennogo plenuma TsK i TsKK VKP(b)*, p. 45.

tion."[130] The seventeenth party congress in January–February 1934 was thus called a "congress of victors."

The outcome of Stalin's revolution from above, like successful revolutions, involved reconciliations of the old and the new. The economic system that the revolution settled for was neither the moneyless product-exchange economy that had been optimistically envisaged and implemented in the heady days of 1929–30, nor a market economy of the NEP type. It was an economy centrally planned in physical terms that awkwardly incorporated money and trade.[131] This basic economic structure survives to the present day. Along with it, the industrial efficiency and quality of the centrally planned economy as it had emerged in the Soviet Union became permanent problems.[132]

The state also came to terms with the "bourgeois" specialists and the older, skilled workers whose service to the "mastery of technology" was now much appreciated. In exchange for their political conformity, if not loyalty, the regime promised material rewards and privileges. Similar implicit, though one-sided, negotiations proceeded in the cultural sphere as well.[133]

The rapid industrialization drive involved great difficulties. They and the way they were dealt with overwhelmed, alienated, and antagonized a number of prominent Bolsheviks over the years. As the difficulties were surmounted, Stalin's opponents found their political edge blunted, their fighting spirit damped, and themselves defeated, as S. I. Syrtsov was reported to have said in 1930: "Subjectively I wanted to help the party and the revolution; objectively I turn out to be in the role of some petty bourgeois neurasthetic."[134] Similar patterns seem to have been repeated on a grander scale in 1931–34.

Some of the former Trotskyists who in 1928–29 had returned to the party apparently began to doubt and waver at that time. K. B. Radek, for example, noted that in 1930–31 he had appraised the situation as follows: "If this general offensive were not slowed down this would, as we defined it by a catch-phrase, 'end like the

---

[130] *4 sessiia TsIK Soiuza SSR 6 sozyva*, 5:27.

[131] For a very useful account, see Davies, "Models of the Economic System in Soviet Practice."

[132] See Filtzer, *Soviet Workers and Stalinist Industrialization*.

[133] Fitzpatrick, "Cultural Politics under Stalin." Note also Dunham's concept "Big Deal" in her *In Stalin's Time*.

[134] Quoted in Gaisinskii, *Bor'ba s uklonami ot general'noi linii partii*, p. 300.

march on Warsaw,' " and "at this fast rate industrialization would produce no results, but would only cause huge expenditure."[135] He returned to the Trotsky camp, he maintained, because, he "shrank from the difficulties that confronted socialism in 1931–33."[136] Many loyal supporters of Stalin also came to have "bitter inward conflict."

One such Bolshevik, A. Barmine, who in 1932 went back to Moscow after two years of diplomatic assignment abroad, was agitated to see that "the condition of Moscow had changed even more than in 1930." He found himself "literally trembling with indignation when I learned that the workers were in such a desperate state fifteen years after the 'proletarian' revolution. I felt ashamed also." Barmine maintained that his case was "not unique" and that for "thousands and thousands of Russian Bolsheviks this period, ending with the bloody years 1937–38, was crucial."[137] The difficulties were such, according to another account, that "in 1931–32 the Rights considered the seizure of power a foregone conclusion. So, at least, we thought." The former "Rightists" were alleged to have sought to create "several Kronstadts" and "achieve corresponding political success."[138]

Whatever the case, the crisis appears to have set both the Left and the Right politically active. In 1932 Trotsky made an attempt from abroad to form a united opposition bloc in the Soviet Union. He was successful, and a bloc was formed of the former Zinovievites, the Sten–Lominadze group, and the Trotskyists. The bloc soon collapsed, however, when some of its major figures were arrested.[139] Furthermore, in late 1932 and early 1933 two factions composed mainly of former Rightists – the M. N. Riutin-A. Slepkov

---

[135] *Report of Court Proceedings in the Case of the Anti-Soviet Trotskyite Centre*, p. 84. See also pp. 249–50 (M. S. Stroilov). "The march on Warsaw" referred to the war with Poland in 1920 in which the Soviet army was routed.

[136] Ibid., p. 544.

[137] Barmine, *One Who Survived*, pp. 201, 207–9.

[138] *Report of Court Proceedings in the Case of the Anti-Soviet "Bloc of Rights and Trotskyites,"* pp. 120 and 169 (V. I. Ivanov and Rykov). "Kronstadts" referred to the Kronstadt rebellion in 1921, which ushered in the New Economic Policy.

[139] Broué, "Trotsky et le bloc des oppositions de 1932," and Getty, "Trotsky in Exile." How strong the bloc was remains unclear. This incident was alluded to in *Report of Court Proceedings. The Case of the Trotskyite-Zinovievite Terrorist Centre*, pp. 71–72. Ian Sten, a former leader of the "Young Stalinist Left," had been implicated in the Syrtsov-Lominadze affair in 1930. According to Getty, in 1933 Trotsky attempted a reconciliation with the Polibureau. See Getty, "Trotsky in Exile."

and the N. B. Eismont, V. N. Tolmachev, and A. P. Smirnov groups – were expelled from the party for advocating a retreat from the economic offensive and the removal of Stalin from his post.[140] Major former opposition leaders, A. I. Rykov, M. P. Tomskii, N. A. Uglanov, G. E. Zinoviev, L. B. Kamenev, and others were implicated at the time for their alleged links with these groups.[141]

By mid-1933, when the crisis appeared to have been surmounted, Kamenev and Zinoviev, who had been expelled and exiled in connection with the Riutin-Slepkov affair, surrendered, condemned their "mistakes," and praised Stalin's "victories."[142] Shortly thereafter Bukharin published an article entitled "Years of Victories" in which he extolled the "victories" of industrialization and collectivization.[143] At the "congress of victors" in early 1934, whatever their private feelings, former oppositionists came out with self-criticism and praise for the revolution's (and Stalin's) "victories."[144]

Clearly there were bases for both respect for Stalin, who as a leader had overcome the grave crisis of 1932–33, and disrespect for Stalin, who as a leader allowed the use of extensive coercion and brutality to cope with the crisis. The oft-quoted rumor that some delegates staged a move to replace Stalin at the congress reflected this latter implication of the "victories." On the eve of the congress, Kaganovich had openly questioned the sincerity of former oppositionists' recantations: "We cannot fully believe them."[145] Bitterness was perhaps mutual.

If so, the former oppositionists were forced to live in a dual state of mind, of ostensible surrender and covert criticism, which the "victors" saw as "double-dealing." No one spoke of this ambivalence more straightforwardly than did Bukharin in his last public

[140] *Pravda*, 11 October 1932; *KPSS v rezoliutsiiakh*, 5:90 (January 1933); and *Vsesoiuznoe soveshchanie o merakh uluchshcheniia podgotovki nauchno-pedagogicheskikh kadrov*, pp. 290–91. M. N. Riutin, A. Slepkov, N. B. Eismont, V. N. Tolmachev, and A. P. Smirnov were all former Rightists or their associates. Broué, "Trotsky et le bloc des oppositions de 1932," contains short, but useful, biographies of these and other oppositionists.

[141] *Pravda*, 11 October 1932; *KPSS v rezoliutsiiakh*, 5:90 (January 1933); and *XVII s"ezd VKP(b)*, pp. 46, 188, 250, 493, 518. See also *Report of Court Proceedings in the Case of the Anti-Soviet Trotskyite Centre*, pp. 150–151, 157, and *Report of Court Proceedings in the Case of the Anti-Soviet "Bloc of Rights and Trotskyites,"* passim.

[142] *Pravda*, 25 May, 16 June 1933.

[143] *Planovoe khoziaistvo*, 1933, nos. 7–8, pp. 117–23.

[144] *XVII s"ezd VKP(b)*, passim.

[145] Kaganovich, *Ot XVI k XVII s"ezdu partii*, p. 44.

speech at the political trial in 1938. Looking back at the preceding decade, he noted:

Psychologically, we, who at one time had advocated Socialist industrialism, began to regard with a shrug of the shoulders, with irony, and then with anger at bottom, our huge, gigantically growing factories as monstrous gluttons which consumed everything, deprived the broad masses of articles of consumption, and represented a certain danger.[146]

Yet, Bukharin stated, their opposition was never consistent, because it

took place amidst colossal socialist construction, with its immense scope, tasks, victories, difficulties, heroism. . . .
And on this basis, it seems to me probable that every one of us sitting here in the dock suffered from a peculiar duality of mind, an incomplete faith in his counter-revolutionary cause [i.e., opposition to Stalin].[147]

Bukharin went so far as to claim that the reason why West European and American intellectuals entertained "doubts and vacillations" about his and other trials taking place in Moscow was that

these people do not understand the radical distinction, namely, that in our country the antagonist, the enemy, has at the same time a divided, a dual mind. And I think that this is the first thing to be understood.[148]

If Stephen F. Cohen is right, Bukharin actually challenged the "official myth, enshrined at the trial, that Stalin's régime and Stalinism were the rightful heirs and culmination of the revolution"; and by "counterrevolutionary cause" Bukharin meant "legitimate opposition to Stalin," and by "a dual mind" an uncompromising spirit.[149] Yet it seemed that the "victorious" Stalin sought to make Bukharin and his associates appear as political double-dealers and waveres who had been determined neither to support the all-out drive for industrialization and collectivization nor to oppose it firmly and consistently.

Historians concur that Stalin was a firmly brutal political leader. The "victory" of Stalin's rapid industrialization drive is often attributed to his success in "rally[ing] both government and people to one common, almost superhuman effort," which the minister of finance

---

[146] *Report of Court Proceedings in the Case of the Anti-Soviet "Bloc of Rights and Trotskyites,"* p. 381.
[147] Ibid., p. 776. See also G. G. Iagoda's similar statement (pp. 784–85).
[148] Ibid., pp. 776–77.
[149] Cohen, *Bukharin and the Bolshevik Revolution*, p. 379.

under Nicholas II, Count Sergei Witte, had failed to accomplish in his industrialization drive in the 1890s.[150] Certainly there is a great deal of truth to this impressionistic view. If NEP aimed at the restoration of an economy ruined by war, revolution, and civil war, a rather undramatic goal, the rapid industrialization drive of the Five-Year Plan symbolized the grandiose and dramatic goal of building a new society. Promoted against the background of the Depression and mass unemployment in the West, the Soviet industrialization drive did evoke heroic, romantic, and enthusiastic "superhuman" efforts. "The word 'enthusiasm,' like many others, has been devalued by inflation," Ilya Ehrenburg has written, "yet there is no other word to fit the days of the First Five Year Plan; it was enthusiasm pure and simple that inspired the young people to daily and unspectacular feats."[151] According to another contemporary, those days were "a really romantic, intoxicating time": "People were creating by their own hands what had appeared a mere dream before and were convinced in practice that these dreamlike plans were an entirely realistic thing."[152]

Western historians tend to ascribe their efforts to the "motivation control" and the "deliberate compulsions" of the party.[153] Clearly exhortation, manipulation, demagogy, and intimidation abounded.

Surprisingly, however, they seem to underestimate grossly the importance of the ideology of Stalin's industrialization, which was promoted as class war. Stalin, far from rallying the entire nation, even split it. Unlike Witte, who had merely dreamed of a strong autocracy that would not have had to rely on any particular class but stand above all classes, Stalin deliberately sought the support of particular political constituencies, the Communists, Komsomols, and industrial workers, by pitting them against the alleged class enemies. It was from among these constituencies that the main beneficiaries of Stalin's revolution, "a new class" or a "new Soviet elite,"sprang.[154] I. Zhukov, who felt he had become a "bourgeois" when lavishly rewarded for his shock work, was but one of such beneficiaries. The class-war ideology of the industrialization drive created a basis for the survival of the regime.

[150] Von Laue, *Sergei Witte and the Industrialization of Russia,* p. 306.
[151] Ehrenburg, *Memoirs: 1921–1941,* p. 221.
[152] Zhukov, *Liudi 30-kh godov,* p. 27.
[153] Von Laue, *Why Lenin? Why Stalin?* pp. 138 and 225.
[154] See Fitzpatrick, *Education and Social Mobility in the Soviet Union,* chap. 11.

It was also among those constituencies, particularly the younger generation who grew up under Soviet power,[155] that "scientific communism" found its sincerest believers. Belief in socialism, according to L. M. Kaganovich, differs from religious belief in that it "is scientific – it is based on our knowledge": "We believe in socialism, not because we wish to, but because we see on the basis of scientific Marxist-Leninist analysis the inevitability of a demise of capitalism and the inevitability of a victory of socialism."[156] This belief, whether religious or scientific, ideologically sustained those many Communists, Komsomols, and workers who, enduring material hardships, took part in the brutal "class struggle." The former wrecker hunter at the Kharkov Locomotive Plant, Lev Kopelev,[157] for example, in describing his participation in the particularly violent grain procurement campaign during the famine crisis, states that he and his cohorts were "convinced that the disaster was not so much the fault of the party and state, as the result of inexorable 'objective' circumstances": "We were convinced that the famine was caused by the opposition of suicidally unconscious peasants, enemy intrigues, and the inexperience and weakness of the lower ranks of workers." So he told himself: "I mustn't give in to debilitating pity. We were realizing historical necessity. We were performing our revolutionary duty." He relentlessly seized grain from peasants.[158] K. Bukovskii, who also took part in the grain seizures, states similarly: "We saw only what we wanted to see. Whether this was a 'hypnosis' or simply our romantic notion (based on belief and conviction) about the surroundings, I do not know; but rather it was still our conviction. . . . we had no doubts whatsoever."[159] Kopelev, Bukovskii, and their peers, who firmly believed in the

---

[155] Interestingly, in the 1930s Trotskyists maintained that "we would hardly be able to attract the younger generation who had been brought up under the Soviet power." *Report of Court Proceedings in the Case of the Anti-Soviet Trotskyite Centre*, p. 181. See also pp. 61–62.

[156] *Partiinoe stroitel'stvo*, 1933, no. 11 (June), p. 9.

[157] See chap. 7, note 38.

[158] Kopelev, *The Education of a True Believer*, pp. 279 and 235. Similarly, Kopelev believed that the "Great Purge" of 1936–38 was a "historical necessity." Ibid., p. 313, and his *Khranit' vechno*, pp. 27–28.

[159] Bukovskii, "Otvet na lestnitse," p. 199. For more detail, see Kuromiya, "Soviet Memoirs as a Historical Source." In the same vein, Grigorenko notes concerning the famine: "I do not accept the justification of ignorance. We were deceived because we wanted to be deceived. We believed so strongly in communism that we were ready to accept any crime if it was glossed over with the least little bit of communist phraseology." Grigorenko, *Memoirs*, p. 36.

victory of socialism through class struggle, were ideologically integrated into the regime.

If Western historians tend to underestimate the importance of the class-war ideology, Soviet historians tend to disregard the tragedy, savagery, and terror involved in the class war. Even after 1931, when the "bourgeois" specialists were rehabilitated, the concept of class enemy was not discarded. As early as December 1931 the chairman of the Russian Republic's Council of People's Commissars, D. E. Sulimov, maintained that the class enemy had changed its tactic in response to a new political situation from frontal attacks to the distortion of the party line from within the government and economic institutions.[160] In January 1933 Stalin contended along the same lines that the "has-beens," or class enemies, "thrown out of their groove," had "wormed their way into our plants and factories, into our government and trade institutions, into our railway and water transport enterprises, and, principally, into the collective farms and state farms."[161] At the April 1933 Metro-Vickers trial, Vyshinsky maintained that having lost the battle, the class enemy now resorted to "the method known as quiet sapping" rather than direct frontal attacks, and that the enemy sought to conceal its wrecking acts by all sorts of "objective causes," "defects," and the contention that they did "not seem to be caused by malicious human intent." Therefore, he noted, the enemy "becomes less detectable, less vulnerable and hence it becomes less possible to isolate him."[162] This appraisal was a politically powerful logic that facilitated police control and enhanced popular vigilance, and also one that caused staggering human and material costs.

[160] *II sessiia VTsIK XV sozyva*, 1:4–5.
[161] Stalin, *Sochineniia*, 13:207.
[162] *Wrecking Activities at Power Stations in the Soviet Union*, 3:41.

Appendix:
Who were the shock workers?

It is difficult to answer this question, partly because statistical data are inconclusive and partly because, strange though it may appear, there was no clear-cut definition of shock workers. It was commonly accepted that shock workers were those who as model workers labored strenuously, carried out the rationalization of production, overfulfilled work quotas, recorded a high productivity of labor, etc. However, it was difficult to define unequivocally the shock worker: in the absence of a well-organized supply system of raw material, tools, energy, and fuel, which frequently interrupted orderly work flows; given the sloppy system of norm setting vulnerable to haggling and tradeoffs between workers and norm setters; and given the feeble authority of the foremen, it was quite easy for workers to feign hard work and pretend to be shock workers. Naturally the political authorities were skeptical of exaggerated statistical data.[1] The following discussion is somewhat hypothetical, but some patterns emerge through statistical analysis.

As Table A.1 shows, by March 1930 half of the industrial workers claimed to be shock workers.[2] This was perhaps a result of the influx of both older, skilled workers and new, unskilled workers into the ranks of shock workers.

[1] *Partiinoe stroitel'stvo*, 1930, no. 2, pp. 21–22. For problems of trade union data, see Belonosova, "Profsoiuznaia statistika kak istochnik izucheniia chislennosti profsoiuzov i tvorcheskoi aktivnosti rabochego klassa SSSR (1917–1941 gg.)."

[2] Sources for Table A.1: for October and December 1929, see *Industrializatsiia SSSR, 1929–1932*, p. 517; for January 1930, see *Materialy k otchetu VTsSPS IX s"ezdu profsoiuzov*, p. 24, and Uglanov (ed.), *Trud v SSSR*, p. 89; for March 1930, see *Kalendar' ezhegodnik kommunista na 1931 god*, p. 268; for May 1930, see *Sotsialisticheskoe sorevnovanie v promyshlennosti*, p. 12; for the remainder, see *Narodnoe khoziaistvo SSSR (1932)*, p. 452.

Table A.1. *Proportion of shock workers (in %)*

1 October 1929	10
December 1929	25
1 January 1930	26–29
1 March 1930	51
May 1930	52
1 November 1930	48.9
1 January 1931	57.8
1 June 1931	65.4

Data indicating the composition of shock workers are available only from the autumn of 1929 on. By this time the movement of older, skilled workers (and, to a lesser extent, unskilled workers) into shock brigades had already started, so that the data reveal a mixed composition.[3] Moreover, the vast professional and regional differences make generalizations about the social composition of shock workers difficult.

Perhaps the most meaningful method of analysis is to identify the initiators and leaders of the shock movement at its early stages, that is, before it was watered down by the addition of massive numbers of workers. This is also a difficult task. Yet it is not impossible to discern some patterns. At the end of 1928, according to the official report of the All-Union Central Council of Trade Unions to the eighth trade union congress, the shock brigades consisted of "young, skilled workers."[4] In May 1929 in Dnepropetrovsk and Kharkov, shock workers were reported mainly as "middle workers" (*rabochie-seredniaki*).[5] As suggested in Chapter 4, they appeared to belong neither to the older cohort of skilled workers nor to the new and unskilled, but to the "core group" of the working class.

---

[3] See, for example, the observation of the composition of shock workers in Kharkov and Moscow in *Izvestiia TsK VKP(b)*, 1929, nos. 26–27 (20 September), p. 16. See also *Industrializatsiia Severo-Zapadnogo raiona v gody pervoi piatiletki (1929–1932 gg.)*, pp. 373, 377–78, and Bezborodov, *Pervye v pervykh riadakh*, p. 34.
[4] *Professional'nye soiuzy SSSR, 1926–1928*, p. 124.
[5] *TPG*, 26 May 1929.

Table A.2. *Age composition of shock workers (in %)*

	22 or younger	23–29	30–39	40 or older
Shock workers	30.2	32.5	22.4	14.9
Workers as a whole	25.0	28.6	23.6	22.8

This hypothesis may be supported by the composition of delegates to the All-Union congress of shock workers held in Moscow in December 1929. Data concerning 550 delegates (80 percent of the shock workers who attended the congress) are available.[6] Sixty percent of them were the leaders of brigades. According to the compiler of the data, there were no particular differences in the composition of the leading and rank-and-file shock workers.[7] The following analysis is based on the data for these delegates, although one has to be aware that by the time the congress met, the influx of experienced and skilled workers had already begun.

First, the majority were male. Women were underrepresented at the congress, accounting for 11 percent, a mere one-third of their proportion to the entire industrial work force. This phenomenon resulted, at least partly, from the fact that women tended to engage in unskilled labor, where the shock movement was less developed.

Second, the shock workers tended to be relatively young (Table A.2). Workers below thirty years of age thus accounted for 62.7 percent of the delegates. In other words, the majority had experienced the October Revolution and the civil war in their teens or younger.[8]

Third, the majority (73.5 percent) of the delegates were party or Komsomol members or candidates.

Fourth, the majority (72.5 percent) of these party or Komsomol members were below thirty years of age, whereas 64.4 percent of

---

[6] The following data are taken from *Politicheskii i trudovoi pod″em*, pp. 351–61, and *Pervyi Vsesoiuznyi s″ezd udarnykh brigad*, pp. 179–86.

[7] *Pervyi Vsesoiuznyi s″ezd udarnykh brigad*, p. 186.

[8] The data on the industrial workers as a whole are taken from Meyer, *Sozialstruktur sowjetischer Industriearbeiter*, p. 139.

Table A.3. *Shock workers by period of commencing work (in %)*

	Before 1905	1906–17	1918–25	1926 or later
Shock metal workers	11.4	33.3	37.8	17.5
Metal workers as a whole	19.7	29.2	31.2	19.9
Shock textile workers	13.8	13.9	55.6	16.7
Textile workers as a whole	27.0	32.2	25.5	15.3
Shock miners	11.8	38.8	43.0	6.4
Miners as a whole	12.1	21.7	32.4	33.8

Table A.4. *Shock and other workers with land holdings (in %)*

Shock metal workers	12.2
Metal workers	20.2
Shock textile workers	6.9
Textile workers	10.4
Shock miners	14.8
Miners	24.6

nonmembers were thirty years or older. This sharp contrast may indicate the influx of older, skilled workers not belonging to the party or Komsomol into shock brigades.

Fifth, those who had first entered industrial work between 1918 and 1925 were most strongly represented (Table A.3). In other words, the majority of shock workers were neither "newcomers" nor older workers. That those who had first entered industrial work between 1906 and 1917 are also overrepresented among metal workers and mine workers may be explained by the addition of older, skilled workers to the shock brigades.

Sixth, the shock worker delegates apparently were more divorced from the countryside than the industrial workers as a whole (Table A.4).

Seventh, the social origin of shock worker delegates tended to be proletarian: those with proletarian roots accounted for 59.0 percent on the average. In the metals industry, where the increased numbers

Table A.5. *Social origins of shock workers (in %)*

	Children of workers	Children of peasants
Shock metal workers	57.0	37.0
Metal workers as a whole	57.0	36.0
Shock textile workers	68.0	20.0
Textile workers as a whole	56.0	40.0
Shock miners	52.0	45.0
Miners as a whole	34.0	62.5

of unskilled workers was conspicuous, the available data show little difference in social origin (Table A.5).

Eighth, the educational level of shock worker delegates was said to be higher than that of the average worker. (Yet, of these "best and brightest of all workers," almost half had only elementary education.)[9]

Ninth, the great majority of shock workers (92.7 percent) were "social activists," holding elected posts in the Soviet, party, union, and other organizations.

This rough analysis of sketchy data suggests that the leaders of shock workers were mainly young and skilled males of proletarian origin who had experienced the revolution and the civil war in their childhood, first entered industrial work shortly after the revolution, and therefore had had several years of work experience and some skills by the late 1920s. Predominantly party and Komsomol members, they were in a position to be critical of both the work culture of older workers and the peasant culture of new arrivals from the countryside.

[9] Lel'chuk, *Industrializatsiia SSSR*, p. 122.

Bibliography

I. Archival sources

Gosplan SSSR, Sektsiia vosproizvodstva, Gruppa kon˝iunktura. "Kon˝iunktura narodnogo khoziaistva SSSR za sentiabr' i 12 mesiatsev 1929/30 g." (cited as "Kon˝iunktura, 1929/30." A mimeographed and numbered copy marked "Oglasheniiu ne podlezhit" is in the "Slavic Unclassified" section of the Library of Congress, Washington, D.C. This seems to be identical with the document in the Central State Archive of the October Revolution and Socialist Construction of the USSR [TsGAOR] in Moscow, fond 374, opis' 1, delo 666).

"Smolensk Archive" (cited as WKP and number. The records of the Smolensk *oblast'* of the All-Union Communist Party of the Soviet Union, 1917–41, were seized in 1941 by the German army and were confiscated from the Germans in 1945 by the American army. This archive is available on microfilm from the National Archives, Washington, D.C. For further information, see *Guide to the Records of the Smolensk Oblast of the All-Union Communist Party of the Soviet Union, 1917–1941,* Washington, D.C.: National Archives and Records Service, General Services Administration, 1980).

"Trotsky Archives" (the papers of Leon Trotsky, Houghton Library, Harvard University, Cambridge, Mass. For this archive, see *Guide to the Papers of Leon Trotsky and Related Collections in the Harvard College Library,* second version [Cambridge, Mass.], 1959).

"American Engineers in Russia" (correspondence, writings, articles, and answers to questionnaires, relating to economic conditions, wages, housing, living costs, and relations with Russian administrative personnel, of American engineers in Russia, 1927–33, Hoover Archive, Stanford University, Stanford, Calif.).

II. Newspapers (place of publication is Moscow unless otherwise noted)

Ekonomicheskaia zhizn'
Golos tekstilei
Gudok
Izvestiia TsIK SSSR
Komsomol'skaia pravda
Krasnaia gazeta (Leningrad)
Leningradskaia pravda (Leningrad)
Molot (Rostov on the Don)
Nasha gazeta
Obshchestvo potrebitelei
Pravda
Proletarii (Kharkov)
Rabochaia gazeta
Rabochaia Moskva
Torgovo-promyshlennaia gazeta (TPG; renamed *Za industrializatsiiu* in January 1930)
Trud
Vecherniaia Moskva
Visti VUTsVK (Kharkov)
Zaria Vostoka (Tbilisi)

III. Journals (place of publication is Moscow unless otherwise noted)

Avtotraktornoe delo
Avtotraktornoe proizvodstvo
Biulleten' Oppozitsii (Paris)
Biulleten' TsKK VKP(b) i NK RKI SSSR i RSFSR
Biulleten' Ural'skogo oblastnogo komiteta VKP(b)
Bol'shevik
Ekonomicheskoe obozrenie
Ezhemesiachnyi statisticheskii biulleten'
Finansy i sotsialisticheskoe khoziaistvo
Gornorabochii
Informatsionnyi biulleten' Tsentrosoiuza SSSR i RSFSR
Inzhenernyi rabotnik (Kharkov)
Inzhenernyi trud
Izvestiia Donskogo okrkoma VKP(b)

Isvestiia Moskovskogo komiteta VKP(b)
Izvestiia Nizhegorodskogo kraevogo komiteta VKP(b)
Izvestiia N. K. Truda SSSR
Izvestiia Severo-Kavkazskogo kraevogo komiteta VKP(b)
Izvestiia Sibirskogo kraevogo komiteta VKP(b)
Isvestiia Stalingradskogo okrkoma VKP(b)
Izvestiia TsK VKP(b) (renamed *Partiinoe stroitel'stvo* in late 1929)
Khoziaistvo i upravlenie
Kommunist (Nizhegorod)
Kommunisticheskaia revoliutsiia
Metall
Metallist
Molodaia gvardiia
Molodoi bol'shevik
Moskovskii proletarii
Na fronte industrializatsii (Leningrad)
Na planovom fronte
Na trudovom fronte
Na ugol'nom fronte (Artemovsk)
Narodnoe khoziaistvo SSSR
Nashe stroitel'stvo
Organizatsiia truda
Organizatsiia upravleniia
Partrabotnik (Leningrad)
Plan
Planovoe khoziaistvo
Predpriiatie
Problemy ekonomiki
Problemy marksizma (Leningrad)
Proizvodstvennyi zhurnal
Puti industrializatsii
Ratsionalizatsiia proizvodstva
Revoliutsiia i kul'tura
Sel'sko-khoziaistvennaia mashina
Shveinik
Soiuz potrebitelei
Sotsialisticheskii transport
Sotsialisticheskii vestnik (Berlin)
Sovetskaia iustitsiia
Sovetskoe gosudarstvo i revoliutsiia prava
Sputnik agitatora dlia goroda
Sputnik kommunista
Statisticheskoe obozrenie

Statistika i narodnoe khoziaistvo
Statistika truda
Udarnik (renamed *Voprosy profdvizheniia* in 1933)
Ustanovki rabochei sily
Vestnik Donuglia (Kharkov)
Vestnik finansov (renamed in March 1930 *Finansovye problemy narod-nogo khoziaistva* and in 1931 *Finansovye problemy*)
Vesnik Kommunisticheskoi Akademii
Vestnik truda
Visnyk profrukhu Ukrainy (Kharkov)
Voprosy torgovli
Voprosy truda
Za industrializatsiiu Sibiri (Novosibirsk)
Za povyshenie kvalifikatsii tekhnicheskikh i khoziaistvennykh kadrov promyshlennosti
Za promyshlennye kadry
Za ratsionalizatsiiu
Za rekonstruktsiiu tekstil'noi promyshlennosti
Za tempy, kachestvo, proverku
Zheleznodorozhnoe delo
Zhizn' Sibiri (Novosibirsk)

IV. Laws, orders, statistical compilations, censuses

Bineman, Ia., and Kheinman, S. *Kadry gosudarstvennogo i kooperativnogo apparata SSSR*. Moscow, 1930.
Direktivy KPSS i sovetskogo pravitel'stva po khoziaistvennym voprosam. Vol. 2 (1929–45). Moscow, 1957.
Ekonomiko-statisticheskii spravochnik Leningradskoi oblasti. Leningrad, 1932.
Gosudarstvennoe predpriiatie. 2nd ed. Moscow, 1932.
Gromyko, E. V., and Riauzov, N. N. *Sovetskaia torgovlia za 15 let. Statistiko-ekonomicheskii sbornik.* Moscow, 1932.
Inzhenerno-tekhnicheskie kadry promyshlennosti. Materialy Sektora truda, ratsionalizatsii i sebestoimosti PTEU VSNKh SSSR. Moscow, 1930.
Itogi vypolneniia piatiletnego plana razvitiia narodnogo khoziaistva SSSR. Moscow, 1933.
Kollektivnyi dogovor zakliuchennyi Pravleniem Oblastnogo Otdela Profso-iuza Tekstil'shchikov Ivanovskoi Promyshlennoi Oblasti, s odnoi storonoi, i Pravleniiami Iv.-Voznes. Tekstil'nogo Tresta, Vladimir-skogo Gosud. Tekstil'n. Tresta, L'notresta, 4-go Gostresta, Bladtek-stil'tresta i Ivgubtresta s drugoi storonoi, na rabochikh i slu-

zhashchikh, kak postoiannykh, tak i vremenno rabotaiushchikh, vsekh promyshlennykh predpriiatii, vkhodiashchikh v eti tresty na srok s 1-go ianvaria 1930 g. po 1-oe dekabria 1930 g. Ivanovo-Voznesensk, 1930.

KPSS v rezoliutsiiakh i resheniiakh s˝ezdov, konferentsii i plenumov TsK. Vol. 4 (1927–31), Moscow, 1970; vol. 5 (1931–41), Moscow, 1971.

Komunistychna Partiia Ukrainy v rezoliutsiiakh i reshenniakh z'izdiv, konferentsii i plenumiv TsK. Vol. 1. Kiev, 1976.

Kontrol'nye tsifry narodnogo khoziaistva SSSR na 1929/30 g. Moscow, 1930.

Na putiakh stroitel'stva sotsializma. Statisticheskii sbornik k III Oblastnomu s˝ezdu Sovetov. Leningrad, 1931.

Narodnoe khoziaistvo SSSR. Statisticheskii spravochnik. Moscow-Leningrad, 1932.

Perepis' rabochikh i sluzhashchikh 1929 g., T. I: Metallisty SSSR. Moscow, 1930.

Piatiletnii plan narodno-khoziaistvennogo stroitel'stva SSSR. 3rd ed., 3 vols. Moscow, 1930.

XV let diktatury proletariata. Ekonomiko-statisticheskii sbornik po g. Leningradu i Leningradskoi oblasti. Leningrad, 1932.

Profsoiuznaia perepis' 1932–1933 g. Vol. 1. Moscow, 1934.

Rashin, A. *Sostav fabrichno-zavodskogo proletariata SSSR. Predvaritel'nye itogi perepisi metallistov, gornorabochikh i tekstil'shchkov v 1929 g.* Moscow, 1930.

Renke, V. P. *Kadry inzhenerno-tekhnicheskogo personala kamennougol'noi promyshlennosti Donetskogo basseina.* Kharkov, 1930.

Resheniia partii i pravitel'stva po khoziaistvennym voprosam. Vol. 2 (1929–40). Moscow, 1967.

Sbornik postanovlenii i prikazov po promyshlennosti. Moscow, 1930–31.

Sobranie zakonov i rasporiazhenii raboche-krest'ianskogo pravitel'stva SSSR, otdel pervyi (I) and otdel vtoroi (II). Moscow, 1924–37. (Citations are by year, otdel, number-article.)

Sostav VKP(b) k XVI s˝ezdu. Dinamika osnovnykh pokazatelei rosta partii mezhdu XV i XVI s˝ezdami. Moscow, 1930.

Sostav VKP(b) v tsifrakh. Vypusk XI. Dinamika osnovnykh pokazatelei rosta partii za 1930 g. i pervoe polugodie 1931 g. Moscow, 1932.

Sotsialisticheskoe stroitel'stvo SSSR. Statisticheskii ezhegodnik. 3 vols. Moscow, 1934, 1935, and 1936.

Spravochnik partiinogo rabotnika. Vol. 7, part 2, Moscow, 1930; vol. 8, Moscow, 1934.

Sud i prokuratura litsom k proizvodstvu. (Rukovodiashchie ukazaniia po okhrane truda i proizvodstva). Moscow, 1930.

Sud i prokuratura na okhrane proizvodstva i truda. Prakticheskoe posobie dlia organov iustitsii. Direktivy partii, postanovleniia pravitel'stva, rasporiazheniia Narkomatov. 2 parts. Moscow, 1932.

Trud i profdvizhenie v Leningradkoi oblasti 1932 g. Statisticheskii spravochnik. Leningrad, 1932.

Trud v SSSR. Spravochnik 1926–1930 gg. Moscow, 1930.

Trud v SSSR. Ekonomiko-statisticheskii spravochnik. Moscow, 1932.

Trud v SSSR. Statisticheskii spravochnik. Moscow, 1936.

Voprosy truda v tsifrakh. Statisticheskii spravochnik za 1927–1930 gg. Moscow, 1930.

Zakonodatel'stvo i rasporiazheniia po torgovle. Moscow, 1930–31.

V. Stenographic reports of congresses, conferences, meetings, trials

A. All-Union party congresses and conferences

XIV s˝ezd VKP(b), 18–31 dek. 1925 g. Sten. otchet. Moscow-Leningrad, 1926.

XV konferentsiia VKP(b), 26 okt.–3 noiab. 1926 g. Sten. otchet. Moscow-Leningrad, 1927.

XV s˝ezd VKP(b), dek. 1927 g. Sten. otchet. 2 vols. Moscow, 1962.

XVI konferentsiia VKP(b), aprel' 1929 g. Sten. otchet. Moscow, 1962.

XVI s˝ezd VKP(b). Sten. otchet. 26 June–13 July 1930. Moscow-Leningrad, 1930.

XVII konferentsiia VKP(b). Sten. otchet. 30 January–4 February 1932. Moscow, 1932.

XVII s˝ezd VKP(b), 26 ianv.–10 fevr. 1934 g. Sten. otchet. Moscow, 1934.

B. Central Control Commission plenums

II plenum TsKK sozyva XV s˝ezda VKP(b), 2–5 aprelia 1928 g. Moscow, 1928. Marked "Na pravakh rukopisi."

III plenum TsKK sozyva XV s˝ezda VKP(b), 25–29 avgusta 1928 g. Moscow, 1928. Marked "Na pravakh rukopisi."

III plenum TsKK VKP(b), iiul' 1931 g. Moscow-Leningrad, 1931.

C. Republic and provincial party congresses, conferences, and plenums

XXIV Leningradskaia gubernskaia konferentsiia VKP(b). Sten. otchet i rezoliutsii. 25–29 January 1927. Leningrad, [1927].

XVI Moskovskaia gubernskaia konferentsiia VKP(b). Sten. otchet. 20–28 November 1927. Moscow, 1928.

Vtoroi plenum MK VKP(b), 31 ianv.–2 fevr. 1928 g. Doklady i rezoliutsii. Moscow, 1928. Numbered edition, marked "Tol'ko dlia chlenov partii."

IX *Dal'nevostochnaia kraevaia partiinaia konferentsiia, 22 fevralia-1 marta 1929. Sten. otchet.* Khabarovsk, 1929.

Drukha konferentsiia Komunistychnoi partii (bil'shovykiv) Ukrainy, 9–14 kvitnia 1929 r. Sten. zvit. Kharkov, 1929.

XI *z'izd Komunistychnoi partii (bil'shovykiv) Ukrainy, 5–15 chervnia 1930 r. Sten. zvit.* Kharkov, 1930 (abbreviated in notes as XI *z'izd KP(b)U).*

Biulleten' 3-ei leningradskoi oblastnoi konferentsii VKP(b). 5–12 June 1930, 11 bulletins. Leningrad, 1930. Marked "Tol'ko dlia chlenov partii."

I *kraevaia konferentsiia VKP(b) Vostochno-sibirskogo kraia. Sten. otchet.* 29 January–5 February 1931. Irkutsk, 1931.

[Kazakhstanskii Kraevoi komitet VKP(b)], *Fevral'skii ob˝edinennyi plenum Kraikoma i KraiKK VKP(b). Doklad tov. Goloshchekina. Postanovleniia i rezoliutsiia.* Alma-Ata, 1931.

D. All-Union Soviet congresses

5 *s˝ezd Sovetov [SSSR]. Sten. otchet.* 20–28 May 1929, 22 bulletins. Moscow, 1929.

6 *s˝ezd Sovetov [SSSR]. Sten. otchet.* 8–17 March 1931, 21 bulletins. Moscow, 1931.

E. All-Union Central Executive Committee sessions

3 *sessiia TsIK Soiuza SSR 3 sozyva. Sten. otchet.* 14–25 February 1927. Moscow, 1927.

3 *sessiia TsIK Soiuza SSR 4 sozyva. Sten. otchet.* 11–21 April 1928. Moscow, 1928.

4 *sessiia TsIK Soiuza SSR 4 sozyva. Sten. otchet.* 3–15 December 1928, 33 bulletins. Moscow, 1928.

2 *sessiia TsIK Soiuza SSR 5 sozyva. Sten. otchet.* 29 November–8 December 1929, 18 bulletins. Moscow, 1929.

3 *sessiia TsIK Soiuza SSR 5 sozyva. Sten. otchet.* 4–12 January 1931, 20 bulletins. Moscow, 1931.

2 *sessiia TsIK Soiuza SSR 6 sozyva. Sten. otchet i postanovleniia.* 22–28 December 1931, 19 bulletins. Moscow, 1931.

3 *sessiia TsIK Soiuza SSR 6 sozyva. Sten. otchet.* 23–30 January 1933, 25 bulletins. Moscow, 1933.

4 sessiia TsIK Soiuza SSR 6 sozyva. Sten. otchet. 28 December 1933–4 January 1934, 28 bulletins. Moscow, 1934.

F. All-Russian Soviet congresses

XIV Vserossiiskii s˝ezd sovetov. Sten. otchet. 10–18 May 1929, 18 bulletins. Moscow, 1929.
XV Vserossiiskii s˝ezd sovetov. Sten. otchet. 26 February–5 March 1931, 18 bulletins. Moscow, 1931.

G. All-Russian Central Executive Committee sessions

II sessiia VTsIK XIII sozyva. Sten. otchet. 30 March–6 April 1928. Moscow, 1928.
III sessiia VTsIK XIII sozyva. Sten. otchet. 21–30 November 1928, 18 bulletins. Moscow, 1928.
II sessiia VTsIK XIV sozyva. Sten. otchet. 20–26 November 1929, 12 bulletins. Moscow, 1929.
II sessiia VTsIK XV sozyva. Sten. otchet. 16–21 December 1931, 12 bulletins. Moscow, 1931.
III sessiia VTsIK XV sozyva. Sten. otchet. 13–20 January 1933, 17 bulletins. Moscow, 1933.
IV sessiia VTsIK XV sozyva. Sten. otchet. 19–26 December 1933, 15 bulletins. Moscow, 1933.

H. Provincial Soviet congresses

Pervyi Moskovskii oblastnoi s˝ezd sovetov RK i KD, 19–23 sentiabria 1929 g. Sten. otchet. Moscow, 1930.
Biulleten' 3-go Leningradskogo oblastnogo s˝ezda sovetov. 17–22 February 1931, 6 bulletins. Leningrad, 1931.

I. Komsomol congresses and conferences

V Vsesoiuznaia konferentsiia VLKSM, 24–30 marta 1927 g. Sten. otchet. Moscow-Leningrad, 1927.
VIII Vsesoiuznyi s˝ezd VLKSM, 5–10 maia 1928 g. Sten. otchet. Moscow, 1929.
VI Vsesoiuznaia konferentsiia VLKSM, 17–24 iiunia 1929 g. Sten. otchet. Moscow, 1929.
IX Vsesoiuznyi s˝ezd VLKSM. Sten. otchet. 16–26 January 1931. Moscow, 1931.

332   Bibliography

VII Vsesoiuznaia konferentsiia VLKSM. Sten. otchet, 1–8 iiulia 1932 g.
    Moscow, 1932.

J. Trade union congresses

VII s˝ezd professional'nykh soiuzov SSSR, 6–18 dek. 1926 g. Plenumy i
    sektsii. Polnyi sten. otchet. Moscow, 1927.
VIII s˝ezd professional'nykh soiuzov SSSR, 10–24 dek. 1928 g. Plenumy i
    sektsii. Polnyi sten. otchet. Moscow, 1929.
IX Vsesoiuznyi s˝ezd professional'nykh soiuzov SSSR. Sten. otchet. 20–29
    April 1932. Moscow, 1932.

K. Individual union congresses

VIII s˝ezd metallistov, 15–28 fevralia 1928 g. Sten. otchet. Moscow, 1928.
VI Vsesoiuznyi s˝ezd gornorabochikh SSSR. Sten. otchet. April 1928. Mos-
    cow, 1928.
Otchet IX s˝ezda profsoiuza rabotnikov zheleznodorozhnogo transporta
    SSSR, 25 maia–4 iiunia 1928 g. Moscow, 1928.
Partiia i X s˝ezd zheleznodorozhnikov o zh.-d. transporte. June 1931, Mos-
    cow, 1931.

L. Other congresses, conferences, and meetings

Ocherednye problemy truda. Trudy I Vsesoiuznogo s˝ezda otdelov ekono-
    miki truda i T.N.B. trestov i zavedenii. 29 June–8 July 1926. Moscow,
    1927.
Vseukrainskaia proizvodstvennaia konferentsiia rabochikh metallistov za-
    vodov Iugostali (28 iiunia-5 iiulia 1928 g.). Sten. otchet. Vol. 1,
    Kharkov, 1928; vol. 2, Taganrog, 1928.
Problemy rekonstruktsii narodnogo khoziaistva SSSR na piatiletie. Piatilet-
    nii perspektivnyi plan na V s˝ezde Gosplanov. 7–14 March 1929.
    Moscow, 1929.
Sotsialisticheskoe sorevnovanie na predpriiatii. Stenogramma ob˝edinen-
    nogo zasedaniia presidiuma VTsSPS s presidiumom VSNKh SSSR i
    predstaviteliami TsK VLKSM, TsK soiuzov i mestnykh soiuznykh
    organizatsii 24–25 iiulia 1929 g. Moscow, 1929.
Pervaia Vsesoiuznaia konferentsiia rabotnikov sotsialisticheskoi promy-
    shlennosti. Sten. otchet s 30 ianvaria po 5 fevralia 1931 g. Moscow-
    Leningrad, 1931.
[Kommunisticheskaia Akademiia, Institut ekonomiki, Sektsiia truda],
    Bor'ba na dva fronta v oblasti ekonomiki truda. Doklad, preniia i
    rezoliutsiia. February–April 1931. Moscow-Leningrad, 1932.

I-oe mezhkraevoe soveshchanie Obl. KK-RKI Urala, Sibiri, Bashikirii i Kazakhstana po Uralo-Kuzbassu. Sten. otchet. May 1931. Sverdlovsk, 1931.

Organy iustitsii na novom etape. 5-oe soveshchanie rukovodiashchikh rabotnikov iustitsii RSFSR, iiun' 1931 g. Moscow, 1931.

Soveshchanie khoziaistvennikov, inzhenerov, tekhnikov, partiinykh i prof-soiuznykh rabotnikov tiazheloi promyshlennosti, 20–22 sentiabria 1934. Sten. otchet. Moscow-Leningrad, 1935.

Sovet pri Narodnom komissare tiazheloi promyshlennosti SSSR. Pervyi plenum 10–12 maia 1935 g. Moscow-Leningrad, 1935.

Vsesoiuznoe soveshchanie o merakh uluchsheniia podgotovki nauchno-pedagogicheskikh kadrov po istoricheskim naukam, 18–21 dekabria 1962 g. Moscow, 1964.

M. Trial proceedings

Ekonomicheskaia kontrrevoliutsiia v Donbasse. Itogi Shakhtinskogo dela. Stat'i i dokumenty. Moscow, 1928.

Protsess "Prompartii," 25 noiabria–7 dekabria 1930 g. Stenogramma sudebnogo protsessa i materialov, priobshchennye k delu. Moscow, 1931.

Protsess kontrrevoliutsionnoi organizatsii men'shevikov (1 marta–9 marta 1931 g.) Stennogramma sudebnogo protsessa, obvinitel'noe zakli-uchenie i prigovor. Moscow, 1931.

Wrecking Activities at Power Stations in the Soviet Union heard before the Special Session of the Supreme Court of the USSR in Moscow, April 12–19, 1933. 3 vols. Moscow, 1933.

Report of Court Proceedings. The Case of the Trotskyite-Zinovievite Terrorist Centre heard before the Military Collegium of the Supreme Court of the USSR, Moscow, August 19–24, 1936. Moscow, 1936.

Report of Court Proceedings in the Case of the Anti-Soviet Trotskyite Centre heard before the Military Collegium of the Supreme Court of the USSR, Moscow, January 23–30, 1937. Moscow, 1937.

Report of Court Proceedings in the Case of the Anti-Soviet "Bloc of Rights and Trotskyites" heard before the Military Collegium of the Supreme Court of the USSR, Moscow, March 2–13, 1938. Moscow, 1938.

VI. Books and articles (in Russian)

Abramov, A. *O pravoi oppozitsii v partii.* Moscow, 1929.

Aksel'rod, V. S. *Kak my uchil's' torgovat'.* Moscow, 1982.

Amosov, A. M. *Otchetnyi doklad TsK ZhD na desiatom s˝ezde zheleznodo-rozhnikov.* Moscow, 1931.

334 Bibliography

Andreev, A. A. *Vospominaniia, pis'ma*. Moscow, 1985.
Antonov, S. A. *Svet ne v okne*. Moscow, 1977.
Arutiunian, Iu. V. "Kollektivizatsiia sel'skogo khoziaistva i vysvobozhdenie rabochei sily dlia promyshlennosti." In *Formirovanie i razvitie sovetskogo rabochego klassa*. Moscow, 1964.
Atlas, M. S. *Kreditnaia reforma v SSSR*. Moscow, 1952.
Avtorkhanov, A. *Tekhnologiia vlasti*. Munich, 1959.
Bakhtamov, I. M. *Kuznetskstroi*. Moscow-Leningrad, 1931.
Barsov, A. A. *Balans stoimostnykh obmenov mezhdu gorodom i derevnei*. Moscow, 1969.
Bauman, K. Ia. *Sotsialisticheskoe nastuplenie i zadachi Moskovkoi organizatsii. Doklad na ianvarskom ob"edinennom plenume MK i MKK*. Moscow, 1930.
Beilin, A. E. *Kadry spetsialistov v SSSR, ikh formirovanie i rost*. Moscow, 1935.
Belen'kii, Z. M. *Rezul'taty obsledovaniia NK RKI kapital'nogo stroitel'stva VSNKh SSSR. Soobshchenie, zaslushannoe na Vysshikh kursakh po organizatsii kapital'nogo stroitel'stva v marte 1929 g*. Moscow, [1929?].
Belonosova, I. I. "Profsoiuznaia statistika kak istochnik izucheniia chislennosti profsoiuzov i tvorcheskoi aktivnosti rabochego klassa SSSR (1917–1941 gg.)." In *Rabochii klass i industrial'noe razvitie SSSR*. Moscow, 1975.
Bespalov, G., and Segal, P. *Komsomol pod znamenem sotsialisticheskoi ratsionalizatsii (opyt Moskvy, Leningrada, Urala i Ukrainy)*. Moscow-Leningrad, 1928.
Bezborodov, S. *Pervye v pervykh riadakh. Sotsialisticheskoe sorevnovanie i udarnye brigady*. Leningrad, 1930.
Bogushevskii, V. "Kanun piatiletki." In *God vosemnadtsatyi. Al'manakh vos'moi*. Moscow, 1935.
Bogushevskii, V., and Khavin, A. "God velikogo pereloma." In *God deviatnadtsatyi. Al'manakh deviatyi*. Moscow, 1936.
Bolotin, Z. S. *Voprosy prodovol'stvennogo snabzheniia*. Moscow, 1930.
Bukovskii, K. "Otvet na lestnitse." *Oktiabr'*, 1966, no. 9.
Bulgakov, V., and Ponomarev, S. *Za perestroiku potrebitel'skoi kooperatsii*. Leningrad, 1931.
Burdov, V. *Profsoiuzy i industrializatsiia*. Moscow, 1929.
Busygin, A. *Pervyi direktor. O nachal'nike stroitel'stva Uralmasha A. P. Bannikove*. Sverdlovsk, 1977.
Busygin, A., *Zhizn' moia i moikh druzei*. Moscow, 1939.
Sversheniia. Moscow, 1972.
Byli industrial'nye. Ocherki i vospominaniia. Moscow, 1973.
Bystritskii, M. G., and Serebriannikov, G. N. *Novaia bronia podrostkov*. Moscow, 1928.

Cheremnykh, V. G. "Zarozhdenie i razvitie massovogo sotsialisticheskogo sorevnovaniia v promyshlennosti Urala (1927–1929 gg.)." In *Ot Oktiabria k stroitel'stvu kommunizma*. Moscow, 1967.

Chistka sovetskogo apparata. K XVI s″ezdu VKP(b). Moscow, 1930.

Chuianov, A. S. *Na stremnine veka. Zapiski sekretaria obkoma*. Moscow, 1976.

Danilov, B. F. *Zhizn'-poisk. Zapiski tokaria-izobretatelia*. Moscow, 1975.

Danilov, V. P., and Ivnitskii, N. A. "Leninskii kooperativnyi plan i ego osushchestvlenie v SSSR." In *Ocherki istorii kollektivizatsii sel'skogo khoziaistva v soiuznykh respublikakh*. Moscow, 1963.

Davydova, N., and Ponomarev, A. *Velikii podvig. Bor'ba moskovskikh bol'shevikov za osushchestvlenie leninskogo plana sotsialisticheskoi industrializatsii*. Moscow, 1970.

Deiatel'nost' organov partiino-gosudarstvennogo kontrolia po sovershenstvovaniiu gosudarstvennogo apparata. Ot XII do XVI s″ezda partii. Moscow, 1964.

Deiatel'nost' SNK i STO. Svodnye materialy. IV kvartal (iiun'-sentiabr') 1928/29 g. Moscow, 1929.

Direktor. I. A. Likhachev v vospominaniiakh sovremennikov. Moscow, 1971.

Drobizhev, V. Z. "O nekotorykh nedostatkakh metodiki izucheniia politicheskoi i trudovoi deiatel'nosti rabochego klassa SSSR v gody bor'by za postroenie sotsializma." *Vestnik Moskovskogo universiteta*. Seriia ix (istoriia), 1964, no. 5.

Glavnyi shtab sotsialisticheskoi promyshlennosti. Ocherki istorii VSNKh, 1917–1932 gg. Moscow, 1966.

"Nekotorye osobennosti metodov upravleniia promyshlennost'iu SSSR v 1926–1932 godakh." *Voprosy istorii KPSS*, 1968, no. 12.

Dukel'skii, S. *Za sotsialisticheskuiu trudovuiu distsiplinu*. 2nd ed. Moscow, 1930.

Dva goda raboty Ural'skogo komsomola. Otchet V oblastnoi konferentsii VLKSM. Sverdlovsk, 1928.

Eikhe, R. I. *Novyi etap i zadachi Sibpartorganizatsii. Doklad i zakliuchitel'noe slovo na V Sibpartorganizatsii*. Novosibirsk, 1930.

Eliseeva, M. I. "O sposobakh privlecheniia rabochei sily v promyshlennost' i stroitel'stvo v period sotsialisticheskoi industrializatsii SSSR (1926–1937 gg.)." In *Izvestiia Voronezhskogo gos. ped. instituta*. Vol. 63. Voronezh, 1967.

Ermilov, V. *Byt rabochei kazarmy*. Moscow-Leningrad, 1930.

Ermilov, V. V. *Schast'e trudnykh dorog*. Moscow, 1972.

Eskin, M. *Osnovnye puti razvitiia sotsialisticheskikh form truda*. Moscow, 1935.

Etchin, A. *Partiia i spetsialisty*. Moscow-Leningrad, 1928.

(ed). *O trudovoi distsipline*. Moscow, 1929.

O edinonachalii. Moscow, 1930.

Evreinov, H. *O svoeobraznom krizise profsoiuzov i ob ikh novykh zadachakh*. Moscow, 1936.

Ezhegodnik sovetskogo stroitel'stva i prava na 1931 goda (za 1929/30g.). Moscow, 1930.

Fabrichnyi, A. *Chastnyi kapital na poroge piatiletki. Klassovaia bor'ba v gorode i gosudarstvennyi apparat*. Moscow, 1930.

Fazin, Z. *Tovarishch Sergo. Stranitsy bol'shoi zhizni*. Moscow, 1970.

Finansy SSSR mezhdu VI i VII s"ezdami Sovetov (1931–1934). Moscow, 1935.

Finarov, A. P. *Kommunisticheskaia partiia – organizator i vdokhnovitel' velikogo trudovogo pod"ema rabochego klassa SSSR v 1926–1929 gg.* Kalinin, 1970.

Frankfurt, S. I. *Rozhdenie stali i cheloveka*. Moscow, 1935.

Gaisinskii, M. *Bor'ba s uklonami ot general'noi linii partii: istoricheskii ocherk vnutripartiinoi bor'by posle oktiabr'skogo perioda*. 2nd ed. Moscow-Leningrad, 1931.

Galin, B. *Perekhod. Kniga ocherkov (1929–1930)*. Moscow, 1930.

Vsegda za mechtoi. Gody tridtsatye i shestidesiatye. Ocherki. Moscow, 1974.

Gastev, A. *Trudovye ustanovki*. Moscow, 1973.

Gavze, F. I. *Razvitie sotsialisticheskogo grazhdansko-pravovogo dogovora (1917–1934 gg.)*. Minsk, 1959.

Gershberg, S. R. *Rabota u nas takaia. Zapiski zhurnalista-pravdista 30-kh godov*. Moscow, 1971.

Gimpel'son, V. E., and Shmarov, A. I. "Ispol'zovanie vnerabochego vremeni trudiashchikhsia Moskvy (20-e–nachalo 80-kh gg.)." *Istoriia SSSR*, 1986, no. 3.

Gintsburg, L. *O khozraschete. K itogam konferentsii rabotnikov sotsialisticheskoi promyshlennosti. Obrabotannaia stenogramma doklada prochitannogo v institute sovstroitel'stva i prava Komakademii 4 aprelia 1931 g.* Moscow, 1931.

Ginzburg, S. G. *O proshlom – dlia budushchego*. Moscow, 1983.

Gladkov, T., and Smirnov, M. *Menzhinskii*. Moscow, 1969.

Gol'tsman, A. *Dorogu initsiative rabochikh. Doklad proizvodstvennykh soveshchanii na sobranii fabrichno-zavodskogo aktiva MK 21/III 29g.* Moscow-Leningrad, 1929.

Govoriat stroiteli sotsializma. Vospominaniia uchastnikov sotsialisticheskogo stroitel'stva v SSSR. Moscow, 1959.

Gudov, I. *Put' stakhanovtsa. Rasskaz o moei zhizni*. Moscow, 1938.

Besedy o kul'ture na proizvodstve. Moscow, 1941.

Sud'ba rabochego. Moscow, 1970.

Gugel', Ia. "Vospominaniia o Magnitke." In *God vosemnadtsatyi. Al'manakh shestoi*. Moscow, 1935.

Gurevich, D. *Za uluchshenie partiinoi raboty.* Moscow-Leningrad, 1929.

Gusarov, V. N. *Nezabyvaemye gody.* Chelyabinsk, 1965.

Iakovleva, E. M. *Razvitie dogovornykh sviazei gosudarstvennoi promyshlennosti SSSR po snabzheniiu i sbytu (1917–1937 gg.).* Dushanbe, 1965.

Ikonnikov, S. N. *Sozdanie i deiatel'nost' ob˝edinennykh organov TsKK-RKI v 1923–1934 gg.* Moscow, 1971.

Industrializatsiia Severo-Zapadnogo raiona v gody pervoi piatiletki (1929–1932 gg.). Leningrad, 1967.

Industrializatsiia SSSR, 1926–1928 gg. Dokumenty i materialy. Moscow, 1969.

Industrializatsiia SSSR. 1929–1932 gg. Dokumenty i materialy. Moscow, 1970.

Iovlev, A. M. "K istorii bor'by partii za perekhod k edinonachaliiu v Krasnoi Armii (1924–1931 gg.)." *Voprosy istorii KPSS,* 1964, no. 12.

Istoriia Kirovskogo zavoda, 1917–1945 gg. Moscow, 1966.

Istoriia "Krasnogo Sormova." Moscow, 1969.

Istoriia Kuznetskogo metallurgicheskogo kombinata im. V.I. Lenina. Moscow, 1973.

Istoriia zavodov. Sbornik. Vol. 3. Moscow, 1932.

Itogi razvitiia sovetskoi torgovli ot VI k VII s˝ezdu Sovetov SSSR. Materialy Narkomvnutorga SSSR. Moscow, 1935.

Ivushkin, N., Serebrianyi, I., and Timofeev, V. *Sorevnovanie na "Elektrozavode."* Moscow, 1929.

"Iz istorii sozdaniia stroitel'noi industrii v SSSR." *Sovetskie arkhivy,* 1967, no. 2.

Izotov, N. *Moia zhizn'-moia rabota.* Kharkov, 1934.

Kaganovich, L. M. *Ob itogakh dekabr'skogo ob˝edinennogo plenuma TsK i TsKK VKP(b). Doklad na partaktive Moskovskoi organizatsii VKP(b) 24 dek. 1930 g.* Moscow-Leningrad, 1931.

Kontrol'nye tsifry tret'ego goda piatiletki i zadachi Moskovskoi organizatsii: rech' na V plenume MOK VKP(b), 19 febralia 1931 g. Moscow, 1931.

Moskovskie bol'sheviki v bor'be za pobedu piatiletki. Doklad o rabote MK i MGK na III Moskovskoi oblastnoi i II gorodskoi konferentsii VKP(b) 23 ianvaria 1932 g. Moscow, 1932.

Ob itogakh ob˝edinennogo plenuma TsK i TsKK VKP(b). Doklad na ob˝edinennom plenume Moskovskogo oblastnogo i gorodskogo komitetov VKP(b) sovmestno s sekretariami R.K. i aktivom Moskovskoi organizatsii 17 ianvaria 1933 g. Moscow, 1933.

Ot XVI k XVII s˝ezdu partii. Doklad o rabote TsK VKP(b) na Moskovskoi ob˝edinennoi IV oblastnoi i III gorodoskoi partiinoi konferentsii 17 ianvaria 1934 g. Moscow, 1934.

Kalendar' ezhegodnik kommunista na 1931 god. Moscow, 1931.

Kalinin, M. I. *Izbrannye proizvedeniia.* Vol. 2 (1926–32). Moscow, 1960.

Kalistratov, Iu. *Za udarnyi proizvodstvennyi kollektiv.* 2nd ed. Moscow, 1931.

Kaplun, M. M. *Brigady na khozraschete.* Moscow-Leningrad, 1931.

Kartsev, V. P. *Krzhizhanovskii.* Moscow, 1980.

Khain, A., and Khandros, V. *Kto oni–novye liudi na proizvodtstve?* Moscow, 1930

Khavin, A. *Kratkii ocherk istorii industrializatsii SSSR.* Moscow, 1962. *U rulia industrii. Dokumental'nye ocherki.* Moscow, 1968.

Kir'ianov, Iu. I. *Zhiznennyi uroven' rabochikh Rossii (konets XIX–nachalo XX v.).* Moscow, 1979.

Koldogovor tret'ego goda piatiletki. Leningrad, 1931.

Kolotov, V. V. *Nikolai Alekseevich Voznesenskii.* Moscow, 1974.

Kommunisty Leningrada v bor'be za vypolnenie reshenii partii po industrializatsii strany (1926–1929 gg.). Sbornik dokumentov i materialov. Leningrad, 1960.

Komsomol. Sbornik statei. Vospominaniia byvshikh komsomol'tsev. Munich, 1960.

Komsomol k XVI parts″ezdu. Leningrad, 1930.

Komsomol na fabrikakh i zavodakh k VIII s″ezdu VLKSM. Po materialam vyborochnogo obsledovaniia fabrichno-zavodskikh i transportnykh iacheek VLKSM na 1 okt. 1927 g. Moscow, 1928.

Konstantinov, A. P., Ivanov, V. M., and Zubarev, V. I. *Leninskie traditsii partiino-gosudarstvennogo kontrolia. Iz istorii sozdaniia i deiatel'nosti leningradskoi oblastnoi i gorodskoi KK-RKI.* Leningrad, 1963.

Kopelev, L. *Khranit' vechno.* 2nd ed. Ann Arbor, Mich., 1981.

Kornilov, A. V. "Povyshenie roli partiinykh organizatsii v khoziaistvennom stroitel'stve (1926–1932 gg.)." *Voprosy istorii KPSS,* 1969, no. 9.

Korotkov, I. I. "K proverke i chistke proizvodstvennykh iacheek." In Iaroslavskii, E. M. (ed.), *Kak provodit' chistku partii.* Moscow-Leningrad, 1929.

Kosior, S. V. *Vybrani statti i promovy* (in Ukrainian). Kiev, 1968.

Krasnikov. S. V. *Sergei Mironovich Kirov. Zhizn' i deiatel'nost'.* Moscow, 1964.

S. M. Kirov v Leningrade. Leningrad, 1966.

Kritsman, L. *Geroicheskii period Velikoi Russkoi Revoliutsii (opyt analiza t.n. "voennogo kommunizma").* Moscow, n.d. [1924?].

Krupianskaia, V. Iu. et al. *Kul'tura i byt gorniakov i metallurgov Nizhnego Tagila (1917–1970).* Moscow, 1974.

Krylov, S., and Zykov, A. *O pravoi opasnosti.* 2nd ed. Moscow-Leningrad, 1929.

Kuibyshev, V. V. *Stat'i i rechi.* Moscow, 1935.

"V. V. Kuibyshev i sotsialisticheskaia industrializatsiia SSSR." *Istoricheskii arkhiv,* 1958, no. 3.

Kuibysheva, G. V. et al. *Valerian Vladimirovich Kuibyshev: biografiia.* Moscow, 1966.

Kuz'min, V. I. *Istoricheskii opyt sovetskoi industrializatsii.* Moscow, 1969.

V bor'be za sotsialisticheskuiu rekonstruktsiiu, 1926–1937 gg. Moscow, 1976.

Vremia velikogo pereloma. Moscow, 1979.

Kuznetskstroi. Istoriia Kuznetskstroia v vospominaniiakh. Novosibirsk, 1934.

Kvasha, Ia., and Shofman, F. *Semichasovoi rabochii den' v tekstil'noi promyshlennosti.* Moscow, 1930.

Lakin, G. V. *Reforma upravleniia promyshlennost'iu v 1929/30 g.* Moscow, 1930.

Larin, Iu. *Stroitel'stvo sotsializma i kollektivizatsiia byta.* Leningrad, 1930.

Lebed', D. Z. *Ukreplenie apparata proletarskoi diktatury; proverka i chistka sostava sluzhashchikh sovetskogo apparata.* Moscow, 1929.

Lel'chuk, V. S. *Sotsialisticheskaia industrializatsiia SSSR i ee osveshchenie v sovetskoi istoriografii.* Moscow, 1975.

Industrializatsiia SSSR: istoriia, opyt, problemy. Moscow, 1984.

Lenin, V. I. *Polnoe sobranie sochinenii.* 55 vols. Moscow, 1958–70.

Leningradskie rabochie v bor'be za sotsializm, 1926–1937. Leningrad, 1965.

Liudi Stalingradskogo traktornogo. 2nd ed. Moscow, 1934.

Malafeev, A. N. *Istoriia tsenoobrazovaniia v SSSR (1917–1963 gg.).* Moscow, 1964.

Markovich, L. *RKK na novom etape.* Moscow, 1933.

Markus, B. *Trud v sotsialisticheskom obshchestve.* Moscow, 1939.

Materialy k otchetu TK KP(b)G. Oktiabr' 1927 g.–ianvar' 1929 g. [Tiflis, 1929].

Materialy k otchetu TsKK VKP(b) XVI s"ezdu VKP(b), sostavlennyi OGPU (k dokladu tov. Ordzhonikidze). Moscow, 1930. Marked "Na pravakh rukopisi. Tol'ko dlia delegatov XVI s"ezda VKP(b)."

Materialy k otchetu VTsSPS IX s"ezdu profsoiuzov. Moscow, 1932.

Materialy k XVIII chrezvychainoi Smolenskoi gubernskoi konferentsii VKP(b), iiun' 1928 g. Smolensk, 1928.

Materialy o rabote profsoiuzov moskovskoi oblasti. Ko vtoroi oblastnoi partkonferentsii. Moscow, 1930.

Materialy ob"edinennogo plenuma TsK i TsKK VKP(b), 7–12 ianvaria 1933 g. Moscow, 1933.

Meerzon, Zh. *Za perestroiku partiinoi raboty.* Moscow-Leningrad, 1929.

Mendel'son, A. S. (ed.). *Vypolnenie plana pervogo goda piatiletki.* Moscow, 1930.

Mikoian, A. I. *Problema snabzheniia strany i rekonstruktsiia narodnogo khoziaistva.* Moscow, 1929.

Prodovol'stvennoe snabzhenie i nashi zadachi; pererabotannye steno-

grammy vystuplenii na rabochikh sobraniiakh po prodovol'stvennym voprosam. Moscow, 1930.

Mishustin, D. *Vneshniaia torgovlia i industrializatsiia SSSR.* Moscow, 1938.

Molotov, V. M. *Stroitel'stvo sotsializma i protivorechiia rosta. Doklad o rabote TsK VKP(b) na 1 Moskovskoi oblastnoi partiinoi konferentsii 14 sentiabria 1929 g.* Moscow, 1929.

V bor'be za sotsializm. Rechi i stat'i. 2nd ed. Moscow, 1935.

Mordukhovich (Mokhov), Z. *Na bor'bu s tekuchest'iu rabochei sily.* Moscow-Leningrad, 1931.

Morin, A. I., Piatakov, G. L., and Sher, V. V. *Reforma kredita. Doklady i rechi na soveshchanii upravliaiushchikh filialami Gosbanka 18–22 iiunia 1929 g. i tezisy Pravleniia Gosbanka (iz stenograficheskogo otcheta).* Moscow, 1929.

Moshkov, Iu. *Zernovaia problema v gody sploshnoi kollektivizatsii sel'-skogo khoziaistva SSSR, 1929–1932 gg.* Moscow, 1966.

Moskovskie bol'sheviki v bor'be s pravymi i "levymi" opportunizmom, 1921–1929 gg. Moscow, 1969.

Moskovskie udarniki za rabotoi. Po materialam obsledovaniia MOSPS i MK VLKSM. Moscow, 1930.

Moskovskii avtozavod im. I.A. Likhacheva. Moscow, 1966.

Mozhina, M. A. "Ekonomiko-statisticheskii analiz riadov raspredeleniia rabochikh po razmeram zarabotnoi platy po periodam razvitiia narodnogo khoziaistva SSSR." In *Statisticheskie modeli i metody v ekonomikcheskom analize i planirovanii.* Vol. VII. Novosibirsk, 1963.

Murashev, D. *Profsoiuzy i sotsialisticheskoe stroitel'stvo.* Moscow-Leningrad, 1927.

Na novom etape sotsialisticheskogo stroitel'stva. Sbornik statei. 2 vols. Moscow, 1930.

Neiman, G. A. *Vnutrenniaia torgovlia SSSR.* Moscow, 1935.

Neizvedannymi putiami. Vospominaniia uchatnikov sotsialisticheskogo stroitel'stva. Leningrad, 1967.

Novye kadry promyshlennykh rabochikh i rabota sredi nikh. (Po materialam obsledovaniia Severo-Kavkazskogo kraikoma VKP(b) i kraisovprofa). Rostov on the Don, 1927.

O rekonstruktsii zavodov Iugostali. Moscow, 1929. Marked "Na pravakh rukopisi."

O Valeriane Kuibysheve. Vospominaniia, ocherki, stat'i. Moscow, 1983.

Olegina, I. N. *Industrializatsiia SSSR v angliiskoi i amerikanskoi istoriografii.* Leningrad, 1971.

Ol'khov, V. *Za zhivoe rukovodstvo sotsialisticheskim sorevnovaniem. Opyt Vsesoiuznoi proverki sotssorevnovaniia brigadami VTsSPS.* Moscow, 1930.

Oprishchenko, A. L. *Istoriografiia sotsialisticheskogo sorevnovaniia rabochego klassa SSSR.* Kharkov, 1975.

Ordzhonikidze, G. K. *Stat'i i rechi.* Vol. 2. Moscow, 1957.

Osnovnye problemy kontrol'nykh tsifr narodnogo khoziaistva SSSR na 1929/30 g. Moscow-Leningrad, 1930.

Ostapenko, I. P. *Uchastie rabochego klassa SSSR v upravlenii proizvodstvom. Proizvodstvennye soveshchaniia v promyshlennosti v 1921–1932 gg.* Moscow, 1964.

Panfilova, A. M. *Formirovanie rabochego klassa SSSR v gody pervoi piatiletki (1928–1932).* Moscow, 1964.

Paramonov, I. V. *Uchit'sia upravliat'. Mysli i opyt starogo khoziaistvennika.* 2nd ed. Moscow, 1970.

Paramonov, N. *Proizvodstvennye soveshchaniia i sotsialisticheskoe sorevnovanie na Urale.* Sverdlovsk, 1930.

Pashukanis, E., and Ignat, S. *Ocherednye zadachi bor'by s biurokratizmom. Doklad v Institute Sovetskogo Stroitel'stva i preniia po dokladam.* Moscow, 1929.

Patolichev, N. S. *Ispytanie na zrelost'.* Moscow, 1977.

Pervye shagi industrializatsii SSSR, 1926–1927 gg. Moscow, 1959.

Pervyi Vsesoiuznyi s'ezd udarnykh brigad. (K tridtsatiletiiu s'ezda.) Sbornik dokumentov i materialov. Moscow, 1959.

Peshkin, I. S. *Dve zhizni Stalingradskogo traktornogo. Sozdanie zavoda i ego vosstanovlenie v poslevoennye gody.* Moscow, 1947.

Platunov, N. I. *Pereselencheskaia politika sovetskogo gosudarstva i ee osushchestvlenie v SSSR (1917-iiun' 1941 gg.).* Tomsk, 1976.

Politicheskii i trudovoi pod'em rabochego klassa SSSR, 1928–1929 gg. Moscow, 1956.

Professional'nye soiuzy SSSR, 1926–1928 gg. Otchet VTsSPS k VIII s'ezdu professional'nykh soiuzov. Moscow, 1928.

Promyshlennost' i rabochii klass Ukrainskoi SSR, 1933–1941. Sbornik dokumentov i materialov. 2 vols. Kiev, 1977.

Rabkina, N. E., and Rimashevskaia, N. M. "Raspredelitel'nye otnosheniia i sotsial'noe razvitie." *Ekonomika i organizatsiia promyshlennogo proizvodstva,* 1978, no. 5.

Rabota NK RKI SSSR ot V k VI Vsesoiuznomu s'ezdu Sovetov. Moscow, 1931.

Ranevskii, I. *V bol'shevistskii pokhod za kachestvo.* Moscow-Leningrad, 1931.

Rasskazy o sotsialisticheskom masterstve. Moscow, 1936.

Ratsionalizatsiia promyshlennosti SSSR. Rabota komissii prezidiuma VSNKh SSSR. Moscow-Leningrad, 1928.

Revoliutsionnyi derzhite shag. Moscow, 1971.

Rezoliutsiia shestogo Vserossiiskogo soveshchaniia po trudu, 10–14 noiabria 1930 g. Moscow-Leningrad, 1931.

Rogachevskaia, L. S. *Iz istorii rabochego klassa SSSR v pervye gody industrializatsii, 1926–1927 gg.* Moscow, 1959.

Likvidatsiia bezrabotitsy v SSSR 1917–1930 gg. Moscow, 1973.

Rozengol'ts, A. P. (ed.). *Promyshlennost'. Sbornik statei. Po materialam TsKK VKP(b)-NK RKI.* Moscow-Leningrad, 1930.

Rubinshtein, G. L. *Razvitie vnutrennei torgovli v SSSR.* Leningrad, 1964.

Sabsovich, L. M. *SSSR cherez 15 let.* 3rd ed. Moscow, 1929.

SSSR cherez 10 let. Moscow, 1930.

Sakharov, G., Chernai, N., and Kabakov, O. *Ocherki organizatsii tiazheloi promyshlennosti SSSR.* Moscow, 1934.

Selishchev, A. M. *Iazyk revoliutsionnoi epokhi. Iz nabliudenii nad russkim iazykom poslednikh let (1917–1926).* 2nd ed. Moscow, 1928.

Seliunin, Vasilii, and Khanin, Grigorii. "Lukavaia tsifra." *Novyi mir*, 1987, no. 2.

Semenov, N. *Litso fabrichnykh rabochikh prozhivaiushchikh v derevniakh i politprosvetrabota sredi nikh.* Moscow, 1929.

Shcherbakova, N. M. "Kvalifikatsionnye izmeneniia v sostave rabochikh metallurgicheskoi promyshlennosti Urala v 1929–1937 godakh." *Uchenye zapiski Permskogo universiteta*, vol. 158 (1966).

Shkaratan, O. I. "Material'noe blagosostoianie rabochego klassa SSSR v perekhodnyi period ot kapitalizma k sotsializmu." *Istoriia SSSR*, 1964, no. 3.

Problemy sotsial'noi struktury rabochego klassa SSSR. Istoriko-sotsiologicheskoe issledovanie. Moscow, 1970.

Shul'man, M. *Nashi dostizheniia na fronte sotsialisticheskogo sorevnovaniia.* Moscow, 1929.

Skobtsov, L. Ia. *Partiinaia organizatsiia Donbassa v bor'be za osushchestvlenie Leninskogo plana industrializatsii strany, 1926–1929 gg.* Stalino, 1959.

Slovo masterov. Moscow, 1949.

Sotsialisticheskaia industrializatsiia SSSR. Ukazatel' sovetskoi literatury, izdannoi v 1928–1970 gg. Moscow, 1972.

Sotsialisticheskoe sorevnovanie v promyshlennosti SSSR. Moscow, 1930.

Sovetskaia intelligentsiia. Istoriia formirovaniia i rosta, 1917–1965 gg. Moscow, 1968.

Sovetskoe trudovoe pravo na novom etape. Moscow, 1931.

Sovety narodnogo khoziaistva i planovye organy v tsentre i na mestakh (1917–1932). Moscow, 1957.

SSSR. God raboty pravitel'stva. Materialy k otchetu za 1928/29 g. Pervyi god piatiletki. Moscow, 1930.

Stakhanov, A. *Rasskaz o moei zhizni.* Moscow, 1938.

Rodnik rabochikh talantov. Moscow, 1973.

Stalin, I. V. *Sochineniia.* 13 vols. Moscow, 1946–51; plus 3 vols. (vols. 14–16) edited by Robert H. McNeal, Stanford, Calif., 1967. The English edition, *Works,* 13 vols., Moscow, 1952–55, was freely consulted.

Stoklitskii, A. *Postup'iu millionov.* Moscow-Leningrad, 1931.

Strievskii, K. *Material'noe i kul'turnoe polozhenie moskovskikh rabochikh. Doklad na IV ob"edinennom plenume MK i MKK VKP(b).* Moscow, 1929.

Suvorov, K. I. *Istoricheskii opyt KPSS po likvidatsii bezrabotitsy (1917–1930).* Moscow, 1968.

Svodnye materialy o deiatel'nosti SNK i STO za I kvartal (okt.–dek.) 1927/28 g. Moscow, 1928.

Syrtsov, S. *O nashikh upsekhakh, nedostatkakh i zadachakh.* Moscow, 1930.

K novomu khoziaistvennomu godu. Pererabotannaia stenogramma rechi S. I. Syrtsova na ob"edinennom zasedanii SNK i EKOSO RSFSR 30 avgusta 1930 g. po dokladam Gosplana o kontrol'nykh tsifrakh na 1930/31 g. Moscow, [1930].

Taskaev, I. *Pervyi traktornyi.* Saratov, 1930.

Tepliakov, Iu. N. *Operatsiiu nachnem na rassvete. O nachal'nike stroitel'stva Stalingradskogo traktornogo zavoda V.I. Ivanove.* 2nd ed. Moscow, 1984.

Tetiushev, V. I. "Bor'ba partii za general'nuiu liniiu protiv pravogo uklona VKP(b) v period XV i XVI s"ezdami." In *Vestnik Moskovskogo universiteta,* Seriia ix (istoriia), 1961, no. 3.

Titov, A. G., Smirnov, A. M., and Shalagin, K. D. *Bor'ba Kommunisticheskoi partii s antileninskimi gruppami i techeniiami v posleoktiabr'skii period (1917–1934 gg.).* Moscow, 1974.

Tomskii, M. *Stat'i i rechi.* Vol. 3. Moscow, 1927.

Profsoiuzy SSSR i ikh otnosheniia k kompartii i sovetskomu gosudarstvu. Moscow, 1928.

Trifonov, I. *Ocherki istorii klassovoi bor'by v SSSR v gody NEPa (1921–1937).* Moscow, 1960.

Uglanov, N. A. (ed.). *Trud v SSSR. Sbornik statei.* Moscow, 1930.

Vaganov, F. M. *Pravyi uklon v VKP(b) i ego razgrom, 1928–1930 gg.* Moscow, 1970; 2nd ed., 1977.

Valentinov (Vol'skii), N. *NEP i krizis partii posle smerti Lenina. Gody raboty v VSNKh vo vremia NEP. Vospominaniia.* Stanford, Calif., 1971.

Vareikis, I. *Osnovnye zadachi vtoroi piatiletki.* Voronezh, 1932.

Vdovin, A. I., and Drobizhev, V. Z. *Rost rabochego klassa SSSR, 1917–1940 gg.* Moscow, 1976.

Venediktov, A. V. *Organizatsiia gosudarstvennoi promyshlennosti v SSSR.* Vol. 2 (1921–34). Leningrad, 1961.

Volodin, G. *Po sledam istorii. Ocherki iz istorii Donetskogo ordena Lenina metallurgicheskogo zavoda im. V.I. Lenina.* Donetsk, 1967.

Vorobei, K. *Odin–za vsekh, vse–za odnogo. Iz istorii pervoi udarnoi brigady na zavode "Bol'shevik."* *Rasskaz brigadira.* Leningrad, 1961.

Voroshilov, K. E. *Na istoricheskom perevale.* Moscow, 1930.

Stat'i i rechi. Moscow, 1937.

Vrediteli piatiletki. Leningrad, 1931.

Vsegda vosemnadtsat'. Donetsk, 1968.

Vsia Moskva. Adresnaia i spravochnaia kniga. Moscow, 1930.

Za tri mesiatsa. Deiatel'nost' SNK i STO. I kvartal (okt.–dek.) 1929/30 g. Moscow, 1930.

Za tri mesiatsa. Deiatel'nost' SNK i STO. III kvartal (aprel'–iiun') 1929/30 g. Moscow, 1930.

Zarabotnaia plata i koldogovornaia kampaniia 1927/28 g. v Leningradskoi promyshlennosti. Leningrad, 1928.

Zavershenie vosstanovleniia promyshlennosti i nachalo industrializatsii Severo-Zapadnogo raiona (1925–1928 gg.). Sbornik dokmentov. Leningrad, 1964.

Zelenin, I. E. "Politotdely MTS (1933–1934 gg.)." *Istoricheskie zapiski,* vol. 76 (1965).

Zeltyn', M. S. "Razvitie form i metodov oplaty truda rabochikh v promyshlennosti SSSR." In *Razvitie sotsialisticheskoi organizatsii truda za gody sovetskoi vlasti.* Moscow, 1968.

Zheleznodorozhnyi transport v gody industrializatsii SSSR (1926–1941). Moscow, 1970.

Zheleznodorozhnyi transport v tret'em godu piatiletki. K X Vsesoiuznomu s"ezdu zheleznodorozhnikov. Moscow, 1931.

Zhiga, I. *Ocherki, stat'i i vospominaniia.* Moscow, 1958.

Zhogin, N. V., "Ob izvrashcheniiakh Vyshinskogo v teorii sovetskogo prava i praktike." *Sovetskoe gosudarstvo i pravo,* 1965, no. 3 (March).

Zhukov, Iu. *Liudi 30-kh godov.* Moscow, 1966.

Krutye stupeni. Zapiski zhurnalista. Moscow, 1983.

Zverev, A. G. *Zapiski ministra.* Moscow, 1973.

Zvezdin, Z. K. *Ot plana GOELRO k planu pervoi piatiletki. Stanovlenie sotsialisticheskogo planirovaniia v SSSR.* Moscow, 1979.

VII. Books and articles (in Western languages)

Andrle, V. "How Backward Workers Became Soviet: Industrialization of Labour and the Politics of Efficiency under the Second Five-Year Plan, 1933–1937." *Social History,* 10:2 (May 1985).

Arnold, Arthur Z. *Banks, Credit, and Money in Soviet Russia.* Columbia University Press, 1937.

Avrich, Paul H. "The Bolshevik Revolution and Workers' Control in Russian Industry." *Slavic Review,* 22:1 (March 1963).

Azrael, Jeremy R. *Managerial Power and Soviet Politics.* Harvard University Press, 1966.

Bailes, Kendall E. *Technology and Society under Lenin and Stalin. Origins of the Soviet Technical Intelligentsia, 1917–1941.* Princeton University Press, 1978.

Barber, John, "Notes on the Soviet Working-Class Family, 1928–1941." Paper presented at the Second World Congress for Soviet and East European Studies in Garmisch-Partenkirchen, Federal Republic of Germany, 30 September–4 October 1980.

Soviet Historians in Crisis 1928–1932. New York, 1981.

"The Standard of Living of Soviet Industrial Workers, 1928–1941." In *L'industrialisation de l'URSS dans les années trente. Actes de la Table Ronde organisée par le Centre d'Études des Modes d'Industrialisation de l'Ecole des Hautes Études en Sciences Sociales (10 et 11 décembre 1981).* Paris, 1982.

Barmine, Alexander. *One Who Survived. The Life Story of a Russian under the Soviets.* New York, 1945.

Bendix, Reinhard. *Work and Authority in Industry.* 2nd ed. University of California Press, 1974.

Berliner, Joseph. *Factory and Manager in the USSR.* Harvard University Press, 1957.

Bonnel, Victoria E. (ed.). *The Russian Worker. Life and Labor under the Tsarist Regime.* University of California Press, 1983.

Broué, Pierre. "Trotsky et le bloc des oppositions de 1932." *Cahiers Leon Trotsky,* 5 (January–March 1980).

Brower, Daniel. "Collectivized Agriculture in Smolensk: The Party, the Peasantry, and the Crisis of 1932." *Russian Review,* 36:2 (April 1977).

"Labor Violence in Russia in the Late Nineteenth Century." *Slavic Review,* 41:3 (Fall 1982).

Brown, E. J. *The Proletarian Episode in Russian Literature, 1928–1932.* New York, 1953.

Carr, E. H. *The Bolshevik Revolution, 1917–1923.* Vol. 2. London, 1952.
The Interregnum 1923–1924. London, 1954.
Socialism in One Country, 1924–1926. Vol. 1. London, 1958.
Foundations of a Planned Economy, 1926–1929. Vol. 2. London, 1971.
The Russian Revolution from Lenin to Stalin (1917–1929). London, 1979.

Carr, E. H., and Davies. R. W. *Foundations of a Planned Economy, 1926–1929.* Vol. 1. London, 1969.

Chase, William J. *Workers, Society and the Soviet State: Labor and Life in Moscow, 1918–1929.* University of Illinois Press, 1987.

Cohen, Stephen F. *Bukharin and the Bolshevik Revolution: A Political Biography, 1888–1938.* New York, 1973.

Daniels, R. *The Conscience of the Revolution: Communist Opposition in Soviet Russia.* Harvard University Press, 1960.

Davies, R. W. *The Development of the Soviet Budgetary System.* Cambridge University Press, 1958.

"Some Soviet Economic Controllers–II" and "Some Soviet Economic Controllers–III." *Soviet Studies,* 11:3 (January 1960) and 12:1 (July 1960).

The Socialist Offensive. The Collectivisation of Agriculture, 1929–1930. Harvard University Press, 1980.

The Soviet Collective Farm, 1929–1930. Harvard University Press, 1980.

"The Syrtsov-Lominadze Affair." *Soviet Studies,* 33:1 (January 1981).

"Models of the Economic System in Soviet Practice, 1926–1936." *L'industrialisation de l'URSS dans les années trente.* (For the full title, see Barber.)

"The Socialist Market: A Debate in Soviet Industry, 1932–33," *Slavic Review,* 42:2 (Summer 1984).

"The Ending of Mass Unemployment in the USSR." In David Lane (ed.), *Labour and Employment in the USSR.* Sussex, 1986.

Davies, R. W., and Wheatcroft, S. G. "Further Thoughts on the First Soviet Five-Year Plan." *Slavic Review,* 34:4 (December 1975).

Day, Richard B. *Leon Trotsky and the Politics of Economic Isolation.* Cambridge University Press, 1973.

Deutscher, I. *Soviet Trade Unions: Their Place in Soviet Labour Policy.* London, 1950.

The Prophet Outcast. Trotsky: 1929–1940. Oxford University Press, 1963.

Dodge, Norton T., and Dalrymple, Dana G. "The Stalingrad Tractor Plant in Early Soviet Planning." *Soviet Studies,* 18:2 (October 1966).

Dohan, Michael R. "The Economic Origins of Soviet Autarchy, 1927/28–1934." *Slavic Review,* 35:4 (December 1976).

Dunham, Vera. *In Stalin's Time. Middleclass Value in Soviet Fiction.* Cambridge University Press, 1976.

Ehrenburg, Ilya. *Memoirs: 1921–1941.* Trans. from the Russian by Tatiana Shebunina in collaboration with Yvonne Kopp. Cleveland, 1964.

Ellman, Michael. "Did the Agricultural Surplus Provide the Resources for the Increase in Investment in the USSR during the First Five-Year Plan?" *The Economic Journal,* 85:4 (December 1975).

"A Note on the Distribution of Earnings in the USSR under Brezhnev." *Slavic Review,* 39:4 (December 1980).

Erlich, Alexander. *The Soviet Industrialization Debate, 1924–1928.* Harvard University Press, 1960.

Ewing, Sally. "Social Insurance in Russia and the Soviet Union, 1912–1933: A Study of Legal Form and Administrative Practice." Ph.D. diss. Princeton University, 1984.

Fainsod, Merle. *Smolensk under Soviet Rule.* Harvard University Press, 1958.

Filtzer, Donald. *Soviet Workers and Stalinist Industrialization. The Formation of Modern Soviet Production Relations, 1928–1941.* New York, 1986.

Fisher, Ralph Talcott, Jr. *Pattern for Soviet Youth. A Study of the Congresses of the Komsomol, 1918–1954.* Columbia University Press, 1959.

Fitzpatrick, Sheila. "Cultural Revolution in Russia, 1928–1932." *Journal of Contemporary History,* 9:1 (January 1974).

"The 'Soft' Line on Culture and Its Enemies: Soviet Cultural Policy, 1922–1927." *Slavic Review,* 33:2 (June 1974),

"Culture and Politics under Stalin: A Reappraisal." *Slavic Review,* 35:2 (June 1976).

(ed.). *Cultural Revolution in Russia, 1928–1931,* Indiana University Press, 1978.

Education and Social Mobility in the Soviet Union, 1921–1934. Cambridge University Press, 1979.

"Stalin and the Making of a New Elite, 1928–1939." *Slavic Review,* 38:3 (September 1979).

The Russian Revolution. Oxford University Press, 1982.

"The Russian Revolution and Social Mobility: A Re-examination of the Question of Social Support for the Soviet Regime in the 1920s and 1930s," *Politics & Society.* 13:2 (1984).

"Ordzhonikidze's Takeover of Vesenkha: A Case Study in Soviet Bureaucratic Politics." *Soviet Studies,* 37:2 (April 1985).

Getty, J. Arch. "Soviet City Directories." Paper presented at the 14th Annual Convention of the American Association for the Advancement of Slavic Studies, Washington, D.C., 15 October 1982.

"Trotsky in Exile: The Founding of the Fourth International." *Soviet Studies,* 38:1 (January 1986).

Graham, Loren R. *The Soviet Academy of Sciences and the Communist Party, 1927–1932.* Princeton University Press, 1967.

Granick, David. *Management of the Industrial Firm in the USSR. A Study in Economic Planning.* Columbia University Press, 1954.

The Red Executive. London, 1960.

Soviet Metal-Fabricating and Economic Development. Practice versus Policy. University of Wisconsin Press, 1967.

Grigorenko, Petro G. *Memoirs.* Trans. from the Russian by Thomas O. Whitney. New York-London, 1982.

Hogan, Heather. "Industrial Rationalization and the Roots of Labor

Militance in the St. Petersburg Metalworking Industry, 1901–1914." *Russian Review*, 42:2 (April 1983).

Holzman, Franklyn D. *Soviet Taxation. The Fiscal and Monetary Problems of a Planned Economy*. Harvard University Press, 1962.

Hoover, Calvin B. *The Economic Life of Soviet Russia*. New York, 1931.

Hough, Jerry F. *The Soviet Prefects. The Local Party Organs in Industrial Decision-Making*. Harvard University Press, 1969.

"The Cultural Revolution and Western Understanding of the Soviet System." In Fitzpatrick (ed.), *Cultural Revolution in Russia, 1928–1931*.

Hunter, Holland. *Soviet Transportation Policy*. Harvard University Press, 1957.

"The Overambitious First Five-Year Plan," with comments by Robert Campbell, Stephen F. Cohen, and Moshe Lewin. *Slavic Review*, 32:2 (June 1973).

Jasny, Naum. *Soviet Industrialization, 1928–1952*. University of Chicago Press, 1961.

Soviet Economists of the Twenties. Names to be Remembered. Cambridge University Press, 1972.

Joravsky, David. *Soviet Marxism and Natural Science 1917–1932*. New York, 1961.

Kataev, Valentin. *Time, Forward!* Authorized translation from the Russian by Charles Malamuth. Indiana University Press, 1976.

Khrushchev Remembers. Trans. and ed. Strobe Talbott. Boston, 1970.

Kirstein, Tatjana. *Sowjetische Industrialisierung – geplanter oder spontaner Prozeß? Eine Strukturanalyse des wirtschaftspolitischen Entscheidungsprozesses beim Aufbau des Ural-Kuzneck-Kombinats 1918–1930*. Baden-Baden, 1979.

Die Bedeutung von Durchführungsentscheidungen in dem zentralistisch verfaßten Entscheidungssystem der Sowjetunion. Eine Analyse des stalinistischen Entscheidungssystems am Beispiel des Aufbaus von Magnitogorsk (1928–1932). Berlin, 1984.

Knickerbocker, H. R. *The Soviet Five-Year Plan and Its Effect on World Trade*. London, 1931.

Koch, W. *Die bol'ševistischen Gewerkschaften. Eine herrschaftssoziologische Studie*. Jena, 1932.

Kopelev, L. *The Education of a True Believer*. Trans. from the Russian by Gary Kern. New York, 1980.

Kornai, J. *Contradictions and Dilemmas. Studies on the Socialist Economy and Society*. MIT Press, 1986.

Kuromiya, Hiroaki. "Production Communes, Production Collectives, and the Labor Movement [in the Soviet Union], 1929–1931" (in Japanese). *Roshiashi kenkyu* (Tokyo), 30 (1979).

"*Edinonachalie* and the Soviet Industrial Manager, 1928–1937." *Soviet Studies*, 36:2 (April 1984).

"The *Artel* and Social Relations in Soviet Industry in the 1920s." Paper presented to the conference, "The Social History of the Soviet Union in the NEP Period," Indiana University, 2–5 October 1986.

"Soviet Memoirs as a Historical Source." In *Russian History/Histoire Russe* (in press).

Lampert, Nicholas. *The Technical Intelligentsia and the Soviet State. A Study of Soviet Managers and Technicians, 1928–1935*. London, 1979.

Lewin, Moshe. *Russian Peasants and Soviet Power*. Trans. from the French by Irene Nove with the assistance of John Briggart. New York, 1975.

"Society and the Stalinist State in the Period of the Five-Year Plans." *Social History*, 1976, no. 2.

The Making of the Soviet System. Essays in the Social History of Interwar Russia. New York, 1985.

Littlepage, John D., and Bess, Demaree. *In Search of Soviet Gold*. New York, 1938.

Lyons, Eugene. *Assignment in Utopia*. New York, 1937.

McAuley, Mary. *Labour Disputes in Soviet Russia, 1957–1965*. Oxford, 1969.

Malle, Silvana. *The Economic Organization of War Communism, 1918–1921*. Cambridge University Press, 1985.

Mehnert, Klaus. *Youth in Soviet Russia*. Trans. from the German by Michael Davidson. New York, 1933.

Meyer, Gert. *Sozialstruktur sowjetischer Industriearbeiter Ende der zwanziger Jahre. Ergebnisse der Gewerkshaftsumfrage unter Metall-, Textil- und Bergarbeitern 1929*. Marburg, 1981.

Mikulina, E. *Socialist Competition of the Masses*. Moscow, 1932.

Mosley, Philip E. "1930–1932. Some Vignettes of Soviet Life." *Survey*, 55 (April 1965).

Nove, Alec. "Was Stalin Really Necessary?" *Encounter*, 13:4 (April 1962).

An Economic History of the USSR. London, 1969.

Nove, Alec, and Millar, James R. "A Debate on Collectivization: Was Stalin Really Necessary?" *Problems of Communism*, 25:4 (July–August 1976).

Radek, Karl. *Portraits and Pamphlets*. With an introduction by A. J. Cummings and notes by Alec Brown. London, 1935.

Rassweiler, Anne Dickason. "Dneprostroi, 1927–1932: A Model of Soviet Socialist Planning and Construction." Ph.D. diss., Princeton University, 1980.

Reiman, Michal. *Die Geburt des Stalinismus. Die UdSSR am Vorabend der "zweiten Revolution."* Frankfurt/Main, 1979.

Rigby, T. H. *Communist Party Membership in the USSR, 1917–1967.* Princeton University Press, 1968.

Rosenberg, William G. "Smolensk in the 1920s: Party-Worker Relations and the 'Vanguard Problem.' " *Russian Review,* 36:2 (April 1977).

"The Democratization of Russia's Railroads in 1917." *American Historical Review,* 86:5 (December 1981).

Schoenbaum, David. *Hitler's Social Revolution.* New York, 1967.

Schwarz, Solomon M. *Labor in the Soviet Union.* New York, 1951.

Scott, John. *Behind the Urals. An American Worker in Russia's City of Steel.* Cambridge, Mass., 1942.

Shimotomai, Nobuo. "A Note on the Kuban Affair (1932–1933). The Crisis of Kolkhoz Agriculture in the North Caucasus." *Acta Slavica Iaponica,* vol. 1 (1983).

Siegelbaum, Lewis H. "Soviet Norm Determination in Theory and Practice, 1917–1941." *Soviet Studies,* 36:1 (January 1984).

"Production Collectives and Communes and the 'Imperatives' of Soviet Industrialization, 1929–1931." *Slavic Review,* 45:1 (Spring 1986).

Silk, Leonard. "Andropov's Economic Dilemma." *New York Times Magazine,* 9 October 1983.

Solomon, Peter H., Jr. "Soviet Penal Policy, 1917–1934: A Reconsideration." *Slavic Review,* 39:2 (June 1980).

Solomon, Susan Gross. *The Soviet Agrarian Debate. A Controversy in Soviet Science, 1923–1929.* Boulder, Colo., 1977.

Sorenson, Jay B. *The Life and Death of Soviet Trade Unionism, 1917–1928.* New York, 1969.

Starr, S. Frederic. "Visionary Town Planning during the Cultural Revolution." In Fitzpatrick (ed.), *Cultural Revolution in Russia, 1928–1931.*

Süß, Walter. *Der Betrieb in der UdSSR: Stellung, Organisation und Management 1917–1932.* Frankfurt/Bern, 1980.

Tatur, Melanie. *"Wissenschaftliche Arbeitsorganisation." Arbeitswissenschaften und Arbeitsorganisation in der Sowjetunion 1921–1935.* Wiesbaden, 1979.

Tucker, Robert C. *Stalin as Revolutionary, 1879–1929. A Study in History and Personality.* New York, 1973.

"Stalinism as Revolution from Above." In Tucker (ed.), *Stalinism. Essays in Historical Interpretation.* New York, 1977.

Viola, Lynne. " 'The 25,000ers': A Study in a Soviet Recruitment Campaign during the First Five Year Plan." *Russian History/Histoire Russe,* vol. 10, pt. 1 (1983).

The Best Sons of the Fatherland. Workers in the Vanguard of Soviet Collectivization. Oxford University Press, 1987.

Von Hagen, Mark. "Schools of the Revolution. Bolsheviks and Peasants in the Red Army, 1918–1928." Ph.D. diss., Stanford University, 1984.

Von Laue, Theodore H. *Sergei Witte and the Industrialization of Russia.* Columbia University Press, 1963.

Why Lenin? Why Stalin? A Reappraisal of the Russian Revolution, 1900–1930. Philadelphia-New York, 1964.

"Stalin in Focus." *Slavic Review,* 42:3 (Fall 1983).

"Stalin Reviewed." *Soviet Union/Union Soviétique,* vol. 11, pt. 1 (1984).

Vyas, A. *Consumption in a Socialist Economy: The Soviet Industrialisation Experience (1929–1937).* New Delhi, 1978.

Weißenburger, Ulrich. *Monetärer Sektor und Industrialisierung der Sowjetunion (1927–1933): Die Geld- und Kreditpolitik während der ersten Phase der Industrialisierung der UdSSR, ihre externen und internen Rahmenbedingungen und ihre Auswirkungen auf das gesamtwirtschaftliche Gleichgewicht.* Frankfurt/Main, 1983.

Wheatcroft, S. G., Davies, R. W., and Cooper, J. M. "Soviet Industrialization Reconsidered: Some Preliminary Conclusions about Economic Development between 1926 and 1941." *Economic History Review,* 2nd ser., 39:2 (May 1986).

Yanowitch, Murray. "The Soviet Income Revolution." *Slavic Review,* 22:4 (December 1963).

Zagorsky, S. *Wages and Regulation of Conditions of Labour in the USSR.* Geneva, 1930.

Zaleski, Eugene. *Planning for Economic Growth in the Soviet Union, 1918–1932.* Trans. from the French and edited by Marrie-Christine MacAndrew and G. Warren Nutter. University of North Carolina Press, 1971.

Stalinist Planning for Economic Growth, 1933–1952. Trans. from the French and edited by Marrie-Christine MacAndrew and John H. Moore. University of North Carolina Press, 1980.

Index